TURMOIL

TURMOIL

THE LIFE & TIMES *of* PHILIP HANKIN

MICHAEL LAYLAND

For more information, contact the publisher at:
TouchWood Editions
Touchwoodeditions.com

Edited by Kate Kennedy
Index by Brittany Vesterback
Cover and interior design by Alex Hennig

CATALOGUING DATA AVAILABLE FROM LIBRARY AND ARCHIVES CANADA
ISBN 9781771514712 (softcover)
ISBN 9781771514729 (electronic)

TouchWood Editions gratefully acknowledges that the land on which we live and work is within the traditional territories of the Lkwungen (Esquimalt and Songhees), Malahat, Pacheedaht, Scia'new, T'Sou-ke, and W̱SÁNEĆ (Pauquachin, Tsartlip, Tsawout, and Tseycum) peoples.

We acknowledge the financial support of the Government of Canada through the Canada Book Fund and the Canada Council for the Arts, and of the Province of British Columbia through the British Columbia Arts Council and the Book Publishing Tax Credit.

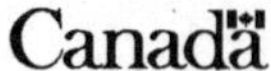

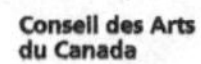

This book was produced using FSC®-certified, acid-free papers, processed chlorine free, and printed with soya-based inks.

Printed in Canada

29 28 27 26 25 1 2 3 4 5

To my wife Jean

Something, in ilka part o' thee,
To praise, to love, I find;
But dear as is thy form to me,
Still dearer is thy mind.

—Robert Burns

Never say die, lad, s'long as there's a shot in the locker!

—Traditional naval exhortation

Contents

Foreword

I was enthralled by Michael Layland's *Turmoil: The Life and Times of Philip Hankin.*

I wish I'd had it at hand many years ago when I wrote *The Wilderness Profound: Victorian Life on the Gulf of Georgia*, my biography of George Fawcett Drabble, an Englishman who arrived on Vancouver Island in 1862. I struggled to make sense of Drabble's career in the confusing and tumultuous 1860s, when political events in the colony were compressed and telescoped into the brief years before British Columbia's entry into the Canadian Confederation in 1871.

Turmoil is the book I needed, with its clear timelines and accessible account of the political history of the Colony of Vancouver Island between Hankin's arrival in 1857 and his departure fourteen years later. Hankin and Drabble were at opposite ends of the colony, but both were involved in the initial mapping and surveying of the island. In their civic and political work, they shared the same broad agenda of creating and extending government infrastructure at colonial and local levels: police, courts, legal apparatus, legislative structure.

Born in 1836 to a landed gentry family in Hertfordshire, England, Philip Hankin had the misfortune to be a younger son of a man experiencing increasing financial difficulties. His father sent Philip's older brothers to venerable Eton and Tonbridge schools, and then obtained suitable commissions or positions for them. But he enlisted Philip, after just a rudimentary education, as a naval cadet aged thirteen. The lad sailed for South Africa almost immediately and thereafter his memoir recorded little about his family.

Philip Hankin's nine-year early naval career involved such adventures as: in 1853 while on HMS *Plumper*, the capture off Angola of a small cutter containing ninety slaves; in the same year, a meeting with explorer David Livingstone, who asked Hankin to accompany him across Africa; and his cooking of a curry dinner for the Queen of the Sandwich Islands.

Hankin arrived at Esquimalt in November 1857, aged twenty-one, a midshipman on HMS *Plumper*. He soon became what he called "personal assistant" to naval hydrographer Captain George Henry Richards, whose coastal survey provided accurate charts for navigation, shipping, and colonization generally. In December 1860, Hankin joined Richards on the surveying vessel HMS *Hecate* and remained with him until the completion of his coastal survey in 1862. If Hankin's BC career had ended there, he would be remembered for his significant contribution to charting Vancouver Island and parts of the mainland coast.

Hankin's naval life in our waters had been a love affair—he recalled being "so charmed by Vancouver Island." He learned several of the local languages and related well with the Indigenous peoples. After leaving the navy, he returned in March 1864, seeking a significant new career on Vancouver Island and in British Columbia.

But his career almost failed to get off the ground. I was fascinated by Hankin's brief foray in the spring of 1864 into the Cariboo gold rush. Layland recounts Hankin's gruelling five-hundred-mile walk to Barkerville, high in the Cariboo Mountains, his stays at roadhouses and "dollar houses," his hunger and desperation. On arrival he slept alone in "an old empty shed" near Barkerville and soon—as just another broke colonist—took what work he could find. Finally, a government officer, G.C.B. Matthew, lent him $60 for the coach ride back to Yale on the Cariboo Road. Five years later, just thirty-three years old, he was making £800 (C$143,000 in 2025) a year as colonial secretary of British Columbia.

Layland takes us down several fascinating rabbit holes of Hankin's years in BC and subsequently. He was the life of the party, the mixer, the showman. In 1861, Richards appointed him aide-de-camp to Lady Jane Franklin, wife of the Arctic explorer, who recalled his performance at Sapperton: "Mr. Hankin bounded on the stage in full sailor's summer costume (all white and blue) flung down his hat, folded his arms, & danced his hornpipe beautifully." He enjoyed performing in front of crowds and was applauded for skilfully reciting excerpts from the novels of Charles Dickens. Hankin was also known for what Layland calls his japes, pranks, and "youthful hijinks," some of them revealing a more complex, less admirable side of his character.

In his professional life, both in navy and government, Hankin was the ideal second-in-command, the consummate right-hand man. He had left school, after all, at thirteen, and his only training was naval. Reprising his role as Captain Richards's personal assistant, he was Governor Arthur Kennedy's chief of police and colonial secretary to Governors Frederick Seymour and Anthony Musgrave. Three times he acted temporarily in charge of the colonial government during critical periods of its evolution. Maybe the Peter Principle applied to his career: he rose to his level of incompetence and no further. His superiors seemed to understand his limitations. He was, Richards wrote, "not fit to be a 1st Lieut. Manner good with men, no great ambition, gentlemanlike & estimable. Knows French, Italian and 3 Indian languages."

Turmoil contains important first-hand accounts of the crises leading to the union of the colonies in 1866, and the colony's more orderly union with Canada in 1871. Layland provides the circumstances and personal ties of these momentous events. Hankin's BC career effectively closes with the end of the colony he'd helped map and survey; he is a colonial figure, not a Canadian figure.

Hankin, Layland shows, was immersed in colonial social networks, both in Victoria and at the highest levels in London. *Turmoil* is full of intercolonial connections, a reminder of Vancouver Island's place in an imperial world. In 1867–68, Hankin was briefly colonial secretary in British Honduras. In 1867, ex-governor of Vancouver Island Arthur Kennedy introduced him to the secretary of state for the colonies, the Duke of Buckingham. Hankin would spend nine years as Buckingham's private secretary (1872–81), including five years when the duke was governor of Madras. Hankin attended the lavish Durbar ceremony of 1877, when Queen Victoria was proclaimed Empress of India.

Hankin is Hardyish in the tragedy of the last decades of his long forty-year retirement, and what Layland calls his depression and "abject loneliness" after his wife's death in 1903, followed by his sad and peripatetic life, his aimless wandering without purpose or roots. He returned twice to live in BC, once in Victoria—which retained a special place in his heart—and once in Vancouver. He almost immigrated to Florida to grow oranges in the 1890s.

Layland builds a narrative around Hankin's interesting but highly selective memoir, written in 1914 when he was seventy-eight years old. The memoir, Layland writes, "contains significant omissions and discrepancies when compared with other contemporary records. It does not give dates for the events recorded," so the chronology must come from other sources: Layland fills in gaps as he goes, drawing on diaries, newspapers, and Colonial Office and BC colonial records. He writes with respect and authority as he peels back the layers of Hankin's life and the discrepancies of his memoir to construct a careful and accurate timeline. Where necessary, he nudges and corrects Hankin's own memories. The result is both high-level political history and a biography of a fascinating and somewhat eminent Victorian.

Layland's style is economical and unpretentious, and his voice is warm and familiar: wise, reliable, and impartial. He brings Hankin and his era to life in precise and spare language. *Turmoil* is written in simple, unadorned, unaffected language and effective prose. Layland's clear authoritative touch is just what Hankin's life requires, free of the lamentable clutter and jargon of academic history.

Hankin's life, deftly told here by Michael Layland, is a reminder that one gifted and unusual person can make a difference in history. Thanks to Layland, Philip Hankin will always be a fixture of our past and *Turmoil: The Life and Times of Philip Hankin* is essential reading for anyone interested in colonial Vancouver Island and British Columbia.

Richard Somerset Mackie
August 2024

Preface

Philip Hankin first came to my attention during my research into the cartographic history of Vancouver Island. In 1862, as a young officer aboard HMS *Hecate*, he made a perilous traverse over the island's northern end and wrote an interesting report supported by a creditable map of his route. His journey merited including in my book *A Perfect Eden* (2016). I also learned that, late in life, he had written a lengthy memoir, the original of which is held the British Columbia Archives in Victoria, BC. I found his story fascinating and wanted to investigate in depth and recount it in a work dedicated to his long and varied career.

*

From June 27 through to October 10, 1954, *The Islander* section of Victoria's *Daily Colonist* newspaper serialized a transcript of the Hankin memoir. In the same newspaper, J.K. Nesbitt wrote brief articles based on the memoir in 1961 and 1965. In 1974, Robert Louis Smith published a scholarly article in *BC Studies*. Focused on Hankin's 1868 appointment as BC's colonial secretary, it called on Smith's research for his MA thesis on Governor Arthur Kennedy and the politics of that era.

Until 2023, the centenary of his death, a full account of the life and complicated character of Philip Hankin had not been told. It was April of that year, and I had been researching and writing this biography for a few years when a bombshell landed: a local publisher reached out to me enquiring if I would care to read an advance copy of just such a book, written by Geoff Mynett, for publication that fall. If so, might I provide an endorsement for the cover? My reaction was total shock mixed with dismay. I felt as Darwin must have done when Wallace's letter arrived requesting his opinion on the latter's theory of natural selection.

Cooler heads helped me realize that the complexity of Philip Hankin's personality, career, and significance merited at least two interpretations, and that I should continue with my project. I have done so, but largely without consulting the earlier book, hoping that its publication will only increase readers' interest in my own account.

Philip Hankin assisted in developing the first accurate marine chart of local waters and in delineating Canada's boundary with the United States. He recorded for the first time a word list of a local Indigenous language. He performed, earnestly and competently, the duties of a government official under three governors, serving as acting head of government on four occasions, and acting as liaison between the government and several First Nations during critical times.

I also wished to draw attention to the many gaps, mysteries, and discrepancies contained within his memoir. The document derives from an enigmatic character faced with many situations of stress and antagonism during his life, as viewed from the distance of decades. I highlight these and puzzle over the possible reasons for those omissions—that is, apart from the obvious lapses of memory to be anticipated from someone in his mid-seventies.

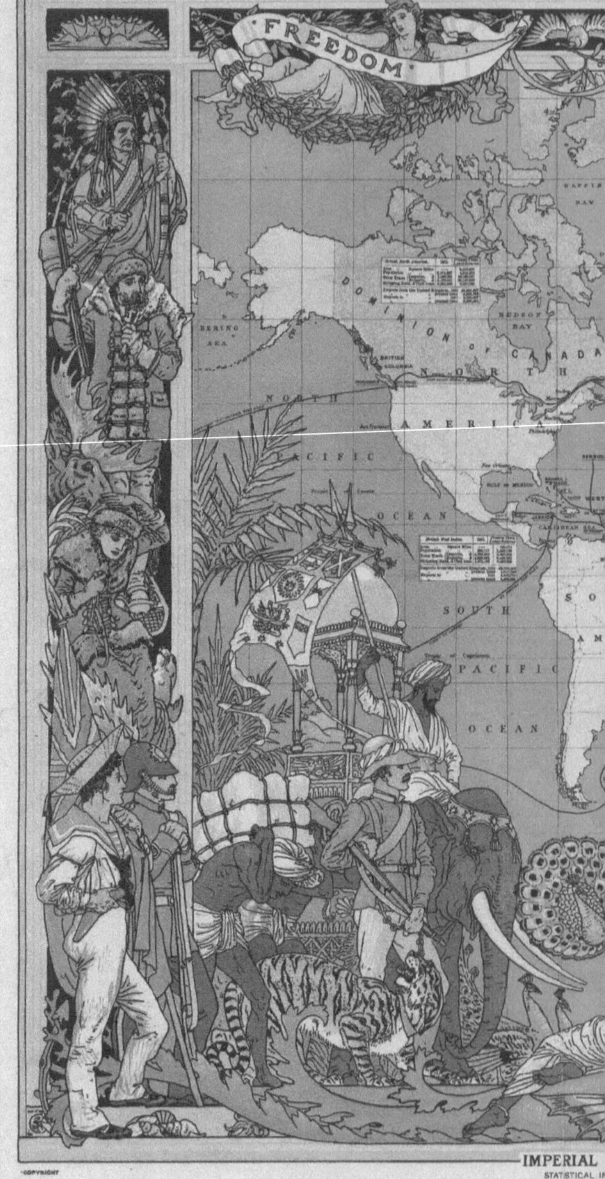

Providing a cartographic backdrop to the life and times of Philip Hankin, this, the so-called Imperial Map, dramatically combines geography and propaganda. Created in 1886, it emphasizes the worldwide extent of British possessions and territories. Reflecting the hubris of the day, it portrays "the Empire over which the sun never sets."

Published in a special edition of the Graphic *illustrated newspaper to mark the Indian and Colonial Exhibition celebrating Queen Victoria's upcoming jubilee, the map also surreptitiously reflects the socialist sympathies of the cartographer, Walter Crane. Lavishly illustrated in the style of the Dutch Golden Age, two centuries earlier, it portrays Britannia dominating the globe, borne in turn on the shoulders of a subdued Atlas who wears a sash reading "Human Labour."*

This theme is continued with the group at bottom left. Well-armed naval and military figures keep watch over symbols of British dominance of India; another soldier in a pith puggaree keeps a firm grip on a snarling tiger with a collar and chain. A heavily burdened coolie dutifully follows behind. An elephant with an elaborate howdah with a turbaned mahout and a banner festooned with stylized escutcheons of British aristocracy completes the scene.

In the western border, three figures represent Canada: a "Plains Indian" replete with feathered headdress, bow and arrow; a trapper in snowshoes; and a young woman in fur-trimmed hat, cape, and jerkin, for some reason clutching her head. Oh, and of course, a bull moose. The extent of Canada includes, according to the map, a sizeable section of western Greenland.

The oceans of the world are traversed by the steamship routes that provided Hankin with diversion for the latter third of his long life. One of these routes appears to indicate that there was plain sailing through Panama, although the canal would not be opened for another twenty-eight years.

The whole essence of the map reflects the times and mood of Victorian Great Britain at the height of the expanding empire. It was within this frame of values that Philip Hankin worked and lived—the context for his life and times.

Introduction

Philip Hankin was barely into his second year when the eighteen-year-old Victoria ascended to the throne of a realm well into its era of social reform and an expanding empire. His long life spanned the reigns of Queen Victoria and Kings Edward VII and George V. For most of his youth, he served his monarch Queen Victoria, her ministers, and nobles in different capacities and in various remote corners of her dominions. He briefly befriended her eldest son, Albert Edward, later King Edward the VII. He spent his retirement traversing the sea routes between outposts of her empire. Late in life he lived in small towns a few miles from where his queen had spent her final decades in reclusive mourning.

Hankin experienced first-hand the effects of the industrial revolution that underpinned the growth of British power, specifically the transition from sail to steam power in the vessels of the invincible Royal Navy. It was also a time of significant scientific progress and social upheaval. The year Hankin was born, Charles Darwin returned from Galapagos, nursing the first inkling of his heretical deductions on the origin of species. During his early years, London saw the growth of scientific societies dedicated to botany, geology, geography, zoology, and other disciplines culminating in Prince Albert's 1851 Great Exhibition and the foundation of the renowned museums of South Kensington. These developments and changes provided exciting scope for him to expand his own horizons.

Britain had recently outlawed slavery, and as a midshipman, Hankin sailed on two voyages to Africa, hunting slavers. He met David Livingstone, who invited him to join an exploratory trek across Africa. He lived long enough to see the conclusion of the "War to End All Wars," but had taken no part. Hankin died in November 1923, having exceeded the life expectancy of his generation by four decades.

The table in appendix 1 puts Philip Hankin's life into historical context, relative to the Vancouver Island region.

Philip Hankin's Memoir

In May 1954, Major General George Randalph Pearkes presented a bulky, untitled manuscript to the BC provincial archivist, Willard Ireland.[1] The document was a memoir written in 1914 by Philip James Hankin, who at the time of its writing was seventy-eight and held the rank of commander (retired) in the Royal Navy. E.L. Britain, the Dominion official resident in Ottawa who ensured Hankin received his pension payments, had sent the document to General Pearkes. Britain told Pearkes of having received the manuscript in about 1920.

The memoir recounts, in remarkable detail, happenings from Hankin's long life. Passages begin with his boyhood in rural England; progress through his service with the Royal Navy, from midshipman to commander; recount the Cariboo gold rush experienced from the lowest rung of the ladder; and stretch into his time as a British Columbia civil servant during the colony's most turbulent years, three times serving as

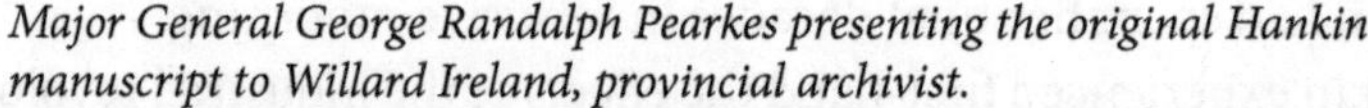

Major General George Randalph Pearkes presenting the original Hankin manuscript to Willard Ireland, provincial archivist.

acting head of government. For ten years he served as private secretary to a duke, five of them during the very apex of the Raj era in India. The latter part of the work is more subdued, as Hankin wound down his life with worldwide travels, including several return visits to his much-loved Victoria.

Mainly chronological, the memoir appears at first reading to be a reasonably fair-minded account of the roller coaster that had been Hankin's life. When writing the memoir, he did not refer to personal journals, as he had kept none, relying purely on his recollections. Closer examination reveals that the memoir contains significant omissions and discrepancies when compared with other contemporary records. It does not give dates for the events recorded, so I referred to other sources to establish the chronology.

I have opted to refer to the protagonist by "Hankin" or "Philip," and occasionally both, depending on the context.

Opening page of Philip Hankin's manuscript memoir.

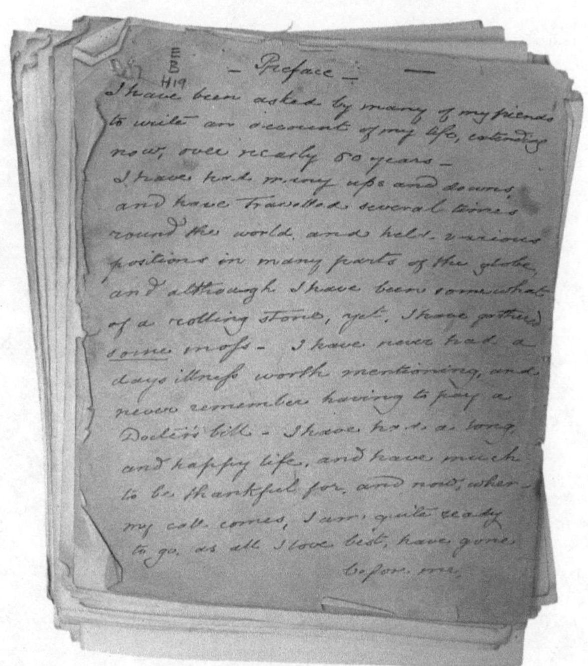

— Preface —

I have been asked by many of my friends to write an account of my life, extending now, over nearly 80 years — I have had many ups and downs and have travelled several times round the world, and held various positions in many parts of the globe, and although I have been somewhat of a rolling stone, yet, I have gathered some moss — I have never had a days illness worth mentioning, and never remember having to pay a Doctor's bill — I have had a long and happy life, and have much to be thankful for, and now, when my call comes, I am quite ready to go, as all I love best, have gone before me.

Adjacent panels of Andrews and Dury's 1807 map showing transportation links for "Sixty Five Miles Round London." Note "Thiel" (Thele) and "Mr. Hankin."

Thele House on Vicarage (later, Roydon) Road; or Stanstead Abbotts, as the Hankin family would have known it. Date of photo undetermined.

CHAPTER 1
A Sad Boyhood

Fierce winds and driving rain lashed the roof slates of Thele House on February 18, 1836. That night, Daniel Hankin's wife Elizabeth gave birth to their sixth child, their fourth son. The elderly attending nurse read the tempest as a portent: "I pity the child; his life like the night will be strange and wild." The omen would prove close to the mark.

Three months later, the lad was christened Philip James in the old Saint James' Church in Stanstead Abbotts. In the church grounds rested a dozen generations of Hankins.[1] The church itself dated from the twelfth century, but the site was sacred in Saxon times. Before that, Romans had occupied an encampment there. The entire area held millennia of ancient history, as evidenced by discoveries of multiple sites of prehistoric occupation. Stanstead manor was once the property of Anne Boleyn.

The village of Stanstead Abbotts lies in the valley of the River Lea in Hertfordshire, some twenty-two miles (thirty-five kilometres) north of London's Charing Cross. It is close to the small town of Ware, which in the nineteenth century provided a convenient and popular resting place for travellers between the capital and Cambridge. The land around was fertile, the principal crop being malting barley to supply the many breweries and hostelries serving the coach trade. The copious, pure water of the Lea provided the other requirement for good beer. Canals built in the industrial revolution efficiently transported barrels of beer to the thirsty multitudes of the city. The Hankin family had, for centuries, been closely connected with all aspects of this profitable business; they were accepted members of the "gentry."

Within Stanstead Abbotts, a mile downhill from the church, lay the house and farm of Thele,[2] the largest landholding in the area. Thele House was a three-storey Victorian construction of brick based on two adjacent cottages and fronted by a high brick wall. It was a substantial house, as befitted the squire of the parish, but was not a mansion. The 1841 census of England recorded that within lived Daniel and Elizabeth Hankin with their many children, three of Daniel's younger siblings (a brother and two sisters), and five long-serving female servants. Philip is significantly reticent about his own siblings in his memoir, providing merely a list of their names and dates of birth.

Between 1830 and 1848, his mother bore fourteen children, of whom four died in infancy. Elizabeth died herself shortly afterward. This continuous series of pregnancies and nursing meant that she had neither time nor energy to care for her children once weaned. Hinting at his lack of motherly love, Philip ironically likened her to the wife of Oliver Goldsmith's Vicar of Wakefield, calling her "a good Breeder."

He devotes more of the initial chapters in his memoir to Daniel, his father, a relationship also devoid of affection. "While my father was always very fond of the newest baby, he never cared for any of us after about 4 or 5," Philip recalled poignantly. He remembered, over seven decades later, how, when he was about five years old, he once held his face up to his father for a good-night kiss. Daniel brusquely rebuffed him with "There, that will do, run away, I never kiss boys!"

Another memory about his father was a peculiar rule about the boys' breakfast. In their farmyard, many chickens and other domestic fowl ranged freely. One of the lads' tasks was to search out eggs laid other than in the henhouses. Despite the copious availability of eggs, Daniel insisted that, for their breakfast, Philip and his brother Charles, two years his junior, were allowed milk, bread and butter, and, between them, a single boiled egg. Although the younger of the two, Charles was the more assertive and usually scooped out the whole yolk for himself.

Philip recalled that his father continually questioned him and his brothers, from the age of five, about their futures. He would declare that they "should all have to work for a living, [he] would not have a lot of lazy boys living at home and doing nothing!" This attitude may have sprung from his father's feelings about his own three siblings who still lived in Thele House. It might also have hinted at more profound problems troubling his father that would surface in later years. But Philip recorded, "This [implied threat] made me very frightened, for I was only 5, and quite expected any day to be turned out of the house."

Normally, one would expect a prosperous farmer, the incumbent master of a large acreage handed down through many generations, to have planned for his succession. He would have identified at least one of his sons to continue the family's stewardship. Such an heir would need years of grooming to prepare for the task ahead, rather than being treated as an expensive burden to be off-loaded at the earliest opportunity. Philip's father sent the three elder brothers away to high-priced schools, destined for other careers. This left Philip, Charles, and Thomas at home, subjected to their father's pressure to leave.

*

In the Hankin household, the only source of tender, loving care came from Daniel's younger sister, the children's aunt Maria, affectionately known as "Ria." A fall downstairs had dislocated her knee, rendering her dependent on a stick or a rustic Bath chair[3] during the day, and costing her any chance of a husband and family of her own. While she did not get on well with the children's mother, Ria was kind to all the children, and they reciprocated her love. Among Philip's fondest memories of his boyhood was going on summer picnics in the nearby woods, the lads pushing Ria in her chair along the paths and lifting her in the chair over the stiles. They would boil a kettle for tea and enjoy seedcake. Philip recalled her as "a kind, sweet-tempered little woman."

Another pleasure was fishing in the River Lea that bordered their garden. Daniel rewarded the boys with threepence per pound for the roach, dace, gudgeon, and pike they brought home for the kitchen. In earlier years, the Lea Valley near Stanstead Abbotts provided Izaak Walton with some of his favourite stretches of fresh water. Walton's *The Compleat Angler*, first published in 1653, became the third most reprinted book in history after the Bible and Shakespeare's works. To his multitude of followers Walton bequeathed the saying "I have laid aside business and gone a-fishing." Although Philip did not mention it in his memoir, he also became adept with the shotgun, a skill to prove useful later, in his naval career.

Philip's early education is a mystery. He mentions being "terribly beaten at the various schools" he attended for failure to comprehend

An illustration of a boy fishing in a 1911 edition of Izaak Walton's The Compleat Angler. *Art by James Thorpe.*

Euclid—meaning geometry.[4] Each summer his father insisted he copy out text from the newspaper. This stood him in good stead for the rest of his life: he wrote grammatically, in a clear hand, and enjoyed corresponding with friends.

For education, Daniel Hankin evidently treated Philip's three elder brothers differently. The eldest was Frederick George, six years Philip's senior, who would be expected, in the normal course of events, to return to continue running the family's estate. He attended Eton College, the most prestigious school in the land. After reading classics at Trinity College, Cambridge, he did not return to Thele. Instead, he took a commission as a lieutenant in the Staff Corps of the British Army in Chennai, then known as Madras, India. He rose to the rank of lieutenant colonel (retired) before returning to become the government inspector of prisons for Islington, London.

The second son, Edward Lewis, was five years older than Philip. Instead of attending college after private school, at sixteen he took a commission as a lieutenant of the British Officers of the Indian Army, to serve in Madras. Edward rose to the high rank of major general before retiring to live in Devon. The third son, Daniel Bell, attended Tonbridge

School, a boarding school for boys, founded in 1553 and later associated with Eton. From there, he studied at a theological college for ordination into the church. For a few years, he served as vicar in the town of Ware, close to Stanstead Abbotts. He later took a similar post in Stoke Newington, in the east end of London.

Between Edward and Daniel Bell came a daughter, Constance Seymour. No record of her education has been found, but there were schools for girls nearby. At age twenty-five, she, too, went out to Madras, to wed Augustus Becher Marsack, an officer with Her Majesty's Fourth Regiment of Madras Native Infantry. She died in India in 1863, having just given birth to a daughter.

*

On one occasion when Daniel grilled Philip on his career intentions, the lad responded: "A grocer." He liked the idea of ready access to treats such as almonds and raisins. This was unacceptable, so he tried again: "A doctor." Daniel poured derision on that idea: "A pretty doctor you would make. You'd kill all your patients!" Soon after that, Daniel's influential friend Sir Henry Ward, a diplomat and politician with contacts in high places, including the Admiralty, remarked that one of the many Hankin sons should go into the navy. Philip, then aged twelve, happened to best fit the role of a midshipman. Daniel informed Philip that he was to have a naval career. The son protested, to no avail. There was one problem: he would need to sit an exam for which his education to date had not prepared him.

The examination to enter the Royal Navy as a cadet comprised writing English from dictation and knowing the first four rules of arithmetic and the "rule of three."[5] While Philip could easily pass the first section, his mathematical skills were woefully below par, showing that he could not have received a primary education comparable to that of his three elder brothers. He would need special coaching.

A clergyman in Harwich, the Reverend John Bull, offered just such tutelage. Philip was sent there for three months and enjoyed it immensely. Reverend Bull was a kindly old man with a gentle wife and three children younger than Philip, and there were three fellow students. The curriculum was not onerous: the boys worked in the garden and had to learn the morning psalm,[6] a few verses at a time, which Philip remembered for the rest of his life. Reverend Bull also drilled them in arithmetic and the rule of three. At the end, Philip's tutor presented him with a small globe, and extracted a promise from him to write to the Bull family from the Cape of Good Hope. In his memoir, Philip recorded he complied. He also noted that he was sorry to leave. Life in a warm, loving household must have been in marked contrast to the one he had known at Thele House.

*

When Philip turned thirteen, his father took him to HMS *Ocean*, a naval shore establishment at Sheerness on the Kentish side of the Thames estuary, to sit for the cadets' exam. A doctor thumped his chest, asked him to cough, and pronounced him free from any physical insufficiency and fit for service. A clerk gave him an examination, which, while perfunctory, included a question involving the dreaded rule of three: "If a ship sails 10 knots in 2 hours, how many knots can she sail in 4 hours?" Notwithstanding Reverend Bull's coaching, Philip was terrified. It had something to do with ships, about which he knew nothing. After wrestling with it for a half hour, he came up with an answer. Finally, he had to write a few sentences from dictation, which he found easy. He was told that he had passed a very good examination and returned home with his father. His mother and family were pleased and congratulated him, which he found "very satisfactory, to say the least of it."

A few days later, a letter arrived from the Admiralty addressed to a Philip J. Hankin Esq. The Lords Commissioners of the Admiralty were pleased to appoint him as a naval cadet. He recorded in his memoir: "How proud I felt."

CHAPTER 2
Learning the Ropes

A second letter from the Admiralty arrived shortly after the news of Philip's appointment. He was to report at once to the officer commanding HMS *Castor* at Chatham Dockyard in Kent. The vessel was then being fitted out for a new commission as flagship to the commander of the Cape of Good Hope Station, Commodore Christopher Wyvill, RN.

Castor was a thirty-six-gun, fifth-rate ship of the line, a full-rigged frigate, with a complement of 275 men. Built at Chatham, it had been launched in May 1832. This was to be thirteen-year-old Philip's first ship.

The Hankin household faced a problem: the instructions were simple—"at once"—but Philip would need to be "kitted out" before he could join the ship. His father, Daniel, acted decisively; he and Philip took the next train to London to call on the established naval outfitters, Silver & Co. They measured him up and would produce the minimum requirement for a cadet's uniform to be sent to Thele House, the rest to follow as soon as possible. Two days later, Daniel insisted Philip parade through the village in his new jacket, ill-fitting trousers, and cap with a gold band, with a troop of village urchins in tow.

The following day, father and uniformed son travelled to Chatham. They located and boarded the *Castor* and Daniel asked to speak with the first lieutenant, commanding the ship at the time. He introduced himself and Philip to the officer, who responded, "All right, he is like a young dog—all his sorrows are to come." He showed them to the midshipmen's mess, and one member politely offered them a glass of ship's rum and some weevil-infested hardtack biscuit. Daniel, after banging

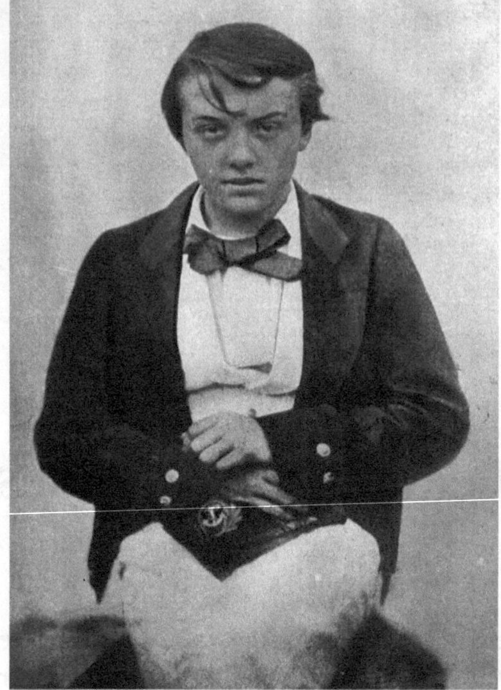

Midshipman Jackie Fisher, a contemporary of Philip Hankin, in tropical dress.

his head on a beam, soon departed with a "Well, goodbye Philip," and a gift of 10 shillings (half a British pound, and worth about C$90 in 2025).

The meagre sums spent by Daniel to kit out and bid farewell to Philip on his naval career were in marked contrast to what he would have needed to provide his two eldest sons, Frederick and Edward, as they embarked on careers in the Indian Army. After their expensive schooling, both would have required sets of costly uniforms and military accoutrements. They would not have needed, however, the private annual incomes of at least a few hundred pounds, depending on the status of the regiment, expected of commissioned officers of the British Army. In India, the costs of living were far lower than in Britain and the army's rates of pay were enough to meet them.[1]

*

The friendly new shipmate, noting the gift, remarked that "ten bob" was not very generous, and that he supposed Hankin's father was not well off. He swiftly relieved Philip of the money as a loan, since he had mislaid his purse, and disappeared ashore with the warning that tea was at four o'clock and he should look sharp or it would soon be gone. The money was never repaid. "Tea," the evening meal, when it came, was just a cup of tea with ship's biscuit for dunking. His messmates advised that this was the last food they would get before breakfast. Breakfast turned out to be tea without milk, coarse brown sugar, and ship's biscuit. Philip was soon to learn the hunger that would persist throughout the voyage.

Within a few days, Commodore Christopher Wyvill came aboard, "a fierce-looking man with a large, hooked nose and a red face. I felt very frightened of him." In early May 1849, a paddle steamer towed them to Plymouth and cast them off, and they set sail for Madeira and the Canary Islands. They took on water, provisions, fresh beef, and vegetables at Tenerife, then sailed to the lonely island of Ascension, anchoring there for two days. The ship's purser bought a quantity of turtles whose meat made a welcome change from "salt junk," and the lads caught a variety of fish, which made a change of diet. After sixty-eight days at sea, they anchored in Simon's Bay, the location of the naval harbour called Simon's Town, just outside Cape Town, at Africa's southernmost point.

During this, his first voyage, Philip would absorb the routines and protocols of the highly structured organism that was a man-of-war under sail. He would begin acquiring an intimate knowledge of the myriad ropes, spars, tackles, and sails that provide power and control to the ship's officers. His young muscles would grow in strength and his reflexes sharpen as he raced up the rigging in response to calls for changes to the sail configuration. He would have learned whole new vocabularies, both nautical terms and profanity.

Simon's Town had been a strategic naval base for the British Empire since the 1790s. Prior to the opening of the Suez Canal in 1869, it commanded the sailing route from England to India and other imperial outposts in the Far East. In 1814, Britain had purchased the region around the Cape of Good Hope from the Dutch government for £6 million (about C$7.7 million in 2025). Six years later, Britain had sent four thousand settlers to the neighbouring district around Port Elizabeth, some four hundred miles (six hundred kilometres) to the east of Cape Town. They declared English to be the official language, replacing the local Afrikaans dialect of Dutch spoken by white European settlers.

By the time *Castor* arrived, most of the Dutch colonist-farmers, known as Boers, had departed on their Great Trek inland to settle north of the Orange and Vaal Rivers. Seven years earlier, the British military had forced the Boers in Natal to move to the Transvaal. Natal was

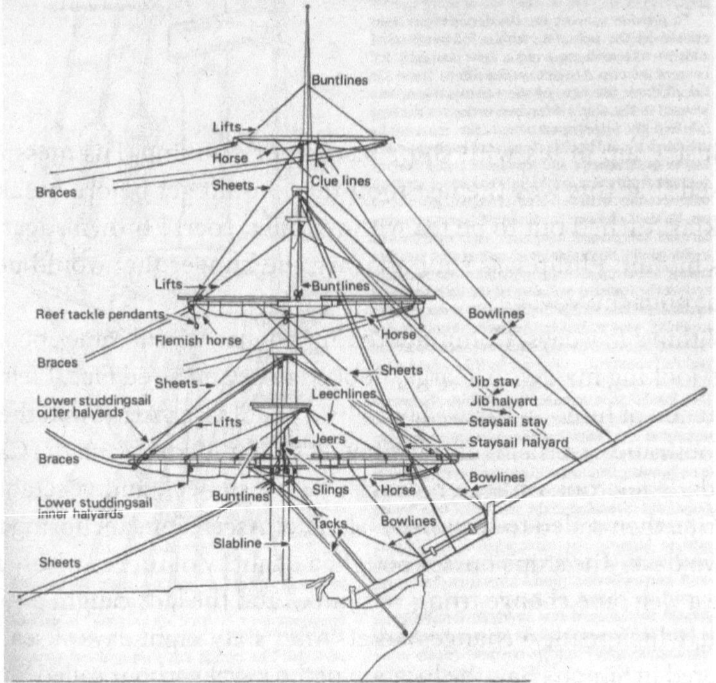

Diagram of the ropes associated with just one mast of a typical naval sailing vessel. Thirteen-year-old Hankin learned all these and more by heart.

incorporated, with the region around Port Elizabeth, into Cape Colony, ruled autocratically by a British governor.

As well as continued military actions against disaffected Boers, there had been unrest among the local Xhosa population, then frequently referred to as Kaffirs (a derogatory word since the twentieth century). This had led to military repression, forming the foundation for the policy of racial segregation. The governor serving at the time of *Castor*'s arrival was Lieutenant General Sir Harry Smith, a soldier who had served with distinction during the Peninsula War and at Waterloo. He was upcountry engaged in aggressive expansion operations in Xhosa territory, as well as in campaigns against Boers near the Orange River.

Things weren't always rough for midshipmen. Philip noted in his memoir that Juana, Lady Smith, the wife of the governor, was hospitable to the "middies" of *Castor*, inviting them, two at a time, to spend a week or ten days with her at Government House in Rondebosch. He would enjoy two such excursions, during which he attended her dinner parties and twice-weekly dances and met many local families. During his time at Simon's Town, he picked up some Afrikaans, which his captain would call upon years later during an awkward diplomatic situation. Philip's facility for learning languages would prove an important asset in his career.

Lady Juana Smith. The Spanish wife of the governor and charming hostess for visiting naval officers at Cape Town.

Lady Juana Smith

Of noble Spanish birth, Lady Smith was descended from Juan Ponce de León, who sailed on the second voyage of Columbus and later explored and charted the coast of what he named *La Florida* on the North American mainland. Juana María de los Dolores de León was just fourteen when Wellington's forces besieged, then stormed, the city of Badajoz, her home in southwest Spain. A strong French garrison were occupying it. Orphaned in the action, she and her sister fled and pleaded with some British officers for protection. A few days later, she married one of them, Brigade Major Harry Smith.

She remained by his side for the rest of the Peninsula campaign, enchanting the officer corps, including Wellington, with her beauty and courage. The soldiers idolized "Juanita." In 1848, Parliament granted her a pension of £500 for her services to the country. Two towns in South Africa were named in her honour, and a third, indirectly, is on Vancouver Island, the town of Ladysmith.

HMS Castor *flying the Commodore's Pennant as flagship at the Cape.*

A few days after *Castor* had anchored in Simon's Bay, another British ship arrived. It was *Neptune*, conveying 150 convicts to be disembarked in the Cape Colony. The resident colonists objected strongly. They felt such miscreants would be a threat to their security and new way of life. Sir Harry advised his superior in London, the Earl Grey, "This is the first occasion on which Dutch and English inhabitants coalesced in opposition to Government."[2]

In the governor's absence, local officials could only ask for clarification from London. In the meantime, the convicts remained aboard *Neptune*, and the colonists lobbied. It was several months before a decision arrived from London. The colonists' case was upheld: the convicts would not be landed at the Cape, but taken to Van Diemen's Land, later called Tasmania, where the penal settlement of Port Arthur was already established.

Soon after *Neptune* departed, *Castor* also lifted anchor for an extended cruise to the Mozambique Channel between the African mainland and Madagascar. Britain's blockade of the slave trade from Africa began in 1808 and lasted until 1870. The Royal Navy's West Africa Squadron, at times several ships strong, was there to intercept the flourishing trade in enslaved people captured in Africa and conveyed to New Orleans or Rio de Janeiro for sale.[3] Most of those vessels operating throughout East Africa, termed "slavers," used the Mozambique Channel.

Under a new law in 1834, ships of the Royal Navy could hunt down and capture slavers on the high seas, release their captives, and sell the ships for prize money, which would be distributed to the captain, officers, and crew of the hunter. Commodore Wyvill was keen to take advantage of the opportunity to improve his own fortune. By 1860 the squadron had captured 1,600 slavers, but at a cost of over 2,000 British sailors dying of various causes during the missions.

Over the next ten months, the cruise took them to several places in the southern Indian Ocean. *Castor* gave chase to several small slaver vessels, but they all escaped. One port visited was Port Louis on Mauritius, where Philip got four days' leave ashore to visit friends of his father who had a sugar plantation nearby.

During the cruise, the midshipmen's formal education continued. A Mr. Jones, their elderly instructor with "very long red whiskers" who was also the ship's clergyman, gave them daily classes in navigation in the commodore's fore-cabin. A cry from the highest yardarm—"Sail on the weather bow!"—interrupted one of his Sunday services. Wyvill called out, "There, that will do Mr. Jones! Grace of our Lord etc., etc., Amen!" He then roared, "Hands make sail!" Every man raced to his station, leaving Mr. Jones alone in his pulpit.

Getting supplies of water during the cruise proved an ongoing problem. It required organizing three of the ship's boats to be ready by three thirty in the morning, with empty casks and provisions loaded for the day, and the men having had their breakfast of cocoa and biscuit. Often it required rowing ten miles (sixteen kilometres) to the shore to find a source of water, usually a river mouth, fill the casks, and row back—a full day's hard work. The water they found was often contaminated. Up to one hundred of the crew fell sick with fever and dysentery, and forty died during the cruise.

Hankin did not succumb to the contagion. His immune system must have been extremely robust. In the preface to his memoir, he proudly claimed, "I have never had a day's illness worth mentioning, and never remember having to pay a doctor's bill." Eventually the ship's doctor warned the commodore that unless he returned to the Cape, he would lose many more of the crew. Frustrated at having failed to secure a single prize slaver, Wyvill reluctantly ordered the course to be set for Simon's Bay.

*

Wyvill, a hard drinker himself, took pleasure in humiliating midshipmen who had not yet become used to liquor. It was his custom to invite a few wardroom officers to dine in his cabin. Occasionally, he would also invite a single midshipman, which they all dreaded. One evening, the steward notified Hankin that he was to attend. Although phrased as an invitation, it was clearly an order.

By now, all of Hankin's clothing was in poor condition. Working in the ship's rigging was invariably hard on cloth. Tar smeared onto the ropes protected them from rot. He laboured to select his least-yellow shirt, brushed and scrubbed it, ironed it with an empty beer bottle, then rubbed chalk onto any visibly dirty spots on the collar. Dressed in his Sunday jacket and waistcoat, he presented himself at the commodore's cabin. Four officers were also invited, making six at table, with Philip's place near the door.

He knew it was the custom to toast one another with wine during dinner. It would be discourteous—an insult, even—to decline. No sooner had the soup been served than the host addressed his young and terrified guest: "Mr. Hankin, pleasure of a glass of wine, Sir?" "With pleasure, Sir," he replied. The steward filled a large glass with strong sherry, and Philip raised it to his lips. "No heel taps, drink it off, Sir, like a man!" ordered the commodore, downing his own in one. Philip knew he had to do likewise.

Throughout the dinner, the other officers repeated the ritual, each toasting the unfortunate Hankin as the commodore bellowed, "No heel taps!" Up to this time, the lad, not yet fourteen, had had little exposure to strong liquor, beyond the odd glass of ale at his father's occasional dinner parties. The five goblets of sherry he had swallowed had the inevitable effect. But the ordeal was not yet over. At the end of dinner, they passed round decanters of port and sherry, and Philip received a large glass of port. "The Queen" was toasted, and all downed theirs in one. A choice of liqueurs accompanied coffee: "Curaçao or Maraschino?" the steward asked. Philip replied with a mumbled "Shure-a-sho."

Philip knew, when the first lieutenant rose, that the dinner had concluded. He got to his feet, bowed to his host, and attempted to leave. He got as far as the door, then fell flat on his face. The sentry picked him up, carried him below to his sleeping place, and left him there, unconscious. Some time later, while still in a stupor, he was shaken awake by an elderly quartermaster. The commodore had summoned him to the quarterdeck. The kindly old man wiped his face with a towel and helped him to mount the companionway. As he came on deck, the ship gave a sudden shift. Philip lost his balance and again fell flat. Wyvill pointed him out to the captain, exclaiming, "That young gentleman's drunk! A disgrace to the Service!" Armed sentries marched Hankin off to walk around the mizzen deck for several hours until he was sober. His further punishment meant forfeiture of two weeks' leave ashore when they returned to Simon's Town.

The entire charade had been a deliberate exercise in humiliation by a Royal Navy flag officer. The purpose seems unfathomable, but such cruelty and blatant abuse of authority appears to have been a regular occurrence under Wyvill's command. Another curious aspect of the affair is that none of Philip's messmates warned him what to expect. In his memoir, recounting the incident, Hankin noted the commodore did not invite him to dine again. It was, he wrote, the only occasion in his life when he ever got drunk. He did, however, fall foul of Wyvill again, later in the voyage.

Meagre and nutritionally lacking as their food had been at the beginning of the cruise, it got progressively worse as the months passed. Philip and his messmates were famished. One day, Philip and another boy peeked through a grill in the quartermaster's storeroom door. They could see a whole smoked ham on a shelf, and their mouths watered. Over the next few days, they sawed through a bar of the grill, then speared the ham with a boarding pike—a stout pole topped with a metal spike—and drew it toward the grill. With a penknife, they carved off a few lumps of ham before it fell to the deck, beyond reach of the pike.

Next morning, when the mess caterer came to collect stores for the midday meal, he discovered the mutilated ham. He suspected it to be the work of middies. He slammed it down on their table, demanding that the culprit own up. Philip and his guilty messmate, although both scared, remained silent. They faced dismissal from the service for such a heinous offence. The caterer removed the damaged evidence and reported the loss, but the perpetrators remained unknown. Philip had had a narrow escape.

*

When they arrived at Simon's Town, several of the sick were invalided home. Philip had to serve his two weeks confined to the ship, but the usual crowd of "bumboat" traders came aboard to offer their wares and services. They were a tailor, a shoemaker, and several washermen who would do his laundry; all for a price, of course. On the cruise for the best part of a year, his clothes were in tatters and his shoes badly in need of repair. He and his messmates all needed to order new uniforms from the tailor, and for Philip, this was a problem.

The arrangements for his pay comprised naval salary of £20 per year, supplemented by £40 from his father. £5 was deducted from his pay to compensate Mr. Jones for his tuition. Philip's net monthly income was £3 6s 8d (3 pounds, 6 shillings, and 8 pence, about C$670 in 2025). The details of Philip's budget were etched into his memory and recorded in his memoir, sixty-four years later. A new uniform suit cost £3 10s, the washing bill for a month was 14s, the mess bill £1 10s. He found it impossible to keep clear of debt. He borrowed from whomever he could, repaying them a little each month. In desperation, he wrote to his father, pleading to be sent £10 (about C$2,000 in 2025) to free him of his current debts, and promising to be more frugal in the future.

The £10 arrived some months later, with a stern letter from his father that Philip considered unfair. Other boys' fathers had contributed £50, but even that would have been far less than the school fees for Eton or Tonbridge provided for Philip's brothers. His father's remonstration about his lack of consideration for his younger siblings particularly stung. He thought about them a lot.

Unfortunately, his father had paid the money through the commodore's bankers, which signalled to Wyvill that young Hankin must have complained about his situation. From his house on shore, he called Philip before him. "How dare you, Sir?" demanded the officer. Hankin explained his financial situation, and the damage that tar in the rigging caused on clothing and the associated expense, but it was to no avail. Wyvill gave the lad a letter for Captain Benjamin H. Bunce of *Castor* banishing Philip to HMS *Seringapatam* for six weeks; on no account was he to be allowed ashore. He was to manage on ship's provisions and wash his own clothes.

*

His punishment was not nearly as salutary as Wyvill had intended. The hiatus in his duties came as a welcome respite after the hardships and dangers of chasing slavers in the Mozambique Channel. The *Seringapatam* was an elderly, twenty-six-gun sailing frigate based on a design from a captured French vessel. In 1850, while Philip served his sentence, it was an anchored receiving ship, or "hulk," intended as transit accommodation for naval personnel not yet allocated to active ships. The masts, rigging, armament, and steering gear had all been removed.

An old salt of a gunner, with his wife on board, oversaw the vessel. They were kind to their young "guest" and invited him to dinner every Sunday in their cabin. The gunner boosted Philip's morale with the time-honoured rallying cry "Never say die, lad, s'long as there's a shot in the locker!"[4]

With his own comfortable cabin, Philip spent much of his days fishing "and had very good sport." Angling skills he developed in boyhood on the River Lea came to the fore. Shrewdly, he kept the gunner's wife well supplied with his catch. It was during this time, forced to cook for himself, that he learned how to prepare fish curry—a skill that would pay off well, later in his career at sea. Relieved of a mess bill and without the need to pay for his clothes to be washed, he could pay off most of his debts. The only downside of his stay was the enforced prohibition on enjoying the hospitality of Lady Smith and her circle of charming settler friends.

*

A little over two years into his service aboard *Castor*, orders arrived from the Admiralty to send four midshipmen back to England, Hankin among them. They boarded HMS *Megaera*, a recently built screw frigate with an iron hull, one of the first such vessels ordered by the Royal Navy. There being no midshipmen's mess, the ship's officers invited the four to join them in the wardroom, so the forty-day journey back to Woolwich passed pleasantly enough.

Three years later, Hankin was awarded the South Africa Medal associated with the brutal Eighth Frontier War, known at the time as the Third Kaffir War, against the Xhosa people. This was a campaign medal issued to all officers and men of the British Army and Royal Navy on active service in the theatre, even if they did not take part in the actual battles. It was to be the only medal Hankin would receive in his career.

South Africa Medal issued in 1855 for service aboard HMS Castor, *Philip Hankin's only decoration. The ribbon is gold with black stripes.*

CHAPTER 3

Ashore, Then Back to Sea

When Philip arrived back in Woolwich in 1852, he found a letter from his father directing him to return to Stanstead Abbotts as soon as possible. Philip's request to the Admiralty to be discharged ashore was granted, and he took the train to Ware, a civilian once more.

Anxious to learn the reason for his father's urgent summons, he was told that, for some time, his mother had been sick with a persistent cough, not thought to be serious. In fact, her condition was far worse than they knew. A week later, his father confided the real reason for calling him home: he was selling Thele House and all the land and emigrating to New Zealand. They were to be pioneer settlers in the new colony, and he needed the boys to come with him to help work the land. The two eldest were both in the army in India, but they could join the venture too, if they wished.

His father explained that the long sea voyage would be beneficial for his mother's health. The plan was to dispose of the property and set out in about eight months' time. He estimated the sale would realize £30,000 (about C$6.7 million in 2025) and that sum should enable them to find and develop an excellent property out there. In the meantime, Philip could not expect to stay at home without a job. Evidently, his father considered Philip's help in preparing a large house and estate for sale not a worthwhile activity for him. Nor was getting the family ready for the life of pioneering in the wilderness of New Zealand. Better that he earn an income. A neighbour and good friend of the family, Mr. Calvert, owned a brewery in London and agreed to find a place for Philip there.

A few days later, with a third-class season ticket, Philip took the train to London and showed up at the brewery near the Tower of London, bearing Mr. Calvert's letter of introduction. The manager appointed him a junior clerk in the office at a salary of £60 per annum. This sounded better than his naval pay, so Philip was content. He was to work from eight thirty until six for one week in two and stay until nine thirty every other week. In those weeks, he would get home at ten thirty. He worked on average fifty-six hours a week for what in 2025 would be £2.80 (about C$5.20) an hour. His duties were not onerous: he was messenger and general dogsbody, but he picked up some knowledge of office procedures and clerical work.

This lasted for five months, until his mother's condition had deteriorated to a point where the doctor could not recommend her making the long journey to New Zealand, and Daniel abandoned the whole plan. Hankin, in his memoir, does not describe any discussion in the family about such a significant relocation and its implications for them. Nor does he even mention the family members present at Thele House during this period that he spent with them. The national 1851 census recorded as residents Philip's parents, sisters Constance, Alice, and Lucy, and brothers Daniel Bell, Thomas, and Graham, as well as his well-loved aunt Ria. Neither his uncle George nor aunt Christiana was listed. Absent, too, was his younger brother Charles, then aged thirteen, perhaps away at boarding school. The census listed no live-in servants, but some of them were surely still present.

Hankin's memoir records no emotion on his part at returning home and reuniting with his family after over two years away at sea. Nor does it note any reaction from them at his reappearance. The commute and long hours of his job in London would have left little time for them to become reacquainted. Aunt Ria expressed her dislike at the smell of tobacco smoke on his clothes, accusing him of acquiring the habit. He explained it was because he had travelled in train carriages with smokers.

His father still showed no interest in having Philip remain and learn to run the farm. Instead, through yet another friend at the Admiralty, he arranged that he rejoin the navy.

The Admiralty offered Philip a choice of two ships, both anchored at Spithead, the Royal Navy's roadstead in the Solent, near Portsmouth: HMS *Agamemnon* or HMS *Sidon*. He chose the latter, a twenty-two-gun, first-class paddle frigate, launched in 1846. He noted a feature he liked was that the middies' mess in *Sidon* was aft of the wardroom, and immediately below the captain's cabin. He was to rejoin as a midshipman. It was 1853, and Philip was seventeen years old.

*

Philip soon fell back into the familiar routine of life aboard and forgot about his spell as a brewer's clerk. Several cadets joined *Sidon* as their first ship, among them, he recalled in the memoir, some who went on to rise to the rank of admiral. He had the good fortune to be assigned to the watch of a sub-lieutenant—termed at the time "mate"—Frank Thomson, whom he later described as "one of the most charming men I have ever met."[1] They formed a friendship that would endure until Thomson's death in 1884. Even after that, Philip remained in contact with Frank's daughter, son, and two grandsons, both of whom became officers in the Royal Navy.

Whenever Thomson had a day's leave ashore, he would take Philip along to stay with his mother, who lived in nearby Southsea and who gave the friends "excellent suppers." She would play the flute accompanied by her son on the piano. During this time, Thomson became engaged to Minnie, sister of another naval officer who, a few years later, would be awarded the Victoria Cross at the siege of Lucknow in India, and rise to the highest naval rank: Admiral of the Fleet Sir Nowell Salmon, VC, GCB. Philip often accompanied Frank and his fiancée to dances at Winchester. He was a natural dancer who loved and excelled at it, recalling at seventy-nine that he "could never resist The Blue Danube waltz."

He remembered attending many dances at the highly fashionable summer resort of Ryde on the Isle of Wight, across the Solent from Portsmouth, and got to know "several charming families." He renewed a warm friendship with a Mrs. Menzies, whom he had earlier met in the Cape when they had invited him to their villa at Sea Point near Cape Town. Mr. Menzies had been chief justice of the colony, and when he died, his widow and family had retired to Ryde. Another mother with a pretty daughter, he remembered, was Lady Douglas.

At this part of writing his memoir, Philip's mood turned from buoyant to melancholic, as he reflected, obliquely, about his own family, probably referring to experiences later in his life: "[Relatives] always want to give you advice, and take liberties, which they would not dream of doing, if they were only friends."

After he had been six months aboard *Sidon*, his mother's condition worsened, and Constance, his sister, took her to recuperate in the sea air at Ryde. This proved unsuccessful, so they returned to Thele House, where she died. Philip's father denied his wish to see his mother one last time before "the summons came," saying that he "should only be in the way." Elizabeth was buried in the Hankin family plot in Saint James' churchyard, Stanstead Abbotts. Philip never mentions having visited her grave.

*

Having been ten months aboard *Sidon* at Spithead, Philip found the lack of action to be tedious, so he applied to the Admiralty requesting transfer to a seagoing ship, and they promptly complied. He was to report immediately to HMS *Plumper*, then fitting out at Portsmouth for a commission to West Africa. He was sorry to leave his messmates, but it proved a fortunate move for him. Within a year, the Crimean War broke out and *Sidon* was actively involved. During the siege of Sevastopol, a Russian shell struck the ship exactly where he would have been stationed had he remained with them. Twenty-two men died or were injured in the explosion. His friend Frank Thomson, newly promoted to lieutenant, had already transferred to HMS *Fury* in the Mediterranean, so he too had a close escape.

Hankin's new ship, *Plumper*, was a small, wooden, auxiliary screw (propeller) sloop of experimental design, a hybrid intended to use a coal-fired steam engine for tactical mobility but rely on sail for long distances. The economical cruising speed under power was six and a half knots. Under sail, the crew lifted propeller aboard, but this complicated arrangement proved inefficient under practical operations. *Plumper* carried six muzzle-loading guns.

Plumper's captain was Commander John Anthony Lawrence Wharton, RN, with Lieutenant Charles John Didham, RN, and Lieutenant Edward Shaw, RN, serving as first and second lieutenants. Philip got on well with all three, but he particularly admired Shaw, "one of the kindest, and best of men. I can never forget him, and all his kindness to me." Shaw was his watch officer and taught him seamanship: how to moor and unmoor a ship, shift topsail yards, and many other skills needed by a young naval officer.

Section of 1851 map *Western Africa* by John Tallis.

Plumper steamed out of Portsmouth Harbour on September 12, 1853, lifted her screw, and set sail bound for the Bight of Benin in West Africa on a mission to intercept slavers. For eighteen months, as part of the West Africa Squadron, they cruised along the coast visiting Liberia, Accra, and Cape Coast Castle. The "Castle" was one of dozens of slave fortresses on the Gold Coast (now Ghana) built as dungeons to hold enslaved people until they were transported to the Americas. In 1853 it was a British possession, so it no longer held any slaves. *Plumper* then sailed west to Ascension Island in the mid-Atlantic, and there, Philip Hankin's fortunes took another turn for the worse.

Married just before his appointment as *Plumper*'s skipper, Commander Wharton wanted to spend time with his new wife, so he applied to be relieved of his command. While they were at Ascension, his replacement arrived, Commander William Henry Haswell. This was his first command, but he already had a few years' experience on the West Africa station. The ship from which he was transferring, HMS *Investigator*, had met an unfortunate end. On a mission to discover the Northwest Passage, it had become trapped in the ice of Prince of Wales Sound and abandoned. Haswell, the first lieutenant, and all the crew returned to

Decorative insert to Tallis's 1851 map *Western Africa*.

Britain in another vessel. Perhaps it was this traumatic experience that made him a martinet, a stickler for detail and impossible to please. Philip recorded that "everyone on board hated him."

Haswell was especially hard on Philip, who had just received promotion to mate, or sub-lieutenant, and so was given charge of a watch; that is, he was the officer on duty for two or four hours. Upon the change of command, *Plumper* returned to the Bight, resuming the hunt for slavers. Philip was not at all happy. "How I hated it all, the hot climate and many men ill with fever, the terrible monotony of the life, and the constant bullying of the captain nearly drove me wild." He wrote to his father's friend at the Admiralty, a Mr. Clifton, to see if he could arrange a transfer to a ship in Crimea, where the war with Russia was raging. The Admiralty responded that if the captain could spare him from his current post, he could return to England.

This displeased Haswell: "So you thought you would get out of the ship, did you?" When Hankin responded, "Yes, Sir," he shook his fist in the junior's face. "Well, Sir, you won't go! I'll see you damned first! Now, go back to your duty!" Some months later, at Lagos, *Plumper* lay at anchor alongside a brig, HMS *Sappho*, that was bound for Australia. Philip asked her skipper, Captain Fairfax Moresby, if he might persuade Haswell to allow him to be transferred to *Sappho*. Haswell's response was negative, but Philip recorded that, had Haswell but known *Sappho*'s fate, he would have agreed to the transfer, for the vessel sailed south and was never heard from again.

On another occasion, Haswell attempted to harm Hankin and possibly condemn him to death. *Plumper* lay at anchor off the mouth of the Congo River. He ordered Hankin to take the ship's whaleboat with five "Kroomen" (local African temporary crew) to investigate if there were any suspicious-looking vessels at Punta da Legna, some 200 miles (320 kilometres) upstream. Haswell allocated no white crew members to the mission, since the estuary was notoriously rife with malaria, and many aboard were already infected. Haswell was evidently unaware of Hankin's robust immune system.

Philip enjoyed the expedition, shooting monkeys, parrots, and other exotic birds, some of which proved delicious: "It was as good as a picnic." Each night he slept aboard the whaleboat, under the awning, and in the mornings, he swigged some quinine-laced wine. After a month,

Studio portrait of Dr. David Livingstone in his later years by Thomas Annan.

he returned to *Plumper*, reporting no slavers seen. He recorded in his memoir: "Haswell seemed much disappointed when, after 14 days, the doctor reported I was quite well."

Off Cabinda, in the north of the Portuguese territory in West Africa, *Plumper* captured a small cutter carrying ninety enslaved people who were sent to the island of St. Helena for release. They destroyed the cutter, since it was worthless as a prize. This appears to have been the only slaver captured during *Plumper*'s three-year commission.

Farther south, they called in at the port of Luanda, the capital of Angola, a major Portuguese overseas province and an important centre of trade. There, Philip met Dr. David Livingstone. The famous doctor, missionary, and explorer was about to embark on a trek of some 1,900 miles (3,000 kilometres) right across the southern African continent to "Quillimane."[2] He invited Philip to join him. The eighteen-year-old found the prospect "most alluring," and begged permission from Haswell, who, again, curtly denied the request. Livingstone completed his epic crossing, the first by a European. He sighted and named Lake Victoria and its falls on the way. Haswell's petulance denied his young officer the chance of participating in one of the greatest episodes of Victorian exploration.

After *Plumper* had completed three years on the commission, the navy ordered the vessel to return home. From Luanda they first headed

Stanford's map of Livingstone's explorations in Central Africa between 1851 and 1873.

for the lonely island of St. Helena, where, for six years until his death in 1821, Napoleon had lived in exile. Philip visited his tomb.

During the fortnight's stopover, Philip took lodgings in a "pretty little farmhouse on the top of a hill, where it was delightfully cool." This brought most welcome relief from the discomfort and oppressive heat of the African coast. The farmer, Mr. Evans, with his two daughters, kept a few chickens and a vegetable garden. When Philip came to leave, one daughter, Lena, presented him with a package of butter, nicely wrapped, for him to enjoy when he was back at sea. He took it as a charming token of affection. He realized his mistake when, soon after he had boarded, a boat brought him a highly scented little note that read:

Dear Mr. Hankin,
I must write you a few lines before you leave, to say how much I miss you, but I hope we shall meet again some day, and with love and kisses,
I am always, your loving
Lena.
P.S.
Please don't forget to pay for the butter—2 lbs. 4 shillings.

Philip sent the money by the boatman, but never heard a word more from his loving Lena. Six decades later, he noted wistfully: "I don't suppose I ever shall."

After stopping briefly at Ascension Island to take on a supply of turtles, three weeks of good sailing brought them home to Portsmouth. As they passed the Isle of Wight, Philip had the middle watch, six to eight o'clock in the morning. It was bitterly cold, in a heavy gale, and he wore only tropical white trousers and a monkey jacket borrowed from the purser. Despite his vivid image of the experience, in his memoir he also noted how pleased he was to drop anchor, once again in Spithead roads, on December 8, 1856. The usual throng of bumboat women soon surrounded them. They offered "bread and butter, cold fried fish, smoked bloaters and other good things. Oh! What a treat it was, after our miserable fare on the coast of Africa, to taste good English bread & butter again." In 1878, W.S. Gilbert was to immortalize one of these women as "poor little Buttercup" in his satirical Savoy opera, *HMS Pinafore.*

The following day, *Plumper* steamed into Portsmouth Harbour to tie up, be inspected by the admiral, and pay off. By then, twenty years old, Philip Hankin planned to study for qualification as a lieutenant.

Poor little Buttercup. Gilbert and Sullivan's depiction of one of the women coming aboard to sell her wares to sailors on their arrival in port.

CHAPTER 4
After Training, Back Aboard HMS *Plumper*

To be promoted to lieutenant in the Royal Navy, a candidate needs seniority—sufficient years of service—and to have passed certain examinations. Regular sessions with an instructor and practical experience during a midshipman's time at sea prepared him for these examinations. Before leaving the West Africa station, Hankin sat an examination in seamanship before a board of three captains. He passed with a first-class certificate. He needed two more: in gunnery, and in navigation. Upon his release from his first voyage in HMS *Plumper*, he would take courses and sit the examinations in each of these, both of which he dreaded.

For navigation, Hankin attended the Royal Naval College in Portsmouth Dockyard. He recorded that he "got through without much difficulty, and obtained a second class certificate." Considering his aversion to Euclid as a schoolboy and his problems with the rule of three, he had clearly made significant progress. Navigation is a practical application of geometry—the principles of Euclid, for ignorance of which he had suffered beatings as a boy. The training he had received from Frank Thomson aboard HMS *Sidon* and Edward Shaw on HMS *Plumper* had produced a remarkable improvement in his mathematical aptitude.

His gunnery classes were aboard HMS *Excellent*, the navy's school of gunnery, also in Portsmouth Dockyard. At the time of Philip's course, 1857, the school was in a dismasted hulk that had once been HMS *Boyne*, a two-deck ship of the line. There was no accommodation aboard *Excellent*, so Philip took lodgings for a month with Mr. and Mrs. Stones, just outside the dockyard gates. Stones was a naval tailor, and his wife took in boarders, usually young naval officers, at 2 guineas—1 pound and 1 shilling, a common unit of payment—per month.

Philip had his own room, "small, but quite comfortable," and the boarders all took meals with the family. Breakfast was always herrings and coffee, and dinner, served at four o'clock as they got back from their classes, was usually boiled rabbit with onion sauce, and a milk pudding to follow. Philip recorded, "It was very good, after the fare I had been accustomed to in a midshipman's mess." Philip remembered the two Stones daughters: "Tilly was about 18 and rather good looking, Dora was a little fat girl, about twelve. She always stood on a chair to say grace, after dinner, making a little curtsy as she said 'Amen!'" He passed gunnery "quite well, for I had a good memory, and had learnt a great deal by heart."

*

One of the Stoneses' other boarders was "an officer named Pender, a very pleasant bright young fellow." He and Hankin became good friends. Daniel Pender was then a second master; that is, a specialist in hydrography, the science of surveying for, and preparing, marine charts. Masters were a separate line of junior officers in the Royal Navy, later called navigating officers, reporting to the Hydrographer of the Navy. Pender had just been appointed to HMS *Plumper*, Philip's old ship, then preparing for a new commission to Vancouver Island. They were to determine the new boundary between British and American territories where the 49th line of latitude north, also called the 49th parallel, met the Pacific. After that, they would chart the coast of Vancouver Island and the adjacent mainland, a project expected to take several years to complete.

As Philip remembered it, Pender suggested, "Why don't you come with us? It will be a jolly trip for you. I know the captain, Richards, well, and if you like I will speak to him about you. I'm sure he will be pleased to have you with him." He was referring to Captain George Henry Richards. Apparently, Pender did not know Richards quite as well as he thought, for when he raised the topic, the captain was adamant that he did not want Hankin since he was not a surveyor. Pender, however, prevaricated when he told Philip of his conversation with the captain. He suggested that if Philip could find a way to get appointed, Richards would be pleased.

Hankin, now twenty-one, liked the idea of a new adventure. Once again, he contacted Mr. Clifton at the Admiralty, explaining what he had understood from Pender to be the situation. Clifton again obliged and Philip received notice appointing him to *Plumper*'s new mission. When Hankin came aboard at Plymouth, the annoyed Captain Richards demanded to know how this had happened. Pender confessed he had thought that his friend would have no chance of arranging the appointment, and so the matter was closed. In the event, Richards was a most reasonable officer, and Philip proved his worth to him.

*

In the section of his memoir covering the first few weeks of 1857, which he spent studying in Portsmouth between his assignments aboard *Plumper*, Philip omitted mention of his family, probably indicating he did not visit them. Some major changes had recently taken place of which he would learn only later.

*

George Henry Richards, Hankin's new skipper, was an exceptional man, a first-rate hydrographic specialist, and an excellent leader. The son of a Royal Navy captain, he had joined the service in 1832 and served in the Pacific, being commended for bravery during the Second Opium War with China. He then assisted in surveying the Falkland Islands and Patagonia. During the subsequent hostilities with Argentina, he won promotion to commander. There followed extensive surveys of the coasts of New Zealand. Between 1852 and '54, as second-in-command to the irascible Captain the Honourable Edward Belcher, he had joined the search for the missing expedition of Sir John Franklin. During that time, he had made extensive solo journeys by dogsled, including one lasting ninety-three days. During this demanding mission, Richards demonstrated great tact and judgement. On his return to Britain, he learned of his promotion to captain.

It had been Richards who first drew official attention to the strategic implications of the United States buying Alaska. He pointed out that the water boundary between British interests on the Pacific coast of North America, and those of the expansionist United States, had not yet been defined. There were no accurate charts of the waters in question. So, aged thirty-seven, Richards received his first command,

Captain George Henry Richards, RN.

HMS *Plumper*, and was appointed deputy commissioner for the Joint Boundary Commission. He was to survey where the agreed boundary, the 49th parallel, met the Pacific and erect a monument marking the place. He was then to make a thorough hydrographic survey of the coasts of Vancouver Island and the adjacent mainland.

*

This would not be the first coastal survey by the Royal Navy in the region. Captain James Cook had briefly visited Nootka Sound in 1778 and marked it on the chart tracking his voyage. Between 1792 and 1795, Captain George Vancouver had come on a mission with limited scope. It was to prove or disprove the existence of a navigable channel from the North Atlantic, across the continent, to a portal on the Pacific. His mission was successful, in that he confirmed it did not exist. Collaborating with a Spanish counterpart mission, Vancouver produced a map of the coastline from California to Alaska that showed Vancouver Island. However, it was not a proper hydrographic survey, lacking depths of water and other navigational information. In 1846 and 1847, Captain Henry Kellet, RN, had brought two ships to the newly constructed Fort Victoria and carried out some hydrographic survey work in the harbour and vicinity.[1]

*

Plumper carried out some steam trials in the Solent on March 11, 1857, achieving six knots, before sailing to Plymouth, where Philip came aboard, to Richards's initial displeasure. The ship needed further work, delaying their departure for Lisbon by two weeks. Philip noted the construction of a new chart room and two more cabins, forming a poop—a raised deck at the rear of a ship. In the Bay of Biscay *Plumper* sprang a leak and, just as they were leaving the Tagus River, the propeller shaft broke, so they had to continue to Rio de Janeiro using sail alone.

Hankin now held the full set of certificates to qualify[2] as a lieutenant once he gained sufficient seniority. Richards designated him the third mate, to keep a watch. The first officer, William Moriarty, had been gazetted lieutenant in 1854, but had no prior experience in hydrographic work. Nor had the second officer, Richard Charles Mayne, gazetted lieutenant just a few months before joining *Plumper*. He had served during the Russian War in the Baltic and Black Sea and had previously visited Esquimalt and Victoria. Under Richards's tutelage, he quickly gained abilities as a hydrographic surveyor. Mayne wrote an excellent book on his four years with Richards, for which the Royal Geographical Society elected him a fellow. He later commanded his own survey vessel and, after retiring from active duty, he was elected a member of Parliament.

At the start of the mission, three survey specialists shared *Plumper*'s cramped wardroom: Master John Augustus Bull, RN, and second masters Daniel Pender and Edward Bedwell, the ship's designated artist. During the voyage, second masters George Browning and John Thomas "Jack" Gowlland joined. Other officers in the wardroom were a surgeon, an assistant surgeon, a paymaster, and a chief engineer, as well as Hankin. There were no midshipmen aboard, but Edward Blunden, a master's assistant, ate with the men. A total complement of a round one hundred men crammed into *Plumper* for the Vancouver Island mission.

*

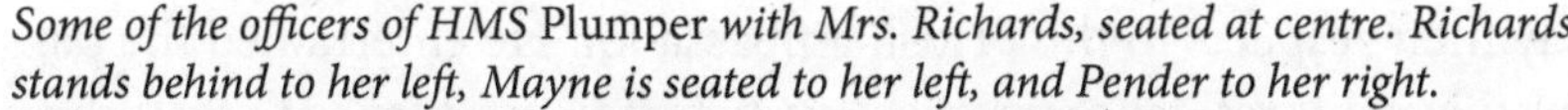

Some of the officers of HMS Plumper *with Mrs. Richards, seated at centre. Richards stands behind to her left, Mayne is seated to her left, and Pender to her right.*

At Rio, the engineers took a further six weeks to make more repairs before *Plumper* could head south for the Straits of Magellan. By that time, it was late July, mid-winter in the southern hemisphere. Their passage through the straits, using the engine, took three weeks, far longer than if they had begun on time and been without delays en route for repairs.

At Port Famine, midway through the strait, *Plumper* paused, waiting for the weather to improve. Philip went ashore with his shotgun, returning with four dozen snipe.[3] Shooting into the flocks was easy, but his supposed hunting skill much impressed his messmates. At another stop, a group of Fuegians[4] approached in a canoe, "a man, two women and a child and very dirty and nearly naked, with the skin of some animal wrapped around their loins." The officers gave them some biscuit and matches, both much appreciated. Captain Richards gave one woman a new pair of warm, knitted socks, saying compassionately, "The poor creatures' feet must be frozen!"[5] Philip believed that the woman had no idea what socks were for.

Hankin recorded that by this time, morale on *Plumper* was high, in marked contrast to his experience under the tyrant Haswell. All the officers had become friends. "Captain Richards was a splendid fellow, and a universal favourite with all. He was a fine navigator, a splendid surveyor, and a very clever man. He was one of the best, and kindest men that ever lived."

Once they had steamed clear of the straits into the open Pacific, they lifted the propeller aboard and set the sails for a hard sail upwind to Valparaiso in Chile. The first officer granted Hankin and Mayne a few days' shore leave, and they agreed to visit the capital, Santiago, about 90 miles (145 kilometres) inland. They hired a rickety cart with two small ponies and found the journey uncomfortable. As protocol required, they called to pay their respects to the British ambassador. He entertained the pair hospitably in his residence for two days, before they returned to their ship.

*

A grey-breasted seedsnipe hunted in Patagonia by Hankin for the pot.

Plumper got underway immediately, setting course for the Sandwich Islands, more correctly known as Hawai'i. Finding the trade wind, they set additional sails and for the next three weeks made seven to eight knots without adjusting the configuration. The crew used the time to paint the ship.

Thirty-six days after leaving Valparaiso, *Plumper* entered Honolulu harbour and anchored. Richards went ashore to call upon Mr. William Webb Follett Synge, the British consul general. The following day, Synge presented the captain to King Kamehameha IV. They arranged that the day after that, the captain and as many of his officers as he could spare would go to the palace for a formal reception. The party, including Hankin, paraded in full uniform to be received by His Majesty and Queen Emma. He noted in the memoir, "His Majesty was very dark, but a good-looking man with the manners of an English gentleman. The Queen was not so dark and very good looking with the most beautiful dark eyes and black hair." Having shaken hands with Their Majesties and listened to the King's words of welcome delivered in excellent English, the officers returned on board.

Philip learned more about Queen Emma: that she was of mixed blood, her mother of Hawai'ian royal stock and her father an Englishman, Dr. Thomas Rook. In fact, her lineage was far more complex. Born in early 1836 just a few weeks before Philip, she had some English blood, but was mostly descended from numerous different noble lines. Dr. Rook had married her childless aunt and they, as was the local custom, had adopted Emma. She had learned perfect English, initially at the Royal School established by American missionaries in Honolulu, and then with an English governess. Well-educated by the age of twenty, she was also an accomplished musician. Emma had spent a week at Windsor Castle as the guest of Queen Victoria.

Not long after the formal reception, Richards received a personal invitation to spend a few days at the royal country residence, some ten miles (sixteen kilometres) outside town, and was told he should bring one of his officers with him. He selected Hankin, and Mr. and Mrs. Synge were also guests. They found the summer retreat to be palatial, handsomely furnished and with "everything done in very good style." Two English footmen waited on their hosts at dinner, attended by several

King Kamehameha IV. Portrait by William Cogswell.

Queen Emma, who graciously accepted and enjoyed a curry lunch cooked by Philip Hankin. Portrait by William Cogswell.

Ladies of the royal family of Hawai'i on horseback. Queen Emma is at the back.

Young ladies of Hawai'i danced the traditional hula for the visitors.

other liveried servants. "The Queen came in a handsome evening dress for dinner, with beautiful jewellery," noted Hankin.

At one point in the dinner Richards mentioned to their hostess that Mr. Hankin was a fine cook and made a delicious curry. In his memoir, Philip does not mention where or when he gained such culinary skills—most probably it was during his "punishment" aboard *Seringapatam*—nor how his captain knew of it. At this, the Queen laughed and said that she was fond of a good curry. Philip politely asked if he might be allowed into the palace kitchen the next day to make a chicken curry for dinner. "The Queen seemed much amused and said, 'Oh certainly!'" He boasted in his memoir: "It was much appreciated. . . . I expect I am the only English Naval Officer who has ever made a curry for the Queen of the Sandwich Islands!" To thank him, the royal couple presented Philip with signed portraits of themselves, which he treasured for the next forty-five years.

Just before *Plumper* was due to leave, the King gave a farewell "Hula-hula" for the officers. Present were several princesses and ladies of high rank wearing "long wreaths of orange blossom and sweet-scented flowers twisted in their beautiful hair. The general effect was very gay and picturesque." Queen Emma did not attend, but there were several English merchants with their wives. The officers and all the locals arrived on horseback, and to Philip's surprise, the ladies rode astride. But "they were decently dressed, not showing their legs. They *looked* like women, not like men," he emphasized.

Everyone sat on mats on the ground at a scenic spot well outside town. They enjoyed a variety of dishes: chicken, turkey, roast pork, and a special delicacy, roast puppy dog. Out of politeness and curiosity, Philip tried the white flesh but was unimpressed. He learned the islanders bred the dogs for the table and fed them only milk. Served with the meal was a sour porridge called "poi," made from the taro plant, and which was a staple of the local diet. There was also "plenty of good champagne."

After dinner, a troupe of a dozen local girls arrived to entertain them with traditional dances. Philip recorded they were "all dressed in pretty native dresses, and necklaces and anklets of flowers. Their dances may be considered by some people not quite correct, but certainly better than the Tango!" At nine o'clock, the party concluded with more champagne. Philip and his fellow officers "mounted their horses and galloped back to Honolulu and went on board."

*

Although Hankin's memoir does not mention it, it is probable that during the long, quieter ocean passages such as between Valparaiso and Honolulu, and from there to Cape Flattery, the two non-survey officers, Mayne and himself, would have received training in hydrography. As first officer, Moriarty had additional responsibilities for managing the ship's condition and operation; it is doubtful that he took the survey training. To prepare them for the survey work to come, the two would have needed instruction and practice in survey mathematics and computation, cartographic draftsmanship, symbology, toponymy, and penmanship. The hydrographic chart normally includes a large quantity of numerals, all of which must adhere strictly to rules about size, style, and legibility, as well as precision in location.

They would need to know a lot more than they had learned as ordinary navigators about the theory of tides, geodesy, and geomorphology. Such instruction likely came from the senior surveyor, Master Bull, and perhaps Captain Richards himself. They would have learned a different way of using the sextant. For normal navigation, to determine their latitude by measuring the altitude of stars, or the sun at noon, mariners hold the instrument vertically. Hydrographers, when carrying out sounding work, hold it horizontally to measure the angle between two stations on shore.

It was late October 1857 when *Plumper* set sail from Hawai'i, bound for Cape Flattery and Vancouver Island.

CHAPTER 5

Hankin's First Visit to Vancouver Island

As HMS *Plumper* steamed into Esquimalt Harbour on Vancouver Island, on November 10, 1857, the band of HMS *Satellite* played a jocular welcome: "Oh, where have you been all the day, my boy Billy?" *Plumper* was about three months overdue because of repairs needed at Lisbon and Rio de Janeiro, adverse conditions in the Straits of Magellan at the height of the southern winter, and their stopover in Hawai'i.

Fifty-four years later, Philip remembered their arrival, waxing poetically:

> *It was a lovely Autumn day when we anchored in Esquimalt. I thought it one of the prettiest places I had ever seen. The maple trees were just getting their autumn tints and a few little cottages with pretty English gardens were dotted here and there along the shores of the bay.*

It must have been exceptionally mild weather for mid-November, for the harbour to have looked like that.

The wooden, twenty-one-gun screw corvette *Satellite* had arrived in June, like *Plumper*, in connection with the Joint Boundary Commission. Her captain, James Charles Prevost, RN, was the senior commissioner for Britain. Supporting him as secretary to the commission was Paymaster Commander William Alexander George Young, RN, who was to play a key role in local government over the next twelve years and have major impacts on Hankin's career.

HMS Satellite.

William Alexander George Young

Before his arrival in Esquimalt aboard HMS *Satellite* in June 1857, Paymaster Young had experienced a stellar career. He had served, with increasing responsibility, as paymaster, purser, and then as secretary to two commodores. During active service in the Crimean War, he served aboard HMS *Duke of Wellington*, a gigantic vessel Hankin would admire during his time aboard HMS *Cadmus*. Young was secretary to the fleet captain of the British Baltic Fleet, a position of enormous responsibility. With ninety-three vessels, this had been the largest ever assembled by the Royal Navy. He was promoted, decorated, and officially commended by his commander.

Young's outstanding record in what would now be termed business administration came to the attention of the Foreign Office. They appointed him as secretary to the British Boundary Commission in New Caledonia, under Captain James Charles Prevost, RN, chief commissioner. He was now aged thirty. His duties, initially, solely concerned the business of the Boundary Commission. *Satellite* also carried a paymaster with two assistants for the ship's routine financial affairs.

Captain George Henry Richards, RN, was Prevost's deputy commissioner with special responsibility for the water boundary. To complicate the technical challenges of the primary mission entrusted to him, Richards now reported to four authorities: the Hydrographer Rear Admiral John Washington; Captain Prevost; a series of admirals serving as commanders-in-chief, Pacific Station; and Governor James Douglas. Richards was to prove fully competent in balancing the requirements of all of them.

The two ships, *Satellite* and *Plumper*, had arrived at a transformative stage in the history of this part of the world. Not only were relations between Imperial Britain and an assertive United States tense, but a flood of American settlers had arrived across the Rockies into the Willamette Valley in Oregon. The Hudson's Bay Company (HBC) had, until then, considered the region to be under its control, and so viewed this flood as a direct threat. They had transferred their regional centre from Fort Vancouver (in what is now Washington State) to a new Fort Victoria, at the southern tip of Vancouver Island.

The British government cautiously assessed the strategic value of their presence in the area. London had entrusted the HBC to establish and manage a colony on the island. Under the leadership of James Douglas—a capable manager of a fur-trading enterprise, but with few resources to call upon—company officials still struggled with these strange new responsibilities. Douglas was grateful for the informal guidance of Paymaster Young from *Satellite*, who was both personable and knowledgeable. Under instruction from his new masters in London, Douglas had recently convened the first Legislative Assembly for the colony on August 12, 1856. The discovery of substantial deposits of coal on the island had come when shipping, particularly naval, was transitioning from sail to steam power. This resource added much to the importance of maintaining a robust British presence on this coast, specifically a naval harbour at Esquimalt.

*

To the south, another major wave of people had arrived in California, lured initially by the 1849 gold rush. San Francisco was, by now, a thriving hub of miners who had struck it rich, merchants and entrepreneurs exploiting that new wealth, and a far larger contingent of unruly newcomers ravenous for the next opportunity to secure their fortune.

The HBC had learned in 1855 of large quantities of placer gold in the gravel bars of the Thompson, the Fraser River's major tributary. Douglas recognized that once news of these deposits reached the ears of the turbulent multitude of prospectors in California, British authority over the region would be challenged. So, in December 1857, he issued a proclamation that the gold mines of the mainland were the property of the Crown and prospecting would only be by permit from the company. He took this pre-emptive action without prior approval from London, but later his government endorsed it.

Victoria was still a small community, comprising a few company officials, most with wives from the Indigenous population; five farms established and owned by the company; and a few more by settlers, mostly ex-company officers. Esquimalt, just getting underway as the home port of the Royal Navy's Pacific fleet, was linked to the colony's capital by an hour's difficult trek along a muddy track or around the coast by dugout canoe. To have two ships, filled with lively young men, attached to these isolated communities added an important dimension to their social life. The resident colonial settlers took care to be hospitable to the visitors.

Philip's memoir recounting the first year of *Plumper*'s mission to Vancouver Island reads like a continuous round of parties and dances. These were held on board, in residences in town, and at the outlying farms and ranches, where lived many daughters. One of those farms, John Wark's, had eight young ladies. Some families even boasted a harmonium or a piano. These social functions—family and guests sometimes numbered forty—were lively, but well chaperoned. At the time of *Plumper*'s arrival, the total non-Indigenous population of Victoria was only about three hundred. There is no sign in Philip's enthusiastic telling of impropriety or conflict, just youthful hijinks.

Hankin recalled many names from those days: "I think I remember all the young ladies on the Island at that time," he wrote. "We thought nothing of walking [to dances] there and back, four or five miles [six or eight kilometres], and often through deep snow with top boots on and our dancing pumps in our pockets, and the girls did the same." While he clearly enjoyed chatting and dancing with many local girls, he did not later recall having held any one of them in special favour. Philip met Governor Douglas and most of the other important men of the community. He dined with them, usually on salmon and mutton, in the officers' mess at the palisaded fort and at their houses.

Before winter prevented survey work by Richards and *Plumper*'s surveyors, there was the diplomatic protocol of meeting with their American colleagues on the Joint Boundary Commission. Prevost and Richards called on their counterpart, Archibald Campbell, at the Americans' camp on Semiahmoo Bay. This was near the spot where the 49th parallel first met Pacific salt water. That same line cut across the tip of Point Roberts, before reaching the Gulf of Georgia, where both sides agreed that the definitive boundary monument should be erected. Those prior discussions hinted that the negotiations might not be harmonious. Campbell was wily and obdurate, and the mild-mannered Prevost was not the robust and confident negotiator needed to counter his stubborn American counterpart.

Wording in the 1846 treaty was ambiguous about where the water section of the boundary was to run. From off Point Roberts it passed from the middle of the Gulf of Georgia, into and through the Strait of Juan de Fuca, and out into the open Pacific. The problem was, through which channel, of the many in the San Juan Islands, should the boundary run? The British side proposed the easternmost, Rosario Strait; their American counterparts argued it should be Haro Strait. Up to this point, available charts were inadequate for a negotiated solution.

For the first part of the 1858 season, surveyors of *Plumper* would need to survey and prepare an accurate and complete hydrographic chart of the archipelago,[1] for use by the joint commission. A secondary, but shorter, task was a chart titled *Semiahmoo Bay and Drayton Harbour*, showing the location of the 49th parallel, both on the bay and at Point Roberts. The plan thereafter would be to chart the coasts of Vancouver Island, beginning with Victoria and the Strait of Georgia.

*

The coverage in Hankin's memoir of this and the survey work for the rest of *Plumper*'s 1858 season is scant on detail and, in places, faulty. Unfortunately, also missing is Richards's own private journal of the mission prior to February 10, 1860. We have, however, Richard Charles Mayne's book, *Four Years in British Columbia and Vancouver Island*, to provide a general guide to what transpired on *Plumper* during what turned out to be a year of momentous change for the young colony of Vancouver Island.

Captain Richards's chart showing the lines of the disputed water boundary through the San Juan archipelago. The easternmost line is the British first proposal, the westernmost is the American counterpart, and the middle is the British proposed compromise.

HMS Plumper *at anchor in Port Harvey, Johnstone Strait, with survey parties about to deploy. A later watercolour of a drawing by Edward Bedwell.*

On December 16, 1857, *Plumper*, bunkers full of Nanaimo coal, had returned to Esquimalt Harbour to batten down for the winter. Richards had secured the use of half a hut there,[2] as a shore base of operations for making their computations and drafting the various charts. To celebrate New Year's Day 1858, the men of *Satellite* entertained their comrades aboard *Plumper* with a dinner. The sergeant of marines presided while officers of both ships looked on. Mayne declared it to have been a very fine affair, much enjoyed by their guests.

Mayne reported in his book how, while forced to await weather good enough for survey operations to begin, they improved the seaworthiness of *Plumper*'s pinnace, the largest of the boats on board. They raised the sides and built a half deck to cover the bow, and they gave it the name *Shark*. They discovered that, unfortunately, in mid-February, winter in Victoria is not over. The improved *Shark* could still not handle the seas and conditions they experienced. Once, the tidal current carried them past the entrance to Esquimalt, "drifting in the night past Race Rocks—it might just as well have been upon them—to Sooke Inlet, twenty miles [thirty-two kilometres] below Esquimalt." On another occasion, caught in a blizzard off San Juan Island, the rigging iced up and *Shark* dragged its anchor. Mayne concluded, "The weather we experienced convinced us that the middle or end of March was quite early enough."

Richards and the men of *Plumper* embarked on the priority work of surveying for the chart of the archipelago needed for the boundary negotiations. Mayne agreed with the British policy that San Juan Island should remain to the north of the boundary. The HBC had established a sheep ranch on the island, since it was free of the wolves that infested Vancouver Island and it offered more land for agriculture than the other islands of the group. Strategically, too, he agreed, "San Juan can be of no use to any country but Great Britain, except for *offensive* purposes, and on the other hand, it cannot be of any use to her, but for *defensive* purposes." He suggested a further reason for wishing to retain possession of San Juan Island: "I have never seen wildflowers elsewhere grow with the beauty and luxuriance they possess here. . . . It was the spot selected by [Governor Douglas's] daughter and niece in which to spend their honeymoons."

The niece Mayne referred to was Cecilia Cameron, the daughter of the governor's sister and Judge David Cameron, the solicitor general. Cecilia had married Young, who was becoming Douglas's indispensable right hand. When the decision makers in London agreed to Young's formal transfer to be colonial secretary, Charles Wilson, a lieutenant of the Royal Engineers, took over his duties as secretary to the Boundary Commission.

*

While Hankin's memoir provides few details of the survey work in the contentious archipelago, it provides a glimpse into the relationship, a year into the mission, between him and his skipper:

> *Captain Richards made me his personal assistant, and I was often away with him on his boat for two, or three weeks at a time. At night we used to anchor the boat in some snug little cove, the men slept on board, and Richards and I had two little tents on shore. He said I was a first rate cook, and I always took care that we had a good supper at night. I generally made him a fish curry of which he was particularly fond, and boiled potatoes which we could often buy from the Indians. There was also plenty of salmon and other fish, and we carried a gun, and could generally get a deer or a grouse.*

*

A series of events brought a sudden change to Fort Victoria's quiet existence at the outermost edge of the British Empire. It began during the summer of 1857. Governor Douglas learned of conflicts developing around the junction of the Thompson and the Fraser River. The local population was at odds with some gold prospectors who had arrived, overland, from the south. The HBC had trading rights only to this territory, called New Caledonia by Captain Vancouver and the company. Douglas was anxious about this American encroachment, but unsure of his authority to intervene.

Despite this reservation, in late December 1857, Douglas proclaimed British authority over the territory, in particular the prospecting and mining for gold. He instigated a mining permit fee of 10 shillings (about C$90 in 2025) per miner per month, payable in advance. He was just in time. The *San Francisco Gazette* reported that US$1 million of gold had been taken from the Fraser River in that year. The following February, Douglas is reputed to have sent 800 ounces of gold to the San Francisco mint for conversion into currency.

Hydrography

Hydrographic survey work, in that era, was carried out by small teams led by one or two surveyors in the several small boats carried by the "mother" ship, which would anchor at a protected location close to the area under survey. Powered just by oars, or occasionally by a small sail, the boats would pass along a stretch of the coastline. The surveyors would first "fix" or survey the location and configuration of the coastline. They would survey and erect beacons on shore, visible from the water.

Next, they would traverse the area of sea off the section of coastline being surveyed, to take lines of soundings, usually in toward the shore and outward. A man in the bow would drop a line, weighted with a lead sinker and marked in fathoms and fractions. As the lead hit bottom and the line came to vertical, he would call out the depth and describe the nature of the sea floor (sand, mud, rocks, coral, et cetera) to be recorded by a note taker. Simultaneously, the surveyors would record the angles they measured between two of three onshore beacons with their sextants held horizontally, and call out the angles to the recorder, who would also note the time from a calibrated watch.

Sailors at the helm and oars worked to keep the boat steady as each set of readings was made—no easy task in rough weather or fast-flowing water. In this way, they collected a series of data points noting time, depth, sea floor, and two angles, which the surveyors later used to calculate the boat's location. Noting the nature of the seabed was important for future users of the chart when they came to select an anchorage.

Later, back at the ship, the surveyors would make their calculations and plot the points in their correct locations onto a draft chart of the area they had covered. They marked each point with the depth (adjusted for tide at the time of the recording). They would then incorporate these sections into a larger chart of the complete area, rather like adding completed sections to a jigsaw puzzle. In this last process, they would edit the number of

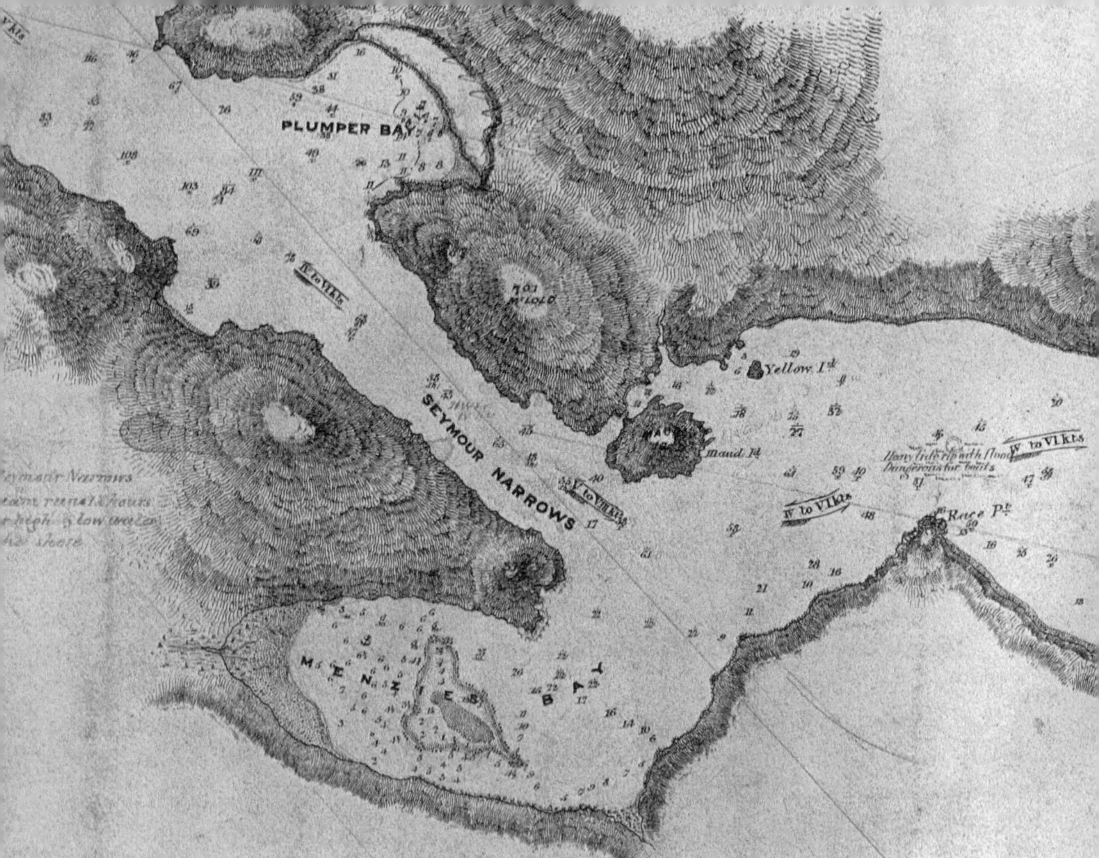

A typical section of a chart generated during the work of Captain Richards and his surveyors. This would then be compiled into the final chart format to be issued. Note the anchorage symbols in Plumper and Menzies Bays.

points recorded to show the minimum necessary to describe the topography of the sea floor for future navigators. The surveyors would interpolate and plot the lines of constant depth to aid that purpose. They also noted and plotted any rocks, at or below the surface, patches of kelp or anything else that might be useful to navigators, such as sources of fresh water, good beaches for landing, and significant landmarks.

Hydrographic surveying in the mid-1800s was a supremely technical process, combining the need for skills in seamanship and mathematics as well as a steady, precise hand for drawing the charts and writing up the notes. Above all, first-rate leadership and well-coordinated teamwork were essential.

A few months later, on April 25, 1858, the paddle steamer *Commodore*[3] arrived in Victoria from San Francisco. To the astonishment of the residents, it discharged four hundred prospectors clamouring for mining licences for the Fraser River. These were just the vanguard. Over the next few months, dozens of ships followed, large and small, seaworthy or not, their decks black with a gold-fevered horde, eventually thirty thousand strong, a hundredfold increase in a year. A raucous tent city suddenly surrounded the village that had been Victoria. Prices for food skyrocketed, as did real estate, building materials, mining tools, and lumber to build boats to take the hopefuls across to the mainland. In addition to prospectors came the inevitable entourage of camp followers: caterers, gamblers, entertainers, even a few honest merchants such as Richard Carr. All sought their own piece of this new bonanza. "Camp cities" of hopeful Americans also sprang up immediately south of the border at Semiahmoo and Point Roberts.

While this invasion was underway, *Plumper*'s surveyors were still at work charting the archipelago. When they returned to base in mid-May, what they found astonished them. Mayne and several other non-involved observers left graphic descriptions of the 1858 tsunamic transformation of Victoria. But not Philip Hankin. To read his memoir, nothing of the sort happened. The events were far too dramatic and far-reaching for even the fuzziest elderly diarist to have forgotten them. Other sectors of the memoir prove he had an excellent memory for even minutiae. The mood of his entries for this period offers no hints of why he would want to erase the entire episode.

*

During the tumultuous summer of 1858, Douglas requested military reinforcements from the colonial secretary in London, who responded by dispatching a large contingent of Royal Engineers. They were to provide both technical infrastructure and armed, red-coated support for his authority. The bulk of this contingent would arrive in April 1859, having sailed around Cape Horn in the longest mobilization ever made by British troops.

The governor made two personal visits to the area of contention. He brought with him a section of marines from *Satellite* for his protection and as a visible reminder of imperial power. *Satellite* took up a position off the mouth of the Fraser to intercept the fleet of prospectors and check that they were all duly licensed. The ship's captain sent his launch to Fort Langley, on similar duty. Douglas had increased the monthly miner's permit to 1 guinea, or US$5—more than doubling it. To dissuade the sailors from *Satellite* and *Plumper* from deserting the ship in favour of the diggings, he promised to double their wages from his colonial funds, but never did.

In July 1858, another British boundary commissioner, Major John Summerfield Hawkins, RE, arrived with a contingent of specialist surveyors from the Royal Engineers, known as "sappers." They were to cut, survey, and mark the land portion of the boundary from Point Roberts to the crest of the Rockies. He, too, made his base in one of the Crimea hospital huts at Esquimalt.

Mayne, who had previously served in San Francisco during a gold rush, described some of the "more unruly of the strange, heterogenous population" who had descended on Victoria: "The new-found wealth of British Columbia had attracted some of the most reckless rascals that gold has ever given birth to." One night in late July, as *Plumper* lay tied up at Esquimalt, the governor sent Richards an urgent call to help

On SS Commodore, *Captain Jeremiah Nagle brought hordes of prospectors to Victoria from San Francisco.*

HMS Plumper *aground off Waldron Island in the San Juan archipelago. Mount Baker in background.*

quell a riot in Victoria. Richards embarked some of Hawkins's sappers in their scarlet jackets, raised steam, and headed for the neighbouring community.

As they left, the ship's doctor was laying out his surgical instruments on the wardroom table, the blacksmith was "casting bullets by the score," and the quartermaster was issuing small arms and ammunition to the men. On arrival at the wharf below the fort, an armed party marched into the square. Richards went to report to the governor, who was already in bed, since the riot had subsided. The governor thanked and dismissed the troops, and "our evening that had begun so fiercely, wound up with a supper in the fort," wrote Mayne.

Hankin, however, made no mention in his memoir of what must have been an exciting episode for everyone aboard. Nor did he recall another drama while he was with *Plumper* that season. In May, while skirting Waldron Island in the archipelago, Richards's ship "took the ground," an acknowledged risk for a surveying vessel working hitherto uncharted waters. The sheathing and bottom received some damage, but they could return to Esquimalt and continue for the rest of the 1858 season and the next.

On May 15, 1858, the *London Gazette* carried the announcement that, having served sufficient time in the service, Hankin, Philip J., was promoted to lieutenant, RN. Such a notice required the officer concerned to return to Britain at once, for reassignment at his new rank. The news did not reach *Plumper* until early October, at the close of the surveying season. Philip greeted it with mixed feelings. He was pleased to get the promotion, but sorry to leave *Plumper*, his messmates, and, particularly, his captain. To offset this, there came a word of encouragement.

During the voyage out and the survey work, Richards had recognized that he needed a new ship. *Plumper* was adequate for work in the sheltered waters to the east of Vancouver Island. It lacked, however, the power needed to cope with the stormy waters of the open North Pacific. He had just learned that the Admiralty had agreed to his request for a larger, more capable vessel. The Admiralty ordered HMS *Hecate* to make ready to replace *Plumper*. Richards, pleased with Hankin's aptitude for survey, assured his protege that he would contact the Admiralty requesting that Hankin be assigned to *Hecate*. He advised Philip that, when he got back to Britain, he should also apply to join that ship.

In August 1858, the British government, ratifying Douglas's preemptive action over the gold region, declared the creation of a second colony on the west coast of North America. It was to include the region on the mainland largely unexplored by Europeans and known by the company as New Caledonia, but with borders only vaguely defined. Douglas, on condition that he sever his ties with the HBC, received a knighthood and was declared governor of both colonies. On November 19, he went to Fort Langley to read his formal proclamation at what was called "The Birth of British Columbia."

*

The passage in Hankin's memoir relating his journey back to England in late 1858 continues in a style that is terse, perhaps even repressed. It reads, "I went down to San Francisco by the mail steamer, and from there by an American vessel to Panama, and crossed the Isthmus by rail to Colón, and then by the West India Mail to Southampton." The single sentence completely lacks his earlier joie de vivre. This, again, is most peculiar.

The trip, which probably lasted about four months, contained several firsts for him. This was his first time aboard an American ship, the first time as a civilian passenger on any ship, his first on a foreign train, and his first visit to San Francisco—and during a time of a city-wide frenzy to get to the Fraser River before all the gold was gone. How many accounts of crossing Panama by rail can have been penned in so brief and matter-of-fact a fashion? Hankin would have spent Christmas and New Year's Eve crossing the Atlantic in an ocean liner, normally providing ample excuses for extravagant celebration.

One curious episode in the journey homeward, while unrecorded, appears to have left an impression on him. While waiting in San Francisco, between ships, he probably stayed in one of the more prominent hotels. When taking meals, he seems to have observed, and admired, the demeanour of the professional waiters. He would later consider this to be a potential role for himself.

*

The replacement who would fill Philip's berth aboard *Plumper* was already in the vicinity. The twenty-year-old second master Jack Gowlland had been with HMS *Ganges* on a surveying mission to the Caribbean and South America. He had just arrived in Esquimalt when Hankin left for Britain. With this transfer, Richards had restored his initial plan to have all his junior officers previously trained in hydrographic survey. Gowlland proved a valuable new member of the surveying team. His log, private diary, and personal letters survive and furnish yet more insights into some gaps and inaccuracies in Hankin's memoir.

CHAPTER 6
Lieutenant Hankin, RN

Referring to his first few days back in England in early 1859, Philip Hankin wrote:

> *I found my father had left Stanstead, and was living at a place called Pertenhall, near Kimbolton [in Cambridgeshire]. I went home at once for a few days, but at the expiration of a week, my father began to fidget, and was always asking me, when I was going to sea again, so I applied for a ship.*

This passage gives regrettably short shrift to a meeting—which would have been around his twenty-third birthday—with so many noteworthy aspects. Evidently, he was unaware that his father had sold Thele House, the home where the family had lived for generations, and moved north-west forty miles (sixty-four kilometres). In 1856, his father had remarried, and Philip now had a stepmother, Jane Hankin, née Keay, and a three-year-old stepsister, Rose. His sister Alice, by then fourteen years old, and his youngest brother, Graham, a year younger, remained with their father, but of the other siblings there was not a word in the memoir.

Philip recorded nothing of his uncle and two aunts who had lived with them at Thele House. His maiden aunts, Christiana and Maria ("Ria"), had used their share of the proceeds from the sale of the family property to buy a house in Clifton, near Bristol. Even if he was given their address, he appears not to have visited them. Apparently, he did not discuss with his father the reasons behind the move, nor his current situation. His ties with his relations in England seemed close to withering, according to his later recollection or his perspective as an old man.

A significant example of that apparent estrangement is Philip's omitting his absent siblings from that part of his memoir. The two eldest, Frederick George and Edward Lewis, had military careers and were serving in the Madras region. Constance, Philip's elder sister, had by then also left for Madras, engaged to be married to another army officer. The third son, Daniel Bell, had taken holy orders, and was at the time a curate in Liverpool. Two of Philip's younger siblings, Charles and Thomas, had travelled to Canada a year earlier, stopping at Montreal. There, two of the most senior directors of the Hudson's Bay Company provided Charles with letters of introduction to Governor James Douglas in Victoria. The brothers made their way to Victoria, arriving in the fall of 1858.

*

The Admiralty's response to Philip's application for a new ship came promptly. He was to join HMS *Cadmus*, a wooden, eighteen-gun screw steam corvette under the command of Captain Henry Shank Hillyar, RN, then at Chatham, preparing to join the Mediterranean fleet. Philip found the first lieutenant, Walter Sidney De Kantzow, to be "a very pleasant man" and noted in his memoir that he retired as an admiral. He also met an old shipmate, Mr. Jones, the bewhiskered clergyman and navigation instructor from his first ship, HMS *Castor*. On May 11, 1859, *Cadmus* set sail on its maiden voyage for Gibraltar and into the Mediterranean. Philip noted that the ship "sailed splendidly."

After joining Vice Admiral Arthur Fanshawe's squadron, Philip admired his flagship, a splendid old three-decker and the first-class ship of the line HMS *Duke of Wellington*. He recorded: "When she was under full sail with studding sails, it was a sight worth seeing." Soon after *Cadmus* joined the squadron, it sailed from Gibraltar to Malta. Hankin noted his pride when, recently promoted to lieutenant, he could show off his seamanship. It was night and he was the officer of the middle watch when a signal came from the flagship that *Cadmus* should take up a new position, ahead and to her "weather" side; that is, to windward. It was a tricky manoeuvre, but he completed it and felt most gratified when the signal came from the mighty flagship: "Well done, *Cadmus*, position very well taken up."

After the squadron had been cruising between various ports in the Mediterranean, including Malta and Naples, for about eight months,

Screw steam corvette HMS Cadmus. *The new Lieutenant Hankin noted the vessel "sailed splendidly" and he was complimented for his manoeuvring of her at night.*

HMS Duke of Wellington *under full sail in the English Channel. Note the studding sails set on the foremast. This warship was twice the size of Nelson's HMS* Victory *and had, until 1855, been the most powerful in the world.*

Philip became anxious to return to Vancouver Island. He feared that Captain George Henry Richards, RN, had forgotten his promise. He was not specific about his reason for this urge to return. His reticence covering that period in his memoir does not shed any light on his true motives. Did he yearn to dance again with the daughters of settlers? Take luncheon on salmon and mutton at the fort? Or to prepare fish curry for his favourite captain? Surely, it could not be to witness again the pandemonium of prospectors in their tent city. Despondent, he resolved to leave the service and make his own way back to Vancouver Island. He wrote to the admiral, requesting his discharge from the navy.

Admiral Fanshawe was astonished and thought that young Hankin must be out of his mind. He ordered that he report to him aboard the flagship. Philip complied immediately and was taken to the admiral's cabin. "What on earth do you want to leave the navy for?" Fanshawe demanded. The reasons Philip gave do not now seem convincing. He told the admiral that he had lost interest, that promotion was slow, and that he thought he might try San Francisco. "And pray, Sir, what do you propose doing when you get there?" challenged Fanshawe. Philip responded, "I am young, and I don't mind hard work. I could get a situation at once, as a waiter at one of the large hotels there." The admiral, incensed, roared: "What! Give up your position as a lieutenant in the Navy and become a waiter? You must be mad!"

The admiral then turned conciliatory. "I will take you out of the *Cadmus*, and appoint you as fourth lieutenant of the *Orion*, a fine vessel, just going to Naples. Don't think anything more about such nonsense as becoming a waiter!" Philip realized his superior was being most gracious, thanked him, and dutifully accepted the transfer to HMS *Orion*.

Orion was indeed a fine vessel: a magnificent second-rate ninety-one-gun screw, ship of the line of the *Hood* class, carrying the battle honour of the Baltic. The admiral had been generous, effectively promoting the disaffected Hankin. Philip found *Orion*'s master, Captain John J.B.E. Frere, RN, to be "an extremely nice man, and a great homeopathist, in which he believed implicitly."

Philip saw an opportunity to ingratiate himself by adopting a similar faith. He bought a chest of little bottles of herbal remedies and used every chance to discuss the topic with his new skipper. Often, when Frere joined him at his watch, Hankin invented complaints and requested permission to go below to take "some Pulsatilla" or some such. The captain, concerned, would agree to take over the watch. Below, Hankin would joke with his fellows at the captain's gullibility. Returning to the quarterdeck half an hour later, he would declare the cure effective, to the captain's "Good night, Hankin, there is nothing like homeopathy!"

It is a story that Hankin, as an old man, recounted with satisfaction, but which reflects poorly on his younger self. It showed his lack of gratitude for Admiral Fanshawe's magnanimity in offering Hankin the position. Also, he repeatedly took advantage of Captain Frere, a kind man showing genuine concern for the well-being of one of his subordinates.

Apart from this unedifying anecdote, the memoir is void of detail about Hankin's experiences aboard a large man-of-war, his fellow officers, or the historic places they visited. While in the Mediterranean, he seems to have gained some command of both French and Italian, but he makes no mention of how this happened. Later in his narrative, Hankin addresses the reader directly, indicating his intention that the memoir was to be read. He must have known that the voyage in *Cadmus* and then *Orion* might considerably interest whomever that reader might be. Why, then, does he fail to describe this period?

Such lacunae in the memoir show no apparent pattern, but they cannot be attributed solely to lapses of memory. For example, Hankin recalled the exhilaration that he, as a young man, had felt in witnessing the spectacle of the *Duke of Wellington* dressed in a full suit of sails, running before a fair wind. Then, reverting to his older voice, he compared such splendour to that of the "immense floating forts" of the "present day" (1914). Today's reader can only regret that Hankin recorded so little of such experiences.

Having related almost nothing about it, he says of the conclusion of *Orion*'s commission only that "at last, orders came for the *Orion* to return to England, and pay off at Portsmouth." It was early June 1860, and Philip went again to briefly stay with his father at Pertenhall. There:

> *In a few days, to my great delight, I received a letter from Captain Richards acquainting me that he had applied for a larger vessel . . . and he had requested that I might be sent out in*

this vessel as first lieutenant. And the next day I received a letter from the Admiralty informing me I had been appointed as first lieutenant to the paddle steamer 'Hecate' and was to join her at Portsmouth, and proceed in her to Vancouver Island.

*

Philip left Pertenhall immediately and at Portsmouth found HMS *Hecate* almost ready to leave. His captain was Commander Anthony Hiley Hoskins, RN, who had been the second officer aboard *Castor* and Midshipman Hankin's watch officer. Hoskins had not been present at the commodore's dinner when the tyrant Wyvill had deliberately made Philip drunk, then humiliated him. Hoskins went on to an illustrious naval career, culminating as an admiral and the Second Naval Lord, decorated with the Order of the Bath as a Knight Grand Cross. *Hecate* departed from Portsmouth on June 25, 1860, headed for Lisbon.

Originally commissioned in 1840, *Hecate*[1] was a wooden, second-class paddlewheel steam sloop with 6 mounted guns and 4 brass howitzers. Hoskins had received his appointment in mid-May. Before that, the vessel had undergone a complete refit at Woolwich Dockyard to modify it for surveying duties. The full complement, as a surveying ship, would be 92 officers and men, 13 boys, and 20 Royal Marines, 125 in total. For the passage out to Vancouver Island, far fewer were aboard.

Hecate was significantly more powerful than HMS *Plumper*. Under steam, it managed 10 knots maximum and 7 at continuous speed from twin, 23½-foot-diameter paddles. Rigged as a brig, it had 2 masts with square sails; for ocean passages with favourable wind, sail power was preferred. With no propeller to hoist aboard, transitions between engine power and sail were far less complicated than they had been on *Plumper*. *Hecate* was 20 feet longer at the waterline than *Plumper* and 5 feet broader in the beam. Their displacements were proportionate; *Hecate*'s was 860 tons against *Plumper*'s 484. As Richards had particularly called for, there was a chart room with space enough for 6 to 8 people to work.

From Lisbon they headed southwest for Rio de Janeiro and, from there, south along the coast to Patagonia, and made ready to transit the Straits of Magellan. Again, it was the southern mid-winter, the weather bitterly cold. Hoskins elected to try an unusual course to enter the Pacific. The Chilean coastline, at its southern tip, is an intricate lacework

Section of John Tallis's 1851 map Falkland Islands and Patagonia. Hecate*'s course from the Strait of Magalhaes (Straits of Magellan) threaded through the channels inside the islands Clarence, Desolation, Adelaide, Hanover, and Wellington.*

of fjords and broken islands, surrounded by snow-covered peaks. The normal exit, having transited the straits westbound, is past Cape Pilar. The route taken by *Hecate*, under steam of course, was to thread through the narrow passages, roughly parallel with the coast, northward as far as the Gulf of Peñas. Hoskins probably chose this as it would be more sheltered from the ferocious westerly storms.[2]

Philip described the experience:

An unusual route, and that passage was rarely taken, for it was narrow and intricate, but it was interesting. The water was very deep, and we could not anchor at night, but always tied up to large trees which grew close down to the water's edge.

They also met some "miserable looking" Fuegian or Kawesqar people, such as he had seen on *Plumper*'s passage. One morning Hankin found that ice, sufficiently thick to bear his weight, had surrounded the ship. He walked around the ship. This was a foolhardy risk for the first officer of a solitary ship with only a minimal delivery crew to take in a remote location, far from help.

*

Hecate stopped briefly at Valparaiso. In harbour during their visit was HMS *Satellite*, on its way home after three turbulent years based at Esquimalt. Hankin knew the captain, James Charles Prevost, and many of the officers. Paymaster William Alexander George Young was not aboard, as he had been ordered to remain in Victoria, on secondment as colonial secretary to Governor Douglas. The two vessels left Valparaiso on the same day, headed in different directions. *Hecate* sailed northwest, bound for the Sandwich Islands. The king received the officers "in much the same ceremony" as had been the protocol on Hankin's earlier visit. The memoir makes no mention, this time, of Queen Emma, or whether King Kamehameha IV remembered Philip from the occasion on which he had cooked chicken curry for the royal couple. In July, *Hecate* sailed for Vancouver Island.

CHAPTER 7
In Absentia: November 1858 to December 1860 on Vancouver Island, While Hankin Was Away

HMS *Hecate* arrived at Esquimalt on December 23, 1860, having made the journey from Portsmouth in just two days short of six months. Philip Hankin was delighted to find "the little *Plumper* was at anchor in the harbour." A week later, most of the crews of the two ships changed places. Some specialist engine-room artificers remained with their original ships, and Lieutenant William Moriarty stayed with *Plumper* for continuity, under Captain Anthony Hiley Hoskins. Taking his place as first officer of *Hecate* was Richard Charles Mayne, and Hankin was appointed second officer. His friend Daniel Pender became the master and senior surveying officer. The pinnace *Shark* was further improved for work on the west coast by being completely decked over and rigged as a schooner.

Within a week, "amid most vociferous cheering from those she left behind," *Plumper* sailed for home. Hankin noted: "I never saw my little ship again. She reached England quite safely but was shortly afterwards broken up."

*

With *Hecate* anchored in Esquimalt, Philip Hankin, now almost twenty-five years old, noted many personnel changes since he had left. Captain

George Henry Richards's wife, Mary, and their infant daughter had joined him, and while they were there, the Richardses had had another daughter and a son christened "Vancouver." They lived in a cottage close to *Plumper*'s (and *Hecate*'s) anchorage in Esquimalt, but soon after *Hecate* arrived, the captain's family returned to Britain, leaving Richards behind.

Among Hankin's previous crewmates, Master John Augustus Bull, who had earlier married Emma Langford, daughter of a prominent HBC farm manager and judge, had recently died, apparently from food poisoning. His place was taken by Hankin's now-promoted friend Daniel Pender. Edward Bedwell, the talented artist, had also been promoted to master. The surveyor who had taken Hankin's place on *Plumper*, second master Jack Gowlland, remained and transferred to *Hecate*.[1]

Plumper's surgeon, David Lyall, an expert botanist, had been seconded to the Boundary Survey, to be replaced by another botanist-surgeon, Dr. Charles Wood.[2] The chief engineer, Charles Wright, who had been aboard *Hecate* on the journey out, remained with the ship. With the departure of HMS *Satellite* in May 1861, Paymaster William Young transferred first to *Plumper*'s then to *Hecate*'s nominal rolls as "additional for special service," meaning as acting colonial secretary to Governor James Douglas.

From the start of his service in the new colony of Vancouver Island, Young had taken an active part in the social circle of Victoria's elite, quickly coming to the attention of the governor himself and his extended family. Douglas appreciated his administrative and business acumen and so had increasingly sought his advice. The dashing and sophisticated naval officer had also caught the eye of Cecilia, Douglas's niece and stepdaughter of Judge David Cameron, later chief justice. In less than a year after his arrival, Young had married Cecilia.

*

Hankin also learned what had transpired locally during his two-year absence—and there was a great deal to learn. After Hankin left in late 1858, the flood of prospectors headed for the gold-laden gravel bars of the Fraser River continued. Curiously, Hankin had witnessed but had not recorded any observations about the start of this influx or its effects on the community. Many of the associated merchants and publicans arriving during that period remained to make Victoria their base for serving the needs of later arrivals. Because of the influx, the demographic profile of the resident population completely changed. Recent arrivals were mostly American, but they included adventurers and scoundrels of many nationalities. Most of them carried pistols and bowie knives—and appeared fully prepared to use them. They outnumbered by far the few families plus company and colonial officials who were already there, even including the naval personnel of ships based at Esquimalt.

One of these arrivals was a Nova Scotian originally named Bill Smith, who had fancifully renamed himself Amor De Cosmos. He brought his photo studio from San Francisco to Victoria to specialize in portraits of miners. In late 1858, he founded a newspaper, the *Daily British Colonist*, which provided him with a platform for his radical views on government. He would mount vigorous, often eccentric, opposition to James Douglas and subsequent colonial and provincial administrators. He was also a controversial politician, later serving for a little over a year as the second premier of the province. The newspaper he founded has continued under various names through to the present day.[3]

On November 19, 1858, Douglas, now Sir James, had proclaimed the second colony on the Pacific coast: that of British Columbia. He and a new judge sent from England, Matthew Baillie Begbie, travelled to Fort Langley, some thirty-three miles (fifty-three kilometres) upstream from the mouth of the Fraser River, to conduct the formal ceremony. This confirmed Douglas's pre-emptive announcement of the previous year for British jurisdiction over the now booming gold rush of the Fraser Canyon and upriver.

Douglas also requested that Young's contribution to managing the additional burden of the second colony be formalized by his secondment from the Boundary Commission to the position of colonial secretary of British Columbia. Douglas had to overcome Young's own reluctance over the paltry salary of £500 per year. The authorities in London had agreed to the transfer, and Young took on multiple duties as auditor for the mainland colony and became de facto colonial secretary of both colonies, an indispensable member of the management team. Douglas would effusively praise Young's "decided business talents" in a confidential memorandum to the Duke of Newcastle, the secretary of state for the colonies in London. Young built a large house close to both the legislature and Douglas's own residence, and went on to assemble a large portfolio of local real estate and business investments.

By the end of 1858, Victoria had a resident population of three thousand,[4] two rival newspapers, and even a paved section of Yates Street.

Sir James Douglas is sworn in as governor of British Columbia at Fort Langley, November 19, 1858. Judge Matthew Baillie Begbie officiates, witnessed by Captain J.C. Prevost, RN, Chief Factor J.M. Yale, and Lieutenant Colonel R.C. Moody, RE. Painting by John Innes.

Miners on the Fraser River had moiled to extract 160,000 ounces of gold, worth the equivalent of C$100 million in 2025.

*

By mid-January 1859, while the weather remained unsuitable for Richards to resume survey operations, *Plumper* was given a new mission: transporting a company of Royal Marines. News of a confrontation between rival gangs of gold prospectors at Yale had reached New Westminster and Victoria. The newly arrived commanding officer of the Royal Engineers' Columbia Detachment was Lieutenant Colonel Richard Clement Moody, RE, also sworn in as lieutenant governor of British Columbia. Moody immediately went to the gold region with Judge Matthew Baillie Begbie to resolve the dispute, which threatened to escalate.

Governor Douglas requested that Captain James Charles Prevost send his marines as reinforcements, to stand by should the matter flare up. *Plumper* carried the marines to Fort Langley. To restore the rule of law to the situation at Yale, termed "Ned McGowan's War," Moody and Begbie opted to first try diplomacy and the power of personality. Bravely advancing upstream, unaccompanied, they were able to resolve the issues, averting the "war." Prudently leaving the company of marines at Langley, *Plumper* conveyed Moody and Begbie back to Victoria.

For the 1859 season, Richards had originally planned to resume the survey of the eastern shores of Vancouver Island, but, again, priorities changed. Douglas wanted better access to and from Victoria and New Westminster to the newly discovered sources of gold, rather than across the border to Washington State. He asked for improvements to the chart of the Fraser River originally made by the HBC in 1827. He needed one that was more reliable for navigation, particularly through the treacherous sandbars off the estuary. There was now considerable marine traffic between the capitals of the two colonies.

Plumper had been at New Westminster on May 24. Annually on this date, members of the British Empire celebrated the birthday of their sovereign, Queen Victoria. Parading were the Sappers under Colonel Moody, RE, the band, and two companies of Royal Marines Light Infantry with a field gun and crew from *Plumper*. At noon, after the royal salute of twenty-one guns, the colonel addressed the assembly "in very feeling and soldier-like terms" to a warm and enthusiastic response from the troops and civilians. After everyone stood to sing the national anthem, they raised three hearty cheers for "our Most Gracious Queen." There was also a Grand Ball in Victoria organized by the officers of *Satellite*, *Plumper*, and the Boundary Commission. Had he been present, Philip would have been in his element.

*

Conditions in the gold diggings were extremely harsh, the cost of food and supplies exorbitant. For much of the year, the weather rendered placer mining impossible. In winter, the river largely froze over. In late spring, the ice and snow at higher altitudes melted, causing the river flows to become torrential. For most of the summer, the water level rose above the gold-bearing bars of gravel. Few prospectors remained at the diggings year-round. Those who could afford it headed back to California to recover and resupply for the next favourable season. Others retreated to the milder climes of the coast and offshore islands, to eke out a living by homesteading—or, as some called it, squatting—until their situation permitted another try at making their fortune.

One such homesteader was Lyman Cutlar, who arrived on San Juan Island in the spring of 1859. He claimed a homestead, as permitted under US law, on an attractive piece of pasture land. He built a cabin, fenced off a small plot with brushwood, and planted some seed potatoes.

Unfortunately, the piece he chose was within the perimeter of Belle Vue, a sheep farm owned by the Puget Sound Agricultural Company, an HBC subsidiary, managed by John Griffin. As well as 1,500 sheep, Griffin had a few pigs, which he let forage freely. Several times, the pigs squeezed through Cutlar's fence and rooted out part of his crop. After complaining to Griffin a few times, he shot one of the intruding marauders in frustration.

Immediately realizing that this meant trouble, he apologized to Griffin and offered what he considered fair compensation. Claiming that the animal was, in fact, a prize breeding boar, Griffin demanded a far greater sum than Cutlar could afford. Griffin informed his superior in Victoria, Alexander Dallas. The dispute over the water section of the boundary remained unresolved, so the island's legal status was moot.

Over the next few weeks, though, the brouhaha over the errant pig escalated. A belligerent American, Brigadier William Harney, became involved, spotting an opportunity to advance his own political career. He mustered four hundred troops supported by several field guns that landed on the island, setting up a fortified camp on Belle Vue farm. Douglas, just as fiery, called on the naval forces then in the region to repel the invasion. *Plumper* and *Satellite* went to collect an armed company of sappers and marines from New Westminster. Those vessels, together with the thirty-one-gun screw corvette HMS *Tribune*, mounted a blockade of Friday Harbour.

Tribune's captain, Geoffrey T.P. Hornby, the senior naval officer on site, stalled in obeying Douglas's order to oust the American forces. It had turned into an armed standoff between two empires: Britannia at the height of her worldwide pre-eminence, and the young pretender proclaiming the Monroe Doctrine of dominance over the American hemisphere.

Fortuitously, two more experienced senior officers arrived on the scene in the nick of time: Rear Admiral Robert Lambert Baynes, commander of the British Pacific Station, and Lieutenant General Winfield Scott, US Army. These wiser heads, both having served in the War of 1812, knew the horrors of modern warfare. They recognized that the solution to the issue would be diplomatic, not military. Between them, they reined in the hotheads on both sides and agreed on a temporary solution until their governments could negotiate a settlement.

Nanaimo in an 1859 sketch by Dr. Panter-Downes of HMS Tribune *seen at anchor. Note the chimney and winding wheel of the coal mine, and the loading pier.*

The Americans could keep their camp at Belle Vue, but were limited to one hundred men, with light weapons only. A similarly sized and armed force of Royal Marines would establish a British camp at the opposite end of the island. This amicable arrangement lasted for the next thirteen years. The "Pig War" was over, and Richards hoped *Plumper* could return to charting the southeastern coast of Vancouver Island.

*

Despite such distractions, during 1859, Richards's survey parties in boats had accomplished a considerable amount of charting. They focused mainly on the harbours and inlets: Esquimalt, Victoria, Nanaimo, Saanich Inlet, Cowichan, Maple Bay, Nanoose, and Baynes Sound on Vancouver Island, and Howe Sound, on the lower mainland.

At the end of August, while based at Nanaimo, Richards received a dispatch from the governor ordering him to return to Esquimalt, again interrupting survey work. *Plumper* left immediately and was steaming south along Trincomali Channel when it struck a submerged rock. Perhaps with a touch of irony, Richards named the hazard Governor Rock. The damage did not at first appear to be serious enough to halt further operations that season. A fleet diver with the flagship HMS *Ganges*, however, inspected the damage to *Plumper*'s hull from the two groundings and recommended repairs at a dry dock. As the nearest was at San Francisco, the ship would need to go there to be made seaworthy.

During the season, they had collected enough raw survey data to spend a productive winter ashore, converting their readings into more than two dozen new charts and harbour insets.

The first part of the winter of 1859–60 was relatively mild on southern Vancouver Island. In mid-February, Richards took *Plumper* south to the dry dock on Mare Island in San Francisco Bay. The damage proved to have been severe: seventy feet of false keel and several sheets of copper had been ripped away, the main keel splintered in several places, and the propeller shaft bent. By late March, repairs completed, they returned to Esquimalt, ready to begin the new survey season. A sudden storm, downing many trees, delayed their start until April 5. They could make their way northward to Nanaimo, but continuing bad weather prevented any survey work. Ten days later, they reached Comox and began sending out survey parties in boats. Mayne and Dr. Wood headed upstream to explore the Courtenay River, while *Shark* and other boats went to Cape Mudge.

For the rest of the summer, *Plumper*'s surveyors progressed up Discovery Passage through the notorious Seymour Narrows, though they did not discover the hidden hazard of Ripple Rock—sounding operations from an oar-powered boat were almost impossible in a current that could exceed nine knots.[5] They recorded a minimum depth in the middle of the narrows of seventeen fathoms (thirty-one metres), which appeared to show clear passage for all vessels. From there, they returned to Nanaimo to collect their messages and refill the coal bunkers.

In the meantime, Richards's boat parties had been working in Bute and Jervis Inlets. Mayne and Dr. Wood started on an overland expedition seeking a new access route to the goldfields from Jervis Inlet. Wood, exhausted, had to give up after a few days, but Mayne again completed an extremely taxing, eighteen-day journey across to the gold rush townships of Pemberton and Hope.

The rest of the 1860 survey season passed without disruption. Work continued along the northern shores of the island. *Plumper* even rounded the stormy tip, Cape Scott, and briefly ventured into Quatsino Sound. It was clear, however, that their trusty ship had insufficient power to operate safely along the rocky, stormy outer coast. The untimely death of the chief surveyor, Master John Augustus Bull, in November cast a sombre mood over *Plumper*'s entire company, relieved only by the arrival, at the close of the year, of the replacement vessel, *Hecate*.

CHAPTER 8
Escorting Lady Franklin

During the first days of 1861, Captain George Henry Richards and his team of hydrographers, now including Lieutenant Philip Hankin, settled into their spacious new vessel, HMS *Hecate*. "My new cabin alone [was] nearly as large as our mess-room of the *Plumper*," remarked the first officer, Richard Charles Mayne. The ship's fittings needed work to prepare for survey operations, but immediately there came a call to search for a new gunboat, HMS *Forward*. The vessel had gone to the aid of a Peruvian merchantman, *Florentia*, in distress near Nootka Sound. HMS *Plumper* also joined the search. All three Royal Navy vessels returned safely, having rescued many of the crew from *Florentia*, which had foundered on the rocks off Friendly Cove.

*

No sooner had Mrs. Richards and her three children left their cottage in Esquimalt to return to Britain than another friend of the family arrived. This was Lady Jane Franklin, widow of the Arctic explorer Sir John Franklin, accompanied by her niece, Miss Sophia Cracroft—called Sophie—with Lady Jane's maid, Sarah Buckland. They were on a tour of North America, funded by the wealthy Henry Grinnell, a shipping magnate.

In February, while preparations for the next season's operations proceeded aboard *Hecate*, Richards entrusted Hankin with a diverting mission. He was to accompany Lady Franklin during her visit to Victoria, New Westminster, and the Fraser River goldfields. His memoir recorded only two minor episodes during the ten-month visit, but Sophie's letters home contained intriguing details of who and what they encountered, revealing unexpected aspects of Hankin's character.

The recent return of a search expedition by steam yacht *Fox* had confirmed the total loss of Franklin's ships *Erebus* and *Terror* in June 1847, and his having discovered the Northwest Passage. Lady Franklin still hoped that someone would recover the letters, logs, and journals from the lost ships. The news had ended Lady Franklin's twelve years of anxiety and considerable expense. Although the news was tragic, it vindicated her husband's name and freed her to indulge once more in what Sophie called her "ungovernable passion for travel." Lady Franklin had come to Victoria primarily to see Captain and Mrs. Richards, but also had other interests in the new colonies.[1]

The ladies arrived aboard SS *Oregon* from San Francisco via Port Townsend early on Sunday morning, February 24—a few days after Hankin's twenty-fifth birthday. During ferociously stormy conditions in the Strait of Juan de Fuca, *Oregon* had crossed paths with SS *Princess Royal*, bearing Mrs. Richards and her children homeward. The captain had been seeing his family away when the visitors arrived at Esquimalt, so first lieutenant Richard Charles Mayne collected and brought them to HMS *Hecate* and settled them into the captain's cabin. The skipper arrived, half an hour later, to greet them in person.

Sophie observed that the ladies, devoutly Church of England (Anglican), were happy to attend the ship's Divine Service that morning. Mayne read the lessons and the entire crew sang well, even the most difficult music. Philip Hankin's tenor voice impressed Sophie, and she noted Richards was visibly affected during the prayers. Captain John Spencer, RN, of HMS *Topaze*, also in the harbour, came to luncheon after the service. Spencer and the ladies had many familial and social connections. Richards appointed Hankin to escort the ladies for the duration of their stay, a choice that proved happy for all concerned. Gowlland recorded, "[Lady Franklin] is a fine, energetic old lady of not more than five [feet] six or seven [inches]—& very amiable & pleasant."

Hankin organized a two-horse covered wagon to convey the ladies and their considerable quantity of luggage to lodgings arranged for them in Victoria. During their ninety-minute journey over a rough track, the ladies, aged sixty-nine and forty-five, felt the biting cold wind despite being wrapped in bearskins and blankets. Alongside them walked Richards and Mayne, in high boots to cope with the deep mud.

The ladies found the lodgings with Mrs. Moses to be "the very best in the place, & really *very* tolerable."[2] Their hosts, Wellington and Sarah Jane Moses, had come to Victoria in 1858 as part of a large group of African American colonists fleeing persecution. He had opened the Pioneer Shaving Saloon and Bath Room on Government Street, and Sarah, "a first-rate cook," managed the hospitality business. The naval community patronized the place well.

Once established in her rooms, Jane received a string of visitors from Victoria society paying their respects. Bishop George Hills, the other person Jane had come to see, was among the first. Her wealthy friend, Miss Angela Burdett-Coutts, had subsidized the bishop generously and had also paid for the prefabricated church shipped to his new diocese. It was constructed of wooden frames with corrugated iron plates for exterior cladding and for the roof. The interior was of redwood from California, with felt and sand between the boards as insulation. Limestone blocks from Salt Spring Island provided a secure foundation. Consecrated in September 1860, the new church could accommodate six hundred worshippers.[3]

The benefactor had asked Jane to report on the progress of the church and on the establishment of collegiate schools for boys and girls, in which Jane shared her interest. So, on their first night in Victoria, they attended evensong at the iron church together with the bishop, the captain, and two officers, including Hankin, from *Hecate*. Accompanied by an organ, an excellent choir battled the noise from an easterly gale raging outside. Sophie noted one pew was reserved for the men of *Hecate*.

The prefabricated "Iron Church" of St. John the Divine in its early state. Attended by the Nagle family and officers of HMS Plumper *and* Hecate.

The Vancouver Island government offices, usually called the "Birdcages," seen from across Victoria's Inner Harbour.

The visitors received many invitations to lunch and dine, including one from Thomas Harris, a successful butcher, whose most important client was the Royal Navy.[4] Hankin poked snobbish fun at the manners of their hosts, but Sophie and her aunt considered them to be "excellent people without affectation of any kind."

They also took lunch with Mrs. Douglas, the wife of the governor, and her married daughters. Sophie recorded, "She has a gentle, simple and kindly manner, which is quite pleasing, but takes no lead whatever in her family." In the governor's absence, William Young, married to Cecilia, Governor James Douglas's niece, took on the role of host. After lunch, he took them on a tour of the new "Birdcages," the government buildings, with a view from a parapet of the harbour and city.

Hankin escorted the ladies to such social events and on shopping excursions. Sophie noted: "He is a very natural nice fellow, with plenty of fun in him. . . . He speaks fluently in Chinook,[5] which is a great comfort here." Sophie knew of Hankin's aunt Christiana, the author of two noted works of the anti-slavery movement. Hankin showed the ladies a one-piece argillite flute ornamented with pewter and mother-of-pearl brought to town by a group of Haida traders, and Jane purchased it.[6] Another trader offered them the fine pelt of a sea otter for only $20, but they declined, as it would be too difficult to get back to Britain.

*

Philip Hankin as a young man, date uncertain.

At the beginning of March, Hankin escorted the ladies on a tour of the Fraser Valley. They boarded the HBC steamer *Otter*, whose captain, William Mouat, gave them the use of his own cabin. Most of the other passengers, headed for the diggings, carried a revolver and a large knife at their belts. Also aboard was "a party of theatrical ladies & gentlemen—one of the former, very pretty."[7] They passed the contentious island of San Juan, and naturally, Jane and Sophie supported the British claim to ownership. Transiting Active Pass, they learned that but for the obstinacy of Archibald Campbell, Richards's American counterpart on the Water Boundary Commission, it would have rightfully been named Plumper Pass. As they left the pass to cross the Strait of Georgia—and as has every visitor before and since—they admired the conical splendour of Mount Baker and the snow-covered peaks of the Coastal Range.

Otter worked its way upstream to what Sophie called "the embryo city" of New Westminster. There, Captain Robert Parsons of the Royal Engineers (known as "sappers"), alerted by Richards of their arrival, waited with a military boat to convey the ladies and their luggage the mile upstream to their impressive camp. They were to be the guests of Lieutenant Colonel Richard Clement Moody, RE, an officer commanding the 164-man-strong Columbia Detachment,[8] and Mrs. Mary Moody. Also staying as a guest in their substantial house was Governor James Douglas.

Government House at New Westminster, constructed by the Royal Engineers, and the residence of Lieutenant Colonel Richard Clement Moody, RE, the lieutenant governor of British Columbia.

The next morning, they were to board *Maria*, a shallow-draft sternwheel steamer of the Anderson company, which had courteously placed their craft at the ladies' service. Their senior captain, a Scot, William Irving, was to provide them special care. After a tour of the camp, they returned to New Westminster, where *Maria* awaited. Parsons also boarded, travelling to inspect the construction of a road beyond Hope and to reconnoitre the mule trail from Yale, the head of navigation below the fearsome canyon. Additionally, two officers from *Topaze* joined, off on a sketching excursion. One of these was the ship's assistant surgeon, Dr. Alexander Rattray.

The ladies were impressed by the 6,000-foot (1,800-metre) peaks that Richards called the Golden Ears based on his suspicion that the double peak guarded the source of the placer gold washed down by the rivers. As the afternoon sun turned the snowy peaks rosy, they passed the sites of New Langley—deserted and replaced by Moody, for strategic reasons, as the capital for the new colony by New Westminster—and Fort Langley, little more than a few huts on stilts and a chapel. *Maria*, unable to reach their planned stop at Fort Hope before dark, tied up to stout trees. Navigating the torrent through a notorious reach with many "snags"—fallen trees stuck tight in the riverbed—was far too dangerous to attempt at night.

In the crowded steamer, three of the six small cabins accommodated the ladies, with four officers in the others. Everyone else bunked down on the floor of the main cabin. The skipper, Irving, and the ship's purser joined the ladies and officers for the evening meal. Sophie noted: "& a very merry party it was, thanks to Mr. Hankin who has plenty of the midshipman left in his composition—but I can't write down the jokes which made our entertainment."

At daybreak they untied and safely negotiated "snag reach," getting as far as the Harrison River leading to Harrison Lake. Prior to the construction of the wagon road through the Fraser Canyon by the Columbia Detachment, this was the principal route to the goldfields. *Maria* briefly stopped for most of the passengers to disembark. The river increased in speed, and in places the sternwheeler could advance only with the help of poling and towing. There were frequent stops to take on more firewood from stockpiles on platforms. They also passed several villages where locals caught and wind-dried the abundant salmon. The party saw a few prospectors, mostly Chinese, identifiable by their conical hats. The men intently worked their "rockers," crude but effective devices separating the gold particles from the river's gravel.

The water level and rapid current permitted *Maria* to get only as far as Fort Hope. The captain felt they might reach Hills Bar a mile below Yale, but the last stretch would be the most difficult. They spent the night tied up at Hope, and the local magistrate, Peter O'Reilly, came aboard for dinner. Once again, Sophie recorded: "Mr. Hankin officiated & amused us infinitely by his love of jam & bad butter."

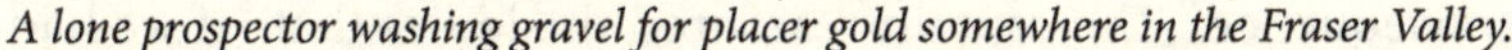

A lone prospector washing gravel for placer gold somewhere in the Fraser Valley.

The next morning, after a visit by the local clergyman and his family, O'Reilly took the ladies and their escort on a tour of the small community. They saw the long-established HBC fort and the courthouse that also served as the church. He showed them samples of placer gold, in use locally as currency. At noon, they reboarded for the attempt to get to Yale.

The next four and a half hours proved fascinating as they passed through spectacular mountain scenery. The vessel *Maria* wound a slow passage past many bars in the river, which had seen the frenzy of the gold rush. All of them showed signs that miners had thoroughly worked them over, with many still in operation. They learned that miners had recovered over £40,000 (about C$7.6 million in 2025) worth of gold from Hills Bar alone. The mining operations varied from lone Chinese prospectors with a pan, to commercial teams of workers employing "flumes"—long, elevated channels made from planks—bringing water from up to four miles (two and a half kilometres), to separate any gold from gravel dug from the riverbanks. What Philip saw and heard in these goldfields must have ignited a small flame in his mind that would grow in insistence to career-threatening proportions.

Someone at Yale had measured the current flow at as much as ten miles (sixteen kilometres) per hour. Sophie described one incident: "A tract of rapids boiling and fuming like a big cauldron. It was, however, in very smooth water that our frail boat struck herself against a rock—the sensation was quite unmistakable." Irving, the captain, and his crew rushed below with blankets to plug what turned out to be a "trifling hole, of no consequence." The captain reassured the ladies that "if we had gone to the bottom, it would have been but a little way after all!" Irving, to the visitors' relief, decided that *Maria* could reach Yale, and did so.

The Reverend William Crickmer, the local clergyman, came aboard to greet them and invite them to dinner. The ladies accepted. They toured the community, evidently still a place of active gold mining with shacks and tents pitched randomly along the beach. The single street was a sea of mud flanked by shops, mostly Chinese-owned. A large Indigenous population surrounded the "town." The visitors noted boxes for drying salmon and a cemetery of mortuary poles carved and painted with traditional designs. There were even some carved figures mocking the dress and postures of the white invaders. They discovered one of the traditional winter houses, a hollowed-out mound of trodden earth, with access by an inclined, notched pole acting as a ladder through the central smoke hole.

The Crickmers, whom Sophie described as "lively, cheerful people," had invited over two dozen local worthies to attend the tea. Hankin enlivened the occasion by first helping Mrs. Crickmer in the kitchen, then play-acting a liveried footman, bringing around a tray of teacups. But he was not finished with his tricks. On retiring to their cabins, Buckland, Lady Jane's maid, having seen her mistress comfortable, went to her own cabin next door. Her shriek brought guffaws from the men's cabins. She had discovered one of the carved figures they had seen earlier peeking out from under her bedcovers. Dr. Rattray had bought the figure from one of the local people. Philip had removed it from Dr. Rattray's cabin and planted it in the maid's bed. Buckland took the jape amiably, laughing with everyone else.

Hankin was still not done with his pranks. After his early breakfast, Philip greeted Sophie with "Come and see this!" He led her to Buckland's cabin, where a strange parcel lay on the bed. He invited her to guess what it was, then drew aside the cloth cover to reveal a tiny baby swaddled tightly to a board. He had borrowed the infant from a local mother for half a dollar. After the ladies had marvelled at the child, Philip restored it to the mother with the gift of a gilt bracelet from Lady Jane.

The following morning, the local HBC agent organized a special excursion for the lady visitors. They travelled in one of the company's large batteau craft manned by ten voyageurs—paddlers who had come west with the company—dressed in their traditional red woollen shirts and hats with coloured ribbons. Two more boatmen in similar attire stood at the bow and stern. Their destination was the canyon as far as the falls. Weaving their way upstream through eddies and whitewater, they passed the site where Captain Parsons was to inspect the construction of the road. After five miles (eight kilometres) paddling and man-hauling the flat-bottomed boat through shallow places, they came to the notorious falls that completely blocked further progress.

The return trip was easier, but just as exciting. The voyageurs sang in chorus as they skilfully negotiated the river's challenges. A banner, newly erected across the narrowest part of the canyon, proclaimed it to be "Lady Franklin Pass." Mr. Crickmer had proposed this name as a courtesy to their visitor, but the authorities never accepted it. Crickmer's formal farewell address to Jane, in a saloon and attended by some twenty men, delayed their scheduled departure from Yale. His rather grandiloquent rhetoric amused Hankin, who committed it to memory, but Jane, ever the gracious lady, thanked the cleric and his fellow well-wishers. After they boarded and the steamer *Maria* departed, there came a volley of shots into the air and cheers to salute their distinguished visitor.

They took stopovers at Hope and Langley on their return before arriving at Sapperton, the Royal Engineers' camp. Colonel and Mrs. Moody invited them to stay once more. During the few days' wait for the scheduled steamer *Otter* from Victoria, Jane inspected some facilities installed by the Royal Engineers' Columbia Detachment. To thank the men of the detachment, Lady Jane requested Saturday be declared a day off, and the colonel granted her wish. The men arranged a farewell entertainment for their visitors for Saturday night at their theatre. Dinner with the Moodys was held early, so all could attend.

The theatre was full when the official party arrived. Many of the men's wives and children were also present. Sophie noted "the Camp being like one great family." A soldier handed them printed programs listing two plays, with songs and dances in between. The cast of the plays was, of necessity, all male, which only added to the amusement. Men with the gruffest voices and wildest whiskers took the female parts. Sophie particularly admired the backdrop, an Italianate view painted by the men. The seven-piece orchestra, led by bandmaster William Haynes, RE, played well, some musicians doubling as singers.

One of the intermediate pieces surprised and delighted the ladies. As Sophie described it:

> *The curtain fell & a hornpipe began & on the curtain rising again, Mr. Hankin bounded on the stage in full sailor's summer costume (all white and blue) flung down his hat, folded his arms, & danced his hornpipe beautifully. You can imagine the reception he got from the astonished audience who knew nothing of his intention. He was encored & very good-naturedly came on again.*

The rest of the event went over just as well. Sophie summed up, "So you can imagine we enjoyed our evening very much."

Next morning, the party boarded *Otter* to recross the strait to Victoria. Richards and Mayne were there to greet them and convey

A sailor dancing the hornpipe. A collectible cigarette card.

them back to their lodgings with the Moseses. *Hecate* was due to visit New Westminster in a few days, at which point Hankin would have to return to his shipboard duties. Back in Victoria, now without Philip in attendance, Lady Franklin and her party went on some excursions to local beauty spots. They arrived back in fine spirits, just in time to dress for Governor Douglas's farewell dinner to them.

A sudden change in the weather spoiled their last day in Victoria. A bitter wind brought snow, preventing visits to bid their many friends goodbye. Nonetheless, many of those friends braved the conditions to visit them for the same purpose. As SS *Panama* steamed out of the harbour on March 24, the flags of the Stars and Stripes and the Union Jack dipped in mutual salute, and the band aboard *Topaze* played "Auld Lang Syne."

Sophie concluded her letter:

> *As a community, the people of Vancouver Island seem a very contented one—enterprising, yet without the grasping of Americans who are never satisfied unless they find themselves pre-eminent; if not alone in the field. . . . The wonderful growth of the colony during its 2 years only of existence, is highly to the credit of its people.*

Lady Jane and Sophie were to return to Victoria nine years later. They would find Philip Hankin again in residence, but in quite a different capacity.

In his memoir, Hankin included two episodes from his months of escort duty with Lady Franklin. The first was the invitation to take tea with the butcher Thomas Harris and his wife. He gleefully recounts how he accurately predicted their greeting and demeanour, snobbishly belittling the couple, who were decent, hard-working people, and worthy citizens. Philip's opinion was in marked contrast to that of the ladies, who correctly judged the true merits of their hosts. The second episode he recorded was the somewhat effusive address presented by the clergyman Crickmer on their departure from Yale. Jane refused Philip's request to copy the text of the address, correctly suspecting that he would hold it to ridicule. He memorized it anyway and quoted it in full in the memoir, with scorn. In doing so, he boasted of his excellent memory.

In fact, apart from the ability to recall such trivia, Philip Hankin's memory appears far from reliable. When compared with Sophie's contemporaneous version of the events, his memoir is often inaccurate. For instance, he mistakenly recalled the whole Franklin episode as being at the end of 1862, a short time before *Hecate* left, whereas it happened in early 1861, soon after he had rejoined Richards's team. He omitted details that surely would have interested him, such as the exhilarating ride through the Fraser Canyon, downstream with the voyageur paddlers in full song; the amazing facilities built and in operation at Sapperton; dinner at the Moodys' with Governor James Douglas, knowledgeably discussing colonial governance; and even his own hornpipe performance.

CHAPTER 9
Adventures Aboard HMS *Hecate*

In early 1861, Lieutenant Philip Hankin, RN, was back aboard HMS *Hecate* under the command of Captain George Henry Richards, RN, an expert in hydrographic surveying. Richards was into his fourth year of a project to survey the coasts of Vancouver Island and the surrounding waters. They carried out the first phases of the project, with several interruptions, in HMS *Plumper*, a sturdy little ship, but not powerful enough for the ferocious conditions to be expected on the west coast. Hankin had been aboard *Plumper* for part of that time and had shown an aptitude for survey work. At Richards's suggestion, after other deployments, he returned with *Hecate* as it came out to replace *Plumper*.

*

The weather on the outer coast of the island was harsher than on the more protected eastern side, so the 1861 survey season would need to start later than previous years; ideally, not before late March. Before surveying could begin, however, an urgent matter required attention. The seasonal spate of the Fraser River carrying large uprooted trees had washed away all the buoys the team had placed in the navigation channel through the Sturgeon Bank off the mouth of the South Arm. To make the channel safe again for the increased maritime traffic, they had to install redesigned buoys and heavier anchor weights capable of withstanding hits from floating forest giants.

The gunboat HMS *Forward* supported *Hecate* for this task, and the two vessels arrived at New Westminster on March 23, to the delight of the residents. *Hecate* was the largest vessel yet to reach the city, and its arrival confirmed that their river would be navigable by merchant shipping. Richards noted that the place was flourishing, with £50,000 annual revenue from customs dues. He declined the city fathers' invitation to a public banquet, pleading pressure of work. He sent surveyors with the ship's boats and *Forward* to position the buoys in the channel. They returned to take dinner with the Royal Engineers at their camp, Sapperton. Hankin, who had been escorting Lady Franklin to the goldfields, rejoined his ship.

After coaling at Nanaimo, they returned to Esquimalt on April 5 to find two new vessels of the Royal Navy at anchor. They were the fifty-one-gun steam frigate HMS *Bacchante*, flagship of the new commander of the fleet in the North Pacific, Rear Admiral Sir Thomas Maitland, and the screw corvette HMS *Tartar*. Richards spent the next ten days briefing the admiral on such matters as building docks and naval stores, and the provision of fresh water. In the meantime, the surveyors calibrated the chronometers and made other preparations for the coming season's work. It was now mid-April, and the weather had turned from a mild winter to a sudden cold snap, followed by a dismal, rainy spring.

Hecate sailed out of Esquimalt and headed out of the Strait of Juan de Fuca in the evening. Richards wanted to know from how far out he could see the new lighthouse at Race Rocks, and was pleased to find that it was still visible from their deck at eighteen or nineteen nautical miles (thirty-three to thirty-five kilometres) distant. After stopping for the morning to fix the position of Port San Juan, they continued around Cape Beale, which Richards identified as the site for the next lighthouse, into Barkley Sound and up the long fjord of the Alberni Canal. They anchored at the far end, close to the Anderson company's sawmill, by then almost built. They had previously reconnoitred this location in *Plumper*, and Richards had arrived there on foot from Qualicum on the eastern side of the island. Guided by an HBC employee, Adam Horne, he had crossed the steep ridge of the Beaufort escarpment.

Governor James Douglas was well aware of the wealth of timber resources that surrounded this strategic and sheltered port. He had discussed with Richards the desirability of locating a route for a road

Race Rocks lighthouse. First lit on December 26, 1860.

between Alberni and Nanaimo. Lieutenant Richard Charles Mayne was to make this his third mission of overland reconnaissance. A sailor and a few packers from the local Tseshaht people accompanied him. Also, a local English settler, William "Eddy" Banfield, volunteered to go with them. Banfield had been a ship's carpenter aboard HMS *Constance*. Noting the potential to use his skills on Vancouver Island, he had taken his discharge from the navy and returned to the island in 1853. He had established a trading business just inside Barkley Sound, had explored extensively, and knew the local people well. The round trip took Mayne's party just under two weeks.[1]

While Mayne was gone, teams led by Hankin and the other surveyors from *Hecate* fanned out in boats to investigate and chart the many lateral inlets along the main channel of Alberni Inlet. The Hankin party charted the eastern sector south to China Creek. In doing so, they skirted a significant hill that Richards named Mount Hankin. Richards had orders from his superior, Rear Admiral John Washington, the Hydrographer, concerning toponyms—the names of places and features shown on the charts. He was to respect the toponyms used by previous explorers, both British and Spanish, and to learn and use the local names wherever possible. For this, he made a practice of hiring local men as interpreter-guides, temporary crew members fed and paid as sailors and given clothing. At the time of naming Mount Hankin, no knowledgeable local was aboard.

Considerably complicating the problem of adopting local toponymy was the extraordinary range of languages spoken by the Indigenous population of Vancouver Island and its nearby mainland. These languages contain a wide variety of sounds difficult for Europeans to pronounce and record on paper. Although the local Indigenous peoples had names for all the geographical features of their territories, writing was not part of their linguistic culture.

There were, and remain, three dominant Indigenous language groups in the region: the Coast Salish, the Nuu-chah-nulth, and the Kwak'wala.

The island's south coast, much of the Strait of Juan de Fuca, the San Juan archipelago, and Puget Sound were the traditional territories of the Coast Salishan speakers.

The west coast from Nitinat (Ditidaht) to the Brooks Peninsula made up the territories of the Nuu-chah-nulth group, comprising fourteen nations (sometimes called the Aht tribes), plus the Makah of Cape Flattery. Their languages, known collectively as Wakashan, have similar roots.

The northern end of the island, down the inside coast as far as Cape Lazo, nearby smaller islands, and the neighbouring mainland were the traditional territories of the Kwakwaka'wakw people, who were known as the Kwakiutl, and who spoke four dialects of the language. Richards had to find interpreter-guides for each of the territories he was working in. He also saw this as an opportunity to teach them the language and ways of the new arrivals.

For the work within Barkley Sound, they recruited a young fisherman of the local Huu-ay-aht community. His Huu-ay-aht name wasn't recorded, but missionaries had given him the name of Thomas Roberts, and aboard *Hecate* he went by the nickname "Friday." He did not prove of value as a seaman, but in Richards's words, Hankin "made a kind of pet servant of him, he went everywhere with him." Philip's primary interest seems to have been in learning Friday's language and making word lists with translations. Friday also knew Chinuk Wawa and provided Hankin with many words and phrases that he incorporated into a word list that has survived.[2] Hankin then extended his knowledge to other related Nuu-chah-nulth, or the Southern Wakashan dialects. Over the next few months, Friday gained knowledge of English. Curiously, Philip did not mention Friday or the word lists in his memoir, nor did he credit Friday as his source for the word lists in the document he submitted to Richards.

Hankin and Friday would subsequently cross paths and work together several more times, though none of these are mentioned in the memoir.

*

The boat parties spent two weeks under miserable conditions. Richards recorded:

> *Not one [day] without rain almost constant & generally heavy breeze. No sun, no sight of hills, very cold and perfect winter. Boats returned all more or less damaged and having done little or no work.*

After the carpenters repaired the ship's boats, *Hecate* left Alberni Canal to anchor within the sheltered inlet of Uchucklesaht. From there, the boats dispersed to survey the multitude of islands, dangerous reefs, and isolated rocks that are a feature of Barkley Sound. Richards pronounced it "the most extensive and broken up place it is possible to imagine." At the end of May, he moved the base of operations to "a very good sheltered place" within the Broken Islands. He noted their surveys would "erase many of the dangers said to exist and find many clear channels. . . . We have also found many good anchorages."

Their next task was to chart the open ocean off the entrance to Barkley Sound and Juan de Fuca as far south as Cape Flattery, in sea conditions where only *Hecate* could operate. They hoisted the boats aboard and Hankin and the other surveyors worked from the ship. They ran a grid of deep-sea soundings that covered the series of sandbanks first noted by the French explorer La Pérouse in 1786, and famous as halibut fishing grounds. They revisited the Alberni mill community for a few days to "put the ship and boats in order" before returning to Esquimalt. They towed a present from the mill owner for the admiral—a new topmast for his flagship *Bacchante*. Richards had left second masters Jack Gowlland and Edward Blunden with the schooner *Shark* and a whaler to reconnoitre the next important inlet, Clayoquot Sound.

In early July, *Hecate* headed north to refuel at Nanaimo, and on the way delivered a quantity of iron boundary markers to now Lieutenant Colonel

John S. Hawkins, RE, the British commissioner for the land boundary, at Point Roberts and Semiahmoo Bay. They also dropped off more markers at Nanaimo, to be delivered by the gunboat *Grappler* to Camp Sumas on the Fraser River above Fort Langley. They continued northward, making stops at Alert Bay, Fort Rupert, and Shushartie, which had been an important trading station during the sea otter boom, but by 1861 was quiet. Richards had wanted to land at Cape Scott, at the northwestern tip of the island, but the timing and weather were unfavourable for measurements. Instead, he steamed by the Triangle Islands to look for potential landing places, but found it too dangerous to get close enough.

Despite it being the height of summer by then, he found the conditions similarly foul as he steamed southeast along the rocky outer shore, taking soundings. It was late in the evening when they reached Clayoquot Sound, so Richards prudently waited at anchor outside for daylight. It was just as well. Some locals came aboard and indicated an entrance to the sound, but when Gowlland came in response to their gun signal, he warned that the entrance suggested by the locals was too shallow for *Hecate*. He piloted the vessel to safety four miles (six kilometres) inside the sound. Evidently, the locals did not appreciate the draft of the ship.

Hecate's boat parties spent the next three weeks continuing Gowlland's survey of the complex Clayoquot Sound, with its many islands, shoals and banks, and several arms, finding them to be "very unlike what is shown on the old chart." The weather remained unconducive to surveying from open boats, and "mosquitos very troublesome."

There was considerable interaction with the local villagers who brought fish and berries to trade. Richards found them to be "a quiet, well conducted people." Gowlland, who had spent six weeks among them, considered them to be "very civil." He noted in particular Wack-la, the chief of the village of Ahousaht, "a fine athletic strapping fellow, about 6 feet [180 cm] high." These comments are in striking contrast to those made by the same officer when describing the Huu-ay-aht of Barkley Sound. Hankin detected and learned the differences between Friday's dialect and those spoken by the people of Ahousaht and other villages within Clayoquot. This knowledge would serve him well a few years later.

While *Hecate* was still based in Clayoquot, a canoe arrived from Alberni bringing their mail, including an official notice of Mayne's promotion to commander. This came as a complete surprise to him, as he had been looking forward to completing the mission with Richards. This meant he would have to leave *Hecate* for redeployment at his new rank as soon as they reached Esquimalt. It so happened that this would be delayed for three months.

Richards needed to take a few more readings at Alberni, then collect Gowlland's party from Nootka, before returning north to finish work at Cape Scott. Meeting a northwesterly gale, however, ruled out hope of landing anywhere at the north end of the island or taking any more soundings. So, after collecting Gowlland, Richards planned to return to Esquimalt via Juan de Fuca, where he needed to fill in some gaps in his set of soundings. By now, it was August 7.

Hecate was running before a strong wind, ten miles (sixteen kilometres) offshore, with the tide, and under full moonlight. The officers of the watch were comfortably fixing their position on the chart every two hours, when suddenly, an hour before midnight, they entered a dense bank of fog—"pea-soup," Mayne called it. They continued on the same course for three hours, which, by dead reckoning, would have brought them to the north side of the entrance and about five miles (eight kilometres) offshore. Richards came onto the quarterdeck. He ordered their speed reduced and asked for the sounding. The depth of fifty-three fathoms appeared to correspond with their calculated position when compared with the grid of soundings they had compiled only six weeks previously.

He adjusted the course to follow the line of the coast of the north shore of the strait, and some five miles (eight kilometres) out. They took soundings each half hour, and the one at four o'clock showed a depth of nineteen fathoms. From their work, Richards felt they must be too close to the north shore for safety, so he ordered a course due south, at a speed reduced to five knots, and stopping to take soundings every ten minutes. He ordered two men to be stationed in the chains at the bow, to keep a lookout and heave the sounding leads. It was also the change of watch, with Edward Bedwell replacing Gowlland on the quarterdeck. At eight thirty in the morning, with the most recent depth of forty-eight fathoms, the captain went below for breakfast.

Two minutes later, Richards heard, "Hard a-port! Stop Her! Reverse the engines!" Rushing on deck, he saw, through the dense fog, his ship strike between two rocks just above the water. A nest of more rocks surrounded them, and there was a heavy swell running. *Hecate* was aground amidships and being twisted and pounded against the rocks with each swell. Gowlland recorded, "Every instant we expected to see her break up amidships."

They did not know their location. Their chart showed no such group of rocks anywhere near their calculated course. Richards ordered all boats lowered, and they were attempting to pull the ship off astern when a canoe approached. Aboard was James Melvin, the captain of an American trading schooner, *Elizabeth*, out of Port Townsend. He informed Richards that they were between Cape Flattery and Neah Bay, on the opposite side of the Juan de Fuca entrance from where they had thought.

The tide was rising, and Melvin advised Richards that the *Hecate* could soon pass between the two rocks and anchor in a small basin where his own ship lay. Richards followed the advice, cleared into the basin and dropped anchors. Since there was not room to swing with the tide, they ran hawsers (very strong steel ropes) out to rocks. By eleven o'clock, piloted by Melvin and his local crewman, and with the ship's boats marking subsurface rocks, *Hecate* escaped the hazard. As they did so, they also emerged from the bank of fog into clear weather. They brought the boats aboard and, with bilge pumps working hard to remove the water flowing in through the damaged hull at eight inches per hour, *Hecate* steamed for the safety of Esquimalt.

Richards surmised that there had been two reasons for their misadventure: There was an unknown countercurrent, separate from the normal tidal flow and possibly generated by the gale, which had carried *Hecate* to the southeast faster than they realized. As well, an additional sandbank must exist in the middle of the entrance, to have given the misleading depth of nineteen fathoms. There had been rumours from local fishermen of such a bank, and it was in one gap in their set of soundings that he had planned to remedy.[3] No one had been at fault. This had been another of those unfortunate incidents only to be expected when charting waters for the first time.

Hankin mentioned the dramatic episode only briefly in his memoir, whereas Richards, Mayne, and Gowlland all described it in detail. *Hecate* had, in fact, had a lucky deliverance from a potentially ship-threatening situation.

The fleet diver from *Bacchante* inspected the damage to the hull and patched the holes with greased oakum, blankets, and sheet lead. Mayne inspected the temporary repairs from inside, pronouncing them "very skillfully stopped," But the structural damage was clearly severe enough to require attention at a dry dock. The nearest one was still at Mare Island, in San Francisco Bay. The admiral ordered Richards to take *Hecate* there without delay. At the end of August, they coaled up at Nanaimo, then headed for California, escorted by the screw corvette HMS *Mutine* in case of a further problem. A few days out, with the weather fair and the repairs holding, Richards signalled to *Mutine* that *Hecate* could proceed alone.

Commander Mayne had earlier reported to the admiral about his next commission. Orders about his replacement had not yet arrived, so Mayne was to remain with *Hecate* until relieved. As its first officer, Mayne was naturally still concerned for the damaged vessel. Also, as he had planned to visit San Francisco anyway, he was quite pleased with that arrangement.

They discovered the situation in San Francisco harbour to be chaotic and riven with the disputes over the Civil War, then in progress, including talk of secession by California. Despite their having officially requested use of the Mare Island dry dock, it would not be available for at least a month. HMS *Termagant*, sent there for repairs, had damaged the dock's structure when it rolled over while entering. Also, a US Navy vessel, *Saranac*,[4] was ahead of *Hecate* in the queue for the dock.

While waiting for the dry dock, Richards visited Lady Franklin, then staying in nearby San Mateo. Then he and Dr. Charles Wood made an excursion on rented horses to Benicia, where they took an elegant river steamer to Sacramento. They found a rowdy state fair in progress and the only accommodation was "a miserable dirty dig hole in the Orleans hotel." The return journey was equally horrendous. Richards wrote: "Glad I was to get onb[d] the ship and get some supper, for I can scarcely say I had eaten since leaving here." They had been away for four days, during which time the officers had worked on their charts and the men kept busy with routine ship's maintenance.

On October 4, *Hecate* entered Mare Island dry dock. What he saw appalled Richards: "Our bottom presented a most ragged and woe begone appearance." Gowlland recorded, "Some of the dockyard officials wondered at our being able to save the ship judging from her severe injuries the great damage she received; the critical position she must have been in to cause them in so many different places; about 50 shipwrights &c were put on immediately and commenced stripping the copper off." However, by the 16th, *Hecate* was afloat once more and Richards commented that "the ship was to all intents made as good as ever."

Mayne left for England a week later. His replacement as first officer, Lieutenant Henry Hand, RN, had joined them in early September. While *Hecate* was undergoing repairs, the officers and crew were granted the use of a receiving hulk—"very strong and serviceable"—as a special courtesy by Captain Gardner, the Commodore of the Yard. Hankin and his fellow survey officers were busy plotting their summer's work and preparing the charts for tracing. Hankin also worked to compile his notes from his discussions with Friday on the Huu-ay-aht and Chinuk Wawa word lists. He was unable to complete them before having to submit them to Richards, who sent them to England.

On some evenings officers received invitations to dine with resident families, but detected considerable anti-British sentiment. Nor was time ashore enjoyable for *Hecate*'s sailors in uniform; rowdies in the many bars would hurl hostile insults. Hankin's memoir only cursorily records the sojourn in San Francisco, except that his captain questioned the bill for repairs when it came. Philip might have recalled his own previous experience aboard a hulk—*Seringapatam* in 1850—but if he did, he made no comment.

CHAPTER 10

Hankin Builds a Monument

After an uneventful return voyage from San Francisco, a refurbished HMS *Hecate* entered and anchored at Esquimalt Harbour on the afternoon of November 1, 1861. HMS *Topaze* and gunboats *Forward* and *Grappler* lay at anchor. Captain George Henry Richards had earlier requested the Admiralty's permission to winter in the Sandwich Islands, which was granted. Because the grounding and dry-docking had cost them two months' work, however, Richards decided not to take up that permission, but to remain to make up some of the time lost.

There was an important job that they could accomplish before winter set in—to construct the granite obelisk on a plinth that would mark the 49th parallel. This would be on the cliff at Point Roberts, the Pacific end of the land boundary between British possessions and those of the United States. It is odd that such a project should be entrusted to inexperienced naval personnel when a large detachment of Royal Engineers, for whom this would have been routine, was available nearby. Instead, Richards delegated the work to Philip Hankin, supported by the bosun and twenty men from *Hecate*'s crew, with the assistant surgeon, Samuel Campbell, on site in case of accidents. Officially a Royal Engineer officer, Captain William Driscoll Gossett, acting treasurer to the Government of BC, was appointed superintendent of the project, but was rarely seen during the construction phase.

After collecting from Victoria the lumber and materials needed for the monument and housing for the work party, *Hecate* crossed to Boundary Bay in mid-November. They landed the equipment and construction crew on the sheltered south side of Point Roberts, where the

HMS Hecate *in Esquimalt Harbour. Watercolour by Edward Bedwell.*

carpenters began by building houses for the officers and the men. With the houses nearly complete, the carpenters returned to the ship, which left for Nanaimo to pick up coal. Loading took an inordinate five days because of the poor management of the facility. Even then, they did not fill the bunkers.

The weather deteriorated, with the wind now a southeasterly gale. *Hecate* made it back to the Point Roberts camp, having been gone a week, to check on the work and to reprovision for two more weeks. The new direction of the wind now exposed the camp to the weather.

The plinth and obelisk were to be built from granite blocks quarried at New Westminster under a contract with a mason, Mr. Thintson. He would bring them to the site by a scow schooner. The first batch of stones had just arrived, but the swell had been too heavy to allow them to be brought ashore until high tide on Monday, when the wind shifted again. They beached the scow, offloaded, and sent back for another batch of stones. The sky cleared enough for Richards to take solar readings to fix the precise location of the obelisk.

The following day, Richards returned to Nanaimo to complete coaling and fill barrels with fresh water. Richards reported, "The weather very disagreeable—either snow or rain." On Saturday, November 30, *Hecate* returned to the site, where Richards found that Hankin and his men had managed to raise all 14 stones to the top of the 200-foot (61-metre) cliff. Also, the party had laid the plinth of granite, 10 feet 6 inches (3.2 metres) square.

Path down the sixty-one-metre-high cliff at Point Roberts. Hankin's party of men manoeuvred thirty-two huge blocks of stone from the beach to the site of the monument marking the 49th parallel.

Richards checked its position. While the orientation was correct, the centre was nine inches (twenty-three centimetres) too far north. Richards faced a dilemma: where to position the obelisk on the plinth. If they placed it in the correct location, it would not be in the centre of the base and would look odd. In the aesthetically preferable centre of the base, however, it would grant the United States a short strip of territory nine inches wider than the agreement. He chose the latter option, "which I thought the better to do for the sake of appearance."[1] Richards took ten of the party back on board and returned to Esquimalt. On December 4, *Hecate* went back to Point Roberts and anchored in the lee of the east side. Despite the fog, from the clifftop Richards and Hankin could see the scow schooner coming toward them.

The next morning, with great difficulty, Richards manoeuvred *Hecate* around to the campsite, exposed to "a whole gale from SE. I have never seen it blow heavier in the strait, with a greater sea. I fear it will go hard for the schooner." Two days later, he steamed back around the point to where the schooner had anchored. *Hecate*'s boats towed it to a pier the team had constructed near the campsite. They unloaded the eighteen stones of the obelisk, five of them weighing over three tons in weight, onto the shore. Before departing for Esquimalt, Richards left Hankin with just ten men to get those stones up the cliff to the site of the monument, which, he acknowledged, "will be a heavy job." It was December 8. He noted, "The Strait full of trees & driftwood, washed off the high water line by the late gales." He made careful notes for the published *Sailing Directions* about how mariners would observe the new lighthouses when approaching Victoria and Esquimalt Harbours from the east.

Richards's journal does not record just how Philip and his small party succeeded in hoisting the thirty-two massive blocks up the cliff, nor how they built the obelisk—neither of them easy tasks—under such appalling conditions. The winter was the coldest on record with the Fraser River at New Westminster frozen over, bank to bank, with ice nine inches thick. They returned to Esquimalt on December 22, having completed the construction. Nor does Hankin mention his obelisk project in his memoir. All that is known is that they erected it in the wrong but visually satisfactory location, where it stands today. The following September, Richards heard rumours that the monument was fast going to ruin, due to it having been built during the frost. He went to investigate and found

The monument marking the 49th parallel at Point Roberts. Erected by Hankin's team.

it to be "in Excellent order." Hankin and his crew, with the mason Mr. Thintson, had done their onerous duty well.

Another Royal Engineer, Lance Corporal J.B. Launders, a skilled cartographer with Colonel Richard Clement Moody's Columbia Detachment, engraved all four faces of the monument.[2]

*

During December, Philip's friend and language tutor, Thomas "Friday" Roberts, who had remained with *Hecate* during the visit to the dry dock, requested leave to visit his family. He promised to return in time for next season's operations.

Richards recorded on December 26, "For the last 10 days the weather has been very fine, cold and frosty. Therm° standing below 30°[F] at night. . . . Victoria harb^r partially frozen over." It continued cold into January 1862, with temperatures as low as 9°F ($^-$13°C) at Victoria and

New Westminster, where ice blocked the Fraser River. Contact between Victoria and New Westminster was effectively severed. Richards recorded, "Indeed, so severe a winter has not been remembered here." The surveyors kept busy preparing charts and sailing instructions, while the crew repaired, painted, and refitted the ship's flotilla of boats.

It was mid-March before first *Shark*, then *Hecate*, could leave Esquimalt. The plan was to meet at Nanaimo. Richards wanted the Royal Engineers to print his charts of Barkley Sound, which were urgently needed, and could not wait a year for a round-trip voyage to have them printed in England. To keep *Hecate* as light as possible to ascend the Fraser, he delayed coaling. He found most of his new buoys still in place, and reached Sapperton, the RE camp, despite thick fog.

Once loaded up with coal, *Hecate* headed north on April 7 to continue with the surveys. They caught up with *Shark* and anchored off Fort Rupert. They found the village much changed since their previous visit aboard *Plumper*. The smallpox epidemic had decimated the population. The effect of rotgut whiskey sold by unscrupulous white traders exacerbated the suffering. According to the resident HBC officer, Hamilton Moffatt, there was no governmental control of this illicit practice.

Moffatt had explored an overland grease or oolichan trading trail that connected the Mowachaht people of Nootka Sound with the village of the Kwakwaka̱'wakw, at the mouth of the Nimpkish River.[3] Moffatt's knowledge of the connection interested Richards, and he got an excellent summary of the local ethnography and languages from him and recorded it all in his journal. He arranged for another old friend from their *Plumper* visit, Rupert Jim, to join them aboard as a translator and guide for the Kwak'wala-speaking regions. The Huu-ay-aht Friday had not reappeared for work by the time *Hecate* left Esquimalt.

Continuous foul weather prevented them from leaving Fort Rupert until April 14, when they got as far as Shushartie and anchored. Their pinnace-schooner *Shark*, although partly repaired during the winter, was still not fit to operate on the west coast. Richards sent Edward Bedwell back with the boat to Esquimalt, to have it brought to fully seaworthy condition. The next day they examined the area around Cape Scott and southward along a rocky coast with heavy surf breaking and no shelter for a vessel before Quatsino Sound. He found a sheltered anchorage just inside the entrance, on the north side, which became known as Winter Harbour.

Next morning, after attempting to leave Quatsino, they encountered an adverse gale and hurriedly steamed back to their anchorage. Richards commented, ruefully:

> *Until May, Gales are the rule—and strong winds from any quarter send surf on the coast and make the shore treacherous for boats. It is under any circumstances and at all times an uncertain coast, and calculated to turn one's hair white—and to inculcate patience.*

That night, Richards renewed acquaintance with Yak-y-koss, a local Koskimo child, whose head had been bound during infancy to distort the skull into a tall cone. He had seen the child during *Plumper*'s visit of eighteen months earlier and came to know her parents. She was now aged about eleven or twelve, still exuding innocent charm, and much enjoyed the attention and presents showered upon her. The parents remembered all the previous members of *Plumper*, and even identified the newcomer, first lieutenant Henry Hand, as a stranger.

The fieldwork associated with the surveys of the northwestern end of Vancouver Island proved hard going. Dense undergrowth of salal bushes carpeting severely broken terrain proved near impassible. Constant freezing rain exacerbated the difficulties faced by land parties. Richards usually included Hankin on his personal crew. The latter recorded nothing of these activities and the miserable conditions in his memoir, merely noting, "I have a wonderful memory." Richards's journal, however, carried several passages describing them.

Seeking a vantage point to provide a view along the coast near Winter Harbour and perhaps sight lines to the offshore islands, Richards and Hankin set out on foot. He wrote:

> *The trail to the sea was passable, but the water being rather high, we could not get along the shore to the* NW *but had to strike inland where I have rarely found such walking in my life: on the tops of banks or along fallen logs, and the bush so thick as to entirely puzzle one. After an hour or two's scrambling, we gained a few hundred yards and again came out on the coast*

scratched and torn and done up—and did not get near the point.

Fortunately for our reputation, it came on to rain & blow from the SEA *so that it would have been useless proceeding. We returned by the rocks, and I determined the next time I tried I would study the tide if possible. But this is difficult country, one moderately fine day in a week at the utmost. Got back at 5* PM, *soaking wet and not sorry to be home.*

This from a man who had made a ninety-day solo journey by dogsled in the Arctic! They had experienced, at first hand, the conditions facing many shipwrecked mariners on the island's stormy west coast. Even if survivors got ashore, they found themselves imprisoned there by an impenetrable barricade of salal and poisonous devil's club bushes. Two days later, they tried again:

Walked across to the outside Coast again, and by dint of climbing precipices and Scrambling thro brush, we managed to reach the point from which Woody Cape[4] *is seen and one of the offlying Islets to the* NW[d] *to which I was able to get true bearings and fix my position. . . . We reached the Ship at 6:30* PM *after a most fatiguing day, having taken four hours to walk a little over a mile, and three to return. It is very difficult to get along the coast by walking at any time—but unless at low water, almost impossible.*

Richards also remarked on the friendliness of the local people and how much they assisted their work:

Our boats are constantly among them, far removed from the ship and quite in their power. They have always been foremost to help them, landing in a Surf a whole village has come down to haul the boat up or to launch her, and they have always shewn the most friendly feeling. I can safely say, having seen & had dealings with almost all the Native tribes in the world, I have never met a more friendly, harmless and well disposed set of people than those on Vancouver Island.

CHAPTER 11

The Hankin-Wood Overland Expedition

Captain George Henry Richards brought HMS *Hecate* south down the west coast from the Quatsino entrance. In passing, he noted the size and complexity of the inlets Klaskino, Klaskish, Nasparti, Kyuquot, and Esperanza. There was a lot more work required to chart this sector than he had anticipated. He found the coast to be

> *studded with Islands and off lying reefs without number, the latter extending some 3 miles [5 kilometres] off the land. . . . I have never seen a coast so cut up as this.*

He planned to concentrate on the outer coast first and chart the inlets later. But before that, he wanted to map the overland oolichan trail between the head of Tahsis Inlet, an arm of Nootka Sound, and the mouth of the Nimpkish River on the island's east coast. Hamilton Moffatt of the Hudson's Bay Company, who had explored it in 1852, had told him of it. George Vancouver, too, had learned of its existence when he met Cheslakees in 1791.[1]

In May 1862, Richards directed Philip Hankin and *Hecate*'s doctor and naturalist, Dr. Charles Wood, to prepare to undertake an expedition from Tahsis to Nimpkish. *Hecate* anchored in a "very snug cove" on Esperanza Inlet, which Richards called Queens Cove. *Hecate*'s flotilla dispersed on charting duties and many local people came to visit. Richards consulted some visiting Mowachaht for advice about the route, since it was their own traditional trading trail. They strongly advised against the idea, explaining that there had been a lot of snow, and the swollen rivers would be impossible to ford. They suggested that from Kyuquot Inlet they would find a far easier route.

Convinced, Richards modified the plan and enlisted the services of four local Ehattesaht men to take the two officers to Kyuquot Sound by canoe. There, they would hire local guides and packers to accompany them across to the east coast to Cheslakees's village at Nimpkish. They expected it would take them three weeks. In the meantime, *Hecate* would work its way back around the north end of the island and await their arrival at Fort Rupert.

The previous year, Hankin had worked hard at learning Thomas "Friday" Roberts's Huu-ay-aht dialect of the Wakashan, or Aht, languages, and he gained fluency as they surveyed the nearby inlets. Wood, in his report of their traverse, noted:

> *I beg leave to offer my testimony to the great energy displayed by Lieut. Hankin who with his previous knowledge of Indian dialects & without an interpreter, within a few days made himself sufficiently master of the Cayuket language as to make our Indians perfectly understand his & my wishes in our progress across the Island.*

Hankin found he could converse with the locals using his command of the Huu-ay-aht dialect[2] but was less successful in persuading them of the urgency to get started. When they finally set off, the locals insisted on returning to their starting point, Actiss, after only a few days because the streams were in full spate.

Hankin had understood that *Hecate* would pass by Kyuquot Sound in a few days, so he resolved to wait for it. Not expecting to relaunch the expedition, he was generous with his food supplies. However, on his third day, the weather having improved, Hankin calculated they could still make the rendezvous with *Hecate* as planned after all. The new team of six men was too few to carry all the kit, provisions, and impedimenta of the expedition; they had to jettison something and would have to forgo any stops for scientific study.

As they started up the Tahsish River for the second time, Hankin realized that his food supply was now limited, but hoped to shoot game for the pot. He also discovered that his packers were both unskilled at overland travel and reluctant. As they struggled through hilly, thickly wooded country, the noise of their passage frightened off any animal worth shooting. The packers had told him that there would be plenty of elk, but they saw none. Heavy rain came on again, increasing the packers' anxiety, but Hankin urged them on. Following a trail, in some places they had to ford the ice-cold torrent.

At one of those fords, he recorded:

The river was about 40 yards wide, nearly breast deep and fearfully rapid. We accomplished the crossing in safety, by all holding on to a long pole and wading into the water at the same time; thus, by our united efforts resisting the force of the current.

Wood's report added that whereupon "the Indians cheered, we joining in, at having got over our first difficulty." Eventually they reached Atluck Lake, where the packers built two rafts to take them all to the far end, with hard paddling. They found the trail again, which led to a second lake, called Hoostan. While they built another raft, Hankin shot a grouse, their first fresh meat.[3]

At the northern end of Hoostan, they found a good trail leading to a third small lake, Anutz. By this time, the officers were reduced to tea and biscuits in the morning, and a shared can of beans and preserved meat in the evening, while the packers subsisted on roots and ferns. After passing through a patch of land "like a neglected English park," which Hankin felt was "available for agriculture," the trail brought them to Lake Karmutsen (now called Nimpkish):

A magnificent sheet of water sixteen or seventeen miles in length, with an average width of one mile and a half [twenty-five to twenty-seven by two and a half kilometres]. It runs in a northwesterly direction into the Nimpkish River, thus completing an entire chain of lakes throughout the Island. I tried it for soundings with fifty fathoms.

They searched unsuccessfully for a canoe, but found on the beach a log, sixty feet (eighteen metres) long, flattened on one side. After launching this and attempting to paddle it, Hankin fitted an outrigger to stop it from rolling, rigged a mast, and hoisted a blanket for a sail. They made

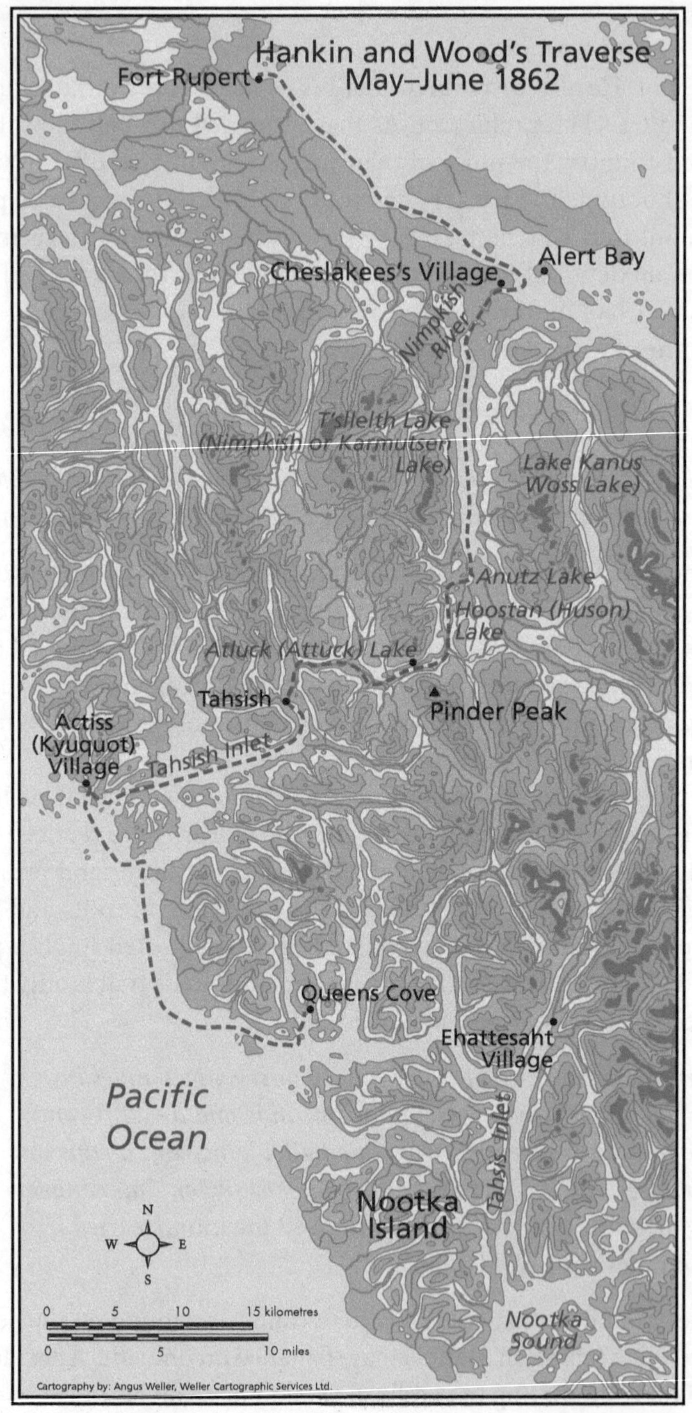

Map showing Hankin and Wood's traverse of the northern end of Vancouver Island.

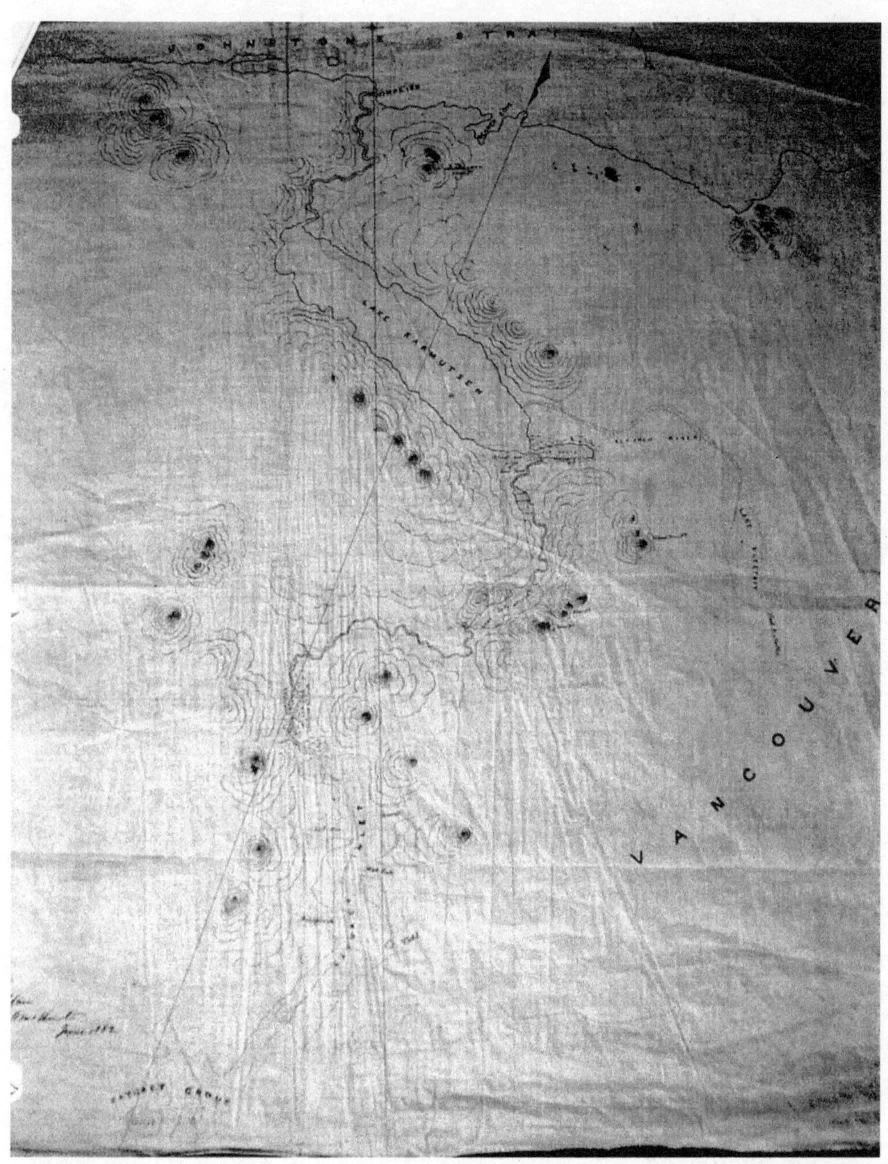

Hankin's manuscript map of their traverse for incorporation in the Admiralty chart #1916.

a few miles before headwinds prevented progress. They rested for a few hours before continuing to the head of the Nimpkish River, which was far too rapid to venture down aboard the log. They would need a good canoe. They found none, but a trail led them to Cheslakees, the main village of the 'Namgis, then known as Nimpkish, people:

> *There are fifteen houses, and many Nimpkish Indians reside here during the salmon season. . . . We found but one canoe here, which we immediately hired, and arrived the same evening at Fort Rupert, where we were most hospitably entertained by Mr. Moffatt until the arrival of the ship.*

Hamilton Moffatt, having explored across the island by an oolichan trail a decade earlier, knew well what the two men had just experienced. From when they left Actiss for the second time, the traverse had taken them nine days. Two days later, *Hecate* arrived, and the two overlanders climbed aboard. Richards recorded in his journal, "The Dr was much knocked up. The season for travelling was too early"—just as the locals had repeatedly warned them.[4]

Smallpox was ravaging the Indigenous population. Villagers had abandoned their homes next to Fort Rupert, fearing contagion. Although Dr. Wood vaccinated all the local people who showed up, several died each day, and there was little Richards or Wood could do to ease the suffering. *Hecate* carried on to Nanaimo, also deserted by locals fleeing the disease, to take on coal before proceeding to Esquimalt.

While in Nanaimo, Hankin and Wood each prepared a detailed report of their traverse. Richards forwarded both to Governor James Douglas, who, later that year, arranged for the *British Colonist* to publish Hankin's. Draftsmen incorporated his map of their route into the published charts. In his covering letter to Hankin's report, Richards informed Douglas:

> *The survey of the greater part of the Western Coast has been completed and several new harbours and anchorages discovered, which, when published for general information, will, I think, prevent a recurrence or lessen the frequency of disasters which have annually befallen vessels navigating this boisterous neighbourhood.*

Philip Hankin described his 1862 overland expedition at length in his memoir. His memory of it, however, was flawed. He remembered it as starting from Nootka Sound, rather than Kyuquot. He did not mention that Dr. Wood accompanied him. Nor did he include the delays with the first team of packer-guides from Actiss. He remembered the names and approximate sizes of the lakes Anutz and Karmutsen, but he also claimed to have "climbed over two mountains some 3000 feet high." That did not happen. They crossed two watersheds, but these were low-lying, although they probably felt much higher due to the difficult terrain.

*

As *Hecate* steamed south from Nanaimo, in mid-June 1862, it passed several vessels headed north full of prospectors intent on getting to the new gold diggings on the Stikine River. In Esquimalt they found two ships just arrived from New Zealand with "emigrants allured here by the reports of the Cariboo gold, deluded, I should say," commented Richards—incorrectly, as it happened. After three frustrating weeks for Richards attending to the admiral and other non-survey matters, *Hecate* left Esquimalt in early July 1862, to resume charting operations.

Hankin's data included in chart #1916. Note that his name has been given to a small range of hills flanking the north side of Karmutsen Lake.

CHAPTER 12

Hecate's Esquimalt-Based Work Concludes

In early July 1862, Captain George Henry Richards's priority was to return to the supposed sandbank that had given them the confusing reading of nineteen fathoms the previous August. Outside the entrance to the Strait of Juan de Fuca, they encountered a fleet of canoes fishing for halibut but could not find the nineteen-fathom spot. They spent two days sounding the extent of the bank. During that time, and twenty miles (thirty-two kilometres) offshore, they came upon a canoe carrying a single all-but-naked fisherman. He paddled up to the ship and asked to be allowed to come aboard. To Philip Hankin's delight, this was none other than the Huu-ay-aht Thomas Roberts, known aboard as Friday.

Gone for seven months, Friday claimed he had tried to return, as agreed, but something prevented it. He begged to be given his old position again and Richards reluctantly agreed. Philip suggested to the captain that this was a case of attachment, for Friday had been the only native islander he had met who had "shewn any gratitude for favours bestowed on him." Richards did not respond, but recorded, "[Friday] soon appeared in Mr. H[ankin]'s best Shirts and Trowsers—nothing was good enough for him, and I believe if he had met his sweetheart after a year's absence, he could not have been more delighted."

The glow of the reunion soon faded. Richards continued:

Three days afterwards [Hankin's] eyes were opened, Friday told him early that he had made a great deal of money thro' being with us formally, that he could now pilot vessels into Barkley Sound and that the little English he had learned was a fortune for him. He had come now to perfect himself in the language—nothing else—and as soon as that was accomplished, he was off like a Shot. Mr. H was much cast down by what he qualified as the slight ingratitude of Friday.

Richards asked bluntly, "Why should he stay with us save for his own advantage?" This episode might be the reason Philip omitted any mention of Friday in his memoir.

*

After stopping briefly at Nootka Sound to reprovision Jack Gowlland's party, *Hecate* returned to Quatsino Sound, arriving on July 12. The cone-headed girl Yak-y-koss and her parents paid their customary visit to the ship and were given their usual gifts of trinkets, cloth, and much-valued soap. Three survey boat parties then departed to examine and chart the multiple arms of the sound. At the close of the month, they again attempted to chart and sound the chain of islands running northwest from Cape Scott. The heavy seas and rock-strewn shorelines combined to make such work virtually impossible. It was far too risky to expose *Hecate* by attempting to pass between the islands, and out of the question for oared boats. Richards abandoned the attempt and returned to Queens Cove in Esperanza Inlet.

A drawing attributed to E.P. Bedwell, likely of Yak-y-koss, the "cone-headed girl" of the Koskimo Nation.

Richards wanted to get a message to Gowlland to let him know they had arrived and that he should join them. After some hard bargaining, he and Friday persuaded three locals to take Friday bearing the message. Meanwhile, Daniel Pender and Hankin would each complete the surveys of the different arms of Nootka Sound. Richards noted, as they were surveying the nearby Nasparti Inlet, the local uses of yellow cedar. "Truly this is a wonderful wood." He admired the canoes, paddles, and furniture they had made from it, and bought some twine they had twisted from its fibres. He thought it would make good rope. He added, "The language of the Indians here is something similar to the Barclay Sound dialect and Mr. Hankin is able to make himself understood knowing the latter."

Gowlland reported that, while anchored at Queens Cove, the Mowachaht, Ehattesaht, and other neighbouring bands paid a ceremonial visit to *Hecate* in a flotilla of huge war canoes, each holding up to sixty men. "Dress[ed] up and Painted Most Extravagantly," they circled the ship three times, chanting and paddling in rhythm, before coming aboard. They presented Richards with a sea otter pelt of mediocre quality, then squatted down awaiting reciprocation.

On August 8, *Hecate* departed from Queens Cove and took the Esperanza route to Friendly Cove, conveying the Mowachaht chief Maquinna[1] and his wife. They then rounded Estevan Point and into the next inlet to the south, Hesquiaht, taking soundings as they went. The boat crews sounded the shallow bay before returning to Esquimalt, to give the men a week's respite. An urgent order from Admiral Maitland interrupted this. He required *Hecate* go to Port Angeles to intercept a boatload of deserters from the flagship. They went but did not find the boat. Apparently, desertion from *Bacchante* had become a serious problem, with up to a hundred men already having "jumped ship." Rumour had it that the reason was the undue severity in the discipline aboard. The temptations of the Fraser and Cariboo gold rushes must also have played their part.

*

About this time William Young's name was briefly transferred from *Hecate* to *Bacchante* on the records of the Royal Navy, still listed at the rank of "Secretary"[2] but effectively employed full-time in the service of the two local governments. Those naval records also record his discharge date of November 11, 1862.

Ten days after the search for deserters came a call from Governor James Douglas. He and his staff were taking a party of eighty settlers to establish farming communities in the Cowichan Valley. He and his entourage would travel in *Hecate*, towing a schooner, *Explorer*, with the settlers aboard. They anchored near a Cowichan village on the shore of the bay. Douglas's party camped near a Catholic church on a nearby hill. Joseph Despard Pemberton, the surveyor, and his aides set about marking the cadastral grids of the selected areas, so that the settlers could each choose a one-hundred-acre parcel to "pre-empt."

Richards noted a high level of apathy among the settlers, who showed little interest in exploring for the places with best agricultural potential. While strolling about the lands, Douglas told Richards that he had held a meeting with the Cowichan Tribes, and they would welcome the settlers. Richards noted that the soil appeared light and clear or only loosely timbered, but he had seen only two or three settlers showing any genuine interest in pre-empting.

After returning to Esquimalt and two days' rest, *Hecate* left on August 23 to survey Saanich Inlet. Richards was most impressed with the district, settled in the previous year or two. Unfortunately, the harsh winter, with three feet of snow lasting six or eight weeks, had caught the farmers without shelter or reserves of fodder for their sheep, and they lost most of their livestock. He felt, however, that those with enough capital for subsistence would soon make up the loss. He and his officers attended the little church, St. Stephen's, and noted a congregation of about thirty souls that Sunday.

After partially coaling, again with much difficulty at Nanaimo, "this ill-regulated establishment," *Hecate* went to meet first master Edward Bedwell in *Shark*. He was charting Bute Inlet.[3] Two other boat parties, provisioned for two months, departed north to chart the entrance to Queen Charlotte Sound. Bedwell, taking provisions for a further six weeks, was to complete the survey of the Bute sector. *Hecate* ran lines of soundings through the channel between Mitlenatch Island and the mainland shore, before returning to Nanaimo for more coal.

In mid-September, *Hecate* returned to Fort Rupert. During the landing, Hankin, as Richards put it, "fell down, knocked my sextant and chronometer over with him and nearly broke his leg—which would not have been half as bad as damaging the instruments." They then headed north and visited Haida Gwaii (then the Queen Charlotte Islands). Richards had to "show the flag" in support of some copper miners who were experiencing hostility from the local Haida people. His excellent diplomatic skills resolved the matter.

He had similar duties at Fort Simpson and the nearby mission at Metlakatla. Some unscrupulous traders were trading bad liquor to local peoples, women were involved, and the ensuing intoxication was causing conflict. Three white men had been murdered. Lieutenant John William Pike, RN, the captain of the gunboat *Devastation,* had learned who the murderers were and had captured some hostages and a quantity of canoes he was determined to hold until the guilty men were handed over for justice. There was a standoff between the large population and the two naval vessels, both running low on coal. Richards's skills at negotiation brought a settlement of sorts, without further drastic action. Pike captured an illicit trading cutter and destroyed three hundred gallons of potent spirit.

Richards navigated through the maze of channels using George Vancouver's charts from 1794. He found them reasonably accurate for his purpose, but these waters saw increasing use by vessels bringing prospectors to the Stikine and the Yukon goldfields. They would need more reliable charts for safe navigation. There was much hydrographic work still to be done. By the beginning of October, *Hecate* was back in Queen Charlotte Sound, verifying the positions of rocks that had caused problems for Vancouver. Richards ran soundings past Hope Island toward Cape Scott, around it, and down the west side of Vancouver Island and into Klaskish Inlet. He recorded of this last: "Bottom very irregular and rocky, by no means an inviting place for a stranger to run for." The local people had all departed inland to their winter villages.

After waiting two days for the storm to ease, *Hecate* emerged into a heavy rolling swell and made the next anchorage in Nuchatlitz Inlet, just south of Esperanza. The survey boat crews spent the next few days sounding the entrances to Esperanza and Nuchatlitz. Parties of sailors cut firewood for the boiler. On October 11, in dense fog, navigating solely by chart soundings, they made for Cape Beale at the southern entrance to Barkley Sound. A sudden break in the fog revealed a landmark and confirmed the accuracy of their charts. They steamed up Alberni Canal and anchored opposite the sawmill. They found four vessels loading up with lumber. The enterprise was now "evidently thriving."

They returned to Esquimalt, again encountering dense fog as they entered Juan de Fuca, but it soon cleared. All *Hecate*'s boat parties joined them within the next few days. Until October 26, the ship underwent refitting and took on fresh water, and the men were able to enjoy some leave ashore.

*

While they had been away, a major event riveted the attention of the male population of Victoria. The liner SS *Tynemouth* had arrived, bearing about seventy young women immigrants from England. The stated purpose was to fill positions as governesses, cooks, nursemaids, and housemaids, but the largely bachelor community snapped up most of them as wives. This was the first of the several "brideships" sent to rebalance the colony's demographics, and the overall impact was beneficial in converting the "wild west" that was Victoria into a more civilized community. The town had recently been proclaimed a city. These highly significant changes to the local civic character passed unremarked in Hankin's memoir.

On November 10, Victoria declared a public holiday to celebrate the coming of age of the Prince of Wales. *Hecate* was a centrepiece of the event. After a procession led by a band to Beacon Hill Park, the ship steamed into the Inner Harbour and at noon fired a royal salute. *Hecate*'s bluejackets fired a response with four howitzers, landed earlier. The evening saw an official dinner, with toasts accompanied by the playing of a band. Bonfires were lit on Beacon Hill and Hospital Point. This was, once again, an extravaganza the extrovert Philip would have relished but did not recall in his later years. This is a significant omission since he met and was befriended by the Prince of Wales himself a few years later during an official visit to Madras (now Chennai), where Hankin would go on to serve.

There was some final work needed at Nanaimo to chart and set buoys in the harbour. They found the coal mines had changed hands. The HBC had sold that part of its business to a private consortium. The new management of the operation was not yet in place, so the handling facilities, tramways, and piers still needed major investment. Richards felt, correctly, that the future for the operation was promising. With an engineer and a capable manager, "it will pay handsomely."

Richards paid a farewell visit to New Westminster, and in his private journal, he contrasted the mood of the population with that of Victoria. There was not the same sense of prosperity and drive. Miners returning preferred to spend their winters in Victoria and just pass through New Westminster. New Westminster citizens of all classes were resentful of what they considered their rival city and quarrelled with anyone who came from, or spoke well of, Victoria. He felt that Colonel Richard Clement Moody, RE, shared the mood of ill feeling. Even so, the town council made a formal address of thanks to Captain Richards for his work in promoting the Fraser River as a navigable channel for commercial shipping.

After coaling in Nanaimo for the last time, Richards and his men, according to Gowlland's journal, received an address of appreciation from the townspeople, and Dr. Charles Wood gave a lecture "appropriate for the occasion." *Hecate* returned once more to Esquimalt, anchoring on December 6. Hankin and Bedwell took their shotguns to the lagoon and returned with "5 or 6 dozen ducks and geese." The next day, Richards received confirmation that he, the ship, and most of the crew were to return home. Master Daniel Pender, soon to be promoted to staff commander, would take the veteran HBC paddlewheeler *Beaver* on charter. Now carrying the designation HMS, it would serve for a seven-year extension to the survey. Funded in part by the two colonial governments, Pender and his crew were to navigate and chart the rock-strewn waters of the intricate channels, islands, and inlets north of Vancouver Island as far as the Alaskan border.

The schooner *Shark*, "fast sailing tender to HMS *Hecate*. Complete with masts, sails and tackling," was put up for public auction in Victoria. The new owner, a Captain Hughes, stated that he would use it for the herring fishery. The following year, the gunboat HMS *Grappler* apprehended *Shark* as it entered Nanaimo Harbour. Hughes was charged with "having repeatedly sold spiritous liquors to the Comox Indians," and found guilty, was fined $500 (about C$21,000 in 2025) and had *Shark* confiscated. Unable to pay the fine, he went to prison for twelve months. *Shark* was sold at auction in Nanaimo, and then for a third time in 1867, and afterward not heard of again.

*

Nanaimo Bastion, township, and mine with ships waiting to take on coal. The sailing craft in the foreground is probably Hecate's *boat* Shark. *Watercolour by Edward Bedwell.*

Master Daniel Pender, RN, in full dress uniform.

HMS Beaver, *reconfigured as a surveying vessel, at anchor off Esquimalt.*

Hankin's memoir recorded that, upon the news confirming *Hecate* was to return home, "I again applied to leave the Navy, for I was so charmed by Vancouver Island, that I thought I would try and get some employment, and end my days there." It was his third time asking to leave, though there is no sign that he made any attempt to seek other employment. Obvious contacts would have been William Young, the colonial secretary, who had been on the nominal roll of *Hecate* for two years, or among other influential members of the community, with whom he had socialized for several years.

According to the memoir, Richards was sympathetic and wrote to the Admiralty. Their answer was that Hankin was needed for *Hecate*'s return voyage. Philip, rather than feeling thwarted, took this as a compliment: "I think I must have been a very valuable officer." It is more likely that Richards, deprived of Daniel Pender and Edward Blunden, could not spare another surveyor from the substantial task of converting the season's fieldwork into charts and sailing directions. They would have to do this during the voyage home. The authorities agreed to Hankin taking his discharge on his return to England.

The *British Colonist*, reporting the imminent departure of the ship, trumpeted:

> *Every nook and cranny of our coast has been explored and mapped. Every current has been marked; an excellent compendium of sailing directions published by Captain Richards, making the navigation of our waters easy. In fact, it is due to Captain Richards and officers, to state that the first thorough survey of our Island has been made by them. Harbors or inlets have been marked on our Island that never existed, and large sheets of water that did not exist were unknown. All this Hecate's Surveying Corps have settled definitely and correctly.*

It is interesting to note the then current view that, before Richards and company surveyed and named all these features, they "never existed." The resident Indigenous people, of course, knew them all intimately, and had had traditional names for each one for untold generations past. That those features had not previously been recorded on the map indicates the ignorance of earlier cartographers, not the features' non-existence.

Even after Richards departed, later explorers and mappers would correct errors or add more information to the sum of incomers' knowledge.

Before the ship departed, the Vancouver Island House of Assembly passed a unanimous resolution:

> *This House desires to express their appreciation of the eminently able and practical manner in which the duties of [the coast survey] have been performed; and that the thanks of this House are due to [Captain Richards and the officers of HMS* Hecate*] for the valuable services thereby conferred upon the colony.*

At seven thirty in the morning on December 28, 1862, HMS *Hecate*, with one of the whaleboats in tow, steamed out of Esquimalt Harbour to the cheers of all the ships they passed, homeward bound. At Albert Head they paused for an emotional moment as now Commander Daniel Pender and his assistant Edward Blunden boarded the whaler, cast off, and "attempted to give us 3 feeble cheers choked with sobs. . . . They staid and watched us until we steamed away out of sight around the Race Rocks, and then pulled slowly back."[4]

CHAPTER 13

Where Corals Lie—*Hecate*'s Return Voyage, Part 1

With the significant exception of a bizarre incident at Batavia, Philip Hankin's memoir recorded scant information about his return voyage to Britain aboard HMS *Hecate*. The omission is most puzzling. The voyage, which occupied the whole of 1863, must have been among the most interesting of Hankin's life—including both his time in the navy and his later years of wanderlust. According to his memoir, he had accepted the refusal of his request to leave the service at Victoria with good grace. He even interpreted it as a compliment, that he was too valuable to be spared. Yet, why he passed over virtually all commentary on that year presents a mystery. It might relate to a disagreeable incident which did him no credit and for which, in retrospect, he felt ashamed.

Unfortunately, Captain George Henry Richards's private journal for that period no longer exists. However, second master Jack Gowlland kept meticulous notes that reveal details of the homeward voyage. He recorded the contributions they made to the charts of the many places they visited. Gowlland described *Hecate*'s visit to Batavia but made only a passing mention of the incident noted by Hankin.

For *Hecate*'s return journey, Richards took a westbound course to resolve some outstanding hydrographic issues. First, however, they needed to eliminate some gaps in existing charts of the American Pacific coast as far south as Mexico with new data, and to visit several reported vigias (uncharted rocks, shoals, sandbanks, reefs, and similar hazards to navigation, above and below the surface that other naval or civilian captains had reported to the Hydrographer, but that had not yet been investigated by trained surveyors). Such reports needed to be confirmed and plotted, or ruled out. This was standard procedure for hydrographic vessels, and prolonged *Hecate*'s mission by several months.

Hankin does not remark on *Hecate*'s voyage having traced a circumnavigation of the globe. He and Charles Wright, the chief engineer, were the only officers aboard for the whole voyage. Few mariners of the era could claim this distinction, and it would have added much to his prestige among his fellows, so the omission is noteworthy. Hankin took pride in his memory and was surely aware of the significance of his having completed the full circle.

*

Hecate's first stop after leaving Vancouver Island in the last days of 1862 was San Francisco. There, the surveyors could calibrate and adjust the ship's chronometers at a private observatory and work on the charts. During the two-week respite the crew took, by watches, twenty-four-hour passes ashore, while others painted their vessel. Gowlland reported that "not one [man] broke his leave, and I do not believe any of them dreamt of desertion."[1] He also observed that the town had "vastly advanced in size and commercial prosperity" since his previous visit. Real estate "eclipses even Victoria in extravagant prices." While they were there, "shiploads of grain and a very handsome subscription in money from the citizens of San Francisco were sent to Liverpool for the poor of Lancashire."[2]

Burning of the steamship Golden Gate, *July 27, 1862.*

Hecate next anchored at San Blas, previously the naval base from which, some seventy years earlier, Spanish vessels had sailed to establish their outpost on Nootka Sound.[3] *Hecate*'s officers found it "entirely deserted in consequence of the civil war raging in the interior." They then began a running survey of the Mexican Pacific coast as far as Manzanillo, where they found an American schooner with a team of divers anchored over the site of a bullion-laden steamer, *Golden Gate.* It had burned and sunk three months earlier with the loss of two hundred lives. The schooner had already recovered a third of the wreck's estimated million-dollar cargo.

Richards and his team made a sounding survey of Manzanillo Bay and the shoreline between the bay and the neighbouring port of Acapulco, which Gowlland described as "situated in a very objectionable position as regards health to their dwellers," with a stagnant lagoon. He also noted that it was a "splendid harbour, capable of containing a fleet of ships perfectly sheltered. The town itself is larger and more approaching to cleanliness to anywhere yet seen on the coast."

They learned that only a week earlier there had been an exchange of gunfire between the city's defensive forts and a French naval squadron that had arrived to water and provision but was mistaken by the Mexicans for a hostile force. The French reaction was swift and punitive, and an armed force headed inland toward Puebla and the capital. Most of the residents fled to the safety of the interior while the fracas took place.

Hecate's next port of call was Honolulu harbour in the Sandwich Islands. They spent the following month on the islands now known as Hawai'i, but Hankin's memoir merely records that they "met many old friends." Gowlland's journal is far more detailed, with the advantage of being contemporaneous. They learned that King Kamehameha IV and his consort Queen Emma were at their country retreat at "Kilau" (Kilauea), on the island of "Owhyhee" (Hawai'i). His Majesty was not well, and both suffered dreadfully from the loss of their only child, their son and heir, only a few months previously. Queen Victoria had been godmother to the deceased prince.

There was a new British consul general, Mr. William Webb Follett Synge, in place.[4] Gowlland found him to be "a most hospitable, splendid fellow, and on excellent terms with His Majesty and the government." There was not, however, any British commercial agent or authorized naval chandler at the port to help them acquire stores or provisions for the ship. Such activity depended on the negotiation skills of the paymaster confronting a local who sounded knowledgeable and helpful at first but soon proved "a most infernal scoundrel."

At the beginning of April, *Hecate* conveyed Synge and some of the court dignitaries to Lahaina, a small port on the island of "Mowi" (Maui), and from there to anchor off the King's house at Kilau. The residence was "a comfortable stone building, built with an eye to light, air and comfort combined." Gowlland learned His Majesty spent most of his time in an adjoining "most luxurious shed, and fishing of which amusement he is both very fond and very expert." Sixteen miles (twenty-six kilometres) from Kilau, the officers visited "Karakakoa" (now Kealakekua) Bay, the site where Captain James Cook had met his brutal death almost a century earlier. "The natives pointed out with great glee the very spot on which his head fell." Gowlland picked up a rock from the place as a souvenir.

After a few days, *Hecate* returned to Honolulu, this time with Their Majesties and a large retinue aboard. The crew fitted out the chart room as the royal stateroom. The ship's company saluted, manning the yardarms, as the royal couple left them to board the awaiting carriage.[5] The king requested that the surveyors make a detailed chart of the entrance to the harbour so that dredging could improve access for vessels drawing up to twenty-five feet (seven and a half metres), such as a frigate. The crew manned their boats in aid of an American whaler that had caught fire just outside the reef. They doused the fire, saving the vessel. On April 20, after a pilot had guided them through the harbour entrance, they disconnected the engines, hoisted sails, and set the course southward for Fanning Island, one of the Line Islands in the South Pacific.

*

At Fanning they found a coral atoll densely covered in coconut palms. It was the property of a Mr. English, who had lived there with his Tahitian wife and several children for the past sixteen years. He had a profitable business in coconut oil, employing seasonal workers imported from other islands. Determining the atoll's location and charting its detail took Richards's team a week, and then, bringing Mr. English and an interpreter, they headed for Humphrey Island. Now called Manihiki in the Cook Islands, it is another coral atoll and one of the most remote inhabitations in the Pacific Ocean.

After a week's slow sailing due, in Gowlland's opinion, to the poor condition of the sails, they sighted Humphrey, a circular strip of coral sand no wider than half a mile surrounding a lagoon. Perhaps four hundred inhabitants lived in a village of houses built from coral stone, thatched with palm leaves. Judging from the several wrecks visible, to anchor outside the village was too dangerous. After determining the position of the island, Richards ordered they steam to another nearby atoll and, again, calculated its true position. Gowlland called it "Reirson," but it is now named Rakahanga, in the Cook Islands. They learned that all these villages suffered frequent raids by pirates seeking slaves for the Peruvian sugar plantations and guano mines. Mr. English—by this time known as "Captain," because he owned a fleet of trading schooners—disembarked. Before leaving, the survey team ran a survey around the perimeter of the chain of islets forming the atoll.

Hecate made similar brief calls for correctional surveys at various islands of Western Samoa and in Fiji. They had crossed the Date Line[6] when, coincidentally, fierce gales of the southern winter hindered their progress westward, ripping several of the sails. Proceeding under sail and steam, they made for Port Jackson, now Sydney, in Australia, to anchor on June 26, 1863.

*

The ship needed a refit, including recaulking the hull and replacing torn sails. After a month's stay, having restocked all necessary stores from the naval commissariat and taking on three hundred tons of coal, *Hecate* left Port Jackson to shape a course up the eastern coast of Australia, keeping about sixty miles (ninety-seven kilometres) offshore. Closer in, contrary currents and eddies "and the charts not being completely surveyed" combined to make the passage dangerous.

They called into Cape Moreton, an island at the mouth of the Brisbane River, the river being the access to the capital of the new Colony of Queensland. The anchorage was safe at the season of *Hecate*'s visit, but easterly winds could drive vessels onto the coral. Nine large vessels lay at anchor, having come straight from Lancaster, England, bringing impoverished immigrants.[7] The wretched passengers were being cared for by the state until they could fend for themselves. The return voyage of those ships of the Black Ball Line was for the highly profitable wool trade. The prosperity of the colony depended on this trade, so resolving the issues of safe passage and anchorage for merchant ships was a top priority.

Hecate passed inside the Great Barrier Reef. The coast, covered in mangrove, was ill-suited for a settlement. The local people menaced them with accurately thrown long spears and amazing boomerangs. Gowlland noted: "Their spears [could] hit a ½-crown [a coin three centimetres in diameter] at 100 yards." Richards soon called off the survey activities.

Previously, Gowlland had recorded in his personal diary that Hankin had fallen ill in early April while they were surveying for potential new ports along the north Queensland coast:

> *Poor Hankin knocked up first with mumps and lately with something else; and insisting with his usual energy in doctoring himself with Cockles pills, nearly overdid it and brought himself to an end; with diarrhea & nausea.*

This contradicted Hankin's boast in the preface to his memoir that "I have never had a day's illness worth mentioning." It is also interesting to note Philip's lack of confidence in the skills of his shipmate and companion on the expedition to cross northern Vancouver Island, Dr. Charles Wood.

Hecate continued the passage up the Queensland coast, passing Cape Flattery. The name must have amused Richards, as it was the same as the one used for the southern portal of Juan de Fuca Strait. Both were toponyms from James Cook's voyages. They continued northwestward, checking vigias and amending earlier charts. They took a line of soundings along their course, adding useful information to the chart otherwise scant on detail. On the last day of August, they rounded Cape York to enter the Torres Strait. Here, the vessel headed west for the southwestern end of the island of Timor, to the Dutch settlement of Kropang (now Kupang).

The Monthly Gazette of Health *in 1821 described Cockle's Antibilious Pills as "half a drachm of extract of colocynth (a powerful laxative) and two drachms of aloes."*

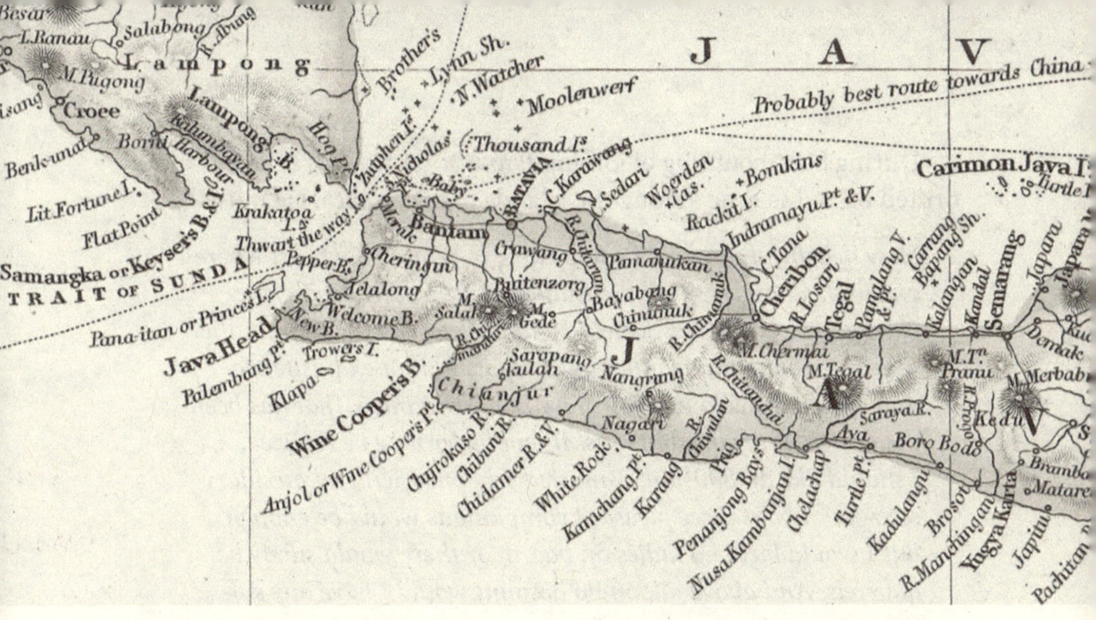

Part of Arrowsmith's 1848 map Asiatic Archipelago *showing Batavia and the Strait of Sunda. Note the hill station Buitenzorg and the infamous volcanic island of Krakatoa.*

They found the fort there to be in decrepit condition, with a well-maintained town of Chinese merchants. Ample supplies of fresh water were there for the taking. The lone Dutch official, or resident, spoke no English nor, according to Gowlland, "showed us any civility whatsoever." After filling their water casks, buying a few chickens and eggs for the officers' table, some fresh fruit, long radishes, and an old buffalo for the crew, they continued westward.

They passed between the islands of Flores, Sumba, Sumbawa, and Lombok into the Bali Sea. Their next stop would be Batavia at the western end of the island of Java, and their course passed along that island's northern coast. Gowlland noted it to be "thickly populated amid beautiful verdant foliage. . . . One could almost fancy himself looking at some fairy pictures." Lateen-sailed prahus, local trading craft, some capable of eighteen knots, crowded the seas.

For anyone but the most jaundiced, the picturesque sights they had seen and the diversity of people met during *Hecate*'s voyage over the previous nine months must surely have cast indelible impressions on the memory. In the section of Hankin's memoir recounting this phase of the voyage, such novel places and events went unremarked. The reader might surmise that the life of a surveyor at sea was, by this time, sadly devoid of any interest for him. The fact that he had recalled that voyage much earlier in his memoir suggests another motive for the omission at this point.

During his recounting of joining *Plumper* for the first time, his mind drifted off to his time among the islands of the tropics. He mused:

> *How delightful it would be to be able to cruise about just where one wished, and visit all the islands of the South Pacific, the Navigator Islands, the Society Islands, the Friendly Islands, the Marquesas and many other lovely spots in that exquisite sea and escape the cold and fog of an English Winter. That has been the dream of my life, but alas! It will never now be realized. . . . I should like an 800-ton, 3-masted schooner, with an auxiliary screw . . . about three pleasant companions would be enough, but I would have no ladies on board, or there would surely be quarrels. And above all, on no account would I have any suffragettes, or they would set fire to the yacht to get the vote. What a comfort it would be to land them on some Island, where they would all be eaten.*

*

On September 21, *Hecate* anchored in Batavia Bay in what is now Jakarta. They found, also at anchor, "an immense fleet of merchant shipping principally Dutch and French, in all little short of 200 sail [vessels]." On their arrival, according to Gowlland's log, "a Dutch officer from the frigate boarded us with the boarding book. Mistook us for the Singapore Mail, shortly expected." Hankin's description of the encounter could explain this misunderstanding. This section of the memoir merits recounting since the incident was the only one he recorded of *Hecate*'s year-long journey home.

Hankin's memory of the itinerary was adrift in placing the episode at Timor. Gowlland's account is more reliable on this, but apparently he was not aware of what transpired when the Dutch captain came aboard. Hankin related:

> *I had unfortunately about 2 years previously mentioned to Capt. Richards one day, in the course of conversation that I could speak a little Dutch which I had picked up some years previously, when I was in the old Castor, at the Cape of Good Hope. So when the Dutch Captn. came on board, I was sent for to act as interpreter. There is a great difference between speaking a little Dutch, and being interpreter, as I soon found out.*

However, I was told to put on my coat and Epaulettes, cocked hat, and sword, and come on deck immediately.

When I got on deck, I found Captn. Richards and the Dutch captain bowing very low to each other and making curious steps backwards and forwards. Looked as if they were dancing a kind of dutch hornpipe. Immediately I appeared on the scene Richards said to me Here you are. For goodness' sake say something to this Dutch captain. He doesn't understand a word of English, and I don't know what to do with him. I replied, really Sir, I can't speak Dutch. Nonsense, you told me you could. Say something at once. One looks like a perfect fool standing here. After meditating a few moments, I suddenly remembered I could say in Dutch, 'Give me some bread please,' well say it, said Captain, that's better than nothing. So I said to the Dutchman, give me some bread, please, and we all took off our cocked hats, and made a low bow.

Now, said the Captain to me—say something else directly. Oh dear, I replied, I really can't say anything else, when I suddenly recollected I could say, 'Give me an orange please' which I did, and we all bowed to each other again and kept walking round, and round in a circle. Well, that's all right said the Captain, but you must say something more, when I remembered I could say 'eighty-eight' in Dutch—Well, that sounds very well said the Captn, Say it two or three times over—it's much better than standing there, looking like a fool. So I repeated, Give me some bread, give me an orange, and eighty-eight when we all bowed again and walked several times round the circle, when at last the Dutch captain said something in Dutch, which I told our Captain, meant goodbye, tho' I had not the slightest idea what it was, and then he went into his Gig, which was alongside the ship waiting for him.

Then Captain Richards turned to me, and said, 'What on earth do you mean Sir, by telling me you could speak Dutch? You made me look like a perfect idiot.' In vain I protested, I had only said I could speak a little Dutch many years ago, but that I had quite forgotten it. In about half an hour, Captn Richards went to return the Dutchman's visit and I was again sent for to accompany him and act as interpreter.

Directly we got on board the Dutch man-of-war, the same ridiculous scene was played again—we first of all made low bows to each other, taking off our cocked hats, and walking round and round. Now go on Mr Hankin said the Captain, say that give me some bread thing. Which I did, and we all bowed again. Now, that next thing Give me an orange, which was immediately done. Now, that eighty-eight, said the Captain, ah that's the best of the lot, and sounds quite Dutchy. When we retreated, bowing and walking backwards to the gangway. When we got on board the Hecate again, the Captain said, It wasn't so bad, as they couldn't say a word of English so we could say something in Dutch!

Then the Captain wrote a flaming letter to the Admiralty, saying he had duly returned the visit, and that the most friendly relations existed between the Dutch Captain and himself! And I have no doubt that the Dutch captain did the same to his Admiralty. I think I did a great deal towards the friendly relations, and perhaps prevented war between England and Holland!

Seemingly Richards forgave his reluctant and hapless interpreter over the episode, since, while *Hecate* lay at anchor for a week in the oppressive heat of mosquito-infested Batavia Bay, the two of them enjoyed a three-day stay at a fine hotel at the interior hill station of Buitenzorg (now Bogor City), swimming in a marble pool and visiting the exotic botanical gardens.

The beautiful, cool hill station of Buitenzorg on Java island visited by Hankin and his captain.

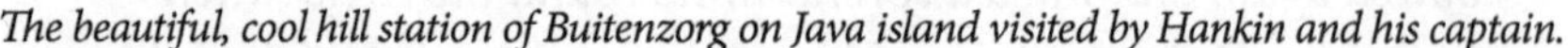

CHAPTER 14

Westabout the Cape—*Hecate*'s Return Voyage, Part 2

HMS *Hecate* steamed out of Batavia at the end of September 1863. As they transited Sunda Strait between Java and Sumatra, their course took them close by a small group of volcanic islands whose 2,600-foot (792-metre) high conical peak was called Krakatoa. This island became notorious twenty years later when it erupted in a salvo of four explosions, supposedly "the loudest sound ever heard by humans." The event ejected a plume of pumice, ash, and sulphur dioxide gas into the stratosphere, causing bizarre, vivid sunsets worldwide for months afterward and darkening the sky for years. It also triggered a trio of tsunami waves up to 100 feet (30 metres) high that travelled around the globe three and a half times, killing over 120,000 people.

Clearing Sunda, *Hecate* headed southwest to catch a narrow band of favourable trade winds. Finding it, Captain George Henry Richards ordered the engines to be shut down and sails hoisted for the long passage across the Indian Ocean. Hankin and the other surveyors returned to the chart room to work on plotting their new findings and on the charts of Vancouver Island, as much as the movement of the vessel under a strong breeze would allow. While within the favourable band, progress averaged a most satisfactory 170 nautical miles (315 kilometres) per day, but there were also periods of calm and of contrary winds. Richards authorized the cooks to access the stock of reserve rations, including, to the delight of all aboard, pickles, to provide a change from salt beef.

Sir George Henry Richards in 1877, when he had achieved the rank of vice-admiral (retired).

After five weeks of variable winds and gradually warming weather, *Hecate* came to anchor in Simon's Bay on the Cape of Good Hope on November 9. Also on station as the guard ship was a fine frigate, HMS *Narcissus*, which had been holding *Hecate*'s mail from England. This included the momentous news of Rear Admiral John Washington's death and Richards's appointment to Hydrographer. The Admiralty ordered his return at full steam.

Over the next two weeks, while the vessel underwent refitting and provisioning and took on extra supplies of coal, the officers visited Cape Town, some twenty-two miles (thirty-five kilometres) away, where the resident British colonials feted them. Visitors to the ship included Her Majesty's astronomer at the Cape of Good Hope, Sir Thomas Maclear, and Mr. Robinson, the surveyor general of the colony. They both inspected and admired the maps, charts, and navigational notes produced during Richards's mission.

After leaving the Cape, they set course northwest for Ascension Island under maximum sail assisted by the engines. According to Hankin, in those days, ships of the Royal Navy on passage did so under their own sail, except for special reasons to be recorded in the log. Only on Sundays were the engines disconnected, and *Hecate* made up to 190 nautical miles (350 kilometres) daily. Arriving at Ascension on December 4, they anchored briefly to take on additional coal.

Keeping to a route close to the west African shoreline to avoid contrary winds, they arrived at the port of Funchal on the island of

Madeira on Christmas Day. They found a small fleet of Royal Navy warships already at anchor. There, Jack Gowlland learned of his promotion to master. London newspapers reported Arthur Edward Kennedy's appointment as governor of Vancouver Island, and Frederick Seymour's as governor of the mainland colony, with New Westminster his base. While the surveyors measured the astronomical coordinates of a point in one Lord Brownlee's garden, *Hecate* took on a further 160 tons of coal. Continuing at full speed for England, they reached the safety of Plymouth Harbour on January 2, 1864, and arrived back at Woolwich on the 7th, to payoff eleven days later.

According to Gowlland's journal, Richards went to the Admiralty to take up his new position. Gowlland himself went home to prepare for his courses in pilotage and navigation. Most of his fellow officers now awaited their next assignment on half pay, except for Hankin and Assistant Paymaster Barclay Corrie. These two "left the service—the former went off to the gold diggings at British Columbia—the latter left and persuaded by his friends, entered again. Through the aid and interest of Captain Richards, [Corrie] was given his seniority back again." Richards added a note to Hankin's service record: "Not fit to be a 1st Lieut. Manner good with men, no great ambition, gentlemanlike & estimable. Knows French, Italian and 3 Indian languages."

Hankin's memoir records his conversation at Woolwich with Richards:

> *[He] was very kind to me and wanted to get me an appointment in charge of a meteorological station at Valencia, and said he would gladly do anything he could for me, so I asked him as a great favour, to try and get me my discharge from the service, as I longed to get back to Vancouver Id. and try and get some employment there. My service on the coast of Africa with Captn Haswell had given me such a dislike to the navy that I had determined to leave it altogether and devote my energies to private enterprise, or some other branch of the public service. In about a week's time, I obtained my discharge, and then went home to my father's house. . . . I was very sorry to leave the ship and say goodbye to all my messmates, for we had spent many happy years together, and we were always the best of friends.*

*

In addition to his journal, clearly intended to remain a formal document of record, Gowlland kept a personal diary in which he was more forthcoming with his opinions of fellow officers, local people, and incidents that occurred during the voyage home.[1] His remarks about Philip provide an interesting and different perspective to the Hankin memoir.

A third component exists of Gowlland's written impressions of part of the voyage. He wrote a series of letters to a young woman, Genevieve Lord, whom he met and briefly courted during his stay in Sydney. In a few of these, he mentions Hankin occasionally, sometimes in less than amicable terms. An entry in Gowlland's diary just prior to their arrival at Honolulu, during discussions over dinner, noted: "Hankins carriboo played out for the present—to suit some other scheme he has got under weigh it has not come to light yet, but will no doubt shortly show itself." This shows that, even before their departure from Vancouver Island, Hankin nursed a semi-secret plan related to the Cariboo gold discoveries. His fellow officers already knew well his penchant for pranks and risky escapades. It also contrasts with Hankin's report of the discussion at Woolwich with Richards, when he declared he planned to seek employment in Victoria.

During their visit to the Sandwich Islands, and following the inspection of the site of Cook's death, Gowlland recorded in his diary:

> *[They] had been invited to dine with Their Majesties. The officers still dressed in their dirty shirts, flannel trousers and no waistcoats sitting down to table with royalty. The Queen however, insisted on us coming in just as we were. I had the honour of sitting on her left, the Captain on her right and Synge took the Vice President's chair. We had a capital dinner. His Majesty however, could not attend, having the day previously had a most severe attack of Paralysis. Champaign to the masthead. Hankin insisted on making a curry, which the Queen admired much. . . .*
>
> *After dinner we lounged into the drawing room and stretched out smoking the King's cigars & drinking his brandy and water, both of which are precious good. Fancy, a poor devil of a second master, stretched out at his ease in a King's drawing room singing songs and smoking cigars, covered in mud and in an everyday rig! The Queen is a regular brick. . . . We wound*

up the night at [Colonel and aide-de-camp to the King] David Kalakowa's house, with guitars, songs, cigars & brandy.

Colonel Kalakowa hosted another event recorded in Gowlland's diary:

A "Hoola Hoola" or native dance for us . . . at an obscure shed some distance out. [Gowlland explains the authorities had forbidden such events, but their host had influence.] Six young girls were dressed up much as our ballet dancers are at home with wreaths of flowers intertwined in their long black hair and bare feet. They stood in a row before the audience, and with their legs far apart, commenced a sort of wriggling motion all over, keeping the shoulders and head [alone] perfectly steady and singing a low moaning sort of monotonous song or chant, beating time with their hands to the tune and to the music behind played by 3 or 4 men who were thumping hollow gourds of an immense size on the ground and likewise singing. As the song proceeded, the motion of the body became more quick and violent, till they appear[ed] to get very much excited.

I cannot say it was a very decent dance as the whole of it hangs on only one subject but looking at it only in the light of a native performance it was most clever and graceful. The young ladies themselves became very affectionate towards the end of the evening so we thought it high time to make ourselves scarce. I don't know whether disgust, pity or admiration was uppermost in my mind on leaving but I think a little of each [would] perhaps be more just. I should however never care to see another.

It is little wonder that the Sandwich Islands proved a popular place to visit and winter over for the officers and crews of British vessels.

*

At Sydney, *Hecate*'s officers met Francis Hixson, recently retired from the Royal Navy and now superintendent of pilots, lighthouses, and harbours for New South Wales. An ex-hydrographic surveyor and close friend of Richards, Hixson had married Sarah, the second daughter of an influential and wealthy politician, Francis Lord. The officers received a warm welcome into Sydney's elite society, in which the Lord family moved. Even though Lord's father had arrived as a twenty-year-old convict from England, his subsequent success as a merchant erased any social disdain for his record.

Gowlland, on arriving at Sydney, learned that his mother had died. In his profound grief, he did not leave the ship for the first two weeks of *Hecate*'s visit. When, eventually, he attended church, it was with Hixson and the Lord family. After the service, Hixson invited him and master's assistant Edward Bedwell back to Masalou, the splendid Lord mansion. He introduced them to the family, including his sister-in-law Genevieve Lord, then seventeen years old and soon to "come out" into society.

For the remaining two weeks until *Hecate*'s refitting and restocking were completed, Gowlland, by then aged twenty, returned several times to Masalou to flirt with Genevieve. Two days after sailing, Gowlland wrote the first of his letters to "My dear Gennie." He mentioned in passing that the Lord girls knew Philip Hankin by the nickname "Larkins," hinting, perhaps, that he still acted the jester. Gowlland signed off this first letter, "your very sincere friend." For the rest of the voyage, he sent off increasingly ardent letters at every opportunity, to a few of which Genevieve responded.

From Batavia he wrote an impassioned declaration of his love that concluded: "Oh don't doom me to despair—forever yours, Jno TG." It was in this lovelorn condition and probably still in grief over the loss of his mother that Gowlland fell victim to the sharp-tongued Hankin's needling. Worse, it happened just as they transited the enervating doldrums of the Indian Ocean. He recorded this sad series of events in his personal diary.

The altercation that arose between Gowlland and Hankin during the long passage across the Indian Ocean provides a revealing insight into a side of Philip's character not visible in his memoir. Apparently, Hankin had been boasting of a picaresque adventure he had had with a young lady in Victoria. Gowlland, who had been close to the family of the lady in question, took umbrage. He pointed out that when the husband of the newlywed lady had learned of the incident, he took a "dangerous looking horse whip, and went all over town looking for 'my friend Sniffles.'" Gowlland noted:

> *I said I thought he had done a very wrong thing indeed in doing as he had done, knowing the easy frail nature of the species to which Mrs J came from. When he turned round on me and said,*

"What the Devil have you to do with it, you dam-d well tried to (making use of a disgusting word) her sister" . . . [I] said, "Hankin you know what you have said is not true; and even if it were anything I told you about that young lady was told under the sacred seal of confidence years ago." "Pho! Pooh!!" says he, "confidence be d-d. I don't believe in such a thing. I have not confidences with anyone." I then replied, "Hankin, I consider you a stinking blaguard."

So much for Philip's claim that "We had spent many happy years together, and we were always the best of friends."

Gowlland demanded a public apology or face the consequences, at which Hankin abjectly "came to my cabin pestering me to forgive him &c. till I told him to go to the devil or some such desperate expression." Hankin did not let the matter rest there. Ten days later, still at sea, Henry Hand, the first officer, discovered some anonymous sheets of paper secreted in his drawer during the night. They were in Hankin's handwriting and with the initials PJH at the bottom. The papers contained scurrilous notes concerning individuals, apparently Gowlland and other officers of the wardroom, but identified just with an initial.

Hand had brought the papers to Gowlland, who considered them to be

certainly most laughable and more a production of a madman than a human right-minded man; but mine was worded in terms so unmistakable and insulting that I could not, (having seen it) look over it. . . . I went to him and said, "Is this your writing and do you mean me?" He immediately snatched it out of my hand and asked how I dared read his private notes, cunning and clever to the last. Although taken somewhat aback, [I] mildly told him that if he did not explain who was meant by the initial letter G—, and substantiate the expression, I should take it to the Captain.

"Certainly you may," he said, and to the Captain we accordingly went. But of course nothing could be made out. He solemnly declared he did not put the papers on the 1st Lieut's table (which I told the Captain I did not believe), and refused to acknowledge who he meant by the initial letter. So what could be done? The Captain said he could not interfere as I

Master John "Jack" Thomas Ewing Gowlland, RN.

> *could prove nothing and it had better be settled otherwise. . . . I wished to show the Captain the kind of dangerous character he fostered as his friend and confidant. . . . Anyway, I lost nothing by the business and he was put in Coventry*[2] *by everyone in the ship. It is a great pity these disagreeable little affairs should occur just as we are going to pay off after such a long and pleasant commission but I am certain there is only one fellow in the ship who tends to promote them, and he has secretly and sneakingly been the cause of every little disagreeability that has ever happened on board of that I am almost confident."*

This most unseemly contretemps with a shipmate could well have embarrassed the mature Hankin; either he wiped most of the voyage from his memory, or he chose not to mention it in the memoir.

*

Gowlland eventually married Gennie Lord. He returned to Australia and was given charge of surveying the coast of New South Wales. In 1866, they christened their first-born son John Vancouver Richards Gowlland. Eight years later, Staff Commander Jack Gowlland was surveying the hazardous entrance to Port Jackson in a small boat. A massive wave rolled in, swamping the craft. He was drowned and received a full ceremonial naval burial.

*

At the conclusion of the commission and payoff at Woolwich on January 18, 1864, HMS *Hecate* went into the reserve. Engineers declared the vessel to be beyond economical repair. In October of that same year, the sturdy ship that had rendered such splendid service to charting the coast of British Columbia was scrapped.

CHAPTER 15
Cariboo Gold Fever

Philip Hankin arrived back in England in mid-January 1864, when he and fellow crew members of HMS *Hecate* were paid off. Despite Captain George Henry Richards's sincere efforts to persuade Hankin to change his mind, he took his discharge from the Royal Navy, having served for almost fifteen years. In a month, he would turn twenty-eight.

The reasons he gave in the memoir for wanting to leave the navy were a desire to find other work on Vancouver Island and his disagreeable experiences as a midshipman aboard HMS *Plumper* under Commander William Henry Haswell, although the latter had occurred early in his naval career. His retrospective account provides no clue that he was afflicted with gold fever. Jack Gowlland's notes suggest that Hankin's nickname "Cariboo" was given to him in his last few months in the navy, and that he had passed the contagion on to the young assistant paymaster, Barclay Corrie.

Philip's father, Daniel, had again moved.[1] Philip found him living at Stiffkey, a small farming community on the north Norfolk coast. The memoir includes no mention of which other members of the household were with their father. Nor is there any mention of Philip's younger brothers, Charles, Thomas, and Graham, who were all then in British Columbia. Once more, Philip found himself in the embarrassing position of having to request money from his father, who was predictably displeased but not ungenerous: "However, he let me have £100 [about C$20,000 in 2025] with the full understanding, I was never to expect another farthing from him—as long as I lived."

Philip had by this time been receiving a lieutenant's pay of £182 per year (about C$37,000 in 2025) for nearly six years, most of which had

The Hankin Brothers: Charles, Thomas, and Graham

The most puzzling aspect of Philip Hankin's memoir is the omission of any mention of his brothers, apart from a simple list of his siblings in the first few pages. His three younger brothers—Charles, Thomas, and Graham—also came to British Columbia and their time there coincided with Philip's on various occasions. It is clear, from other records, that there were interactions between Philip and the others, but he does not record them in his memoir, written much later.

Charles, although younger, seems from childhood to have been more assertive and better educated than Philip. This could have been behind Philip's apparent grudge, later exacerbated, perhaps, by the latter's success at Barkerville and in the malting business. Daniel Pender's letter to Captain Richards in late March 1864 confirms that Philip and Charles were apparently close when they visited him together. Philip's lack of reference to Charles's presence at the meeting highlights a deliberate decision to cut mention of his brother from all but the earliest section of his memoir. This antipathy could have had its origin in an unmentioned falling-out at Barkerville during the few weeks following their meeting with Pender.

There is no apparent reason, however, for animosity by the elderly Philip toward either Thomas or Graham. They were both much younger than himself, and less successful. Graham's life was short, tragic, and without accomplishment. Of his three brothers, Philip seems to have been in the closest contact with Graham. He socialized with the Nagle family, whose circle provided Philip with much of his social life in Victoria, and was cared for when sick by Mama Nagle. He also celebrated Philip's marriage to Isabel and shared a close bond with Jessie, Isabel's younger sister.

The Nagle family also knew both Charles and Thomas. So did Captain Richards and Philip's close friend and shipmate, Daniel Pender.

been served at sea. His necessary expenses would not have been heavy, and, from the memoir and journals of fellow officers, he does not appear to have lived extravagantly. For reasons unknown, Philip appears to have been unable to save any of his pay.

*

The memoir continues:

> *I was very grateful for the money, and left for London, where I stayed in lodgings for a week, bought a few clothes, and took a 3rd class passage to Colon, [on the Caribbean coast of Panama] by one of the West India packets, a paddle-steamer. It was certainly rather rough, but I was fortunate enough to make friends after a few days with the officers, who, when I told them I had just left the Royal Navy, were kind enough to invite me to mess with them, which was much better than messing with the steerage passengers who were a very rough crowd. The passage to Colon took about 21 days. I crossed over the isthmus by train to Panama [City]. I remember it took 4 hours in a very slow and crowded train, and what with the heat and hundreds of mosquitoes, and millions of flies of every sort and kind I can't say it was enjoyable.*

He found that the bimonthly steamer to San Francisco had just left, obliging him to spend the next two weeks in the only hotel, "a very dirty place and full of mosquitoes." Six years earlier, as he returned

Illustration from Panama in 1855 *by Robert Tomes. The railroad, opened in 1855, preceded the canal by fifty years.*

Main street in Barkerville.

Miners standing at a typical mining windlass. The small man, second from left, is Billy Barker.

home upon promotion to lieutenant, he had followed this same route in reverse, but he made no comment in his memoir on the conditions then. Apart from the discomfort, he was in danger from insect-borne, tropical diseases—two decades later, over twenty-two thousand workers constructing the Panama Canal succumbed to yellow fever and malaria.

From Panama, while awaiting the next ship, he wrote a letter to Gowlland, who commented in his journal:

> *Corrie sold [Hankin] a pretty dog—after promising to go then backing out at the last moment. Bad as Hankin has proved himself, I never thought so badly of him as to think he would sell his friend; and Corrie professed to be so for him; so that poor Philip who relied so on Corrie will be dreadfully cut up.*

Gowlland's slang now renders his comment ambiguous, but it hints that Philip had fully expected Barclay Corrie to resign and accompany him "back to the Colony." It is another example of Philip's omitting from his memoir a painful breakdown in a personal relationship. Odd, too, that Philip should confide such a private matter to a man from whom he had recently parted with such bitter words.

His funds, including the £100 from his father, were "fast melting away," so he again took a third-class passage aboard an American ship. This too, proved uncomfortable. His fellow passengers in steerage were "very rough miners and all kinds of Loafers [who] were making their way to the gold fields of California." Understandably, he preferred to sleep on deck rather than in the fetid air below. The food was awful and the service worse. "We dined at noon, all standing up at a swinging table, and the knives and forks were chained for fear they should be stolen." But, as he recalled in his memoir, "I was young, in excellent health, and quite prepared to rough it." The discomfort lasted a further two weeks, and at San Francisco he had better luck with his timing. He could take immediate passage on a packet, a small, speedy vessel bound for Esquimalt.

*

Hankin's account of his life during the spring of 1864 is the most enigmatic section of the memoir. It is also quite long. He devotes forty-one pages to this period, compared with only eleven to cover *Hecate*'s year-long voyage returning from Victoria to Woolwich. He gives only vague dates for the various events in this period, but other sources provide a reliable timeline. To understand the extent and degree of the differences between his version and the other sources, it is as well to first summarize the memoir, beginning with his arrival, now as a civilian, at Esquimalt.

On his arrival, Hankin visited HMS *Beaver*, anchored in Esquimalt Harbour, and met with Daniel Pender. He also met old friends in Esquimalt and Victoria. He discovered that, while still amiable, they no longer afforded him the respect he had enjoyed as a naval officer. Failing to find employment, and despite a severe shortage of money—less than $25—he "made up [his] mind to go to the Cariboo . . . a very small town of Barkerville." On his arrival at Fort Yale by steamers, unable to afford the $50 for a seat on a rough wagon, he set out to "hike the 600 miles." In fact, it would have been much less than that to the goldfields.

Backpacking with just two blankets and a few provisions, and drinking from the river, he walked between "dollar houses." These so-called hotels would offer a meal of "beans and fat bacon, with bread or a biscuit, and very thick coffee . . . good or bad it was always a dollar." Other nights he slept rough, making it to Barkerville in just twenty days. He recalled it was May, the "weather fine and not very cold," and he occasionally fell in with a companion headed on a similar quest.

He found Barkerville "quite a little settlement" with several small hotels and saloons. There were log cabins with miners, some of whom had good claims and were "taking out a considerable quantity of gold." Several feet of snow covered the ground. Not having eaten for twelve hours and down to his last half dollar, he entered a small establishment and warmed himself by the stove, ordering "some bread and butter and hot coffee." At dusk, he left and walked out of town to find "an old empty shed" in which he slept soundly, wrapped in his blankets.

Next morning, hungry and penniless, he remembered ruefully how his messmates, when they learned of his intention to resign his commission, had warned him, "There is no pipe to dinner on shore!" As he recalled his time aboard *Hecate*, he noted a tear on his cheek but brushed it away, repeating the words of the old gunner aboard *Seringapatam*: "Never say die, lad, s'long as there's a shot in the locker!"

Farther down the creek, he found a man at the head of a mine shaft working a windlass to raise a bucket filled with slurry, which he washed in a rocker to separate any gold dust. The man looked unwell, so Hankin offered to take over, to which the man reluctantly agreed. After a few hours of hard work, the man's replacement arrived, so he invited Philip to come and share their supper and offered the floor beneath his bunk as a place to sleep, which Philip accepted. He found the log cabin warm and the other four members of the outfit welcoming. Philip had tasted no food for the previous twenty hours, so he relished the Irish stew and mugs of tea. To repay his hosts, Philip arose at three the next morning, relit the fire, and had breakfast ready for them to begin the day's labour. The men were appreciative, and called him "a bully boy, with a glass-eye," which Philip realized was a compliment.

After "a month or six weeks" of housekeeping and cooking—without pay, since the mine was not very productive, though he was fed and sheltered—Philip realized that he needed to earn some money. Fortunately, another mine nearby struck a lead that paid three hundred ounces per day, and the owners needed someone to manage their books. They hired him at $15 per week to weigh each day's output of dust and deposit into the bank. He parted on good terms with the original group and the comfort of their cabin floor, to take a tiny room in a nearby "hotel" with a small bed, a chair, and a washstand. It cost a dollar per night plus another dollar for two meals. This left him with a dollar each week, with which he treated himself to "one very bad cigar and one glass of rum and water." After another "month or six weeks" the lead dried up, as did the need for his services.

Still devoid of savings, Hankin decided the Cariboo was not for him. Better to return to Victoria and seek a job with the government. Fortunately, in Barkerville he had met a government officer, "a Mr. Matthews," whom he had known in earlier days, who generously lent him $60 for the fare. He had to hike the thirty-five miles (fifty-six kilometres) from Barkerville to Quesnel, along a trail through the forest, where he "did not see a human being or an animal and very few birds." The trek took him twelve hours. For $40, he booked an outside seat on a Royal Mail wagon leaving for Yale the following morning. The seats were three abreast on rough planks, exposed to the weather, aboard "a very rough, shaky conveyance, drawn by 4 unbroken horses." The journey took three days and nights, with occasional brief stops to change horses. He wrote, "I never in my life remember feeling so tired, or such an intense longing for sleep."

At Yale, he took a room in a small hotel, "fell asleep, and never moved for 27 hours." The following morning, he boarded a little sternwheeler for New Westminster. His only clothing was "a rough old flannel shirt and a pair of long Wellington boots with the legs of my trowsers tucked inside as miners wore them." Also aboard was Archdeacon Henry Press Wright, whom he had met during his days in the navy. Wright, who was travelling with his wife and pretty daughter, recognized him and, as they shook hands, noted, "I'm afraid you are not one of the lucky ones." Philip had to agree. The kindly cleric counselled, "*Nil desperandum*, something will turn up," and invited him to stay with them for a few days at their home in New Westminster. Philip demurred on the grounds he was in no fit state "to sit at table with ladies." "Stuff and nonsense," came the reply, and the offer was repeated.

Philip gratefully enjoyed the Wrights' hospitality for two days and noted, "I shall never forget their kindness as long as I live." After this brief respite, he crossed over to Victoria, arriving "with about seven dollars in my pocket, which was every farthing I had in the world." Wondering how he would survive, he took the cheapest room he could find and set about calling in search of work of any description, claiming, "I would do it better and for half the money anyone else asked." At last, he secured a temporary position as a replacement clerk with the prominent firm of lawyers Drake and Jackson at $20 per week. Delighted at this change in his fortune, he wrote, "How earnestly I hoped the clerk would never recover from his illness . . . perhaps not very Christianlike, but it was natural." He worked diligently, even during the customary long lunch hour enjoyed by the other clerks.

All too soon, Philip's hopes were dashed. The clerk he was replacing recovered his health and returned to his duties. Mr. Montague William Tyrwhitt-Drake said he had been well pleased with Hankin's work and gave him "a written testimonial to that effect." Philip resumed his search for employment. He had saved some of his wages and rented a tiny furnished cottage at $15 per month. He lived frugally, shopping, cooking, and cleaning for himself. He noted complacently that, in contrast to many others in similar circumstances, he took "very good care never to be seen in the gambling and drinking establishments of Victoria by day or night." He acknowledged that his lack of special qualifications hindered his search.

Despite Philip's misgivings over his lack of qualifications, he was not unemployable. The letter of recommendation from one of the leading lawyers in town would have been of considerable benefit. Also, unknown to him, he had another powerful ally, Captain George Henry Richards, RN. Although the *Hecate* had left these waters over eighteen months earlier, the high regard for Richards and his work persisted in town. Apparently, Richards, on hearing from Pender about Hankin's sorry situation, had written to the new governor, Arthur Edward Kennedy, endorsing the good qualities of his former officer. Among these, he would have mentioned that Philip had a working command of Chinuk Wawa, or Jargon, spoken by most of the local people, plus several dialects of the Wakashan language of the island's west coast. This latter knowledge was exceptional among the colonist community, as Kennedy would have realized.

Eventually, Hankin called on the interim colonial secretary for Vancouver Island. The former secretary William Young, who had left with his family for a year's leave in England on May 16, had been replaced by Henry Wakeford. Hankin requested that his name be registered as an applicant for employment in the government service. Kennedy would have seen his application. Two weeks later, Hankin received a letter offering "a junior clerkship in [the colonial secretary's] office, at a salary of eighty dollars per month." He rejoiced: "how happy I felt and how rich!" He calculated that the salary was equivalent to £190 per year, more than he had earned as a lieutenant in the navy. "I commenced my duties the following day."

*

Notwithstanding the vagueness of this period in Hankin's memoir, it is possible to put accurate dates to both ends of it. Daniel Pender maintained regular correspondence with Richards during the work aboard HMS *Beaver*. This took two forms: formal reports on the progress of the survey work and administrative matters such as negotiations with the local government, and a series of informal, private letters as between close colleagues.[2]

Pender reported to Richards, in an informal letter dated March 31, that, during a discussion aboard the flagship HMS *Cameleon*:

A messenger came to say that an intimate friend of mine had come by the packet—not having heard from Hankin since Hecate arrived in England, I had hoped he would have changed his intention of leaving the Service & had persuaded myself that he would have remained. However, on landing at Esquimalt I had immediate reason to prove myself mistaken, for there as large as life stood Philip Hankin and his brother Charles, looking as natural as though he had just come onshore from Hecate & was merely going to Victoria for a stroll.

Not only does this note provide the date of Philip's arrival back in Esquimalt, it also proves clearly that Pender and Richards both knew that Charles, and probably Thomas, Hankin were present in the colony. By this time, Charles would have been well known throughout Victoria society as a successful miner in the Cariboo. Pender's note continues:

Poor fellow [Hankin] has a long stroll before him & so he will find—I took him off to lunch & tonight he sleeps onboard & will do so until he goes off to British Columbia which will be about a week. A more insane act I cannot conceive a man in his position guilty of, viz giving up the Navy. But, as he told me today he does not repent, & on the contrary looks forward to making a fortune. I have nothing more to reproach him with—I think it heinous that had he rec^d^. a letter which I wrote to him in Novr. last telling him how his brothers had been going on &^tc^.—he would not have come as he is.

This part of the letter seems to refute Philip's intentions, as given in the memoir. He wrote that his plan was to seek work in Victoria, but according to Pender, Philip told him that it was to get to the Cariboo.

It also hints that his friend knew Philip's finances were low. On April 14, Pender again wrote informally to Richards, updating him about Hankin. A letter from Hankin from New Westminster had reported he was in good spirits and that on the 9th he had been headed upcountry:

I was very glad to get him away from here for on seeing some old faces & familiar things, I fancied for the step he has taken. If, however, his health holds good, he may get on.

Another naval officer noted Philip Hankin's return to Victoria. Lieutenant Edmund Hope Verney, commanding the gunboat *Grappler*, had arrived in Esquimalt in May 1862, and knew the officers of *Hecate* well, including Hankin (just two years his senior). He wrote a series of letters to his father relating the events, places, and people he experienced. His entry for March 26, 1864, included:

I am sorry that Hankin has left the Service: he has arrived today: I always strongly disapproved of it when he spoke to me on the subject, and had hoped that his better sense would have guided him when he returned to England: however, we shall see how he prospers.

That was Verney's last (and only) mention of Hankin in his letters through to his departure in June 1865. By that time, Hankin would have re-established his reputation in both naval and civilian government circles.

A notice on page 2 of the *Daily British Colonist*, August 30, 1864, provides a date for the conclusion of Philip's Cariboo venture:

Appointment.—Mr. Philip Hankin, late a Lieutenant in the Royal Navy and acting under Capt. Richards in his surveying expeditions to this coast, has received an appointment in the Government offices.

Thus, the duration of Philip's journey to and from the Cariboo must have been a little over three months, from April 8 through to mid-July. Clues in the memoir, however, place his arrival at Barkerville at about May 20, his job with the second group of miners lasting from the end of June through to mid-August, his return to Yale, rest, and river trip to New Westminster at about the end of that month, and his return to Victoria by the first week in September.

Other aspects of his account merit question. The first is his route to the goldfields. He started his hike from Yale. This was not the usual route taken by Cariboo-bound prospectors. Most of them took the route via Harrison River and Lake to Port Douglas. During his earlier trip with Lady Franklin, he had watched the miners aboard leave the paddlewheeler to set out on this route.[3] From Port Douglas, the route led by Seton Lake to Lillooet, where it would join the Royal Engineers'

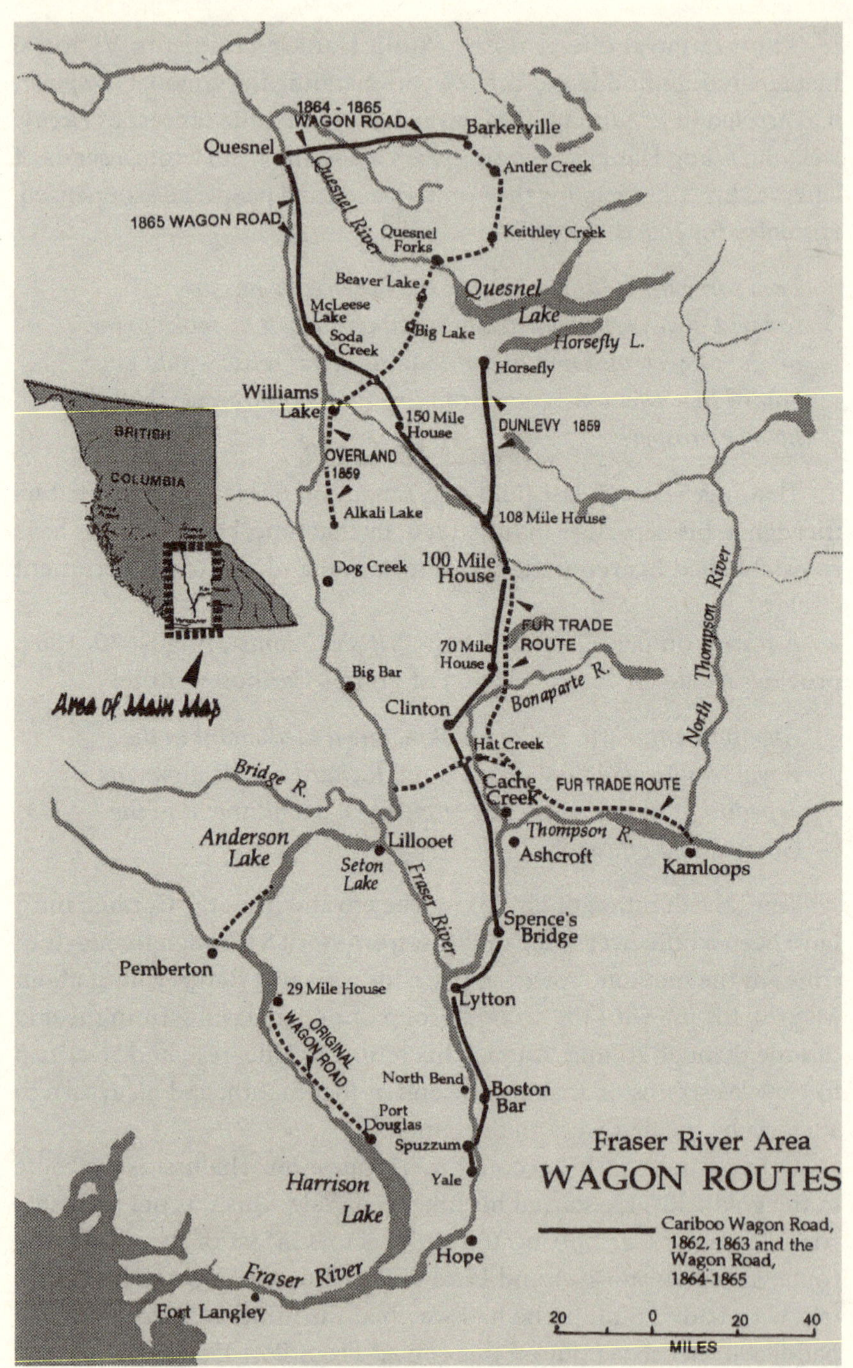

Map of the various routes to the Cariboo by Lillian Wonders.

Cariboo Wagon Road, then under construction. Thence it led to Williams Lake, Quesnel, and the mining towns along Williams Creek.

The route from Yale to Lillooet would have been through the Fraser Canyon and far more difficult. The memoir provides no clue of the locations en route. He makes no mention of snowshoes, which would have been essential for the thick drifts he would have encountered, especially at the higher altitudes. It is doubtful that he had had prior experience of their use. The weather for that year was relatively mild, but even so, the thaw would not arrive for at least two months. The return route was more straightforward. The new road would have ideally suited the postal cart.

Either of these routes to Williams Creek would, at that season, have been crowded with many hundreds of returning miners and hopeful greenhorns such as himself. There was also a vigorous freight business, usually by pack train of mules or by wagon, bringing provisions and equipment for the thriving stores servicing the mining operations. His description of this traffic—"Sometimes I would overtake some man . . . and be a little company for each other"—is unconvincing.

So too are his descriptions of the two small mining groups who took him in. There was ample work available for casual labourers all along the creek at, according to several contemporary accounts, $10 per day. There was absolutely no need for him to have spent "a month or six weeks" as a housekeeper and cook for space on the floor of a warm hut. Similarly, a mere $15 per week for his services as bookkeeper and treasurer to a temporarily profitable mine seems questionable. Even his description of finding a derelict shed buried under five feet of snow to provide rudimentary shelter on his first night at Barkerville just does not ring true. Adding to this implausibility, Hankin's recounting of the discussion between him and the first group of miners reads more like a boy's adventure yarn than the tale of a man who, for the previous fifteen years, had been an officer in the Royal Navy.

After that brief meeting with Philip and Pender, Charles returned to Barkerville. The timing and his route are not known, but in mid-June the *Mining Register* listed the transfer of one full undivided interest in the Barker claim from Charles to H.P. Walker (for, presumably, his client, Judge Matthew Baillie Begbie, a surreptitious investor in the syndicate). Charles also asked the gold commissioner for one month's leave of absence for seven of their thirteen men "due to water"—presumably, flooding in the shaft. On June 20, the *British Colonist* carried a letter, dated June 1, reporting that "the mining prospects of [Williams] creek were never more flattering . . . great results may be safely predicted. . . . The claims are nearly all at work . . . and, The Barker Co. are sinking a new shaft."

The trusting acquaintance from his earlier days, "Mr. Matthews," who lent Philip $60 for the fare back to Victoria, is identifiable as G.C.B. Matthew.[4] At the time, he was a district magistrate, and later he became registrar to the Supreme Court. Matthew would have known the Hankin brothers and judged that his loan to one of them was secure. His trust was justified by repayment as soon as Philip was financially able.

*

The most blatant and perplexing omission from Philip's memoir is the complete absence of any mention of Charles or either of his other brothers being in Victoria or Barkerville during that time. He deliberately or subconsciously expunged all three from his memory. This strongly suggests that, for reasons unknown, his relationship with Charles had become embittered. Otherwise Charles would surely have either welcomed and supported Philip's participation in the Barker syndicate, including acquiring a suitable outfit and arranging that they travel together for the start of the 1864 summer season, or firmly discouraged his going there at all. If the latter, would he not have provided subsistence for Philip while he sought more suitable employment in Victoria?

Charles meeting Philip on his arrival at Esquimalt and accompanying him to meet Pender shows that, initially at least, there was some communication between the two brothers. Nowhere does the memoir offer any clue as to the reason behind the apparent lifelong breakdown in the relationship. And what of Thomas and young Graham? It is all most peculiar.

Governor Arthur Edward Kennedy. In office between March 1864 and October 1866.

CHAPTER 16

Liaison Officer to a Massacre

Less than a week before Philip Hankin returned from England and met with Daniel Pender in late March 1864, another figure landed at Victoria who was to have a major influence on the course of Philip's life. This was Arthur Edward Kennedy, appointed governor of the Colony of Vancouver Island, replacing Sir James Douglas, who had served for six years. Kennedy, born into the Irish gentry and educated at Trinity College, Dublin, had spent twenty years as an infantry officer in the British Army and eight in the Colonial Service. He had already been governor of the Gambia and Western Australia, distinguishing himself as a vigorous administrator with a low tolerance for corruption and inefficiency. He was highly regarded in the service, and the Victoria press greeted his appointment as a welcome change from the HBC's still-powerful influence.

During his two previous postings, Kennedy had witnessed the distress caused to Indigenous communities by the consequences of incoming colonists. His concerns were chiefly about imported diseases and alcohol. He had instigated measures to mitigate such misfortunes and brought his concerns to the new assignment. He learned that repeated waves of smallpox and measles had devastated the defenceless communities on the island, and that the selling of bootleg liquor to the local people was rife.

Kennedy quickly came to realize that there was a fundamental problem for the colony: insufficient income to fund an effective government. Douglas and his colonial secretary, the former naval officer William Young, had diverted revenues from the mainland goldfields to cover both sets of civil servants. Now the two colonies had separate governors and budgets. Vancouver Island was on its own, needing urgently to access local sources of funding. Kennedy had faced this problem before. He put out a challenge to the island's business community: if they would recruit a team to explore the island's natural resources—searching particularly for minerals ready for exploitation—and raise private funding toward such a survey, he would cover their investment from his treasury, two for every dollar they secured.

The town took up his challenge. In June 1864, the nine-man Vancouver Island Exploring Expedition, under the command of a Scottish botanical collector, the self-styled "Dr." Robert Brown, set out on their quest.[1] They discovered a small goldfield on the Leech River, triggering a rush of prospectors. They also found several viable deposits of coal, but these were nowhere near profitable enough to stave off the next few years of dire economic hardship for the island.

*

Philip Hankin's priority on returning from Barkerville to Victoria sometime in July 1864 was finding a job. The first one he secured was only temporary, filling in for a clerk with lawyers Drake and Jackson. While it lasted only a month, they provided him with a glowing reference that helped when he applied to the government service.

To apply for, and then show up for, both positions, Hankin must have had to dress presentably. It would have been unacceptable for him to arrive dressed as he had been when he came down from the goldfields and met Archdeacon Henry Press Wright, but he could not afford any new clothes. He must have relied on those he had left in storage, including the suit, shirts, and shoes he had bought in London. He would also have shed the full set of whiskers and shaggy locks customary at the diggings.

The timing of Philip Hankin's application for a position with the government of the colony was fortuitous. Young, an upright and most serious officer, knew Hankin, but more than likely would have considered him immature and lacking *gravitas*—a bit of a jester. Philip's foolhardy decisions to resign his commission and then to risk and lose everything in his foray for Cariboo gold would have only reinforced this view.

Young's temporary replacement, Henry Wakeford, would not have known the applicant personally. His only information about Hankin's character or abilities came from Captain George Henry Richards's letter of recommendation. He would have passed the application to Governor Kennedy, together with Richards's and Tyrwhitt-Drake's endorsements.[2]

In government service, as at the lawyers' office, Philip was punctilious in his duties. He was the first to arrive and the last to leave; he brought his own lunch and kept his midday break to under an hour. He proved quick and reliable in managing the files and was respectful and courteous to his colleagues. But here, the memoir loses the chronology of what occurred next.

*

Hankin had served a little over a week in his new position when a serious incident on the island's west coast radically changed the trajectory of his career. Altercations between Indigenous people and isolated British traders and settlers were of growing concern in Victoria. One such incident involved William "Eddy" Banfield, a trader who lived at the southern entrance to Barkley Sound. Banfield had been a valuable source of information about the west coast Indigenous communities when Douglas had been in office. In October 1862, the trader had been the victim of an honour killing by Klatsmick, a Huu-ay-aht man.[3]

An announcement in the *British Colonist* of September 10, 1864, drew attention to another tragedy. Some locals arriving in a canoe reported a civilian trading sloop, *Kingfisher*, had been attacked, plundered, burned, and sunk near the large Ahousaht village of Marktosis in Clayoquot Sound. The skipper Stevenson, the mate Wilson, and a local interpreter had been murdered. A few days later, another trading vessel arrived from Alberni with further news. The crew had learned "through native sources" of the incident, which confirmed, in gory detail, a violent attack by the Ahousahts, led by their chief, Cap-Chah.[4]

*

Up to this point, the Ahousaht people did not have a reputation for such atrocities. In 1855, Eddy Banfield had reported to then-Governor James Douglas:

> *I have had frequent opportunity of observing their manners, to strangers they are morose, to a resident white man, they are*

as kind as could be expected. A firm moral influence has more power on them than Colt's Revolvers, or Bowie Knives.

Richards noted in 1861, when he was charting Clayoquot Sound:

There appear to be a considerable number of Natives at this place, and quiet, well conducted people.

Jack Gowlland, who had led HMS *Hecate*'s advance party into the sound, noted, significantly:

They are named the 'Ahousahts'; the Chief's name is Wack-la—a fine athletic strapping fellow about 6 feet high; they are very civil and bring us great quantities of Salmon to trade.

The attack on *Kingfisher*, however, was a last straw for the government. The new governor, Arthur Edward Kennedy, decided it was time to assert their authority and displeasure at piracy or other attacks on white men. Kennedy called a conference with Rear Admiral Joseph Denman—commander-in-chief, Pacific Station, whose flagship HMS *Sutlej* was anchored in Esquimalt—about the situation and measures to be taken.

Denman agreed to send his support ship, HMS *Devastation*—a six-gun paddlewheel frigate, similar in size to *Hecate,* under the experienced commander John W. Pike—to investigate and report back. He was to use caution and only open fire on the locals if fired upon. Accompanying the mission were Horace Smith, superintendent of police in Victoria, and, as interpreter, none other than Thomas Roberts, or Friday, who had been aboard *Hecate.*[5] Before approaching Marktosis, the Ahousaht village deep within Matilda Inlet in Clayoquot Sound, to look into the *Kingfisher* incident, Pike was to investigate the murder of Banfield in the Huu-ay-aht village on Barkley Sound.

On September 28, Friday piloted *Devastation* to the Huu-ay-aht village. Pike brought him and a lightly armed escort in two boats ashore to palaver.[6] The party landed to confront a horde of armed warriors, ready for battle. Following a brief scuffle, they took a chief's daughter as a hostage. They exchanged her for three suspects connected to the Banfield case, including Klatsmick. Seizing some canoes, the shore party returned to their ship with no shots fired from either side. Pike then crossed the sound to a village that had been the scene of yet another incident and recovered a stolen pistol.

At both Barkley Sound villages, Pike and Friday calmed the locals, whom, earlier, a malicious trader had agitated. The trader had warned them that the navy would immediately attack their villages with cannon. Pike listened to the locals' complaints about mistreatment by traders and assured them that the government only wished to maintain law and order, peaceably if possible.

Devastation then proceeded to Clayoquot Sound and approached Matilda Inlet on Flores Island, where the *Kingfisher* had been attacked. There, Pike found a new situation. About two hundred warriors, distributed strategically at places around the inlet, laid an ambush for any landing party. Pike assessed the situation. He reasoned that although he had the firepower to get ashore and capture the miscreants, he could not do so without loss of lives. As ordered, he withdrew to await the admiral's response to his report, which he promptly sent back to Esquimalt.

The admiral was astonished and affronted by such an impertinent challenge to the Royal Navy. He had, however, other pressing matters on his mind and his resources were meagre. As commander-in-chief of a fourteen-vessel squadron, he had responsibility over a vast area of ocean. A civil war raged to his immediate south, posing potential threats to Esquimalt and his squadron.

Denman had earlier suggested that the colonial authority permanently deploy a quantity of armed gunboats. He commanded two small

Gunboat HMS Forward.

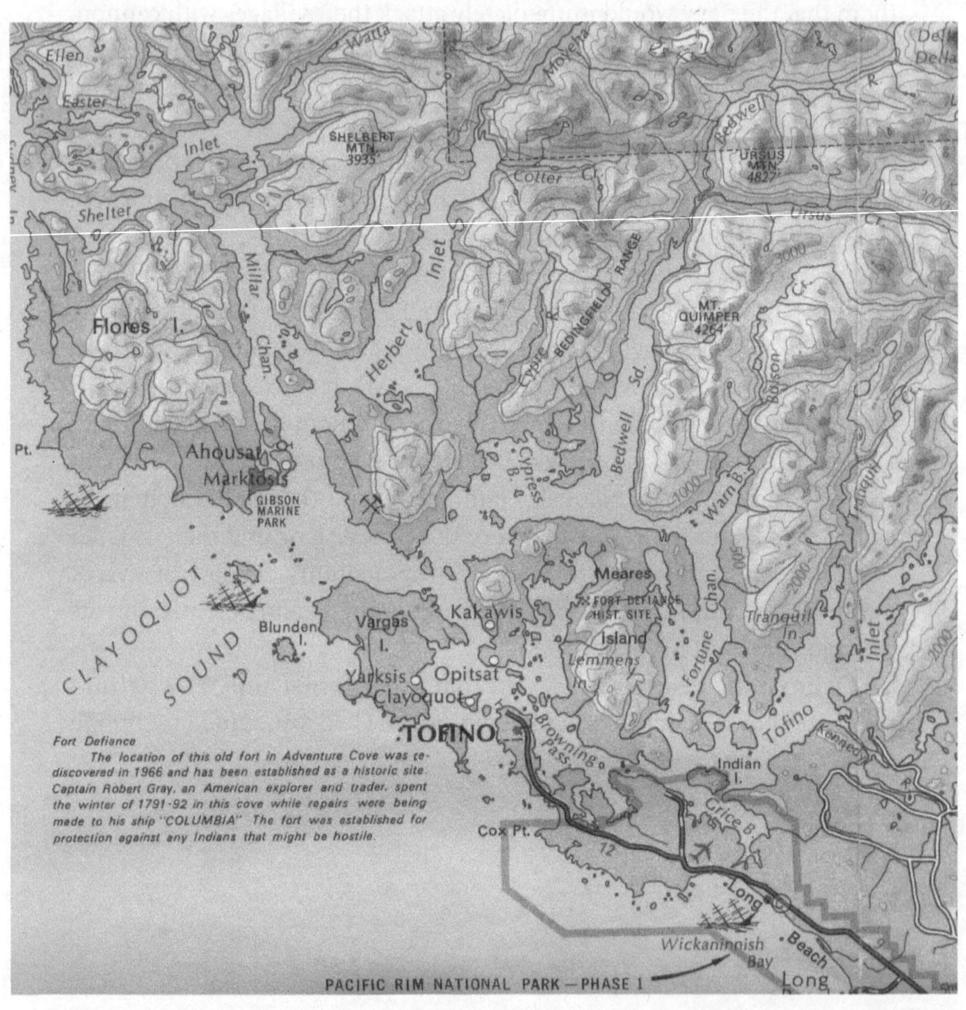

Topography of Clayoquot Sound and vicinity. Section from Vancouver Island (South) in Backroad Mapbook series.

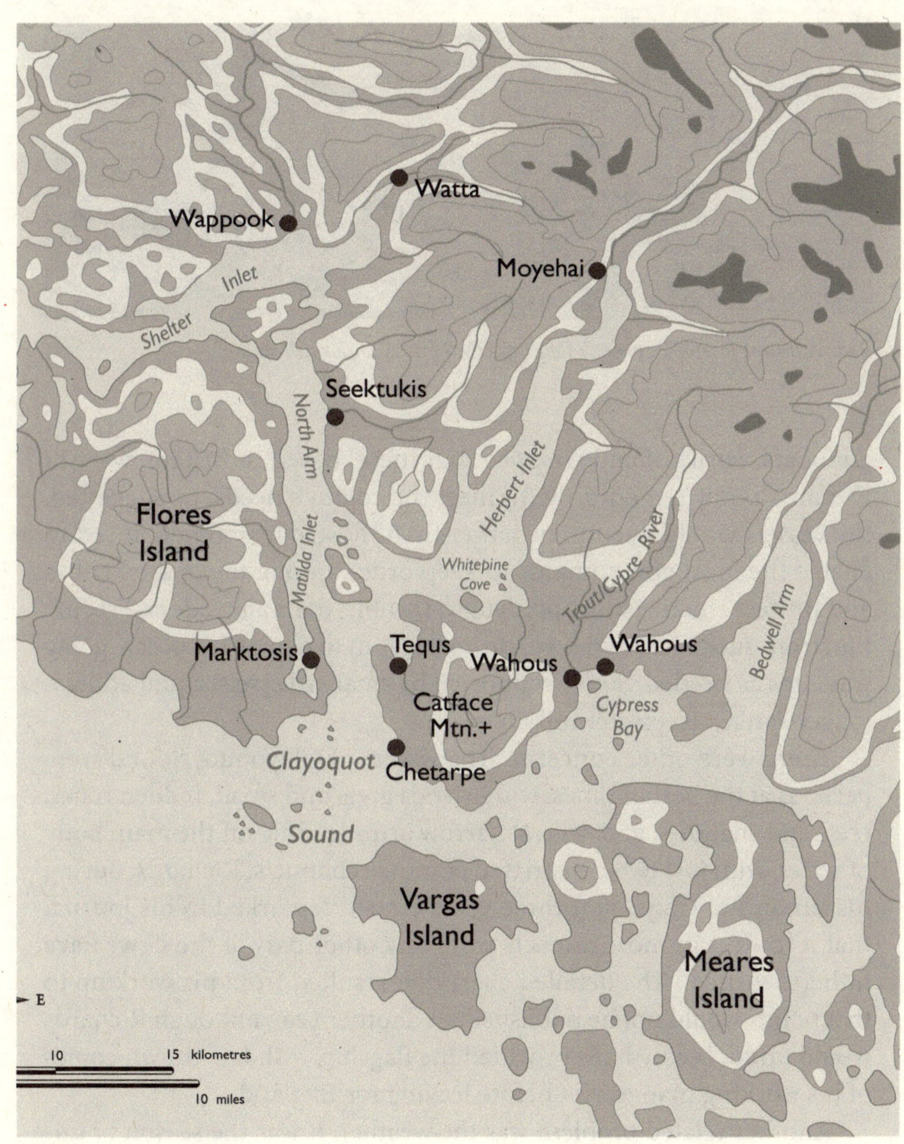

Villages of the Ahousaht Nation in Clayoquot Sound.

Rear Admiral Joseph Denman's flagship HMS Sutlej *under full sail.*

gunboats, *Forward* and *Grappler*, but these, based in Britain, were in Esquimalt only temporarily. To meet the colony's needs, he suggested, the vessels would need to be larger than those currently deployed to enable the local governments to keep order among the coastal tribes and protect them against predatory, trouble-making traders. Freeing him from such local duties would enable him to deploy his ocean-going warships as needed. *Sutlej*, supported by smaller vessels, could address longer-range, deepwater missions.

There were other concerns. The waters of Clayoquot Sound were perilous at the best of times, with islands great and small, hidden rocks, reefs and shallows, and several narrow arms leading off the main body of water, with just two constricted entrance channels. Richards, during his surveys of Clayoquot three years earlier, remarked in his journal that it "differs in most respects from any other part of the I$^{d.}$ we have hitherto visited." The detailed chart that resulted from his work up to that point[7] would not be published for another year, although Richards would undoubtedly have provided the flagship with fair-drawn copies of his working manuscript before leaving for England.

Another related problem was the weather. It was the season of unpredictable equinoctial gales and fogs. Navigating the waters of the west coast of the island, never straightforward, would be especially fraught. *Sutlej*—a fifty-gun, fourth-rate, screw-assisted frigate, 180 feet long and drawing over 16 feet—would be the largest vessel ever to have entered Clayoquot Sound. For the admiral to justify taking his flagship into

Artist's impression of the Huu-ay-aht man Thomas "Friday" Roberts dressed as an emissary with a ceremonial paddle.

such a hazardous situation, he would need a compelling reason. But Denman, famously a man of decisive action, felt fully supported by the ex-soldier Kennedy, who had even offered to come with them. In the end, Kennedy did not take part.

Despite his misgivings, Denman took *Sutlej* to investigate. He first secured an official request from Governor Kennedy for Action in Aid of the Civil Power. Kennedy again provided Police Superintendent Smith, Friday, and now his new clerk Hankin to act as interpreters and mediators with the Ahousaht people. It must have come as a welcome surprise for Denman to learn that he now had one of Richards's survey officers available to assist his navigators.[8] *Sutlej* headed directly for Matilda Inlet, accompanied by the gunboat *Forward*, to join *Devastation.*

They arrived to discover that the Ahousaht people had deserted the village of Marktosis inside the inlet and dispersed to several other villages throughout the sound. At Seektukis, a village midway up North Arm (later named Millar Channel), Hankin and Friday went ashore. Despite the admiral's urging them to carry at least a pistol, they were unarmed. After keeping a single man talking, Hankin called up two of the boat's crew to come and take the man prisoner. Back on board, Denman and Pike, with Hankin and Friday, interrogated him. The man acknowledged that he had witnessed the attack on *Kingfisher* and provided valuable intelligence. This included confirmation that Cap-Chah had led the ten-man gang of attackers. He named several villages that could be hiding members of the group, one farther up North Arm as well as Wappook and Watta on Shelter Inlet, accessible only with difficulty from the head of North Arm. Another village, Moyehai, lay at the head of Herbert Inlet. Denman sent Pike to Moyehai to check and report back.

On Pike's arrival at Moyehai, volleys of musket fire greeted *Devastation*'s boats. As ordered, Pike retreated and informed Denman of the opposition he had met. The admiral ordered Pike to take *Devastation* and destroy the villages of Seektukis, Wappook, and Watta, but not to fire on the inhabitants unless fired upon. Denman moved *Sutlej* to Moyehai, where he positioned the massive ship with half of its fifty gun ports open, menacing the village. He sent Friday ashore dressed as an emissary and carrying a large and decorated ceremonial paddle. Friday delivered Denman's simple message: Give up the miscreants and the ship would withhold its fire. Refuse and he would obliterate the village and seize their canoes. After a palaver on the beach, Friday returned to report that the villagers remained defiant and scornful. Denman recorded:

> *I then ordered a heavy fire to be opened on the village and on the surrounding bush to clear it and then sent in the gigs to complete the destruction of the village under cover of the ship's guns and those of the heavy boats.*

Denman's tactics were to first bombard the area with *Sutlej*'s heavy guns, then send in boats armed with incendiary rockets to burn the houses and their contents. A shore party, under covering fire, would land to destroy or tow away any canoes they found still intact. The rockets were weapons of devastating efficacy when directed upon close-packed dwellings, made largely of cedar planks, and on stores of food essential for survival through the upcoming winter.

Bombardment by cannon, followed by incendiary rockets, was an unwarranted overreaction to men simply defending their homes and families. This was not a salutary lesson but blatant brutality. It condemned generations of an entire Nation of several hundred people to famine and hardship, although few officials at that time in Victoria would have viewed it as unjust. The wholesale loss of their canoes was a severe

The bombardment of an Ahousaht village by incendiary rockets fired from ships' boats. Watercolour taken from a sketch in Illustrated London News.

punishment on the Ahousaht. For these coastal people, dependent on sustenance from the sea, and distributed over many locations accessible only by water, canoes were essential both to their livelihood and to the social intercourse between their extended families.

Five hours later, with Moyehai levelled, *Sutlej* steamed back to Matilda Creek, bringing twelve captured canoes, to rejoin *Devastation*. Pike had found artifacts from *Kingfisher* in all the places he had similarly destroyed but apprehended none of the wanted gang. The man previously interrogated had told them that Cap-Chah himself lived at Wahous village on Cypress Bay on a low-lying isthmus between Herbert and Bedwell arms, or nearby, on the Bedwell itself. Denman ordered Pike to destroy those two villages and seize any canoes. During the attack, they saw Cap-Chah, wearing a blue jacket—part of *Kingfisher*'s trade goods—and leading some villagers away from the action. Meanwhile, Denman ordered the deserted villages of Marktosis and Tequa to be burned.

Denman mounted a surreptitious attack specifically targeting Cap-Chah. Placing a guard in Cypress Bay, he sent Lieutenant Hugh Stewart, RN, with a strong party of armed sailors and marines from *Sutlej* to White Pine Cove aboard *Forward*. This lay on the far side of Catface Mountain, forming the southern tip of the peninsula between Herbert and Bedwell arms. According to a report in the *British Colonist*, Philip Hankin accompanied the raiding party. Just before dawn—guided by some Clayoquot, local enemies of the Ahousaht—the party crossed the marshy isthmus by a three-mile trail to what remained of the twin Wahous settlements on Cypress Bay, by then a collection of crude, temporary shelters hidden in the bush.

Leaving a party deployed to catch any fleeing villagers, Stewart led his primary force stealthily toward the shelters. Just as they were about to attack, the dogs of the village barked the alarm, arousing the residents, who fled into the surrounding bush. They fired at their attackers, but the marines were better armed and disciplined. After a brief exchange of fire, the villagers vanished deeper into the dense salal understorey, leaving ten dead. The marines suffered no loss. They captured one of the wanted gang members and wounded Cap-Chah twice, but again he escaped.

Forward then went to the head of North Arm, with Hankin and Friday still aboard. Lieutenant the Honourable Horace Lascelles, RN, carefully navigated his gunboat though the narrow and justifiably named Rocky Pass into Shelter Inlet. This was where their first captive had told them some members of the gang had fled. At one village, probably Watta, the locals surrendered a second gang member. They also informed the officers that a falling rock, dislodged by the bombardment, had killed another of the gang. The gunboat returned and delivered their new captive to *Sutlej*.

On one occasion when the negotiators went ashore to palaver, a man rushed at Hankin brandishing a knife. The intended victim swiftly wrenched the weapon away from his attacker. This, apparently, was the only time the Ahousaht molested the two emissaries during the action.

It had become clear that even the combined firepower of three warships was not enough to extract Cap-Chah from his forest refuge. Denman needed a different approach. He released his two captives and gave them some blankets and tobacco with a message for their people: If Cap-Chah and the remaining attackers were surrendered to justice, he would take no further reprisals on the villages. If, however, after one month, none turned up, "forcible measures will be resumed." *Forward* remained in the area for a week to accept any such rendered fugitives, but none appeared. Lascelles felt that once the dispersed Ahousahts returned to rebuild their villages, the plan might work. It did not work out that way. There was no further hostility, but neither the gang members nor their leader surrendered or were given up to the authorities. However, Hankin was to meet Chap-Chah a year later and the two would reconcile.

Admiral Denman had failed to achieve the prime aim of the sixteen-day action: to apprehend and bring to justice the leader and his "band of pirates" responsible for attacking *Kingfisher* and killing its master and crew. He was at pains, however, to word his report, dated October 11, to Kennedy in positive terms:

> *It is with great pleasure that I inform you that the service in which 69 canoes have been destroyed and about 15 men killed, has been performed without the slightest injury on our side.*

He makes little mention of any injuries or death caused to the women and children of the nine villages obliterated, except for one wounded little girl who, with her parents, he was bringing to Esquimalt for medical attention.

He concluded his report by commending Pike and noting "that Mr. Smith, superintendent of Police, has rendered essential service and deserves my thanks." Smith was there to take into custody any apprehended suspects and bring them before the court in Victoria. Admiral Denman was far more effusive in his praise for Philip:

> *I cannot close my letter without expressing very strongly the great assistance I have received from Mr. Hankin, whose coolness and presence of mind have been of the greatest value. I consider him most especially qualified to deal with the Indians, who know him well and by whom he is very much liked and trusted. He is also an excellent interpreter, and with the aid of Friday, the means of communication have been all that I could desire.*

The *British Colonist* published Denman's report, in full, including the paragraph paying tribute to Hankin. Everyone of influence in Victoria would certainly have read and noted it. On October 14, Kennedy sent a report to his superior in London about the various cases of unrest and aggression to white men by the Indigenous communities of the west coast. He attached the report from Denman. He noted:

> *I feel confident that the forbearing yet firm and effective proceeding taken by the Admiral, will be productive of the best*

results. The Natives on this coast will require constant and regular supervision till they are impressed with the danger of breaking the Law, and the certainty of punishment. . . . Mr. Hankin who is so well spoken of by Admiral Denman is a gentleman to whom I have lately given temporary employment in the Colonial Secretary's office and knowing his expertise on the west coast I offered his services to the Admiral. Mr. Hankin was recommended to me by Captain Richards under whom he served in the Royal Navy. I hope to put Mr. Hankin in a better position when a suitable opportunity offers.

Just such an opportunity would not be long in coming.

Denman's effusive mention of Hankin's splendid performance under a hostile situation extended to his recommending that he be reinstated at his former naval rank. He even suggested that Hankin would make a most suitable commander for one of the larger gunboats that he was proposing. He suggested the government permanently station them in the area for coastal protection and liaison with the Indigenous peoples. The Admiralty accepted the first recommendation and reinstated Lieutenant Philip Hankin, RN, effective February 4, 1865. Both governors Kennedy and Seymour welcomed the second idea, in theory. The former, however, viewed it to be out of the question if the costs were to be borne by the colony. Colonial authorities in London, reluctant to make an exception for these two colonies for fear of many similar requests, would not provide funding for such vessels.[9]

*

Philip's own recollection of the events of the Clayoquot action, as given in his memoir written half a century later, does not always match the details from other sources. His chronology incorrectly places it such that he was already superintendent of police. That appointment would come later, and because of his performance during the events. He makes no reference to the participation of Horace Smith. He misremembers the location of the action as being in Nootka Sound, not Clayoquot. Nowhere does he mention the name Ahousaht. As in the rest of the memoir, he omits any mention of Friday, who was clearly present and closely associated with his own activities as interpreter and emissary.

In his telling, Philip does not note Denman's initial deployment of *Devastation* to investigate, before committing *Sutlej*. He recalled that his own participation came from the admiral's request to the governor for "someone who knew something of the Indian language." He boarded *Sutlej*, and as soon as they arrived at the (Ahousaht) village, the admiral had asked his

> *opinion as to the best steps to take. He talked of firing on the village, but I begged him not to do so, and said that if he would allow me, I would land in the ship's Dinghy, with only two men. I had some trouble to get the admiral to consent to this, but I said No, I would not be shot, just landing in the way I proposed, and that firearms would be of no use whatsoever, for we could see with our glasses all the Indians, about 2,000 of them all in their warpaint and evidently very excited. . . . I said I wanted nothing but my walking stick, as I knew the Indian character. . . . At last, the admiral consented.*

The Hankin memoir is confusing about which village they first confronted. It cannot have been Marktosis at Matilda Creek, which had been deserted by the time *Sutlej* arrived. None of the other accounts mention seeing anywhere near that many warriors at any of the villages. Richards's chart shows the main village called "Ahousaht" as lying on the southwestern side of Catface Mountain opposite Matilda, now known as Chetarpe, and notes "250 inhabs." Richards depicted and named only major villages. Hankin also appears unaware that Denman ordered a strict rule of returning fire only after being fired upon. Philip continued that, after landing, he

> *walked straight up to them and managed to make them understand what the big ship had come for, and said that if they did not give up 'Kupcha' the chief of the tribe, who we held responsible for the killing of the white men, there would be great trouble as the Admiral would fire his big Guns, and their villages would be destroyed, and many of them killed. They answered, they could not give up Kupcha, as he had escaped into the bush, which I did not believe.*

Hankin identifies the leader and chief of the tribe as "Kupcha," clearly the same man as "Cap-Chah" in Admiral Denman's report. This differs from Wack-la, the name of the chief reported by Gowlland. Hankin returned to *Sutlej* and reported on his conversation:

> *The Admiral asked what I would advise being done, if he should destroy the village? I said No, but land a party early the next morning, and surround the village, taking as many Prisoners as we could, and retaining them as hostages, until Kupcha should surrender.*

Hankin forgot, or deliberately omitted, the bombardment of several villages with cannon and incendiary rockets. He continued his account describing the overland attack on the Trout River villages of Wahous (see map on page 167), launched several days after the first call for the surrender of Cap-Chah. His version also differed in several significant ways with Denman's and other reports, mostly enhancing the significance of his own role:

> *Accordingly, I landed next morning at 3 o'clock with about 300 men, and endeavoured to surround the village; this, would, I thought, be not difficult, and it would have been quite successful had it not been for the barking of several small dogs which gave the alarm! The Natives all took to the Bush at once, and my men were very anxious to have a shot at them as they ran away, but I would not allow it, and gave orders that there was to be no firing, unless the Indians first fired on us. I had taken no firearms with me, but I took up a position on top of a rocky eminence about 100 feet high, so that I could see everything, and gave the necessary directions. Two or three bullets whizzed by me, and one of our men was slightly wounded. I then gave orders to return the fire, and three of the Indians were killed, but the Bush was very dense, and they all very quickly made their escape.*

It is most improbable that Denman would have given command of an assault party of sailors and marines to a civilian, even if he were an ex-naval officer. Aboard *Sutlej* there were competent officers, naval and marines, who would have rightly objected to having their authority over their men subordinated. The party was nowhere near three hundred strong, but just forty sailors, thirty marines, and six Clayoquot guides. In the memoir Hankin concluded his account of the episode:

> *The village was destroyed, and I returned to the ship, but the Indians had received a lesson which they never forgot, and never again attempted any attack on any small trading vessel.*

This is not at all surprising, considering the enormity of damage visited on the Ahousaht people, their dwellings, canoes, reserves of food, their livelihood and social structure, by such a savage demonstration of imperial might.

The officers of HMS Sutlej. *Admiral Joseph Denman leans on the rail at upper level, centre.*

CHAPTER 17

Reinstated and New Responsibilities

On October 23, 1864, Master Daniel Pender, RN, aboard HMS *Beaver* at anchor in Esquimalt Harbour, wrote a hasty, informal note to Captain George Henry Richards, his superior and close friend, back in England:

> *At Noon and shortly after the [gunboat] Forward with Hankin came in from the West Coast. With some letters in my pocket, I met him onboard the Sutlej, the whole matter was turned over by us. We went and saw Govr. Kennedy who agreed that the best step he could take would be to get back into The Navy.*
>
> *Adm. Denman has from Hankin's services on the West Coast at Clayoquot offered to do anything for him, even to assist in his re-installation and further recommends him for Command of one of the Gun Boats as at present attached to the Colony which he considers desirable. This evening the Admiral has . . . drawn himself a draught which . . . will sa[v]e the expense of Hankin going home and in the interim he will retain his appt. in the Colonial Office of £200 pr Annum.*

Hankin clearly enjoyed his ten days aboard HMS *Sutlej*, comfortable in the familiar, structured world of the wardroom and quarterdeck of a naval vessel. He wrote:

> *I received the greatest kindness from everyone on board, the Admiral asking me to dinner almost every night.*

The memoir recorded Denman sent a letter to both the Admiralty and the Colonial Office in London that read:

I consider the whole success of the Expedition entirely owing to Mr. Hankin. He shewed the greatest zeal, intrepidity, and intelligence, and displayed a Knowledge of the Native character, which impressed me with the highest opinion of his value.

Philip noted, modestly:

It did not seem to me that I had done anything to deserve such praise, but it was my good fortune to have served in the 'Hecate', and to having had an opportunity of learning something of the Indians and their language.

Here, again, Hankin's memoir loses track of the sequence of events, jumping forward a year. Evidently, Denman's letters resulted in Philip being reinstated at his rank without loss of seniority, and the extension of his appointment with the local colonial secretary's office for one year.

It is not clear what his new role and duties were supposed to be, but the next few weeks were, for him, a time of considerable ease. His improved status was such that he could befriend the chief clerk, Edwin Nesbitt, and they agreed to rent a "delightful little, furnished cottage" together. They hired a Chinese servant, a combined cook, housekeeper, launderer, and gardener, who proved excellent. These arrangements now allowed him to live in reasonable comfort, while saving part of his salary for the purchase of "some decent clothes." His old friends in Victorian society accepted him once more, and he was "often asked out for a high tea with a little dance afterwards."

The memoir recorded that "Sir Arthur Kennedy[1] was extremely good to me, and he was one of the most delightful men I ever met." The personable Philip also got on well with the governor's wife and two daughters, and he delighted in receiving frequent invitations to dances at Government House. "I was always a good dancer and used to enjoy these parties very much." He had fully recovered his verve as a charming and gallant young naval officer, at ease in the finest of social settings.

One of Hankin's first tasks after returning from Clayoquot was to act as translator in a court case related to another incident where Indigenous people were accused of attacking whites. Apparently, two men from the Huu-ay-aht Nation had been part of a group that attacked a party of five sailors from a civilian vessel anchored at Alberni sawmill. The attack had taken place farther down the inlet, near Barkley Sound. Hankin translated for the defence that the five men were deserters from their ship and that Edward Stamp, owner of the mill, had offered a bounty of $20 for each deserter caught and returned. Two well-respected white men, Peter Francis, a trader at Port San Juan, and Dr. Robert Brown,[2] both confirmed that they knew of this bounty. The Huu-ay-aht Thomas "Friday" Roberts testified through Hankin that four years previously, Stamp had given him $20 for the return of two deserters from another ship.

A few days later, Philip was again called upon by the court, this time as an expert in Indigenous matters. This new case concerned another Huu-ay-aht man, Klatsmick, accused of murdering an English settler, William "Eddy" Banfield, two years earlier.[3] Peter Francis was a witness for the Crown, stating that Klatsmick had confessed the murder to him, believing it justified under traditional custom. Hankin also explained to the court:

> *[He] did not think [the Natives] understood the nature of an oath. [He] had frequently questioned them and found their only faith was in salmon and berries; they did not believe in the existence of a God, in the ordinary acceptation of the term, or any future state.*

Hankin's testimony was no doubt influenced by his experiences with the Ehattesaht paddlers, who beached him and Dr. Charles Wood early, prior to their overland expedition[4]; and with the Kyuquot packers, who refused to continue on his first attempt; and with Friday, who failed to return to *Hecate* as agreed. The judge acquitted Klatsmick, apparently on these grounds, setting an awkward precedent for the colonial authority.

*

In November 1864, Charles Hankin sent a letter addressed to the acting colonial secretary (Wakeford) seeking "employment in the Service." This, too, is puzzling. By this time, Charles was wealthy, a member of a successful syndicate at Barkerville, and had quit a government position to do so. Why would he wish to reapply? Governor Arthur Edward Kennedy saw the letter and noted, "Ask Mr. H. to call upon me." Wakeford later noted, "Which he did 22.11.64." The following month, Graham Hankin submitted a similarly worded application. Kennedy again noted, "Let me see him," and Wakeford, "Done 13.12. 64." The governor accepted neither application. It seems it was not customary, in those days, to specify the nature of the position sought, or attach any statement of qualifications or experience. Philip probably knew of his brothers' applications, but he did not mention them in his memoir.

The following season, Charles was back in charge of the Barker claim. The *Cariboo Sentinel* reported they had eight men at work setting up a new wheel and sinking a new shaft "with prospects of good pay." For the 1866 season, he was no longer listed as foreman, but there were still eight shares and, according to the *Sentinel*, just four men at work sinking a new shaft.

CHAPTER 18
A Policeman's Lot, Part 1: Promotion

Throughout November 1864, a trial took place that fascinated the population of Victoria. Horace Smith, the superintendent of police, was arrested and accused of systematically extracting bribes from several of the town's larger drinking establishments. Gambling in them was prohibited, but in return for regular payment, Smith would turn a blind eye. He was also under suspicion for "running," or selling, rum to Americans, then under Prohibition. At the end of the month, in the final trial before the Supreme Court, the jury, having been sent back several times by the judge, could not reach a unanimous verdict, and so the case was dismissed. By then, however, Smith had resigned his post in disgrace.

Daniel Pender, with his ear in the right places, privately informed Captain George Henry Richards a week before the trial:

> *Hankin is still in the Colonial Office & is about to have the appt. of Commissioner of Police made vacant by the resignation of Mr. Smith, who has been allowed to retire, being unable to refute certain charges of bribery brought against him. I agree with you in thinking Hankin is better off in a permanent ground berth here than he would be in the Navy. He gets on very well indeed with the Gov*r. *and has very good prospects.*

Events proved Pender correct in substance but confused about the actual position. Prior to this change, the police chain of command had been Chief Commissioner Augustus Pemberton,[1] who was also a stipendiary magistrate, reporting directly to the governor, with Smith, as superintendent, being appointed by and reporting to the commissioner. Reporting to Smith were a Sergeant Hill and a varying number of constables and gaolers. Smith had come up through the police ranks and had served in this position since 1859.

The announcement came on a Friday evening immediately before the Christmas break. Pemberton was relieved of his duties as chief commissioner, suspected of complicity in Smith's nefarious activities. He was not replaced but would continue as police magistrate. Philip Hankin would replace Smith as superintendent. Reporting to him, as inspector, would be George Welsh. Thus, Hankin would report to acting colonial secretary Henry Wakeford on all police-related matters.

From his earlier experience in West Africa and Australia, Governor Arthur Edward Kennedy knew a colony needed a competent, adequately funded civil service to function effectively. This included magistrates and a police force staffed with trained, properly paid, and uniformed officers who would be key to conserving peace and order in the colony. The estimates for 1865 included the provision of two horses, enabling two constables to be mounted, adding to their effectiveness and authority.

Amor De Cosmos, editor of the *British Colonist*, wrote on December 23 in support of the new configuration of the police force:

> *We see no grounds for cavilling at the changes thus introduced by His Excellency. Mr. Hankin has had considerable experiences in colonial affairs and is thoroughly versed in the habits, customs and languages of the aboriginies. He has been tried in emergencies and shown undaunted pluck in facing treacherous foes. He is young, but that is no fault, and what he at present lacks—an intimate acquaintance with all the blackguards, renegades, law-breakers, and loose-fists in the community, will come to him in due season, whether he seeks to cultivate their acquaintance or not.*

The journalist dismissed Philip's fourteen years in the Royal Navy plus time among prospectors for Cariboo gold, when he would have come across quite a few bad apples. Evidently, neither Kennedy nor De Cosmos considered Hankin's total ignorance of civil or criminal law to be any impediment for his appointment as police chief. Concerning the new inspector, De Cosmos continued:

> *[About] Mr. George Welsh, late in the employ of the Bank of British Columbia and formally in the Police Force . . . it is needless to speak; he is well known, and probably no better selection for the post could have been made.*

In mid-January 1865 Kennedy presented to the Legislative Assembly of the colony the proposed financial estimates for the year, prepared by acting colonial secretary Wakeford.[2] They included the police department "in the course of being reorganized. . . . The annual salary allotted to the superintendent [$1,940, about C$54,000 in 2025] is considered no more than adequate for the officer whose is the responsible duty of preserving the public peace." The police department included the gaol and the press gang, plus detachments at Nanaimo, Sooke, and Esquimalt. Inspector Welsh would receive $1,200 (about C$34,000 in 2025). There would also be four sergeants, a medical officer on call, a gaoler, a superintendent of convicts, an armourer, constables (on foot and mounted), wardens, and a cook. There were allocations for uniforms, quarters, fuel, lighting, and medical attention for members of the force.

The estimates included an allowance of $750 for travelling expenses for the superintendent, reduced in the debate to $500 (C$14,000 in 2025), showing that the legislature preferred he focused on crime prevention and law enforcement activities in Victoria at the expense of the other communities.

Philip's promotion brought substantial responsibility. His annual salary, paid locally and equivalent to £485 (about C$100,000 in 2025), appeared to be significantly more than he would have received as a senior lieutenant in the navy. His task, however, was daunting. The force up to that time was riddled with corruption; the town of Victoria, while nowhere near as murderous as those in the US "Wild West," was still unruly, full of saloons catering to itinerant prospectors, thieves, and renegades. Hundreds of prostitutes and rum-runners operated blatantly and with impunity. As well as upholding the law in Victoria and the other centres of settler population, he was charged with policing the coastal communities where there was no other representative of the law. Illicit trade in rotgut whiskey to the Indigenous population and other conflicts with shady traders generated major sources of unrest among them.

On his first day in the new job, Philip found "the jail in a filthy state and no kind of discipline. Had the jail thoroughly cleaned and used a great quantity of coal tar and whitewash." During this "new broom" process, he discovered an invaluable ally in "one of the sergeants, Macbride, who had retired from the Army. He was a splendid fellow, and always loyal and true. And we got on very well together. His son is now [in 1914] Sir Richard MacBride."[3] The new superintendent lobbied to build a sanitary drain from the prison to Bastion Street. The streets of Victoria in those days acted as the open sewer system.

Philip undertook, as an early initiative, a preliminary census of the colony. He counted that in the greater Victoria area and Esquimalt, there were 4,485 males and 2,114 females of all races. He also estimated 300 at Cadboro Bay and a total of 1,800 in Saanich, Alberni, Cowichan, and Nanaimo. Clearly, he seriously underestimated the number of Indigenous people.

Early in Hankin's period as superintendent, he suffered an expensive embarrassment. The *Daily Chronicle* for February 24 reported an incident under the jocular lead "Another Jail Bird Escapes in Borrowed Plumage." A prisoner—a seaman serving two months—was assigned to work as personal servant to the police chief. One evening, while Hankin was taking dinner with his friend Daniel Pender aboard *Beaver*, the prisoner spotted an opportunity to escape. According to the article:

> *He dressed himself in one of Mr. Hankin's Sabbath day suits, with a white shirt, stand-up collar and neck-tie to match. Providing himself likewise with a carpet-bag, in which he stowed the contents of a wardrobe for future use and, lest he should come to want on the way, stealing $90 [C$2,400 in 2025] from a cash box and three gold watches, the 'bird' flew out of the window, slid down the water-pipe, and took the road to Esquimalt, where he embarked on the steamer yesterday morning for Portland.*

Hankin discovered the loss the following morning.

*

Laurel Point and the Inner Harbour, Victoria, 1864. The Nagle residence is to the right of the prominent arbutus tree at right of picture. Watercolour by Edward M. Richardson.

The family of Captain Jeremiah Nagle played a significant role in Philip's social life. Born in Ireland, Nagle had gone to sea as a boy and risen through the ranks to that of master mariner. The family had been pioneer settlers in New South Wales and New Zealand before coming to California. There, for two years, Nagle skippered the steamer *Commodore* on a regular run between San Francisco and Victoria, bringing prospectors, merchants, and sundry speculators to seek opportunities offered by the Fraser River gold rush.

On his appointment as harbourmaster, Nagle bought his family a comfortable house in James Bay with its own wharf on what became Belleville Street. Together, Nagle, his fellow Irishman surveyor Joseph Pemberton, and Captain Richards comprised the Lighthouse Board. After a few years, Nagle lost his job because of accounting irregularities originating before his tenure. He then set up as a successful shipping agent and speculated in the real estate boom. Nagle also bought a farm out at Sooke where two productive seams of copper ore were discovered and briefly exploited.

In 1865, the Nagle family included three eligible and sociable daughters, Susan, then aged twenty-five, Jessie, twenty-one, and Isabella, usually known as Isabel and sometimes as Belle, nineteen. The eldest daughter, Kate, aged thirty, had married an older man, William Patten, who managed the dry dock at Mare Island in the Bay Area. Both *Plumper* and *Hecate* had gone to Mare Island for repair. It is probable that Philip had known the family since his first arrival eight years earlier, although, surprisingly, nowhere in his memoir does he mention them. Susan kept an informative diary from which some key years are missing, the pages having been destroyed, for reasons unknown, by a servant. Fortunately, her volume for 1865 is largely complete and reveals significant details about Philip's personal activities during a critical period not covered in his memoir.

While the uppermost strata of class-conscious Victorian society never fully accepted the Nagles as people of quality, they were popular in most circles and respected as honourable and sincere churchgoers. Jeremiah served as justice of the peace for Vancouver Island and later for Victoria. He was also a churchwarden at Christ Church. The Nagle home formed an important hub in the social life of several naval officers, including Philip and Lieutenants Henry Fox, commander of the gunboat *Forward*, and Edmund Hope Verney, of the corvette *Tribune* and the gunboat *Grappler*. Henry Fowler and Edwin Nesbitt, Philip's colleagues at the colonial secretary's office, moved in the same circle, as did the young Graham Hankin. Graham enjoyed a close if platonic friendship with Jessie Nagle. The family and their circle regularly attended the Anglican church of St. John the Divine, the "iron" one of such interest to Lady Franklin during her visit,[4] and where the Reverend Robert J. Dundas conducted services.

*

In mid-March, in response to a long-standing request from the Huu-ay-aht people, Superintendent Hankin took passage aboard the steamer *Thames* to investigate the situation at Alberni and Barkley Sound. The white population associated with the Alberni mill had nearly all departed, fearing imminent danger. He spoke with the local inhabitants—who were afraid of retaliatory raids by the Ahousaht for having assisted the naval action of the previous year—and assured them of official support.

In April Hankin, in his capacity as senior police officer, went with HM steam sloop *Cameleon* to visit the new settlements at Cowichan and Comox. He and Commander Morton Jones, RN, found the settlers had few complaints about the local peoples, unless they had been supplied with liquor. Under the influence, they were said to become entirely irresponsible for their actions, sometimes murdering Europeans. Whiskey, apparently, was readily available from Victoria and brought there in canoes and by illicit traders in small schooners.

Commander Jones urged that the law needed to be represented locally as soon as possible. A fishing party of "U-cul-taws"—We Wai Kai, Lekwiltok, or Ligwildaxw—from Cape Mudge had been raiding settlers' potato plots. The officer assembled the offenders and lectured them sternly, ordering them to return to their village and saying that he would send a gunboat to verify compliance. Commander Jones concluded his report to Kennedy:

Mr. Hankin has been of great service from his knowledge of the language, and tact and judgement displayed in communicating with the Indians.[5]

Over the summer Philip visited the west coast inlets a few more times, usually aboard the gunboat *Forward*. These missions provided logistic support to the second phase of the Exploring Expedition, now led by ex-corporal John Buttle. Returning from one of these sorties, Philip brought some samples of placer gold panned by the team along Bear Creek off Clayoquot Sound.

Unfortunately, these traces of pay dirt triggered an immediate rush to the creek by a large, motley group of would-be prospectors. Many lacked experience of the work and had only vague information as to the location. They soon returned empty-handed and furious, blaming Buttle for their failure. Buttle, a serious, honourable man, was mortified to discover, upon returning to Victoria after a successful exploration, that his reputation had been unjustly tarnished. He wrote a long letter of explanation, published in the *British Colonist*, and, after the mission was completed for the year, left in disgust with his family for California.[6]

Not all Philip's duties as police chief related directly to law and order. On May 24, the Queen's birthday, he joined the Reverend Alexander Charles Garrett[7] in persuading several of the local Indigenous groups to take part in the celebrations. Governor Kennedy gave them appropriate gifts of welcome, and each "Tyhee" (Chinuk Wawa for headman) responded with an address that the *British Colonist* described as "being somewhat remarkable for the sturdy independence of their tone and the shrewdness of some of the remarks."

On the harbour, the Indigenous groups raced in their canoes,

presenting the most novel and attractive feature of the day. Nine large canoes each with twelve brawny [paddlers] started from

Rock Bay Bridge to the finish line . . . the crews standing up in their canoes urging forward their light craft with loud shouts, and the paddles of the entire fleet keeping perfect time with each other. The prize, a bale of blankets, was borne off by the victorious Songishes [Songhees].

*

In early May, Susan Nagle noted in her diary that she, Jessie, and Isabel went to see Mr. Hankin's rooms, and he invited them to take tea there a few days later, which they accepted. She wrote:

Mr. Hankin and Mr. Fowler came for us in a boat to save us the walk. We had a very nice tea and returned about eight o'clock. The two gentlemen . . . intend taking us all up the Arm in a boat and not returning till evening.

Two pages from Susan's diary for early June were ripped out. They must have contained significant developments, for the next undated entry brought intriguing news:

[Papa and Mama] took tea at Mr. Hankin's . . . and yesterday evening they went for a pull up the Arm with Mr. Hankin and Sir Lampton Loehne, who is stopping with him. It is settled that they [Philip and Isabel] are to be married about the 12th of Aug., its being Isabel's birthday.

A romance had blossomed between the two, and Philip's invitation to Isabel's parents for tea had been to seek their permission for the marriage. Philip was then twenty-nine, a decade older than his fiancée.

A few days later, Susan—who from then on began to refer to "Mr. Hankin" as "Philip"—wrote:

Isabel and Philip went for a long ride and when they returned about seven, Philip asked me to go for a canter round Beacon Hill. I did not wait for a second invitation but was ready in two minutes. Our canter ended in a gallop as hard as we could go round the course. I enjoyed it greatly. I had not been on horseback for more than two years. . . . [A few days later she wrote:] Mr. Hankin was to leave this morning in the gunboat for the

Isabel Hankin, née Nagle, at the time of her wedding.

> *north, to be away from 10 days to a fortnight. I believe they are to be married about the 1st of August. They are to spend their honeymoon in Saanich. Jessie and I are to be the bridesmaids and Mr. Fox and Mr. Fowler groomsmen. The wedding is to be a very quiet one. The wedding is to be at home, not only on Papa's account [Captain Nagle had recently broken his leg and ribs in a carriage accident] but it will be a great savings of expenses. We shall not have anyone here except Aunt and Nellie and the groomsmen, Mr. Fox and Mr. Fowler.*

*

As Susan had recorded, on June 19 Superintendent Hankin returned to Clayoquot Sound aboard *Forward*, redeploying John Buttle and his team of explorers, and planning "to visit various Native Tribes." Having arranged a rendezvous with the Ahousaht at their newly rebuilt village, they first visited Cypress Bay. Eight months earlier, during the assault by the overland party, rocket fire had destroyed two villages in the bay. In his report to Kennedy, Hankin noted:

No attempt had been made to rebuild them, the remains of several dead bodies were lying scattered about and the whole place presented a scene of great desolation.

They attended the planned meeting at Chetarpe Village,

an entirely new settlement on Vargas Island . . . and found nearly all the Ahousaht Tribe assembled numbering upwards of 200. They appeared to be busily employed making new canoes, they informed us 80 were destroyed by the Sutlej. 'Cupcha' the chief was present but, on our landing, concealed himself in the bush and refused to come forward.

After waiting about half an hour and sending several messages to him, he ventured [on a promise he should not be made prisoner] to make his appearance. He was evidently very much frightened, and it was some time before we could reassure him. He is a fine, well-built man about 40 years of age, of a most villainous countenance. He showed us his wounds in his leg and shoulders, which appear to have been very severe although quite healed now and repeatedly asked if 'our hearts were good towards him?' We assured him of our friendship and protection so long as he behaves well to the whites, but on the other hand, told him that any such treachery or misconduct on their part would meet with inevitable punishment.

We distributed among them presents of soap, tea, sugar, and biscuits and parted with renewed protestations of friendship. Their houses were newly built and, although they informed us some few of their tribe were away fishing, yet this is now the principal, in fact, the only large village of the Ahousahts. Our visit to this tribe struck me as being one of no small importance it having removed all feeling of mistrust on the part of the Ahousahts and established friendly relations between Native and the Whites.

*

Upon being officially informed by the Colonial Office in London that the Admiralty had agreed to Hankin's reinstatement as lieutenant, Kennedy wrote back requesting that Hankin be allowed to continue in his appointment as superintendent of police for one year. The Admiralty duly granted the extension in a confirmation letter dated June 8, 1865, but the effective date is not clear. The question of his salary is also vague, but Philip's memoir implies he received payment from the civil list as a colonial police officer rather than a naval officer—a situation that was to prove unfortunate, as he would now be subject to local budget decisions.

In July, William Young, the former naval officer with the retired rank of commander, returned from his year's leave to resume the office of colonial secretary for Vancouver Island. His acting replacement, Wakeford, became colonial auditor. This changeover came during a heated discussion between the city council and the governor over deployment of the convicts' chain gang. The council wanted the convicts to be used to clean the streets of Victoria, supervised by the police force. Kennedy resisted because it would demoralize the force and they would lose respect.

Philip submitted a detailed plan for a reconstructed police force that included qualifications and required standards for constables. Several serving members who failed to meet the standard were dismissed. Under his policy, executed by Superintendent Hankin, the force had been remodelled and trained to perform proper police duties throughout the island. De Cosmos argued, illogically, that "in this happy period when crime is reduced to a minimum, when the services of the force are not so frequently called into requisition as formally, it is surely as little as can be expected that its members be as much as possible utilized." Kennedy won that argument, but it served to only increase the growing conflict between elected politicians and the governor.

*

Hankin made two more trips resupplying Buttle and visiting Indigenous communities on the west coast, one in late July, immediately prior to the wedding—to Susan's displeasure:

> *It is most annoying when they are to be married so soon . . . but fortunately [Philip] got back in time for the original wedding day, which was the third of the month. They were married about ½ past eleven. Capt. Fox was my groomsman & Mr. Fowler Jessie's. We had breakfast directly after & then danced for a short time, but it was too warm to do more than a few quadrilles and lancers.*[8]

At half past four the bride & groom started for their cottage at Esquimalt, and we accompanied them on horseback.[9] *. . . We remained at the cottage for a short time & continued our ride. . . . We got home about ten, had some tea and finished off with a dance. The next two days we were very tired, and we are only just recovering.*

[Later] Graham came back [from church with Jessie] & had dinner. In the afternoon we walked down to see Philip & Isabel at the cottage. It seems very strange to think of Isabel's being married. I can't realize it yet. She is very happy and advises me to follow her example.

This last entry is poignant, as Susan's diary had earlier hinted at regret over a disappointing love affair of her own a few years previously, and concerns over her increasing years as a spinster.

The August 4, 1865, edition of the *British Colonist* carried a small, paid announcement:

MARRIED
In this city on the 3rd instant, at the residence of the bride's father, by the Rev. E. Cridge, Philip James Hankin, Lieutenant, R.N., and Superintendent of Police, son of Daniel Hankin, Esq., of Pertenhall, Kimbolton, Huntingdonshire, to Isabella Gertrude, fourth daughter of J. Nagle, Esq., of Victoria, Vancouver Island.
San Francisco and English papers please copy.

Not until well after the event did Hankin's memoir make a passing reference to the fact that he had married. It appeared to come as an afterthought:

[I received a communication] acquainting me that the Lords Commissioners of the Admiralty had been pleased to re-instate me in the Navy, and promote me to the rank of Commander. They added I must be prepared to return to England at once, when I would be appointed to a ship, or else placed on the retired list. As I was at that time holding a very good appointment in Victoria, worth nearly £500,[10] *and had only been married two months . . . I decided to go on the retired list and remain where I was.*

This recollection appears muddled. His reinstatement was as lieutenant and it had come prior to the marriage, being effective in early February 1865. The Admiralty approved Kennedy's later request for an extension to Hankin's leave of absence to continue in the government appointment—for two further years. Their approval of this request, dated April 1866, showed that then, Hankin still held the rank of lieutenant. News of his promotion to commander could not have come before that summer, by which time his situation in Victoria had taken a significant turn for the worse. His reaction to it would have been quite different to that described in the memoir.

Philip Hankin's service record shows that he was "Compulsory retired April 1, 1870" with "Retired pay, under 40 years of age, £109-10-0 p. annum." His retired rank would have been as commander.

*

Philip erroneously noted in the memoir that at the time of the wedding Captain Nagle was still the harbourmaster of Victoria. Nagle maintained his shipping agency office on Bastion Street "next to the Police barracks." Two weeks after the wedding, he offered "for sale or lease" the family's nine-room residence, plus a water lot and wharf ninety feet long, with a large-size bathhouse on Belleville Street in James Bay. He also offered a mortgage on the property at one and a half percent per month. The house did not sell and was twice offered at auction, eventually selling in early November "with all its furniture" to a Dr. W. Dickerson, the former (and disgraced) coroner.

The Nagle family had once been financially comfortable but had fallen on harder times. The copper mining business at Sooke had failed. Fourth daughter Isabel probably brought no dowry or personal wealth to the marriage and had no training to enable her to work. Susan had taught at a small school to help with the family income. Her diary does not record the selling of the Nagle family home, nor to where they moved. She noted in mid-October that "Isabel and Philip seem very happy. They are at the Barracks." This hints that, probably for economic reasons, the couple had vacated their Esquimalt cottage, so carefully redecorated, to take advantage of the apartment in the police building on Bastion Street near the site of Fort Victoria, to which Philip's position entitled him. In addition to quarters, he received free coal, gas, and a servant.

The police barracks in Victoria. Superintendent Hankin and his bride had an apartment on the upper level.

While there is no record of Pender informing Richards of Hankin's marriage to one of the Nagle daughters, he would have done so immediately. Pender knew that this topic would have particularly interested Richards, since he and Harbourmaster Nagle had worked together, deciding the crucial matter of positioning Vancouver Island's first lighthouses. In his next letter on record, Pender discussed the couple as though it was no longer news to Richards.

*

In early November 1865, Kennedy requested a show of force by the navy to support settlers in the Comox Valley. Raiding parties of Laich-kwil-tach from the village of We Wai Kai at Cape Mudge had been stealing potato crops and destroying fences. The Cape Mudge community were fierce rivals to the local K'ómoks People and of a different language group. Admiral Denman felt that a meeting of the settlers should first be called to discuss the problem and action to be taken.

He ordered a squadron of *Sutlej*, *Sparrowhawk*, and *Clio* to steam for Comox immediately. The screw dispatch gun vessel HMS *Sparrowhawk*, under the command of Commander Edwin Augustus Porcher, RN, had arrived on station only a few days earlier. Accompanying Denman and Porcher ashore for a meeting with the local settler community, according to Porcher's diary, were a "Mr. Philip I. Hawkins (the Superintendent of Police & Governor of the Gaol at Victoria) and Dr. Comrie." Clearly, this meant Philip Hankin and that the admiral had not fully briefed Porcher. Peter Comrie was ship's surgeon aboard *Sparrowhawk*. It was the season of storms and getting three miles (five kilometres) upstream on the swollen Courtenay River in canoes was difficult. However, they found many settlers had gathered in the mission chapel and, after lunch, addressed the matter at hand.

Denman understood Kennedy's intentions were to persuade the Laich-kwil-tach people to desist from raiding the settlement and return to Cape Mudge. To their surprise, many settlers disagreed with this, fearing the absence of Laich-kwil-tachs would only encourage the K'ómoks to overcharge for fish and other provisions. Besides, they said, the thefts were really only trifling. In a vote, nineteen settlers wished the Laich-kwil-tach to remain, against eleven wishing them gone. Denman, after meeting with Claylick, the chief of the Laich-kwil-tach, aboard *Sutlej*, and guided by Hankin acting as interpreter, persuaded him to withdraw his people for a few months, after which they could return. The chief had earlier been captured and held in chains and menaced by a midshipman who mimicked that he was to be hanged. Now, showered with gifts and promises of being made a policeman, he undertook to have his people return to Cape Mudge. *Sutlej* and *Clio* returned to Esquimalt and *Sparrowhawk* visited settlers in the Cowichan Valley.

Cary Castle, the north end of the governor's residence in Victoria, recently enlarged to include a ballroom.

CHAPTER 19

A Policeman's Lot, Part 2: Demotion and Dismissal

After a long delay in the construction and fitting out of the new Government House, now with a ballroom attached, His Excellency the Governor and Mrs. Arthur Kennedy gave the first Vice-Regal Ball. The evening of October 26, 1865, saw what the *British Colonist* later described as "beyond doubt the largest, the most sociable, and in all respects the most successful re-union that has taken place in the colony." Attending were heads of the civil departments, officials in both colonies, officers of the Royal Navy and a visiting American warship, officers commanding the two garrisons in the disputed but now peaceful San Juan Island, and several hundred civilians. Couples danced to a quadrille band.

Two days later, the paper listed many of the guests, including "C. Hankin Esq., Superintendent of Police and Mrs. Hankin" (surely the misprint would have annoyed Philip) and Miss Nagle, one of his new sisters-in-law. Daniel Pender, who was in town, apparently did not attend. There followed a sumptuous supper, speeches, light entertainment, and more dancing until three thirty in the morning, when everyone stood to sing the national anthem. For reasons unknown, Philip made no mention in his memoir of this important social event and his attendance with his new bride.

*

In December, stipendiary magistrate Augustus Pemberton prepared and presented a summary report on the number of cases in Victoria sent for trial, itemized by type of offence between the end of September 1864 and the end of November 1865. This was not the total number of accused arraigned by Hankin's force, just the number that were not dismissed by the magistrate.

The senior court found thirty-one cases worthy of consideration. These included: two cases of "keeping a common gaming house," which Hankin's predecessor, Horace Smith, would have overlooked; two "disorderly houses," or brothels, of which there must have been many dozens in operation; three "assaults with intent to kill," no murders; five "receiving stolen property"; one "riot"; and two "breaking gaol."

The city would have been, by then, reasonably law-abiding when compared with its earlier history, thanks to Kennedy's policy and Hankin's management. To the same report, Superintendent Hankin appended a summary of the costs of the gaol during the same period. The daily average of prisoners confined was forty-six, at an average daily cost of 59 cents per person. From this, he deducted the estimated value of the labour of the prisoners at 12 cents per person per day, giving a net daily cost of 47 cents each.

*

The year 1866 began disastrously for Kennedy and Hankin and ended with both departing Vancouver Island. The economy of the colony was in deep depression and factions within the Legislative Assembly spoiled for a fight with the establishment.[1] The essential problem remained the same: lack of adequate revenue to fund the costs of government, including the civil list. Complicating this were arguments over who should set the budget—the governor and colonial secretary or the elected politicians—and who had the responsibility to set and collect taxes to pay for everything. Inevitably, the deficit mounted, as did the colony's debt burden.

In January, a correspondent for the *Times* of London noted changes for the worse in Victoria: "A large proportion of buildings of every class [are] unoccupied . . . trade dull and diminished in amount . . . bankruptcies numerous and 'skedaddlers' [fugitive debtors] abundant, money scarce and the employment of labour limited."

The Treasury building, one of the "Birdcages," with an anonymous ironic caption. Photograph by F. Dally.

These were not the only issues. Uncertainties over the impending union of the two colonies, Vancouver Island and British Columbia, loomed large behind all policy discussions. How was this to be managed? Where would the capital city be: New Westminster or Victoria? How to reconcile the public debts? Who would serve in the new, single administration? Which governor was to remain? How would they treat any officials not brought into the united government? How to apportion authority between London and the new colony? What laws should apply, and how would they be enforced?

Apart from the Indigenous peoples, the populations of both colonies still consisted mostly of transients and recent arrivals, with scant knowledge and experience of the processes underlying democratic elections and responsible governance. Thus, they held little respect for such niceties.

Kennedy, aware of the deteriorating financial situation, presented his Estimates for 1866 for the approval of the Assembly. He had reduced the total from $314,000 to about $206,000 (C$8.6 million and $5.7 million respectively in 2025)—a decrease of 34 percent from the previous year. Members of the Assembly, however, were in no mood to co-operate. Their earlier attitude of sullen obstinance now became one of outright opposition. Their reply drastically cut both the number of civil servants and the salaries of those remaining.

Their version of the civil list abolished eleven senior positions, including the surveyor general, the treasurer, the auditor, the registrar of the Supreme Court, the governor's private secretary, and several specialized clerks. Among the latter was Henry Fowler, who had been Philip's groomsman. Kennedy pointed out to his superiors in London that "meritorious public officers appointed by the Queen have been summarily dismissed without compensation."

In his dispatches home, Kennedy identified the Assembly's strategies behind the changes:

> *The refusal to recognize or provide for the offices of Surveyor General and Treasurer is a foolish attempt to deprive me of the services of these gentlemen in the Legislative Council. . . . The desire of the Assembly to legislate and govern without reference to other branches of the Legislature is very clear. . . . I fear [they] look to the neighbouring Territory for precedents where 'vigilantes' administer justice, and 'difficulties' are adjusted with the revolver and bowie knife. . . . I think the time has arrived when the existing form of Government should be reconsidered and amended, if Vancouver Island is to be permanently retained as a British Colony. Two years' experience has convinced me that the House of Assembly, as at present constituted, is not capable of using constitutional power in a respectable manner.*

The police department came in for particularly vindictive wrath by the Assembly. They cut the office of superintendent, demoting Hankin to inspector. Welsh, who had been in that role, was now sergeant, and they eliminated all but five constables for the entire colony. Kennedy, in another dispatch to London, observed:

> *I have induced Mr. Hankin to retain his office as head of the Police in the hope of his position being improved in this respect. The salary voted for the office Mr. Hankin holds is $1,200, only little more than double the wages which a common labouring man receives in this Colony, where all the necessaries of life are enormously high. I may remark that Mr. Hankin is especially useful in dealing with the Indian population.*

Kennedy also noted: "In Victoria alone, with a mixed population of 5 or 6,000, there were 85 licensed drinking houses, many of which are in addition brothels and gambling houses." The reduced force and one magistrate would henceforth "be exempted from all Executive control and placed at the disposal of the City Council, a Body who have heretofore shown a greater tendency to violate than to uphold the law."

There was to be no representative of the law at Nanaimo "with a population of 800 exclusive of Indians," nor any for the west coast of the island. Kennedy added:

> *You will observe that the Assembly propose to leave the Indian population to 'execute their own laws,' that is, to murder each other without let or hindrance when inflamed by drink, the sale of which to Indians they propose to legalize. . . . It will be remarked there is* <u>*no other*</u> *available force in the Colony beyond the moral support afforded by the presence from time to time of some of Her Majesty's Ships. Robberies are frequent and 'the knife' often resorted to in drunken quarrels. . . . The Police Magistrate of Victoria adjudicated upon 1,583 cases between September 30, 1864, and November 20, 1865. The number of prisoners undergoing sentence in the gaol varies from 50 to 60—desperadoes of all nationalities—and the absence of any force beyond a gaoler and a few warders to suppress any outbreak is courting danger which will more than probably occur.*
>
> *There are, moreover, 800 stand of arms*[2] *given to the Colony by HM Government and at present in charge of the Police without any guarantee against their being seized. The very small number of resident British population renders the reduction or abolition of the Police force a still graver and more significant fact. . . . [Hankin] has brought [the police force] into a state of efficiency and decency.*

Kennedy attached a horrendous report by Hankin describing a district of Victoria falling within police jurisdiction:

> *There are about 200 Indian prostitutes living in Cormorant, Fisgard, and Store streets, in a state of filth, and dirt beyond all description. On entering one of their shanties in the afternoon, I have seen 3 or 4 Indian women lying drunk on the floor, nearly*

naked, covered in blood, and their faces cut with broken bottles, with which they had been fighting. . . . The stench emitted from these dens is abominable, and is sufficient to cause some loathsome and contagious disease.

Whiskey sellers, prostitutes and bad characters are to be found in this locality, and unfortunate sailors coming on leave from their ships are allured here by the Indian women and robbed. If it were not for the constant supervision of the Police, it would be dangerous for any respectable person to walk through these streets either by day or night.

In early February, Kennedy responded to the Assembly's resolution that drastically pruned his Estimates with a long, formal letter informing them:

[I have] already dispensed with the services of fourteen public officers paid from General Revenue, including two stipendiary magistrates. . . . I have induced the Superintendent and Inspector [of police] to retain their offices for the present time on the insufficient salaries voted for the inferior offices, deeming this course absolutely necessary for public safety. . . . I think it highly injudicious to reduce the salary of public offices so as to render no longer an object of ambition to men of ability and respectable station to hold them.

Hankin had little to say in his memoir about such difficulties in his second year in the police force. Daniel Pender, however, mentioned them in a private letter to Captain George Henry Richards in England:

The Legislators of this place are going on the <u>wholesale retrenchment</u>, cutting down official salaries, discharging &c, &c—at a smart rate. Poor Hankin has had his pay reduced to $1,200 per annum & extra work imposed, but he has had the gratification of seeing the man who was loudest in the House for cutting off salaries, one Dr. Dickson [sic], whom you may remember being summarily dismissed from the office of Coroner for (what has not transpired but it is generally supposed) making himself too obnoxious in the House as a salaried man. Mr. De Cosmos is at the head of a set of republicans & they are doing all they can to go to war with the Governor.

Another voice raised to support the "retrenchment" of the police force was that of Leonard McClure, an Irishman and editor of the *British Colonist* (owned by Amor De Cosmos). Both De Cosmos and McClure were members of the Legislative Assembly (MLAs). On one occasion, soon after the reduced budget had taken effect, someone calling himself "Watchman" ranted in a letter to the newspaper about how his house had been burgled. When he reported it to the police, demanding prompt action, he was affronted when Inspector Hankin explained he had no one available to send, reportedly adding, "Perhaps Mr. McClure and Mr. De Cosmos might send a man to search." McClure used editorial space in a diatribe against the performance of the police, repeating the suggestion that it be placed under the control of the City Council. As an MLA, McClure, a few weeks later, called for "a committee of the House to enquire into the condition of the Police Department."

Before that committee could begin its hearings, another complaint was raised against Hankin. The proprietor of the Commercial Hotel in the centre of Victoria, Isaac Turgoose, brought a claim for defamation against Superintendent Hankin. He sought $5,000 (about C$148,000 in 2025) in special damages for slander. His case alleged that Hankin had described his hotel as a "perfect nuisance, a notoriously bad one, and the common resort of prostitutes." Defending him was a Mr. Wood, barrister with Drake and Jackson, where Philip had briefly worked as a clerk on his return from the Cariboo.[3]

Also in defence, the attorney general "claimed that the remarks were made in the Police Court by Mr. Hankin in the discharge of his duty as a public officer and was therefore a privileged communication. He made them in answer to a question from the magistrate during a case against Turgoose." The chief justice agreed that Mr. Hankin was doubly privileged—as a witness and as a public officer—and that the plaintiff had no case against the defendant.

Meanwhile, the enquiry committee had met and heard testimony from several ex-members of the police, dismissed by Hankin in his efforts to improve the quality of the force. They, of course, all felt the situation under Horace Smith had been far better.

The police enquiry tried to bring Hankin before them but, with the support of the governor, he was able to stall long enough to allow more pressing matters to come to the fore. The dire financial situation of both colonies had become a crisis. Bankers cut off credit. The Colonial Office in London decided Kennedy was correct that the only solution was the unification of the two colonies. This was generally approved by people on the island but opposed by the mainland colonials.

Governor Frederick Seymour was then on leave in Europe but available for discussions on the issue with London. He secured relatively favourable terms for New Westminster. All agreed, for a population the size of a small English town, two governors and two sets of officials were uncalled for. On August 6, 1866, Queen Victoria gave royal assent to "The British Columbia Act."

The act meant that the Colony of British Columbia effectively absorbed that of Vancouver Island. Victoria was no longer to be a free port. Henceforth, the taxation system in place on the mainland would apply on the island, and the Legislative Assembly in Victoria would be discontinued. There would be a new Legislative Council, part elected and part appointed by the colonial authority, sitting in New Westminster. The governor for the united colony would be Frederick Seymour. When the news reached Victoria, it shocked the population, particularly the MLAs, who saw their livelihoods about to evaporate.

*

There is little on record about Philip and Isabel's private life during those turbulent times. He does not refer to it in his memoir. Susan Nagle's servant destroyed her diaries for that year and for most of 1867; and her other sister, Jessie, had not yet begun a journal. There is, however, a private note from Pender to Richards, dated July 8. In it, he noted:

> *Philip Hankin is crying out about the decline of the place, but it is in part the result of his reckless disposition & partly I fancy from the fact that he finds married life in Victoria an expensive amusement. Mrs. Hankin has improved so much, but dresses &c. &c, cost money here. . . . I am in hopes that soon the colonys will be united with an economical staff of Govt. officials & Crown Colony form of Govt. Then I firmly believe the place will flourish, at present property in Victoria is low because the rivers in B.C. are too high for the Gold to be got out, and all the hordes of traders must go bankrupt. But in this month, August & later the Big Bend, and Cariboo mines will yield largely, judging from the most reliable information I can obtain.*

Mrs. Isabel Hankin. Portrait taken on one of her visits to San Francisco, probably 1870.

These comments hint of a letter missing from the record, in which Pender reported Hankin's wife, Isabel, as being unwell. From her photographs, she appears to have been a small-boned, delicate woman. Her sisters' diaries record their frequent maladies, suggesting the general constitution of the Nagle daughters was not robust.

With the impending new regime and the expiration of the Assembly's legitimacy, Kennedy and his superiors in London agreed to shelve all the issues over the Estimates. Governor Seymour and the executive of the united colony, once it took shape, would work to resolve them.

*

For ten days in August, Kennedy took Hankin on a visit to the major Indigenous and settler communities around the island. Coasting traders had complained of harassment by some Indigenous people. Admiral Joseph Denman provided HMS *Scout*, a twenty-one-gun, three-masted screw corvette, to take the party. Captain John Adolphus Pope Price, RN, commanded the vessel. After leaving Esquimalt, their first call was to what had been the Stamp sawmill at the head of Alberni Inlet.

HMS Scout. *Conveyed Governor Kennedy on his farewell circumnavigation of Vancouver Island, accompanied by Philip Hankin.*

There are some intriguing clues that Thomas Roberts, the Huu-ay-aht man known to Hankin as Friday, also took part in the Kennedy expedition. In 1867, a year after the Kennedy party had been there, two Anglican missionaries from the Columbia Mission, Henry Guillod and the Reverend Jules Xavier Willémar, arrived in Alberni to establish a mission and school. Willémar, in his report issued in 1868, noted:

> *On our way to Victoria & before leaving Barclay Sound we saw two fishing stations occupied by some of the Ohiat tribe. At one of them we were able to stop for several hours and found a great many Indians, amongst them the first Chief of all the tribe who was thoroughly delighted to see us. There also we found a young man who understood Chinook perfectly—the only one we met during our visit. I had a long conversation with him in the presence of the chief & several others—none of whom understood Chinook at all, but the young man interpreted all I said. I explained to him who we were, why we had come amongst them.*[4]

In a separate report, Guillod noted that, while at their new Alberni mission on September 10, 1867:

> *Canoe of Ohy-ahts arrived. Charles Friday, who was interpreter on the Scout a few years ago, and understood Chinook very well, came to see us. . . . He seemed disappointed we were not living with his tribe. He said they were the largest, and told us he wanted to come to school.*

The young man, Charles Friday, exceptionally fluent in Chinuk Wawa, certainly appears to have been the same person noted by Willémar, and who had claimed he had been aboard *Scout*. Neither the lengthy reports in the *Colonist* and *Chronicle*—written anonymously by one of *Scout*'s officers, perhaps Captain Price—nor Hankin's memoir mentions Thomas "Friday" Roberts having been aboard, but this was most probably the same man who had been with Hankin on both *Hecate* and *Sutlej*. A further clue is a brief note by Frederick Dally, the photographer who accompanied Kennedy aboard *Scout*, who wrote that while *Scout* was fog-bound before heading into Alberni Inlet: "Friday [August 11, 1866]. A Barclay Sound native came on board this morning."[5] Again, it seems most likely that the man Dally referred to was the same Thomas Roberts who had worked with Hankin.

At the Alberni mill site, Kennedy and his party were distressed to find what had once been a thriving settlement now totally devastated. Cottages with carefully tended gardens had fallen into ruins, overgrown with weeds. A solitary European settler, the caretaker Drane, watched over the rusting machinery of the mill. Farther upstream of the Stamp River, another loner, the tenant farmer Charles Taylor, cared for a small herd of healthy-looking cattle.

The day following the visit to the derelict mill, *Scout* steamed to Uchucklesaht village, where the party met the locals, gave them some blankets and ship's biscuit, and enquired into their condition. Kennedy reported receiving what he claimed was a common request: for a government agent to be stationed among them to protect them and properly relay any grievances they had. Unable to leave Barkley Sound because of fog and adverse seas, they visited Village (now called Effingham) Island, where the entrepreneur Gilbert Sproat had set up a salting operation for the abundant local codfish, which were sent to Victoria in the small schooner *Codfish*.

Scout's next port of call was in Clayoquot Sound, the Ahousaht village. They met the chief, Cap-Chah, who had been a principal figure in the *Kingfisher* incident. Similarly to Hankin's last enounter with Chief Cap-Chah, the group noted severe scars to his leg and shoulder, wounds received in the action but now healed. They gave him some blankets and tobacco for distribution among his people.

After anchoring for the night in Hesquiaht harbour, they called into Friendly Cove at the mouth of Nootka Sound and landed. They met the

Mowachaht villagers, presented the usual gifts, and heard the request for a resident agent.

Afterward, *Scout* steamed around Nootka Island into the narrow Esperanza Inlet, where, Dally reported, they scraped a "round-topped rock which carried away fourteen feet of the ship's false keel." They anchored for the night in Queens Cove, memorable to Philip from his time aboard *Hecate*. The next day, they steamed north for the shelter of Quatsino Sound and anchored. En route, they experienced familiar west coast conditions: thick fog, drenching rain, and heavy surf beating onto a broken, rocky shore. There, they found a steamer, *Kate*, whose captain, Waller, was trading for salmon.

The next day, the weather cleared fine for their journey around Cape Scott through the Goletas Channel to Fort Rupert (near what is now Port Hardy), where they found at anchor the HBC steamer *Otter* (a larger vessel, replacing the *Beaver*). Kennedy and Hankin landed to visit the fort and the nearby community of Nahwitti (now called Tsaxis). Dally noted that the village was the largest on Vancouver Island with several hundred inhabitants. Philip would have remembered this place well from four years earlier, when he and Dr. Charles Wood had concluded their overland adventure to cross the island (see chapter 11), noting the villagers then suffered dreadfully from the smallpox epidemic.

It took the whole of the following day for *Scout* to reach Tribune Bay on Hornby Island, where they anchored. Next morning, they headed for Comox. The governor and Philip rode around the area on borrowed horses, calling into settlers' farms. According to an article in the *British Colonist*, of August 21, 1866, Kennedy "enquired most kindly into their wants, and evinced great interest in their farms, stock &c. Nearly all the settlers spoke cheerfully of their prospects and appeared contented." They wanted a road from the settlement to the bay and some economical method of getting their produce to market. They had raised some splendid hogs and poultry but could not find a market for them in Victoria, except at a significant loss. This struck the visitors as odd, since the city imported bacon and butter in significant quantities. They considered that there was a business opportunity for a commissioned agent to handle the produce for the settlers as a group.

"Most of the settlers were single men and complained bitterly of not being able to find wives, as bachelor life is not conducive to comfort." This is in interesting contrast to the earlier generation of HBC men, who readily married local women. In a nearby stream, abounding in trout, officers from the ship caught some magnificent fish. The author of the published account of the trip, most probably Hankin, commented, "This is altogether a most flourishing little settlement." They next called in at Nanaimo, noting, "the town had wonderfully improved during the last three years. Its progress appears slow, but sure." This is a clue that the author of the *Colonist* article was Hankin, since no one else aboard would have seen Nanaimo in 1863. There were no ships in the harbour waiting to load coal.

Their next call, to the Cowichan Valley, was on a Sunday, and so the governor's party attended service at the parsonage. Thirty-nine people were present. Afterward, Kennedy and Hankin again toured the local farms on horseback. One farm particularly impressed them with its magnificent crop of oats and about twenty head of fine cattle. The owner, a Mr. Alexander, who had a wife and family, appeared to thrive and prosper. He had previously farmed in Britain and Australia, but "infinitely prefers this, and is perfectly contented with the spot he has chosen." Kennedy also met with the local Somena people and discussed with them their concerns about land. They wanted resolution about what land they were to have. Before returning to Esquimalt, the party called in to Salt Spring Island and visited the farm of a Mr. Booth.[6]

Their circumnavigation of Vancouver Island had covered 800 nautical miles (1,480 kilometres). Kennedy reported that whiskey traders were the primary source of trouble. This voyage, aboard a ship of the Royal Navy, must have come for Philip Hankin as a blessed relief from the chaotic anxieties associated with being a policeman. Taking one consideration with another, the latter half of his two-year stint of constabulary duties was "not an 'appy one." Fourteen years after these events, Gilbert and Sullivan would release their comic opera *The Pirates of Penzance.*

*

"A Policeman's Lot Is Not a Happy One" is a popular song from Gilbert and Sullivan's comic opera The Pirates of Penzance. *A cigarette card portrays the character.*

Soon after the party's return, news about the union of the colonies reached Victorians, causing great consternation. Vancouver Islanders, having considered themselves the primary colonists, now learned they would become the lesser of the two populations. Kennedy's situation was now that of a "lame duck," with diminished status in the community. Seymour was still in Europe, but Kennedy promptly announced he was stepping down and returning to Britain in late October 1866, before his successor returned.

Instead of the customary grand farewell banquet, an ad hoc committee organized a ball in the name of the citizens of Victoria. Lumley Franklin, the mayor, chaired the committee. At $5 a ticket, they would hold it in the assembly rooms, a short way out of town. The naval ships and the HBC provided material support with decorations, music, and refreshments. About 230 people attended, including Admiral Denman and the officers of the other ships in harbour, ex-governor Sir James Douglas, and senior government officers, all with their ladies. The article listed Philip and Isabel as present, as well as Graham Hankin, but none of the Nagle family, nor Daniel Pender. Kennedy penned a brief but diplomatic and courteous note of appreciation to the mayor and "so many honourable men and their estimable families." A few days later, the *British Colonist* carried the note together with a positive account of the event and its participants.

On the eve of Kennedy's departure for Britain on October 23, the twelve heads of departments of his administration, including Hankin, delivered a formal address to him. It expressed their collective regret at his premature retirement from the post, their appreciation of his services, demeanour, and zeal, and their best wishes for his future.

*

Before leaving, Kennedy wrote a letter to Seymour recommending Hankin's services be retained. On the day following the Kennedys' sailing, William Young sent a dispatch to the Earl of Carnarvon in London formally informing him Governor Kennedy had "transferred the administration of the government to [me] as the Senior Member of the Executive Council, pending the Union of Vancouver's Island with British Columbia." Chief Clerk Edwin Nesbitt would act as colonial secretary.

*

Frederick Seymour served as governor of mainland British Columbia between 1864 and 1866, then of the united colonies until his death in June 1869.

Seymour, aware that the decision made in London displeased the population of Victoria, arrived there on November 7 with his new wife. He reported being received "with great coldness, but no disrespect." In marked contrast, when he travelled to New Westminster a few days later, he found the reception there to be "most loyal and gratifying." On November 19, he issued, simultaneously in both locations, the proclamation of the union of the colonies. He admitted to Carnarvon that "there was no enthusiasm or excitement shown in either town." Hoping to allay the fears of Victorians over their loss of the House of Assembly and status as a free port, Seymour spent the following month in Victoria.

During this period, Seymour announced his selection for government officers, confirming his strong bias in favour of those from New Westminster. For colonial secretary, he nominated Arthur Birch, the man who had stood in for him during his fourteen-month leave of absence. Young was to be, temporarily, treasurer. Among other officials of Kennedy's team let go, Seymour gave Philip Hankin a dispatch to hand carry to London, which declared:

[The bearer] had been highly recommended by Mr. Kennedy and by Rear Admiral Denman. My own limited knowledge of him leads me to regret that the absolute necessity for retrenchment in the public Departments compels me to deprive my Government of his services.

Seymour would later come to regret the wording of this dispatch. Philip recorded in his memoir that he had been told his "services would be dispensed with in three months' time." Realizing he could not fight the matter:

I merely wrote a civil note requesting that my services might be dispensed with at once. In reply, I was told that my request to resign my appointment would be granted, and that I should be given 3 months' salary and the passage for my wife and self would be paid to England. In a week's time, we started via Panama and New York for England.

A later letter from Seymour recorded that Hankin's severance package "from the impoverished funds of the Colony [was] £51 11/- as compensation for loss of office and £165 for passages for wife and family to England."

The morning before they sailed, December 13, 1866, the *British Colonist* carried a brief notice of Hankin's departure:

[He] will be succeeded by Mr. Brew, or Capt. Pritchard of New Westminster. Mr. Hankin has proved an efficient and honest officer.

CHAPTER 20
Colonial Secretary in Belize

On Philip Hankin's arrival in London in January 1867, he presented Governor Frederick Seymour's supportive dispatch to the officials at the Colonial Office. They were sympathetic to his situation. One of them commented, he "may very probably be a fit candidate for any similar appointment which may fall vacant." Such comments, added to incoming dispatches, were termed "minutes." Another added, "The Union came very hard on such cases." Once again, Hankin's financial situation was dire. He was down to a single £5 note. Initially, he and his wife booked into the Great Western Hotel for two nights while he looked up some contacts. Fortunately, George Reay, the brother of his father's second wife, "was exceedingly kind and invited us to stay with them" in their commodious house nearby.

He also called upon Arthur Edward Kennedy, who was still in London and preparing to take up a new position as governor of Sierra Leone in West Africa. Kennedy invited him to come to the Colonial Office, where he would present him to the Duke of Buckingham. He did so, generously praising Hankin's work. After Kennedy left them alone, the duke questioned Hankin for about ten minutes and concluded by assuring him he would hear back in a few days and that "he might be able to offer me some employment."

His Grace the third Duke of Buckingham and Chandos, orator and statesman.

The Duke and Duchess of Buckingham

Richard Plantagenet Campbell Temple-Nugent-Brydges-Chandos-Grenville, third Duke of Buckingham and Chandos (plus several other subsidiary, hereditary titles) was a British soldier, politician, and administrator born in 1823.

After attending Eton and Christ Church College, Oxford, he joined his local yeomanry regiment, rising to the rank of honorary colonel. Entering politics in 1846, he was a loyal member of the Conservative party, and friend and subordinate to Benjamin Disraeli.

In 1857, his father, the second duke, was declared bankrupt, so Richard resigned his seat in Parliament. They managed to keep the stately home by selling off much of the estate and household treasures. Four years later, on his father's death, Richard became

The south facade of Stowe House, circa 1880. Residence of the Dukes of Buckingham and Chandos.

the third duke and entered the House of Lords, gaining a reputation as a skilled orator and statesman. He chaired the executive committee for the Great Exhibition of 1862. In 1866, appointed Lord President of the Council, he became concerned with foreign and colonial affairs. He then became the secretary of state for the colonies.

He married Caroline Harvey, daughter of the sheriff of Buckinghamshire, in 1851, and they had three daughters, Lady Mary, Lady Anne, and Lady Caroline Grenville.

The family's primary residence was the grand mansion, Stowe House. Their London home was Chandos House in Cavendish Square. Both of these were designed by Robert Adam.

Mrs. Isabel Hankin. Date and location of portrait uncertain.

An invitation to return to the Colonial Office soon arrived, and officials showed Hankin to the duke's room. He wrote in his memoir:

> *His Grace said he could offer me the Colonial Secretaryship at Belize, British Honduras. The salary would be £600. The previous holder of that office, Mr. G.C.B. Matthew,*[1] *had just died of yellow fever, so his successor would need to leave England as soon as possible. . . . I responded, 'with many thanks to your Grace, I accept the appointment with much pleasure, and I can be ready to start at four o'clock tomorrow morning!' The duke smiled and said, 'It will be soon enough if you go by the next steamer to Havana. From there you will find some vessel to get you to Belize.'*

The duke then invited the Hankins to dine at Chandos House, his London residence, where he presented them to the duchess, Caroline, and her three daughters, Mary, Anne, and Caroline, the Ladies Grenville. "They were all most kind and charming in every way and made us feel quite at home." A week later, the couple boarded a steamship of the West India Line, bound for Havana in Cuba. During his brief stay in Britain, Hankin had not tried to introduce his wife to his father. Nor does he seem to have contacted his old mentor, Captain George Henry Richards, RN. A few weeks after their having left Victoria, Isabel's sister, Jessie, noted in her diary that Isabel had not been well and that a "sea voyage would restore her to health."

The journey lasted two weeks, including a brief call into the island of St. Thomas. Here, Isabel contracted yellow fever[2] and became seriously ill. The newlywed couple stayed for three days in a hotel in Havana. The British consul directed Hankin to a local doctor with much experience in this disease. The doctor's skill prevailed, and he advised a period of convalescence on the far side of the island, where the air was fresher and cooler. There, they spent the next six weeks.

From Cuba they made a complicated and disagreeable journey by train, small cattle boat, and, finally, by an even smaller schooner. They crossed the Gulf of Honduras, battened down for twenty-four hours in a tiny, hot, stinking cabin during a tropical storm, and finally landed in Belize Town, the capital of the new colony of British Honduras.

*

On arrival, Hankin presented himself to the lieutenant governor, John Gardiner Austin,[3] and explained why they had been delayed in Cuba. Mrs. Austin and their two daughters were "a charming family, received me most kindly." Another officer, Mr. Graham, the treasurer, invited the Hankins to stay with him and his wife until they could find their own accommodation. The only place available was owned by a local lady, Mrs. Hume. The house was not very comfortable, but the rent was only $6 a month, and it was about a ten-minute walk from Hankin's office. A broad ladder, called a staircase, with about thirty steps, led up to the front door. There were no shutters or blinds, but Mrs. Hume assured them she had ordered shutters from New Orleans. The beating sun was a problem, but the Hankins hung an old curtain to provide some relief.

They soon discovered that a goat, a turkey, and some chickens were frequent invaders into the house, eating any food left out. Hankin found the climate, while hot and enervating, reasonably healthy, apart from occasional epidemics of yellow fever and cholera. Everyone slept under

Belize Town, capital of British Honduras. An inset to Tallis's map of Central America, 1851.

British Honduras

British Honduras, renamed Belize in 1973, is a nation on the Caribbean coast of Central America. Forming the southeastern corner of the Yucatán Peninsula, it has a land area approximately three-quarters that of Vancouver Island, half of which is mountainous; the rest is swampy, lowland plain. The extent of its coral reef is second only to Australia's Great Barrier Reef.

Dense, tropical hardwood forest once covered much of the interior. For three thousand years, from 1800 BCE to 1200 CE, this area formed part of the Mayan civilization. For centuries following European contact in the early years of the sixteenth century, it was a rambunctious cauldron of pirates, buccaneers, renegades, and survivors of shipwrecks, with the settlers, mestizos, creoles, and Indigenous descendants of the Maya all in conflict. "Baymen," or freelance loggers, and slave-owning barons exploited the rich forest resources. The lowlands were later cleared for vast sugar plantations, operated with imported African enslaved people and Mayan bonded labour.

The overall character of the population became far closer to that of the Caribbean than the rest of Central America, with an English-based creole as their primary language. Independent since 1981, Belize is a member of the Commonwealth, with King Charles III as ceremonial head of state. Currently, it is a tourist destination due to the vibrant coral reef.

mosquito nets, but tiny sandflies could squeeze through the mesh and inflict painful bites.

Not long after the Hankins' arrival, there came a major uprising in the north. A band of Guatemalan Maya had raided the mahogany camps, taking hostage several of the loggers and demanding ransoms and "protection money." Governor Austin sent a small detachment of the troops stationed in the colony to restore order. Outnumbered by the invaders, they retreated ignominiously, losing several horses and mules in the rout.

When the news reached Belize Town, the government declared martial law, which added to the general sense of agitation. The authorities in Jamaica sent reinforcements under a Colonel Harley. He overcame the few remaining invaders and recaptured the horses and mules, but found that the raiders had put villages and plantations to the torch. The populations had vanished. There were also fears that wealthy "filibusters" from the southern United States intended to take over the country and introduce slavery. The morale of the colony's settlers was extremely low, and the economy was in ruins.

Hankin did not record these incidents in his memoir. A series of short, anonymous bulletins in Victoria's *British Colonist*, however, did report them. The series had begun in early March 1866, with a full-column comparison between the two colonies, pointing out the similarities, apparently written by someone with knowledge of both places, most likely G.C.B. Matthew. It is doubtful if that first article attracted Hankin's attention, since it predated his involvement with the Central American colony and problems closer to home fully occupied his attention.

*

Back in Victoria, Jessie recorded in her diary that, in mid-September, another of Philip's brothers, whom she called Charlie, had been in town for ten days. She noted:

> *I like him better than Philip & I am sorry he has gone away, for I should have liked to learn more of him. We went for a ride of thirty miles [forty-eight kilometres] to Saanich with Graham & Mary Skinner. I enjoyed it very much, though I was very tired yesterday.*

By 1867, Charles Hankin was a significant figure in Cariboo gold mining, with interests in several syndicates. After their outing to Saanich, Charles returned to work and was not mentioned in Jessie's diary again.

Frequently noted, however, was the youngest of the Hankin brothers, Graham. He was clearly a close friend of the Nagle family, especially Jessie. She recounted their many outings as a group, and recorded the slow, sad deterioration in his health. In late November 1868, Jessie noted:

> *[Graham] was very ill with a liver complaint and inflammation of the lungs. Mama has been taking care of him. I went with Eddie to see him and take him something to eat. I'm almost afraid he won't be able to dine with us on Christmas day.*

Except for a few weeks as a temporary clerk in the law firm of Drake and Jackson, Graham does not appear to have had a job. He lived, presumably, on limited savings or perhaps revenue from his brief spell at Barkerville. Another possibility is that Charles provided ongoing support. Whatever their source, his funds were sufficient for him to travel to the Sandwich Islands and later to San Francisco, seeking healthier climes during the winter months. As he left for the second trip, he told the Nagles that he did not expect to return to Victoria, but Jessie noted she thought he would.

*

After the Hankins had been in British Honduras a few months, London recalled Lieutenant Governor Austin to England. He had sold a large piece of local real estate to an American syndicate, to the Colonial Office's disapproval. They reassigned him as colonial secretary in Hong Kong. Until a new governor could be installed, Hankin became administrator of the colony. Isabel continued to suffer the after-effects of her fever, or perhaps a recurrence of an earlier ailment. The local doctor advised that she return to Britain for further recuperation. She could travel with the Austin family, and a Royal Navy warship conveyed them all to Jamaica, where they boarded a passenger liner.

The memoir makes no mention of what provision Hankin made for Isabel's time in England—financial, accommodation, doctors' bills, general caregiving, an allowance for clothes, et cetera. She knew no one there apart from those she had met in the brief time between arriving from

Victoria and leaving for the Caribbean. These were the Reays, in whose house on Westbourne Terrace they had stayed, and the Buckinghams. The Kennedys had already left for West Africa for him to take up his new position as governor of Sierra Leone. Most probably, she would have returned to the Reays. From hints in letters from Susan and Jessie, the duchess learned of Isabel's return and occasionally invited her to stay at Stowe House. The Hankins' separation would last for the next eighteen months, until Philip returned from British Honduras.

Sir James Robert Longden replaced Austin. He had been governor of Dominica and, before that, president of the Virgin Islands, making him a seasoned Caribbean administrator. Hankin found his wife, Alice, who had been born in another of the islands, St. Kitts, to be "charming, a great addition to our small society." Hankin resumed his duties as colonial secretary, controller of customs, and clerk to the council.

*

Soon after the changeover of lieutenant governors, Hankin, now unaccompanied, gave his first formal dinner party and Lady Alice "graced it with her presence." As related in the memoir, the Hankin household had just a single servant, "Miss Jiner," a cook and housekeeper, the daughter of a Belizean mother and a long-departed British sergeant. Hankin's planned menu for the dinner included tinned soup, a tin of cold salmon, and a large roast turkey. Unfortunately, Hankin had overestimated Miss Jiner's culinary abilities. As soon as the guest of honour arrived, they sat down for the first courses. He wrote:

> *Then there was an awful pause for about ten minutes. Feeling very nervous, I tried to keep the conversation going, then called out in as gentle a voice as I could assume 'Miss Jiner, is the turkey not ready?' She popped from behind a screen and called out, 'I no go bodder wid de turkey. I trow him ober de warl!!'*

Happily, the guests, including her ladyship, took the situation well, laughing it off and claiming they were not in the least hungry. Hankin's only remedy was to tell Miss Jiner to open two cases of sardines, make some thin slices of bread and butter, and to pour more champagne, "which fortunately was very good. The Colonial Secretary's first official dinner party is not forgotten to this day."

*

Susan learned from one of Isabel's letters, written around mid-April 1868, that the duke had enquired if she thought Philip would accept the post of colonial secretary in Sierra Leone. Isabel, aware of Philip's fervent wish to leave British Honduras, accepted on his behalf. The new appointment would have to wait, however, until his replacement could arrive. According to the memoir, the duke had informed him of Kennedy's request for Hankin to join him in Africa and offered him the post at a salary of £700, a £100 increase. Hankin accepted immediately, understanding the need to await his replacement. In mid-July, a Colonel Hunt arrived. He had previously served as private secretary to Governor Austin. After a brief handover, Hankin could begin his return journey to England.

He chose a novel route. He first took a small steamer to New Orleans, where he caught "a larger and more comfortable boat up the Mississippi River." It was one of the immense sternwheelers famously plying the river in that era. For six days, he enjoyed the comforts of a stateroom and the elegant dining room. Each night, the boat would tie up to the riverbank, allowing the passengers to enjoy dinner and dancing to the band aboard.

At one of those occasions, "a remarkably pretty girl," who danced well, caught Hankin's eye. Another passenger introduced them, and Hankin requested

> *the pleasure of the next waltz. She looked at me from head to foot and replied 'Well, Sir, you may dance the square dances right nice, but I guess you are getting pretty fleshy for the round ones!!' I couldn't help laughing, however we had one or two dances together, when she said to me 'Well, Captain, you are a real elegant dancer and I've just had the tallest time with you, aboard this boat, that ever a Yankee girl had,' which I suppose was meant as a great compliment.*

Philip Hankin was then into his thirty-fourth year and, despite a thickening girth and receding hairline, had clearly not lost his prowess on the dance floor nor his personal charm.

He disembarked at Memphis, then boarded a train to New York, where he took passage aboard a transatlantic liner. By that year, with the development of sleek, steel-hulled, coal-fired, screw-driven vessels,

The Mississippi sternwheeler John Streckfus.

the journey time to Southampton was down to eight days. He arrived in London in early October to learn that Isabel had been a guest at Stowe for a month. The duke invited him to join her for a week before he was due to take up the Sierra Leone post. The plan was for Isabel to remain in England for the first year, since she had still not fully recovered. The climate of the West African coast, the notorious "White Man's Grave," was also rife with tropical diseases.

He had not been at Stowe more than a few days when the duke advised him that a vacancy had just opened in Victoria. Governor Seymour had requested that someone take the position of colonial secretary, since the incumbent was in only an acting capacity. The duke offered the position to Hankin, at an annual salary of £800, a further increase of £100 over the rate for Sierra Leone. He noted in the memoir, "This was, of course, splendid, and most thankfully accepted." Isabel, too, welcomed the chance to see her family.

Before leaving, Hankin made an excursion to Regent Street in London, perhaps to visit his tailor, and bumped into a familiar figure from Victoria, Alfred Waddington. He was an entrepreneur, promoter, and politician, best known for his ill-fated scheme to build a road to the Cariboo from Bute Inlet. It had proved an impossibility because a canyon and near-vertical waterfall blocked the route. The construction crew had become embroiled in a battle with the resident Indigenous peoples, triggering the notorious Chilcotin War. Waddington was in London attempting to raise support and finance for a railway through the same route. He learned Hankin was a guest at Stowe and appointed colonial secretary in Victoria. He reported this news in a letter to George Pearkes, a lawyer and an associate, "as I suppose you know."

In less than a week, on November 4, 1868, the Hankins boarded a liner for New York, thence to Panama, where the trans-isthmus railway had just been completed. From there, via San Francisco, they headed once more for Victoria.

CHAPTER 21
A Controversial Appointment

Philip Hankin was probably unaware of the drama behind his appointment, or the impending furor it would provoke. While he and Isabel had maintained a regular correspondence with members of the Nagle family, the latter would not have been privy to the political undercurrents.

It all began with Arthur Birch, Governor Frederick Seymour's colonial secretary, resigning to return to Britain. Initially, he had been a junior clerk in the Colonial Office in London, seconded to the new colony of British Columbia. He had given Seymour loyal service over the previous three years. The governor, hoping to have Birch return, requested that the Colonial Office in London grant him six months' paid leave of absence instead. The officials under the Duke of Buckingham and Chandos, the secretary for the colonies, rejected this arrangement. On July 15, 1867, Birch left, returning to London with no loss of seniority.

Within the administration of the newly united colonies, Seymour had promised William Young the new position of chief magistrate of Vancouver Island, and told him that if and when Birch left, Seymour would replace him as colonial secretary. Young's desire to preserve his heavy investment in a home in Victoria complicated his position. He could not afford a second home in New Westminster, needed if he were to become colonial secretary. The Legislative Assembly's vote to move the provincial capital from New Westminster back to Victoria eliminated this difficulty.

Young was highly qualified, having been a paymaster in the Royal Navy, twice serving as the chief administrator and accountant for an admiral commanding a large fleet, including during warfare. The navy had then seconded him to the Foreign Office, having nominated him as secretary for the British delegation to the 49th Parallel Joint Boundary Commission. Soon after he had arrived, Young had been assigned to Governor James Douglas to act as his colonial secretary, first for Vancouver Island, then for the new colony of British Columbia as well. He had continued serving under Governor Arthur Edward Kennedy, but just for Vancouver Island. In all these roles, he had performed with distinction. By this time, Young had served in this part of the world for almost ten years, apart from one well-deserved long leave home.

Seymour, however, nursed reservations about Young's loyalty. Members of the faction surrounding Seymour at New Westminster, particularly Birch, had influenced his views. This group was the rival to their counterparts in Victoria. Despite his initial concern, after Young had been in the position for three months, Seymour confirmed to London that he was to continue in the role.

Without question, Young was a member of the highest social and governmental circles in Victoria. He had married Douglas's niece, Cecilia, and was by now a close confidant to the former governor. Seymour's doubts over Young concerned any bias that favoured the interests of his Victoria colleagues over those from across the Strait of Georgia. Would he be able to act professionally and impartially? Young was dissatisfied with his salary and the fact that he was without the benefits of a permanent position. However, he continued to perform his duties conscientiously until the situation was resolved. Buckingham had previously requested a report from Seymour about Young. The duke expected to confirm the appointment to colonial secretary, which would mean that Young would receive the full salary from the date he took over from Birch.

A major aspect of the rivalry between New Westminster and Victoria concerned which of them should be the capital. Seymour strongly favoured New Westminster, but in the spring of 1867, he put it to a vote by the new Legislative Assembly. The pro-Victoria faction, although in the minority, won the vote by thirteen to six, through some devious pranks played on an inebriated Captain William Franklyn, the member for Nanaimo. Without ratifying the vote, the annoyed Seymour consulted with London, who left the matter up to local decision. In the second session a year later, he put the same question to the vote. Again, Victoria

William Alexander George Young, bearded, seated on the ground at left, with his wife, seated to his left, children, and visitors.

prevailed. On May 25, 1868, London endorsed the decision. Victoria was now, officially, the capital of British Columbia. Seymour and the New Westminster faction were not pleased.

One immediate result was that property prices in the Royal City plummeted dramatically. Members of the Assembly and government officers, having invested in homes there, found themselves destitute and needing accommodation in the new capital. Through Seymour, they petitioned London for compensation, to no avail. Since it had been a local decision, it would need to be resolved locally. The local coffers were bare and credit unobtainable. Exacerbating the difficulties were two major fires: first at Barkerville, then followed by the whole of Government Street, Victoria's commercial centre, going up in flames. Both resulted in huge financial losses. London declined Seymour's application for a further loan of £50,000, and his request annoyed the officials.

Under these stresses and not thinking as clearly as he had previously, Seymour wrongly suspected Young of having influenced the two votes for Victoria. On June 5, he sent a dispatch to London:

> *I would venture to request that Your Grace will not appoint Mr. Young to the permanent office of Colonial Secretary without some further communication from me. I find Mr. Young clever and energetic, but he is so mixed up in the affairs of Victoria that I cannot give him the entire confidence which a Governor should repose in his Colonial Secretary.*

Frederick Seymour with a kitten.

This letter arrived in London on July 16 and made its way through the chain of officials to Buckingham, eight days later.

The duke's senior official had appended a minute to the incoming dispatch: "Your Grace should fill [the position] by direct appt." The duke agreed and directed a reply: "In reliance upon your opinion, I shall endeavour to select some other well-qualified person for the appointment of Colonial Secretary." The duke's response was dated July 28. Philip Hankin had just left Belize on his return to London, prior to taking up his new appointment in Sierra Leone. Buckingham's dispatch did not address what was to happen to Young.

That dispatch had arrived in Victoria by mid-November. Seymour realized there had been a miscommunication and hastened to reverse the decision. The mails being slow and unreliable, he added a line to a telegram:

> *Do not remove Young yet. . . . I am afraid I expressed myself too strongly. . . . After working for upwards of a year with [Young] I have been unable to find out the slightest unfaithfulness on his part, and I must certainly state that I find him clever, hardworking and useful. . . . The Legislative Session is approaching and it would*

be difficult for a man new to the Colony to conduct the business of Colonial Secretary.

It was now too late. By the time the message had arrived in London, Buckingham had already acted. On October 6, he wrote informing Seymour that he had "appointed Mr. Philip Hankin, RN, Colonial Secretary of Sierra Leone, to be Colonial Secretary of British Columbia at a salary of £800 a year." A week later, he followed it up by giving Hankin's departure date as November 4. A week after that, he enclosed the Queen's Warrant for Hankin "in the room of Mr. A.N. Birch." The decision had been made. The duke had earlier responded brusquely to Seymour's telegraph, "It is not possible for me to interfere. . . . Lieut. Hankin having left this country for British Columbia on 4th November, I have no opportunity of delaying his arrival."

While Hankin was still at sea, on his way to Victoria, Seymour made one last attempt to impede the changeover. He sent a dispatch pointing out that the legislative session was in progress. Inducting a new presiding member of the legislature, with no handover, would seriously threaten the work already accomplished, and that still had to be covered. Buckingham minuted, "Which I suppose means he will not induct him until the legislative business is over."

*

Rumours of London's impending removal of Young and his subsequent replacement by Hankin arrived in Victoria in mid-November. Young was among the first to hear them. He immediately queried Seymour on their truth and about the implications for his own future. The governor responded that the rumours "were not unfounded" but ducked Young's personal question. On November 26 Young wrote a temperate, yet firmly worded, twenty-two-page formal letter to Seymour. In it he set out, with dates and documentary citations, his many-faceted claim to the post, or an equivalent or superior new position. He concluded with the request that Seymour "forward it to the Secretary of State [Buckingham] and in your and his hands I leave it with abiding faith in the perfect justice of the issue."

Seymour did not respond to Young's letter but attached it to his next dispatch to London. That dispatch, dated three days after the letter, was in two parts: first, a vitriolic, personal deprecation of Hankin, followed by an endorsement of Young's case. The attack on Hankin's character and history appears to show Seymour's snobbery. Taken at face value, it seems contrary to his previously stated reasons for not including Hankin in his list of officers for the united colony. His earlier letter of reference had read: "My own more limited knowledge of him leads me to regret that the absolute necessity for retrenchment in the Public dep^{ts}. compels me to deprive my Gov^{t}. of his services." But Seymour's wording might also be read as a diplomatic rejection. He described Hankin, on his return from Barkerville, cruelly but not without justification as "a dead broke miner." He also noted, again with accuracy, that his police employment had brought him into contact with the lowest classes of the community.

Seymour added, "He has married into a family with which it would not be pleasant for some ladies to associate. He is personally extremely unpopular." All these claims, while containing elements of truth, were questionable reasons for disqualification for the post. The Nagle family were of the respectable, churchgoing middle class. While they were not intimate with the topmost echelon of Victoria's society, mainly centred around Douglas and his family—as was Young—the Nagles socialized with such prominent families as the Stamps and the Creases.

As for Hankin's personal popularity, a vociferous few would, no doubt, object to his appointment. These fell into three groups: those who had opposed the two previous governors and the whole concept of colonial rule; the publicans, hoteliers, and shady traders who had suffered under his and Kennedy's stricter application of the law; and the supporters of Young, opposed to unjust treatment of him.

Seymour's revised opinion about Young clearly contradicted his earlier concerns, which had centred around his reliability and independence from influences by Victoria's old elite. He agreed with Young's claim that he had been "assured of the Colonial Secretaryship or a situation of equal value," adding that, "I confidently state that in him you will possess a valuable public Servant . . . but I imagine that he would be still more useful in a new scene of action where he would start free from all prejudices and partialities."

The Colonial Service officers in London minuted their thoughts on Seymour's latest dispatch as it circulated. One felt that "any annoyance or difficulty that may fall to the lot of [Seymour] he most fully deserves." Another noted the support for Hankin from such authorities as "Captain

Richards, Mr. Kennedy, Admiral Denman, and Judge Needham,[1] if the testimonials are true, Lt. Hankin is just the man for the place." A third official commented, "Revolting from the consequences of [Seymour's] own act, he tries to get out of them by depreciating Lt. Hankin against whom, as far as I can see, there are no real & personal grounds of complaint." Yet another observed that a man whom Seymour "somewhat unnecessarily calls a 'dead broke' miner, really shews little else than enterprise." The general view was that they send "a snubbing letter" to Seymour and that they should wait and see how well Hankin's appointment worked out.

As for Young, the consensus was that his case was strong, and that "we are bound to place [him] in as good a position as that which he has been unfairly deprived."

A major problem, raised by Seymour, was the salary of the colonial secretary. Established practice decreed that, from a newly appointed officer's departure from England, he would receive half the regulated salary until he had presented his credentials to the governor, whereupon he would go on full salary. The outgoing officer would go on half salary as soon as his replacement's embarkation until his own arrival in London and reassignment to a new post. In this special case, the officials proposed Young remain on full salary until Hankin took over. The senior official, Undersecretary Sir Frederic Rogers, minuted, "[Seymour] has made the difficulty & he sh^{d}. be left to get out of it." Buckingham added, "I agree with FR."

*

All these deliberations took until early May 1869. In the meantime, the predicted uproar in the Victoria press grew, starting in late November with the news of the replacement decision. The Nagle family received the news by letter from Isabel and were, naturally, delighted, but concerned about the hostile reception Philip might meet. As they had feared, it was immediate. The *British Colonist,* on November 23, 1868, carried three items related to the news about Hankin. The first was a brief report:

> *Mr. P. Hankin, formerly Superintendent of Police, of this city, has been gazetted Colonial Secretary of British Columbia vice Birch.*

To which the editor added: "What next? And next?" The second item occupied three column inches in the editorial section, decrying the appointment as

> *Another evidence of how little the feelings of the Colonists are taken into consideration by the Colonial Government. . . . The whole system of Government with which we are favored [is] like a left-handed blessing. . . . [As for Hankin himself,] as the head of our Police-force he proved certainly much more ornamental than useful. . . . His manner was extremely arrogant and overbearing to all who approached. . . . We congratulate Governor Seymour upon the able and amiable acquisition to his staff.*

This concluding remark was, of course, sarcastic. The third was a letter to the editor written by "A.DeC.," that perennial gadfly to the governing authority, Amor De Cosmos, journalist, newspaper owner, and fiery politician. He wrote, tongue firmly in cheek:

> *The unexpected announcement on Saturday has given rise to considerable discussion. Now, sir, I am one of those who consider the new appointment as a fortunate circumstance for the Colony, as it will bring very forcibly under public notice how little Mr. Young has done during the ten years that he has been at the head of the Executive Council. . . . While awaiting the speedy inauguration of self-government, give Mr. Hankin an opportunity to prove whether he has the capacity and statesmanlike qualities . . . before he is condemned; for at best, his term of service will be but brief under the present regime.*

De Cosmos, a democrat, had long opposed the rule by what he called the "company-family compact" of the HBC and Douglas, and by the Colonial Service.

The next day, November 24, the discussion continued in three letters to the editor, expressing differing opinions. The first, responding to De Cosmos's letter of the previous day, strongly supported the retention of Young:

> *I am one who considers the new appointment a very unfortunate one for the Colony—nay more, the greatest insult yet offered to this Colony by the Government, perhaps unwittingly. . . .*

No one, as far as I know, has the smallest confidence in Philip Hankin's ability, but all assert him to be an unfit man, to say the least. . . . It would be as well to get up a petition to the Governor, urging him not to appoint Mr. Hankin until His Excellency has communicated with the Home Government, and urge upon the Government the desirability nay, necessity, of cancelling the appointment.

The letter was signed just "H." One possible writer could be Dr. John Sebastian Helmcken, a former HBC physician and politician who was married to one of Douglas's daughters and therefore a member of the exclusive clique.

The second letter, signed by "FAIR PLAY," supported Philip, noting that the editorial had failed to acknowledge that

Mr. Hankin has served for the last eighteen months as Colonial Secretary of British Honduras, and that as late as the 1st of October last, he was gazetted Colonial Secretary for Her Majesty's settlement of Sierra Leone. May we not presume, from his appointment, that he has given satisfaction at the Colonial Office in England to those who were in a position to form an opinion about him? . . . Mr. Hankin does not owe his appointment to influential relations or connections, but simply to his own personal merit and to those friends his merit has won for him, and your comments on his appointment appear hardly fair.

The third letter, signed by "AN OLD COLONIST," also responded to "A.DeC.", accusing him of wanting to keep himself prominently before the public. The writer praised Young's "tried and faithful service" in the hour of the province's greatest need. He called for

a very respectful [public] remonstrance against the wrong done to this Colony, to say nothing of that to Mr. Young himself unless indeed a position far in advance to that which he now holds should be offered to him. . . . Citizens of Victoria, make yourselves heard in a constitutional manner, and believe, it will not be in vain.

The following day, the editor of the *British Colonist*, Leonard McClure, continued to attack Hankin. He posted a full-column, ranting editorial, replete with bombastic statements supported by "almost unanimous opinion," "all the public of Vancouver Island," and "everyone," but devoid of substantive evidence. He derided "FAIR PLAY" for his views and denigrated Hankin's experience in British Honduras as "the government of Indians, half-bred Spaniards and the descendants of runaway negro slaves." He pronounced Hankin's role in charge of the police force as "arrogant in his demeanor towards citizens, tyrannical towards his inferior officers, and publicaly [*sic*] insulting in his intercourse with the magistrates; his inefficiency as a detector of crime was notorious." All this vitriol was in marked contrast to the editor's own words upon Philip's return to England, just two years earlier: "Mr. Hankin has proved an efficient and honest officer."

On November 26, another letter writer, signing himself "FAIR PLAY IS A JEWEL," chimed in with, "A torrent of indignation has been poured by a few individuals on the injustice of the Imperial Government in appointing Mr. Hankin as Colonial Secretary, over the head of Mr. Young." The writer also wanted to "denounce the wrong done to one of the most able, energetic and popular men the Government and the public have ever had." He was referring, of course, to Young.

Another letter on the same day, signed "JUSTICE," pointed out that Young had voted for the order of 1867 that

> *wiped [Vancouver Island] out of existence . . . [and] enabled the Governor of the Mainland to dispense with the services of the Island officials only . . . this nefarious act, by reason of which many other deserving officials besides Mr. Hankin were deprived of their vested rights. By the recent appointment, I am glad to see that Mr. Hankin did not at the same time lose his remedy.*

In early December, Sir James Douglas wrote to his daughter Jane about the happenings in Victoria and the impending developments around the position of colonial secretary:

> *Is Young to be recalled and sent elsewhere to make room for a younger [by nine years] and certainly less experienced man? Young is in a great way and will possibly have to leave the Colony. The Governor is very sore about the appointment, protesting it was made without his concurrence or even being*

consulted about it. Be that as it may, it was certainly in his powers to have prevented it. The Nagles, I am told, are in high feather about Hankin's appointment, though I do not see that it [would] do them much good.

This letter reveals Douglas was unaware of Seymour's dispatches expressing reservations about Young's independence from his own clique. The Nagles' reported pleasure at the news was probably more related to having Isabel back among them than any preferences Philip's position might bring them. In fact, the Nagle family, having followed the comments in the press, were most concerned at the probably hostile reception that awaited the couple. Jessie recorded:

The appointment has caused a great excitement, and many are very much against him. He will have a great deal of trouble at first with officials, as well as the townspeople.

Late in the evening of December 31, during a fierce southeasterly gale, the packet boat *Active* coming from Portland had to be diverted from entering Victoria Harbour as scheduled and land at Esquimalt. That same night, an American bark, *Delaware*, ran aground near Fisgard Light as it ran for cover in Esquimalt. Disembarking for his fourth arrival on this coast was Philip Hankin, accompanied by his wife, Isabel.

CHAPTER 22

In Limbo

Philip and Isabel Hankin landed at Esquimalt late on New Year's Eve, 1868, in appalling weather. It provided a stormy portent to the reception Philip would face from his new boss, fellow officers of the government, the press, and the populace. Exacerbating the dreadful conditions was a total absence of transportation to Victoria. A Grand Ball was in full swing at Government House, and all carriages were busy conveying participants to and from the festivities. Passengers from *Active*, including children, faced an arduous hike, with their luggage, in the dark, over ten miles (sixteen kilometres) of muddy track to the town.

Fortunately, the storm abated. There were several hotels and roadhouses on their route—the Steamboat Exchange, the Coach and Horses, and another aptly called Halfway House—where some of them might have found shelter for the night. Susan Nagle's diary recorded that the Hankins walked as far as the "first bridge" at Rock Bay before meeting a carriage. If they walked, they would have left any heavy trunks and cases with a cartage company to bring to them the next day.

In Victoria, they booked into the St. Nicholas hotel. Philip, by this time, knew of the hostile reception awaiting him. He fully expected to be ordered back to Britain forthwith, and so did not want to settle in anywhere before his future became clearer. He also needed to be in the centre of town to meet Governor Frederick Seymour to present his credentials. Susan and Jessie Nagle met the arrivals the following day. Susan's diary recorded, "Isabel is looking as well as can be expected after her long voyage. She has grown I'm sure a couple of inches since leaving here. Jessie & myself appear such mites beside her & even Philip looks smaller." Jessie merely noted, "Isabel & Philip arrived on the 31st both looking very well." The next day, Sunday, the Hankins attended morning service at their familiar church of St. John the Divine before joining the Nagle family for lunch.

Despite Hankin sending immediate word of his arrival to Seymour, they did not meet until January 6, when Seymour invited him and Isabel to dinner at Government House. Even then, the governor did not accept the credentials but hinted that he was still in discussion with London about the appointment. Philip's memoir recorded that Seymour later offered him the position of chief commissioner of lands and works. Sensibly recognizing his complete lack of qualification for such a technical role, he declined. The incumbent, Joseph Trutch, an engineer and surveyor, was accused of a conflict of interest. He partly owned a highly profitable toll bridge over the Fraser Canyon on the wagon road to the Cariboo.

The Legislative Assembly comprised the council or cabinet of senior officials, ex officio, and representatives, both appointed and elected, from centres of population, or districts, on Vancouver Island and the mainland. They were all men, owners of property, of European ethnicity, and professing primary allegiance to the British Crown. Women, Indigenous people, Asians, and non-loyalists were not accepted as representatives or MLAs. The key role of the colonial secretary was as the presiding member, or speaker, of the Assembly. Between Young and Hankin, the former was, by far, the more experienced negotiator. Seymour thus faced a double dilemma: if he failed to accept the decision made by the Colonial Office, he would be guilty of insubordination. He had, however, the pressing need to have his legislative agenda, including some crucial financial bills, negotiated through the Assembly.

Were he instead to obey orders and immediately replace Young with Hankin, getting his agenda passed would be more difficult, if not impossible. By keeping Young's services for the session, but reducing his salary by half, he must have expected Young's motivation to weaken. Seymour's already straitened budget could not afford two full salaries for a colonial secretary. As would soon come to light, his health was not good enough to combat London, nor to resolve the apparently insoluble conundrum locally. An increasing dependence on alcohol also impaired his judgement and drive.

Even though he had received, in mid-January, the Duke of Buckingham's order to appoint Hankin, Seymour still attempted a compromise. He would pay Hankin his full salary, effective from his arrival, but stall on accepting his credentials. He would maintain Young, also at full salary, for the session, and hope London would reverse their decision. They could allow Young to remain as colonial secretary and reassign Hankin elsewhere. He gave no hint of this risky plan to Young, who was left to assume his letter pleading his case was now tacitly accepted, and the matter settled for good. Young gave his full efforts and skill in handling Seymour's agenda. His assumption and trust were to prove unjustified.

*

In hindsight, Seymour could have appointed Hankin commissioner for Indian Affairs. This would have both filled an urgent need and taken advantage of Hankin's knowledge of Indigenous languages and his experience in negotiating with local communities. His talents in this area were on record in the testimonials by Admiral Denman and by Seymour's predecessor, Arthur Edward Kennedy. No one else with such skills was available to Seymour. He was soon to regret the lack of such an officer, which caused him serious problems, even hastening his untimely death. There is no sign that Seymour knew of, or appreciated, this natural fit that would have resolved multiple difficulties. It is most probable that Hankin and London would have welcomed this resolution to the situation. Young, too, would have supported such an appointment, and with it, his own confirmation.

The Colonial Office was already considering a stern reproach of Seymour for his mishandling of an affair involving a lethal dispute between Indigenous groups on the northern coast. It began with a letter dated May 1868, from William Duncan, a British missionary who had arrived in 1857. He had established a community of converts among the Tsimshian people at Metlakatla at the latitude of Hecate Strait. The surveyor, Captain George Henry Richards, had suggested the sheltered location to Duncan in 1862.

Metlakatla mission and community. Watercolour by Lieutenant Porcher, RN.

Five years later, Seymour visited and admired the success Duncan had achieved. He sent a glowing report to London and received encouragement from Buckingham: "I read with much satisfaction." Duncan's latest letter, however, brought bad news. During a multi-group gathering on the lower Nass River one month earlier, long-standing grievances ignited, exacerbated by the presence of alcohol. Six local men were shot, five of whom died.

As their tradition required, reprisals ensued. The fury was such that it fell upon a canoe of four innocent converts from another mission, Kincolith, killing three and carrying off the fourth, a boy. Duncan feared that all-out war was imminent. It threatened the several Christian communities in the region. He wrote that it would be "fatal to the further spread of civilization." He pleaded with Seymour for an urgent demonstration of British justice. Seymour forwarded Duncan's letter to London with a cover note saying that Admiral Hastings[1] was currently in the area, aboard HMS *Sparrowhawk*.[2] "He will, I have no doubt, furnish assistance to Mr. Duncan." Seymour had earlier provided *Sparrowhawk* with an elderly ex-HBC man, George Blenkinsop, to act as interpreter, but the governor had no means of speedy communication with Hastings.

HMS Sparrowhawk, *a speedy, light warship.*

Officials in London minuted Seymour's dispatch as "most lamentable." They notified the Admiralty that Buckingham considered the matter to be "of great moment that [these] infant settlements of native Christians sh[d.] not be allowed to be destroyed." Hastings, unaware of the duke's policy on the question and uncertain of Seymour's wishes, hesitated in taking direct, forceful action.

In late July, Duncan wrote again to Seymour, reporting that *Sparrowhawk* had visited twice. Her captain, Edwin Augustus Porcher, "was not prepared to take any steps. . . . He looked on the matter simply as an Indian quarrel." Duncan, who was also a magistrate, was most disappointed. He had assembled a strong case against some perpetrators but needed the support of the navy to enforce the law. Seymour replied to Duncan that the naval ships, including Daniel Pender's HMS *Beaver*, had made the visits "without any instructions from me." He considered that the authority available to Duncan should have sufficed.

Seymour's dispatch to London, dated November 30, described developments around Metlakatla. His wording showed his attitude to the affair. He felt it "was almost entirely taken out of my hands." This caused great displeasure in the Colonial Office. By the time it arrived, the Earl of Granville had replaced the Duke of Buckingham as secretary of state for the colonies. This reflected the changeover in governments from Benjamin Disraeli to William Ewart Gladstone. Over the next two months, the dispatch circulated among the officials. They minuted their condemnation for Seymour's approach: "Anything but satisfactory"; "I cannot imagine Seymour not being able to find someone he could have trusted to accompany the *Sparrowhawk*"; "[he] treats the matter . . . in a very abrupt & unsatisfactory manner . . . I have seen but little in regard to the way of dealing with Indians."

They minuted comments on Blenkinsop's opinion that "missionaries were not to trouble themselves about the murder of Indians but to keep to 'their business' . . . and in this view of a missionary's duty, Mr. Seymour appears to me contemptuously to acquiesce." They contrasted this instance with the "stirring and expensive operation," referring to the reprisal action against the Ahousaht three years earlier. Although the latter incident was

> *in redress for injuries against European subjects of HM, whom I w^d. observe are not more entitled to rely on the gov^t . . . than those Indians who have forsaken their savage mode of life & placed themselves under what they suppose to be the protection of British Law.*

Granville sent this blistering reply to Seymour's dispatch in early March 1869. By the time it arrived in Victoria, other matters had moved on.

*

Seymour's risky stratagem of disobeying London's order to replace Young with Hankin paid off, at least initially. The Legislative Assembly proceeded smoothly with the agenda, debating and passing bills according to the governor's priorities. That they did so was because of Young's experience, skills, and motivation. On January 18, Seymour sent a telegram to London informing them that "there is an improvement in revenue. The Legislative Body is in session and that everything is tranquil." Sandford, the undersecretary, minuted, "Satisfactory. Clearly no Hankin revolution." Apparently and mistakenly, he assumed Seymour had appointed Hankin, as instructed.

Philip, frustrated over the uncertainty of his future, but for once well paid, accepted an invitation from Captain Edward Stamp to stay with him at his residence. Stamp was a wealthy entrepreneur, a close friend of Jeremiah Nagle and his family, and had known Hankin since the earliest days of his Alberni sawmill. Susan often referred to the house as "The Hill" in her diary. It was on Park Street, close to the Birdcages, the popular name for the legislative buildings.

William Alexander George Young, commander, RN (retired). A significant figure in the governance of the colony, an able administrator, and a member of James Douglas's extended family.

After one long editorial diatribe in early January, derogatory to Hankin and praising Young, the *British Colonist* eased up on its criticism. It had failed to reflect, it claimed, the generally favourable opinion about Hankin's character and personality. The subject of the editor's earlier ill will still enjoyed a wide circle of supportive friends in the community.

In mid-February, ex-governor Sir James Douglas mentioned Hankin and his unfortunate situation in another letter to his daughter:

> *Nothing has yet been done in Young's case—he still acts as Colonial Secretary—though Hankin has been here two months waiting to be sworn in. The poor Governor has got into a pretty mess and hardly knows what to do. He won't see Hankin, though the poor fellow is not to blame for taking a good appointment when it was offered.*

At about the same time, Daniel Pender, who had recently received promotion to staff commander, wrote privately to Richards: "Hankin not installed. Gov[r.] trying to get the appt cancelled."

Having stayed as guests of the Stamps for two weeks, Philip and Isabel rented the James Bay house of a Captain William Hales Franklyn, who had just received the post of civil commissioner in the dependency of the Seychelles in the Indian Ocean. Franklyn had only recently set up in business in Victoria as an auctioneer and real estate agent. After a life at sea as a master mariner in the merchant marine—as had been both Nagle and Stamp—he had retired to run a successful farm in Cedar, near Nanaimo. He had served as justice of the peace in that community since 1860 and was also the appointed MLA for Nanaimo.[3]

*

Hankin, perhaps as a relief from the uncertainties of his situation, began a new activity. He gave the first of a series of public readings at the Mechanics Literary Institute. The institute had started in Scotland during the 1830s and spread as a concept throughout Britain and the empire, arriving in Victoria in 1864. The goal was the general intellectual benefit of middle classes, achieved mainly through public lectures. Some speakers even illustrated their talks with slides projected by the splendid innovation the oxyhydrogen lantern. Other efforts included musical recitals, reading rooms with books and newspapers, a lending library, original poetry competitions, and debating societies. Philip's name was on the bill just three weeks after he arrived back for the grand opening of the institute's new premises.

As the last item before the interval, Hankin gave a dramatic reading, "a selection from Boz" by Charles Dickens. The *British Colonist*, in its review of the event, recorded:

> *The spacious hall was crowded with a large and intelligent audience [mentioning several prominent members of society]. Mr. P. Hankin's [contribution] was capitally rendered and gave universal satisfaction. The gentleman's imitative powers are fine, and he threw all the life and spirit into the selection that the author appears to have intended it should possess.*

Over the following weeks, he presented more of Dickens's works and epic poems by Sir Walter Scott and others.

In his memoir, Philip recalled his frame of mind during this period:

> *I had not asked for this appointment, but thought I should be very foolish to refuse a good appointment because, with some people, it was not popular. So, I said to myself, do your best, and live it down, which, after a time, I succeeded in doing.*

Fort Street North in Victoria. The two-storey building at left houses the Mechanics Literary Institute, a popular venue for lectures, recitals, and light entertainment.

After six weeks in limbo, Hankin wrote a personal letter to Buckingham, letting him know about the situation. By then, the Earl of Granville had replaced the duke as secretary of state, and so Buckingham passed Hankin's letter to the Colonial Office.

Susan blamed the poor mail service for the delay in confirming Philip's appointment:

The general opinion is that all the letters and despatches which have left England during the last two or three months are either destroy'd or are tumbling about the plains, owing to the trains being blocked up by the snow. It is very stupid of the people at New York sending the letters in the winter by that way instead of by steamer. We should then get our letters regularly.

Irregularities in the mail service were certainly a factor in the poor communication between Seymour and the Colonial Office.

*

At the close of the legislative session in mid-March, Seymour informed London:

I have carried all the bills to which I attached importance. . . . I found it indispensable to keep on Mr. Young as Acting Colonial

Secretary. We should never have got the Financial Bills through with Mr. Hankin as Presiding Member.

Granville responded, referring to the sentence about keeping Young, "I must refer you to my confidential Despatch of 19 April." That earlier dispatch, couched in a censorious tone, had stated:

I learn from private sources that Mr. Hankin had been six weeks in the Colony . . . but of this I have received no information from you, and I am left to conjecture whether the disastrous consequences foretold by you have arisen or are likely to arise. . . . I desire to know whether that course [appointing Hankin] has been taken and if not, what has been done, and with what result.

These dispatches from Granville crossed with one from Seymour, dated April 8:

Not having received any answer to my despatches [listed as dated between November 16 and December 12], I have determined to incur no longer the responsibility of keeping Lieutenant Hankin, RN out of the office of Colonial Secretary to which he was appointed by Royal Warrant. I have issued a Commission to him today and have sworn him into office.

London's only minute to this dispatch was "Ack[nowledge] receipt." By this time, the officials, including Granville and Buckingham, had exhausted their tolerance for Seymour's inconsistencies, poor judgement, and insubordination. His term as governor was due to expire, and they had already identified a replacement for him: Anthony Musgrave, who had been governor of Newfoundland since 1864.

*

Just before Philip learned that, at last, he was to be installed as colonial secretary, he and Isabel received an invitation to a social luncheon followed by dancing aboard HMS *Zealous*, the recently arrived flagship of Admiral Hastings.[4] The event seemed to confirm, in naval circles at least, that Philip was no longer considered a pariah. He still held the naval rank of lieutenant.

HMS Zealous, *the first ironclad warship to be based at Esquimalt.*

News had recently arrived that the Admiralty had ordered the base for Britain's Pacific fleet to be transferred from Esquimalt to Valparaiso in Chile. This would be a terrible blow for the social life of the community. Susan's diary recorded the news with dismay. She probably spoke for many Victorians when she added:

> *Everything seems to be conspiring against us in this poor little place, & there will be nothing for us but Confederation [with Canada] or joining the Yankees, equally disagreeable measures.*

This dilemma would become the single greatest topic of debate for the next two years. Fortunately, Hastings believed the strategic importance and vulnerability of this colony required the constant protection of *Zealous*, as well as *Sparrowhawk* and the smaller gunboats.

Hastings's primary concern was the threat of attack by the Fenian Brotherhood. This was an Irish-American movement seeking Irish independence by provoking conflict between Britain and the United States. Their strategy was to seize British Columbia and other colonies to trigger a war between the powers. There had been several alarms sent through diplomatic channels that Fenian forces were assembling in San Francisco. Local preparations were to put the militias at Victoria and New Westminster on standby, and position gunboats to protect both communities. Ships' captains vetted crew members for Fenian sympathizers. Hastings reasoned that these measures alone would not provide sufficient deterrence. A stronger show of force was essential. He would keep his primary ships based at Esquimalt.

*

A few weeks later, Susan noted in her diary:

> *I went for a pull [excursion in a rowing-boat] up the arm [the Gorge] on Saturday with the Hankins, Daniel Pender & a Mr. Harmon also on board the Beaver. He seems a very nice young fellow. D.P. is looking very old he has fallen off greatly in the last few years, the difference between him and Philip is very marked, altho' there is only two years' difference in their ages [Philip the junior], anyone would think there was ten. I can't help having a great regard for old Dan, nevertheless, seeing him always takes me back to old times.*

Pender had recently added a staff commander's third gold ring to his sleeve. Since his long detachment aboard *Beaver* was expected to be concluded shortly, the usual requirement to return to Britain for redeployment at the new rank was waived.

CHAPTER 23

Proving His Worth

During Philip Hankin's time in limbo, he and Governor Frederick Seymour became better acquainted. He described their relationship in his memoir: "Mr. Seymour was not very polite to me at first, but after a short time, we began to get along very well." The latter progressively understood that much of what he had read about the new arrival in the *British Colonist* and heard from enemies of Arthur Edward Kennedy, his predecessor, had been biased and exaggerated. Lieutenant Hankin was clearly not the uneducated, contentious social outcast he had been painted. This was a gentleman.

The Assembly was now in recess with the governor's legislative priorities safely accomplished. Seymour felt more comfortable entrusting the key role of colonial secretary to someone of unknown ability, imposed upon him against his wishes. Once in office, the now Honourable[1] Philip Hankin began to familiarize himself with the issues currently facing the government. He would have realized, however, that his new superior was not a well man, under much stress and with a serious alcohol problem.

William Young, on learning of Seymour's belated decision to obey the duke's order to appoint Hankin to the position that he had considered settled as rightly his, was, understandably, deeply hurt. The news came with no sign of what was to become of him. He immediately wrote a polite yet heartfelt letter to Seymour. In it he requested the governor send a copy to the secretary of state, together with an endorsement of "my public conduct during the [three years] I have been a member of your government, and which Your Excellency has already so pleasingly communicated to me."

Seymour, as requested, forwarded Young's letter but added minimal comment by way of affirming Young's invaluable service. After referring to his earlier remarks on Young back in November, he noted, "I certainly hope that Your Lordship . . . will be enabled to offer Mr. Young employment, if not promotion, in another of Her Majesty's Colonies." Seymour closed, "I shall write further on this subject." He intended, one would hope, to prepare a glowing testimonial for the man who, earlier, he had so grievously misjudged, a loyal officer who had managed the business affairs of the colony through a trying financial situation. The position of treasurer had remained unfilled as a result of economic and political pressure.

The undersecretary added a minute, "Wait for letters & Mr. Young," but his departure was not as immediate as Seymour thought, and events prevented the promised further letter. So Young found himself in limbo and on half salary for the next several weeks. Hankin's memoir omitted any interaction with Young, and indeed anything about his initial period in the position.

*

Similarly, Philip recorded nothing about his appearances at the Mechanics Literary Institute. These continued after his appointment, and his reputation as a talented raconteur grew with each performance. Less than two weeks after taking up the new position, he gave readings from two of Dickens's works. The first was the "affecting little story," the history of little Dombey from *Dombey and Son*. The long, gushing review in the *British Colonist* described how it was

> *read in the clear, distinct tones, modulated to suit the person represented as speaking, pleasure than that of hearing Mr. Hankin in these charming readings. There could be no doubt as to the effect on the audience. Everyone was deeply moved and applauded Mr. Hankin at the close with hearty goodwill.*
>
> *Mr. Hankin then read The Schoolboy's Story by Dickens, with his wonderful facility and clearness of enunciation. The effect on the audience might be distinctly noted in the changing expression of the faces of the listeners, and their wrapt* [sic]

Early legislators, circa 1869. Hankin is seated on the balustrade, left of centre.

> *attention. Mr. Hankin was frequently applauded during the recital, and at the conclusion received the unanimous and loud expression of general appreciation. . . . The audience included a great number of ladies, who seemed to enjoy the entertainment with more than ordinary zest.*

*

At the end of April, Hankin was sworn in as a member of the Executive Council. His position of colonial secretary meant he would be presiding member, and second-in-command to the governor. In mid-May, he was elected to the private committee organizing the Grand Regatta to celebrate Queen Victoria's birthday, to be held later that month. William Young and Joseph Trutch also served on the committee.

*

For Seymour, May 17 started out a most depressing day. A long-delayed dispatch from Lord Granville arrived, the one that reacted to his report of his handling of the murders near Metlakatla. It conveyed a forceful reprimand:

> *Your despatch seems to me to be far from satisfactory. . . . I do not understand [your] statement that the matter 'was entirely taken*

out of your hands.' [It was your duty to] resume your proper relation in regard to the Administration of the Country, and to set right what had gone wrong. . . . I much regret that the inaction of your Government in the present instance contrasts strongly with the stirring and extensive operations . . . when an outrage was committed on European Subjects of Her Majesty in 1864.[2]

It is not clear whether Seymour had already planned to revisit the north, or if Granville's blistering rebuke prompted his immediate action. He boarded HMS *Sparrowhawk* for Metlakatla. Hankin later reported that, before joining the voyage, "His Excellency [Seymour] had been in a delicate state of health, suffering from extreme debility, but no danger was apprehended by his Medical advisor." His personal secretary-aide, a Mr. Lowndes, accompanied the governor, and the chief commissioner of lands and works, Joseph Trutch, also joined the party. Trutch had been sworn as a magistrate, as had the captain of *Sparrowhawk*, Commander Henry Wentworth Mist, RN.

At Kynumpt Harbour, a few miles north of Bella Coola, they encountered HMS *Beaver* under the command of Staff Commander Daniel Pender. He came aboard to greet the governor and stayed for dinner. He told them that the trading schooner *Nanaimo Packet* was again in the Nass area. It was up to its nefarious business of selling liquor to the local

Commander Henry Mist, RN, new skipper of HMS Sparrowhawk, *taking Governor Seymour to Metlakatla.*

Indigenous people in return for furs. This vessel had been the source of the alcohol that had inflamed the festivities on the lower Nass River the previous year, triggering the conflict.

Trutch's report also noted that Seymour was unwell when he had come aboard, but that once at sea, his condition seemed to improve. Nine days into the voyage, they anchored off Metlakatla. They prudently awaited the mission's leader, William Duncan, to come aboard and pilot them into the harbour.

Seymour accepted Duncan's invitation to inspect the settlement the following day. He, with Trutch, Mist, and Lowndes, went ashore to be greeted by a uniformed guard of honour. They toured the settlement with its school, church, and trade workshops, and even visited some of the residents' houses. The following day, they held a long conversation with Duncan, discussing the quarrel between the Tsimshian and Nass peoples. Duncan hoped to bring their chiefs into a peaceful negotiation under the authority of the governor. Seymour agreed to this plan.

Before ascending the Nass River, they called into the nearby HBC trading post, Fort Simpson, where they met Robert Cunningham, the company's local agent. Cunningham had just returned from Hazelton, on the upper reaches of the Nass. He had been visiting his business partner there: none other than Philip's brother Thomas Hankin. Cunningham considered the plan "judicious" and felt both sides were eager to return to their previously good relationship, provided it could be done without loss of face, and through an authoritative peacemaker.

The following day they entered the Nass River and anchored off the Kincolith mission. They planned to ask the nearby villagers if they had acquired liquor from the *Nanaimo Packet*, the suspected source. Trutch took the captain's gig upstream to visit the Nass villages, with Lowndes and Duncan as interpreter. They explained they carried an important message from Seymour for the assembled chiefs of the Nass:

> *[The governor] was much grieved at the evil work that had been going on for some time. He was there as a peacemaker between themselves and their Tsimshian neighbours. He invited the chiefs to travel aboard Sparrowhawk with him down to Fort Simpson. There, they would meet and resolve all the difficulties fairly, and before him.*

The gig's party, accompanied by a small flotilla of Nass chiefs, returned downstream and boarded *Sparrowhawk*. Several of them confirmed they had bought liquor from the *Nanaimo Packet*, the same man who had supplied them the year earlier. Captain Mist seized the vessel and towed it to Fort Simpson. On June 2, representatives of both sides discussed the events, and compensation due from, and to, each group. After two hours, the parties settled the matter, and the magistrates drew up a formal document, in effect a peace treaty between the Tsimshian and the Nass. Everyone signed and the governor affixed his seal. The governor sternly told the chiefs that, henceforth, they must live under English law and, if they should take lives ever again, they would be punished.

Sparrowhawk returned to Metlakatla with *Nanaimo Packet* in tow. In the schoolroom set up as a court, the two magistrates, Mist and Trutch, sat in trial against the master and crew of the schooner. It lasted two days, resulting in a guilty verdict. The penalties were: the schooner forfeited; the master fined $500; and each crew member fined $10 (about C$13,800 and C$275, respectively, in 2025). The schooner and its cargo would be taken to Victoria and sold.

*

Meanwhile, back in Victoria, the governor's absence provided his new colonial secretary, Philip Hankin, with an excellent opportunity to become familiar with the files and issues of his office. In this, he had two other public servants in support: Charles Good, deputy colonial secretary, and David Charles Maunsell, private secretary to the governor. Maunsell held strong opinions and a good grasp of the interfactional conflicts that bedevilled the combined colony. Initially dubious about the man parachuted in from London, he warmed to Hankin once they had worked together and he became fully supportive.

It is doubtful that the previous incumbent, William Young, would have been co-operative in a handover, but his record keeping would have been impeccable and accessible. Although the responsibilities in Hankin's new role would have been far greater than those he faced in the equivalent office in British Honduras, his experience there would certainly have been of value. Also, he was knowledgeable about the history and geography of the region, and already knew most of the key people of influence.

*

On May 24 and 25, the city of Victoria held grand celebrations of the Queen's official fiftieth birthday. There were three sporting events. First, there was horse racing at the Beacon Hill track, with five races on the card.[3] The following day, Olympics, a local baseball team, hosted a game against their American rival, Rainier. Organizers timed the game to finish so spectators could also attend the primary event. This was the Grand Regatta, which Hankin had helped organize. The patron, His Excellency, could not attend since he was still aboard *Sparrowhawk* in the north.

The races took place on the Gorge, some distance out of town. The paddlewheeler *Leviathan* twice towed a string of boats full of watchers, bringing, the paper estimated, "six or seven hundred people," and even more came by road in every imaginable conveyance. The weather had been fine for the racing the previous day, but it turned to rain. The populace, however, was not deterred from enjoying the occasion, even when the landing stage constructed near the starting line sagged under the weight of enthusiasts, soaking many feet.

The program listed ten races of different configurations, including one for Indigenous canoes, all with trophies and cash prizes. For unknown reasons, the canoe race did not take place. One event was a sort of race, between men mostly from the navy, in "tubs"—half barrels, powered by a paddle or shovel. The craft, virtually unmanageable, capsized frequently, causing much hilarity. William Haynes, ex-bandmaster of the Royal Engineers' Columbia Detachment, led the Volunteers' Band. They provided military and operatic music suitable for the occasion. As at Beacon Hill, several "refreshment booths tended to increase the gaiety of the occasion." Despite the large number of people enjoying themselves, there was not a single breach of the peace.

*

The following morning, Young auctioned the contents of his house. These included furniture, glassware, china, engravings, piano, three carriages, livestock including horses, and his scientific instruments. That evening, at St. Nicholas Hall, the mayor of Victoria chaired a splendid dinner. Virtually all notable men of the community attended. The dinner was to recognize the service of William Young over the previous dozen years. Perhaps significantly, Hankin was not on the list of those attending, nor was ex-governor Sir James Douglas. To follow the meal, guests heard a long series of toasts and responses. The mayor proposed toasts to the health of the Queen, the Prince of Wales, the president of the United States, and to Governor Seymour, which was "drank standing and with cheers."

The mayor then proposed the health of the guest of the evening, the Honourable William Alexander George Young. The toast was "drank with three times three cheers and 'For He's a Jolly Good Fellow!'" Two evenings later, on May 29, the volunteer firemen of the city assembled, each carrying a flaming torch. Preceded by a band, and followed by a large crowd, they marched in procession across the James Bay bridge to the Young family's home. On a signal from their chief, they gave three hearty cheers. Young appeared on his balcony to thank everyone and assure them that, wherever he went in the future, he would always remember Victoria's Fire Brigade. The brigade members enjoyed appropriate refreshments. Everyone sang "God Save the Queen" before re-forming to cross the bridge back to the city.

A storm affected the scheduled arrival of the mail steamer *California*, which delayed the departure of Young and his family. Hankin had assured him that the colonial treasury would pay the passage for himself, wife, and family to England. They eventually sailed for San Francisco from Esquimalt on June 7. Before leaving, Young left a letter to Seymour in the hands of Hankin. Prior to that, there had been an exchange of telegrams with London about possible new positions for Young. At the end of April, he had learned of an upcoming vacancy for a colonial secretary

The front of William Young's well-appointed house. He sits with his son in a trap while his wife watches from the balcony.

at Demerara, a part of the Guianas populated by British planters. He applied for it through Seymour. Granville responded, "Request not vacant. Offer Young Stipendiary Magistrate at British Guiana." Since this position was far inferior to his recent one, Young turned it down, requesting compensation for loss of position through no fault of his own.

*

On June 5, as *Sparrowhawk* started across Queen Charlotte Sound headed for Skidegate, Governor Seymour came on deck briefly, apparently quite well, but soon retired to his cabin. They visited the Haida village nearby, admiring the line of carved poles, sixty feet high and four feet in diameter, outside each lodge.

As they left Skidegate, the ship's engineer noticed problems with the screw bearings and, heading into a strong breeze, they made slow progress. They found *Beaver*, still at anchor in Kynumpt Harbour, and Pender came aboard. He brought letters for the governor from a Mr. Feake, the HBC manager, and two white settlers at Bella Coola. They feared an imminent attack by the locals and requested that the governor visit before returning to Victoria. A note from Captain Lewis of the HBC vessel SS *Otter* supported their plea. Seymour felt that, since Bella Coola was on their way, they should go there if Captain Mist considered the ship's condition and supply of fuel permitted. Mist agreed, anticipating that they could take on additional coal before reaching Nanaimo. After a few hours' speedy run, *Sparrowhawk* anchored at Bella Coola that night.

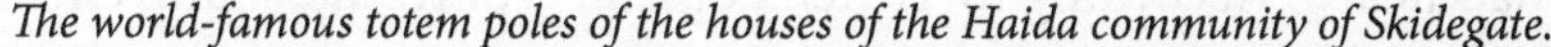

The world-famous totem poles of the houses of the Haida community of Skidegate.

The HBC manager, Feake, and the two settlers, Fletcher and Clayton, came aboard immediately and explained the situation to Trutch and Mist. The governor, exhausted from having had diarrhea for three days, could not attend to business. The two magistrates listened to the complicated saga of events, including assaults on a white man, George Pearse. They then asked Feake to get word to the chief of the Bella Coola people, to bring the accused man before them on board the ship the next morning. Mist also arranged with Feake to supply forty cords of wood for the ship's boilers.

That night, with Dr. Peter Comrie and Lowndes in constant attendance, Governor Seymour's condition worsened. At a quarter to ten the next morning, June 11, he ceased to breathe. The captain would have preferred to leave for Esquimalt immediately, but without the requested supply of wood, he feared they might not make Nanaimo. As the wood needed to be felled, bucked, and split, it did not arrive until late that evening. Even then, the strong breeze and river current prevented canoes from delivering the wood to the ship.

In the meantime, the party summoned to appear before the magistrates arrived and assembled on the quarterdeck. The principal chief was visiting a distant village, so Tom Yakokias, a well-dressed young chief, represented him. Five years earlier, the governor had rewarded the young man for good conduct. Trutch, not wanting to tell them of Seymour's death, explained that the governor was ill, and that he had asked them to speak on his behalf. Feake repeated his and the settlers' complaints before the group. Trutch then asked the young chief to respond to what they had heard. According to Trutch's official report, the young chief responded:

> *There were some few bad men among them, but the tribe were generally very friendly to White People. Some of the Indians from the interior whilst at Bella Coola last winter had talked with these bad people of his tribe & had tried to concoct a plan for killing & stabbing the White People, but the great Majority were entirely opposed to such wickedness. . . . He was certain since a Man of War had come up there wd. be no fear of the White People being further injured.*

As to the specific assault, Trutch continued, it was a quarrel between two wicked men. The white one, George Pearse, was a supplier of liquor. The judgement was to take the local man, whose name was unrecorded, in the quarrel for trial in Victoria, unless he paid a deposit of ten blankets as security for his future good behaviour. They locked the man in the brig for a few hours until his relatives delivered the blankets. Trutch told the chiefs he would report all these proceedings to the governor. They should not feel the government was indifferent to the well-being of the few white people. If such incidents happened again, they would hold the chiefs responsible. A warship would come and punish any crimes. Trutch recorded they seemed to fully understand and agree to the justice administered. Feake, the settlers, and the young chief provided depositions against Pearse, the seller of liquor. After the hearing, Trutch, Lowndes, and the ship's officers visited the main village of nine lodges, housing some two hundred people.

By two thirty in the morning, the wind had died down. Despite loading only seventeen cords of wood, Mist got *Sparrowhawk* under weigh. They next anchored off Fort Rupert but did not communicate with the shore. There was a small coal mine nearby. They hoped to load enough coal here to avoid calling in at Nanaimo. Unfortunately, the low tide prevented them from getting to the mine's jetty. Rather than wait for six hours for high water, Mist continued south. They got to Nanaimo and took on enough fuel to get them to Esquimalt, arriving at ten thirty p.m. on June 13. Trutch and Lowndes immediately headed for Victoria, bearing the news of Governor Seymour's death.

CHAPTER 24
The Administrator

Awakened on June 14, 1869, with the news of Governor Frederick Seymour's death, Philip Hankin faced a hectic day. In the twenty-year history of the colony, this was the first death of a serving governor. The protocols of the Imperial Colonial Service, however, covered such an eventuality. With an immediate and smooth transition of authority, the business of government would proceed uninterrupted. As the senior member of the Executive Council, Hankin took command as acting head of government. He would serve until London nominated a replacement governor and that person arrived to relieve him.

The first action was his formal swearing-in. He wrote and signed two documents: an oath of allegiance to Her Majesty Queen Victoria, and an oath to "faithfully and duly execute the office of Administrator of the Government in and over the Colony of British Columbia." Henry Pering Pellew Crease, who now became the senior member of the Executive Council, and Chief Justice Joseph Needham witnessed the formality. Hankin then promoted Charles Good, who had been his deputy, to acting colonial secretary. He invited David Charles Maunsell, who had been private secretary to Seymour, to continue in the same role for him, and he accepted.

Once sworn in, he sent a telegram to Lord Granville informing him of Seymour's death, that he had "assumed the Government pending instructions," and that he proposed Mr. Good to take his place as colonial secretary. He followed up with a dispatch summarizing the circumstances of the death, pointing out that it had followed visits aboard HMS

Sparrowhawk to Metlakatla and other settlements on the northwest coast. He attributed the cause to "an attack of Diarrhea" that occurred on June 10. He confirmed he had taken the oaths to assume the office of administrator.

He explained that the mail boat was due to leave immediately, so greater detail would follow this brief report by the next mail. He also sent dispatches requesting confirmation of the appointments of Good and Maunsell, and acknowledging receipt of packages of dispatches from London addressed to the late governor. He and Maunsell hastened to read those dispatches in case they contained matters of urgency. Some of those incoming messages, dated as early as April 10, were late in delivery, and some were marked "Confidential." One, dated April 19, was the reprimand for Seymour's expressed opinions about Hankin and the reluctance to appoint him as colonial secretary in place of William Young.

Hankin noted in his memoir that, as acting Administrator, he received the same salary as Governor Seymour, £4,000 a year. In fact, he misremembered; the rule decreed that a temporary replacement should have only half that of the office vacated. Still, £2,000 represented a significant boost to his income. He reflected that just three[1] years previously he had landed in the colony with just 25 shillings[2] (£1.25 or $6, or about C$165 in 2025) in his pocket. He also recalled and took comfort from a German proverb, *Armut ist keine Schande* (poverty is no shame). The same man who, only five years earlier, had dossed down hungry and penniless in a derelict shack outside Barkerville now held the highest office in the colony. He was just thirty-three years old.

Hankin also realized that his elevation in status could create resentment or jealousy among his colleagues and others. Susan Nagle had just received an appointment as a teacher in the school at Yale but had not yet left Victoria. In her diary, she recorded her shock at the news of Seymour's death and her sympathy for his widow. Curiously, she omitted Philip's, and consequently her sister Isabel's, now-elevated position, and their much-improved financial situation.

The following day, the *British Colonist* discussed the news at length. The editorial focused on Hankin, noting how he, although relatively young, had some experience in such a role, having temporarily acted as administrator for British Honduras during an interval between governors. The article concluded:

Members of the band of the Royal Rifle Volunteers. Bandmaster William Haynes is in the centre holding a clarinet.

> *One of the finest opportunities that we have ever known fall to the lot of an aspiring man, is now within the grasp of Mr. Hankin. An exhibition of energy and diplomatic tact, after so long a period of Colonial somnolency, will achieve for him an enduring fame.*

The ambiguous last sentence seems to imply that Hankin would have greater discretion in directing the affairs of state than was the case. London would continue to dictate policy and limit the local scope for action. Also, the dire financial position of the colony left little room for any novel approaches.

The same edition of the paper also carried an announcement of the funeral arrangements for the following day. Spelled out in the official *Gazette Extraordinary* were the order of procession, salutes by ships' guns, and the tolling of church bells. The coffin was to be placed on a gun carriage, flanked by pallbearers, and followed by members of the Fire Brigade and Rifle Volunteers, then naval personnel, clergy of various denominations, the mayor and council, civil servants, legislative and executive councillors, the administrator (Hankin), and, last, the public, all two by two.

They would march in slow time to a band playing Handel's "Dead March" for the quarter of a mile between the naval hospital and the naval cemetery for the interment service and the firing of a rifle salute over the grave. The procession would then return to the hospital, in reverse order and now in quick time, before dispersing. The officials, brought to Esquimalt aboard the chartered steamer *Enterprise*, were to return the same way.

*

On the morning of June 15, a telegram arrived from London responding to Philip's report of the death of Seymour. It read: "Mr. Musgrave is appointed Governor, you may announce that he will proceed to British Columbia immediately." For some months, people had known that Anthony Musgrave was nominated to replace Seymour, but this was expected to happen the following November in order for Seymour to gain enough service to qualify for his pension, then retire. As it was, London sent Musgrave, then serving as governor of Newfoundland, a telegram instructing him to proceed to Victoria without delay.

Musgrave, born the son and grandson of colonial administrators in the West Indies and eight years Philip's senior, had been studying law in London when he had been called back to the Caribbean to be colonial secretary for Antigua. He had held a series of positions of increasing responsibility in that region until his appointment to Newfoundland in 1864. There, he worked to rescue the fortunes of the impoverished but proudly independent colony through confederation with the other British North American colonies, the new Dominion of Canada. He was now tasked with bringing British Columbia into a similar relationship. A widower, his two unmarried sisters and his nephew, also named Anthony, accompanied him. His only son, who was fourteen years old, was in England attending Harrow School.

The new appointment represented a significant promotion for Musgrave. He had been receiving half the salary listed for British Columbia. He accepted and requested permission to come to London for a few weeks beforehand. London sent an immediate disapproval. Evidently, the Colonial Office lacked confidence in Hankin's capacity to take on the duties as administrator for more than a limited period. The lack of support for Hankin by senior figures in the colony, as reported by Seymour, seemed to have had a residual effect in London.

*

Before boarding the steamer *California* on June 7, William Young had left a letter with Hankin, addressed to Seymour. He had requested it be forwarded to Lord Granville in London. It now fell to Hankin to process it. He duly sent it on to the earl, together with a note reporting the colony had paid the money for Young's passage back to England along with his wife and family. Young's letter pointed out that he had received no reply to his earlier plea. This requested a year's leave of absence on half pay to arrange the next phase of his career. He was still only forty-three years old and in good health.[3] He felt that under the circumstances, he was entitled to either a significant appointment or a substantial pension.

The minutes appended by the colonial officials to Young's letter were sympathetic to the concept of a gratuity for losing the position he held upon the union of the colonies. They recognized, however, that a better solution would be to find him another acceptable position within the service. There seemed to be an opportunity about to arise in Ceylon.

By the same batch of outgoing mail, Hankin responded to the confidential dispatch from London berating Seymour for not appointing Hankin as colonial secretary. He pointed out that Seymour had already complied with the order and appointed him to the position. He added: "No disastrous consequences have arisen, neither do I apprehend the slightest possibility of any arising." Sir Frederic Rogers, the permanent undersecretary, minuted, wryly, "Rather irregular that it should have fallen to Mr. Hankin to open this despatch."

*

Joseph Trutch had accompanied Seymour aboard *Sparrowhawk* on the investigatory voyage to Metlakatla. Toward the end of the month, he presented his report on the voyage to his new superior, Administrator Hankin. It was in two parts: a chronological account of the activities of the party with an accompanying summary of the various outcomes of the matters investigated, and recommendations for future action. He noted, briefly, the dysentery and death of Seymour, without discussing the cause. Philip immediately forwarded both documents to London, adding only a closing note: "All has been quiet here, and no inconvenience has arisen to the Public Service from my having assumed the Government of the Colony."

The officials in London appended several lengthy minutes to the documents. Rogers wrote the final comment:

> *I should ackn^{e} this very interesting report, and express satisfaction both at the prompt manner in w^{h} Mr Seymour started for Metlakatla on receiving L^{d} G[ranville]'s dph of the 7th March and at his success in accommodating a quarrel, w^{h} if left to itself m^{t} have produced very serious results in asserting the cause of improvement among the Indians. Gov. Seymour certainly died in the perf^{e} of a good work.*

Conventions of the era governed discussion of personal matters, in particular illness and demise, of the sovereign and her representatives. The professors Akrigg, in their 1977 book *Gold and Colonists*, brushed aside such delicacy when they investigated the true cause of Seymour's death. They quoted the report of Dr. Peter Comrie, the medical officer aboard *Sparrowhawk*, who had attended Seymour during the days leading up to the death. Comrie had noted:

> *Governor Seymour . . . had for some time been debilitated. I found him suffering from gastric irritation, nervous tremors, sleeplessness, and other symptoms of alcoholism. . . . The evening of his death he succeeded in getting hold of a bottle of brandy and drinking it off.*

Trutch would have known the truth but provided the more diplomatic version for public consumption. The newspapers similarly reported the sad news. However, it seems probable that Hankin and the senior echelons of the small community of Victoria also knew what really transpired. It is not clear whether the Colonial Office learned of Dr. Comrie's report or accepted the tactful wording of Hankin's telegram and dispatch.

Joseph Trutch's position as the chief commissioner of lands and works had been under review. There was a perceived conflict of interest over his part ownership of the Alexandra toll bridge. At the beginning of July, he handed Administrator Hankin a letter. In it, he affirmed he had now divested himself of all his interests in the bridge; he requested that the secretary of state be so informed. A document from the Bank of British Columbia, attesting to the sale and dated January 5, supported Trutch's affirmation. Maunsell, who had been the governor's private secretary, had continued in that office under Hankin. He confirmed Seymour had intended to notify London about the matter immediately on his return from Metlakatla. Thus satisfied, Hankin felt justified in forwarding the letter from Trutch, with the bank's attestation, to Granville. He stated he considered that there was no longer any reason to prevent Mr. Trutch from continuing in his position.

*

In early July, two French warships sailed into Esquimalt on a courtesy visit. They were the twenty-gun steam frigate *L'Astrée*, accompanied by the four-gun dispatch, or gunboat, *La Mothe Piquet*. The frigate bore the flag of Rear Admiral Georges Charles Cloué. Captain St. Hilaire commanded the smaller vessel. The admiral paid the customary call on the local head of government. The next day, Philip returned the visit, accompanied by Trutch, Good, and Mr. Lowndes. As they came aboard, the ship's band played "God Save the Queen." Philip explained he could not receive the admiral at Government House as the late governor's widow still occupied it. Instead, Philip invited him and his officers to his own residence that evening. According to international protocol, as the Hankin party disembarked from *L'Astrée*, they were saluted with thirteen guns, and HMS *Satellite* returned the courtesy.

Philip recalled in his memoir that the formal salutes "inflamed the angry Passions of my friends in Victoria more than ever. . . . They would not understand that it was not <u>me</u> they were saluting but the office I held." As well as the formal dinner offered by Hankin to the French officers, an impromptu afternoon picnic at Colwood for them was arranged by Staff Commander Daniel Pender, a few other naval officers, and the Reverend Frank Gribbell. Rear Admiral Cloué could not attend, but the two French captains and Philip and Isabel Hankin were among the sixty who enjoyed "a bountiful collation." Afterward there was "singing and dancing etc. until an early hour in the evening. Hayne's band was in attendance. The affair was most creditable to all concerned."

The visit did not please everyone. A few "leading citizens" who tried to get aboard *L'Astrée* were turned away. Affronted, they penned an angry letter to the *British Colonist*, which published it but added an editorial note suggesting they must have been mistaken, since "the French are proverbial for politeness." The following day, the admiral welcomed anyone from Victoria who wished to visit his flagship. That evening, *L'Astrée*'s band gave a concert ashore attended by the administrator and the chief justice with their ladies and many naval officers and other officials. After a week, the flotilla departed, bound for the Sandwich Islands via San Francisco. Hankin reported the visit to London, stating, "My relations with the Admiral have been most cordial and friendly."

While the French ships were in the area, Hankin learned of a further tragedy at Ahousaht. It derived from the brutal naval action against the villages some three years earlier.[4] The ships had fired salvos of incendiary rockets, intending to set fire to the houses, stores of food, belongings, and traditional items of the tribe. Some of those rockets seem to have landed but failed to ignite at the time. Villagers had discovered them later in the undergrowth. Mistakenly thinking the canisters contained gunpowder that they could use in their muskets, one of the more adventurous men attacked a canister with a chisel, watched by his companions. Unfortunately, the contents were not black powder, but an incendiary mixture containing phosphorus. The mixture, designed to explode and burn on contact with the air, did so, killing three, seriously injuring four spectators, and destroying the surrounding houses.

*

At the end of June 1869, intelligence reached Administrator Hankin that a notorious Fenian Brotherhood troublemaker, George Francis Train, was in San Francisco and threatening to mount a two-thousand-strong armed invasion of the colony. The British and Canadian governments took the Brotherhood seriously, although rifts between the group's factions diminished the potency of the threat. The British consul in San Francisco telegraphed the news, through Royal Navy channels, that Train had left there for Portland and "might be expected in Victoria." A plan was already in place to prepare for such an event, which Hankin then set in motion. The gunboat *Forward*, normally based in Esquimalt, anchored in the harbour, the Rifle Volunteers mustered to stand by, and magistrate Augustus Pemberton and police inspector Bowden were briefed.

Hankin learned that the steamer *Wilson G. Hunt*, on an unscheduled sailing due to arrive early in the morning of July 10, listed Train on the passenger manifest. On the ship's arrival at one a.m., Bowden went aboard to confirm that Train was there, and learned the man was asleep. Five hours later, he watched the suspect disembark with four companions and he followed them to the American Hotel. Bowden reported seeing him in discussion with the hotelier and several other men. Train then strolled about town for a few hours, before re-embarking. The steamer left at nine that evening, with about a hundred people watching from the wharf.

According to Bowden's report, Train "conducted himself with propriety whilst here." The *British Colonist* noted Train had "an egotistical swagger and self-conceited smirk which are anything but pleasant." Train had hinted that he expected to be elected president of the United States in 1872. He left a note to the editor that concluded, "Regret that cannot meet your people at the theater or lecture hall today." Hankin ordered the *Forward* and the Volunteers to stand down. He advised London of the visit, attaching reports by Pemberton and Bowden, with the newspaper clipping. He concluded: "I see no reason to apprehend any disturbance."

*

That month, Susan Nagle took up her post as a teacher in a twenty-two-pupil school at Fort Yale. She lodged with her cousin Helen, known to the family as Nellie, who had married Joseph William McKay. He was a mixed-race HBC stalwart, faithful ally to James Douglas, and an explorer and fur trader. McKay had supervised the company's interests in the Nanaimo coal fields and had been an elected legislator. At the time, he oversaw the company's operations throughout the Kootenay, Cassiar, and Stikine districts.

*

In mid-July, Mrs. Seymour sailed for England, accompanied by the faithful Lowndes and the Reverend and Mrs. Hayman. News arrived that the new governor Musgrave's arrival was delayed. The *British Colonist* speculated that this was to allow him to see Newfoundland join the Canadian Confederation. In fact, that would not happen for another

The signature of Administrator Hankin atop an official certificate.

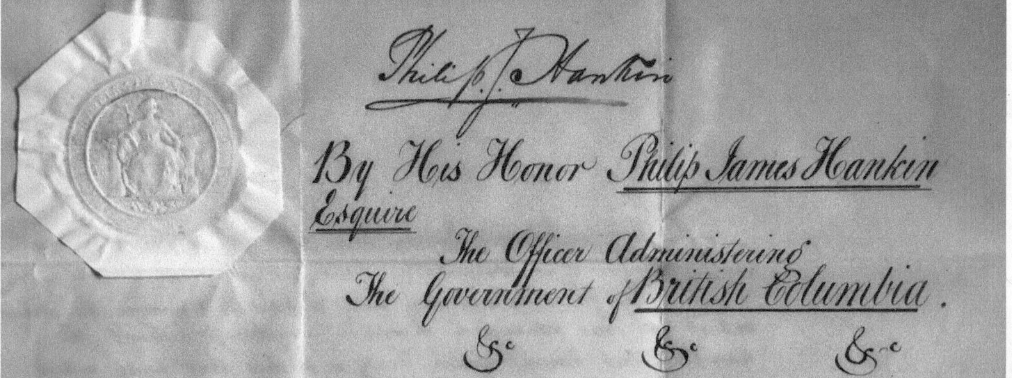
Philip J. Hankin

By His Honor Philip James Hankin Esquire

The Officer Administering The Government of British Columbia.

&c &c &c

eighty years. Rather, he had been waiting to hand over Newfoundland's governorship to Stephen Hill. Musgrave departed from Halifax on July 17. He travelled to New York, then overland to San Francisco by train. The journey impressed him with the importance of a transcontinental rail link, a factor of significance in the negotiations to come. The newspaper article concluded, remarkably:

> *Meantime matters go on smoothly under Mr. Hankin, who, we honestly believe, is striving hard to make the most of very small means.*

CHAPTER 25

Colony to Province, Part 1: Preparation

On August 10, 1869, in one of his last official duties as acting head of government, Philip Hankin received the formal salute of Rear Admiral Thomas Turner, US Navy, arriving aboard USS *Pensacola* on a brief visit. HMS *Satellite*, as one of its last formal actions in Esquimalt, exchanged gun salutes with the visiting vessel. The admiral came ashore to call upon the senior officer of the local government, and Administrator Hankin returned the compliment by visiting the flagship.

Early on the morning of August 23, *Satellite* again fired its guns, this time to salute His Excellency, Governor Anthony Musgrave, on his arrival. Administrator Hankin, with the captains of *Satellite* and HMS *Sparrowhawk*, William Henry Edye, RN, and Henry Wentworth Mist, RN, received him as he landed. They drove immediately to Philip's residence for breakfast. Musgrave's party included his two sisters and his nephew Anthony.

Afterward, the new governor drove to Government House to begin his official duties. In the afternoon, he first made a formal call on the executive committee at the Birdcages. Later, he and his nephew marched in procession to the Supreme Court with an escort from the Rifle Corps and a band, with Hankin and David Charles Maunsell, the private secretary, in attendance. Watched by a packed courthouse, Chief Justice Joseph Needham solemnly administered the oaths of office. "His excellency's prepossessing bearing and appearance, clear and emphatic tone

Governor Anthony Musgrave.

of voice" pleased the audience, which greeted him with "hearty and long continued applause." He then returned to Government House, which would be his residence for the next two years.

With Musgrave's swearing of the oath, Hankin reverted to his position as colonial secretary. He had served as administrator for nine weeks.[1] Charles Good returned to his old position as his deputy. Musgrave announced that his nephew, Anthony, would be his private secretary, in place of the long-serving Maunsell. The new governor asked the Colonial Office in London to find a suitable place for Maunsell elsewhere in the service.

From before his arrival, Musgrave's salary had been a contentious issue. The local press and many of the elected members of the legislature had long complained, with justification, about the salaries of Victoria's colonial officers, including that of the governor. They considered that the salary bill placed too heavy a burden on the colony's limited funds. Appointed by "the Crown," in effect the Colonial Office, the officers received salaries under their empire-wide scale. The Crown, however, did not pay those salaries; each colony's budget had to cover them. Over the years, this had resulted in deficits, underwritten by debts to the Crown, to be repaid in annual instalments. A Crown agent locally administered a separate fund of London's money.

The cost of living in Victoria shocked Musgrave. It was far higher than in Newfoundland. What to him had appeared a reasonable salary was now significantly diminished in real terms. This came to a head when Hankin informed Musgrave that, in addition to the £4,000 salary from British Columbia, his predecessor, Frederick Seymour, had been drawing £1,000 from the Crown fund. Seemingly, earlier secretaries of state Carnarvon and Buckingham had allowed this.

This news had implications not only for Musgrave, but also for Hankin. His salary during his nine-week tenure as administrator related directly to that of Seymour. This would have meant an additional £86 5s for Hankin. Musgrave raised the matter in a dispatch to London. He suggested that if the addition to Hankin's payment as administrator was made from Crown funds, it would not affect the colony's budget. He felt that locals would not object to his own remuneration being the same as his predecessor's, and pointed out the significant increase in his cost of living justified this.

The news of Seymour's arrangement astonished the officials in London. Apparently, he had been drawing this additional money for the past two and a half years, undiscovered by audits. They asked Carnarvon and Buckingham for their views on the matter, then referred the matter to the British Treasury. In the meantime, they cancelled the planned allowance of £500 for Seymour's widow. They eventually decided that the additional £1,000 drawn by Seymour was not formally approved; therefore, neither Musgrave nor Hankin was entitled to the extra. They requested a full accounting of the money Seymour had claimed. Hankin had earlier asked London if the British Treasury would pay the costs of Seymour's funeral. London replied that such a payment would not be made from Crown funds, but if the Legislative Council voted to pay the costs, the Colonial Office would not object.

While Musgrave was not happy with this decision, he fully agreed with the Colonial Office's priority for him. He was to help bring about the union of British Columbia with the Dominion of Canada. He knew that local opinion was mixed, with a few Vancouver Islanders preferring annexation to the United States. He suspected that he would find more support on the mainland, but he wanted to verify this personally. He needed to do so prior to the next session of the legislature, and before winter prevented travel. Musgrave was a man of reputed energy and

Governor Musgrave and his group visiting the Royal Marines' camp on San Juan Island. Musgrave is seated at right, Hankin seated at centre.

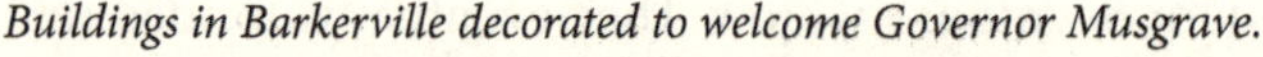

Buildings in Barkerville decorated to welcome Governor Musgrave.

action. Despite having barely recovered from his five-thousand-mile journey from Newfoundland, he crossed to the mainland just two weeks after having arrived in Victoria. Philip Hankin, Commissioner of Lands and Works Joseph Trutch, Captain Delacombe of the Royal Marines,[2] and the Reverend Dr. W.E. Hayman accompanied him.

After briefly visiting the now much-diminished New Westminster, they inspected the new lumber-based communities at the mouth of the Fraser River: Hastings, Gastown, Burrard, Jerry's Cove (now Jericho), and Moodyville. By September 11, they had reached Yale to stay overnight at the McKay family residence, where Philip's sister-in-law Susan Nagle lived. The following day, Hankin and some others returned to Victoria. The governor and Trutch carried on upcountry. Travelling by Barnard's Express stagecoach and on horseback, the two visited Lytton, Ashcroft, and Barkerville.

Here, the gold miners gave the governor and Trutch an enthusiastic reception. Fifty firemen in uniform escorted them through multiple ceremonial arches of fir boughs with banners proclaiming WELCOME in English and Chinese. Fireworks and guns blazed their salutes. Musgrave, having confirmed firm support on the mainland for union with the Dominion, could then retrace his journey. Reaching Yale by October 9, they stayed another two nights with McKay, but took meals with the gold commissioner, Peter O'Reilly. Susan noted in her diary that she found Musgrave to be "a very nice man we are all delighted with him and are quite sorry he has gone. It is strange how much one can get to like a person even in a short time." He returned to Victoria on October 14, having been away for over five weeks.

Musgrave reported to London immediately about the tour, enclosing the texts of his addresses to local dignitaries and their responses. His overall impression on the "condition and future prospects of the colony" was better than he had been led to believe. Gold mining was now proceeding well and was free from the "scum of the population which has been floated off." Businesses of all kinds were thriving, and for agriculture "there is scarcely a limit to the productiveness of the soil." The rearing of stock, similarly, "with no finer Cattle or Sheep. . . . Probably next year there will be little, or no beef imported in Victoria." He concluded by noting the favourable comments in the addresses he received to the concept of confederation with Canada. He warned, however, that these "cannot be taken as the unanimous opinion of the white population," especially of those on Vancouver Island.

*

Dispatches from London brought news of William Young. The first, sent on September 13, informed Musgrave—who would not have known Young except from records generated by Seymour—of official approval for payment of his passage back to England. It also mentioned that Young had accepted the position of assistant colonial secretary in Jamaica, then one of the most important British colonies. This meant that his claim for a gratuity for loss of office was not justified. The dispatch of November 3 reported that the treasury had reviewed the case and now recommended that "a gratuity equivalent to not more than six months' salary should be voted to Mr. Young."

A probable cause for the reversal of opinion was a letter to Viscount Cardwell, a former secretary of state, from Sir James Douglas. It read, in part:

> *As a rapid, clear-headed, hardworking man of business, Mr. Young has few equals and his character is, in all respects, irreproachable. He is, moreover, a very sensible fellow, most able, and trustworthy to the last degree.*

Such an endorsement from "the father of British Columbia" would have effectively countered all Seymour's denigrations.

*

In mid-August, Lord Granville, then secretary of state for the colonies, wanted to clarify the options for anyone in British Columbia who was decidedly against, or wavering about, confederation with Canada. He sent a dispatch to Musgrave, directing that he publish his statement on the issue. He had sent the same text to Sir John Young,[3] the Governor General of Canada. The dispatch arrived in late October, and Musgrave instructed his colonial secretary, Hankin, to have it distributed to the press immediately. The *British Colonist* published it on October 30, 1869.

In twelve paragraphs Granville explained that, at last, the two vast territories governed by the Hudson's Bay Company, Rupert's Land and the North-Western Territory, were to be united with Canada. This would mean that all British possessions on the North American continent, except for British Columbia, would make up the Dominion of Canada.[4] This raised the question: Should this westernmost colony join, or remain apart from, the Dominion? He acknowledged:

> *Sentiment in the colony does not appear unanimous . . . but the prevailing opinion was in favour of union. . . . Such was the opinion of Her Majesty's Government. An important factor would be the construction of, 'a British line of communication between the Atlantic and Pacific oceans.'*

Granville chose not to go into the details of such an agreement, leaving it for the two parties to negotiate directly. Of particular importance would be "the condition of Indian Tribes and the position of government servants." Those "servants" will have been quite sensitive to their future under confederation. They remembered the callous treatment of some of their colleagues—including Hankin—when the two colonies had united only a few years previously. Granville closed by directing Musgrave to "take such steps . . . for promoting the favourable consideration of this question."

On October 30, Musgrave responded with his own thirteen-paragraph dispatch. He informed Granville that, although he would have preferred to wait until the December meeting of the Legislative Council, he had published the message from London. Someone in Canada with a motive to favour the unification project had already leaked copies of that text. No doubt this influenced Musgrave's decision. Even though he had been in the post a short while, he recognized that the issue was far more complex and difficult than had been the case for the Maritimes. He understood that opinion in Canada held it that the chief opposition would be from the official members of council. He pointed out that these officers, while apprehensive about their futures, had not openly declared opposition. His own view was that offering them suitable pensions or positions would remove any such opposition.

There was more to the matter than just the opinions of the government servants. There would be other factors to confront and resolve. Among them was the status of Victoria as a free port. Business interests in Canada had lobbied hard for that. However, duty-free import of cheaper products from below the border would disadvantage local farmers and ranchers. He also pointed out the provincial demographics. The total white population was less than ten thousand. Many of these were not British subjects and therefore might support annexation to the United States. Others would have come west from Canada and be less in favour of rejoining a regime they had left. British immigrants, other than those sent out by the government, would need to be convinced of the benefits confederation held for them.

Apart from the demographic complexity, they would need to resolve the financial questions. The colony was already heavily in debt. With such a small population, repayment through taxation would not be possible. The local cost of living was already twice that in Canada. The grant-in-aid from Britain of 80 cents per head of population would not cover the cost of effective government for such a vast area.

Musgrave reminded Granville and his officials that the Rocky Mountains presented a formidable barrier for a transportation link to Canada. This was a far greater hurdle than the Gulf of St. Lawrence was for Newfoundland. The colony would require the building of at least a wagon road, if not a railway, as a critical condition for union. He pointed out that the colony had already,

> *by its own unaided energy and resources,*[5] *constructed an astonishing road from Yale through the canyons of the Fraser River to Lytton . . . to the Cariboo, over which I have recently travelled for five hundred miles [eight hundred kilometres]. It was not unreasonable to expect the Dominion to complete that link.*

Musgrave concluded by warning London (and Canada) that "the details and terms of the proposed union are by no means easy to be arranged." He undertook to bring the matter to the next session of the legislature. "I shall prepare with the aid of my Council some plan of Union as a tentative proposition." Once the issues had been fully and fairly argued, he could report more fully on what he had just presented, which was "a superficial view." He copied Sir John Young on the dispatch, to inform him of his, Musgrave's, current "impressions on the question which has naturally so great an interest for [Young's] government."

Without having seen Musgrave's reply to Granville's dispatch, public opinion in Victoria, as reported by the *Daily Colonist*, was immediate and angry. It appeared clear to many that Britain was washing its hands of the colony. If they elected not to join Canada, they would be left to their own devices. Those employed in the civil service interpreted the dispatch as an ultimatum. If the colony voted for confederation, how might they be treated? Should they stay or make other arrangements for their future?

In mid-January 1870, Musgrave followed up his long dispatch of October 30 with a private note to Charles Cox, a senior administrator in the Colonial Office. In it, he reminded Cox of their brief connection, years previously, and solicited a personal favour. He was most concerned about some contents of his dispatch, intended to be frank and confidential, being made public. He asked that, if it were to be printed, would Cox kindly arrange to "cut out some passages which it might do harm to make public?" He explained, "I am working away as well as I can, but many matters seem to me to be in a dreadful mess and to have been understood by nobody, yet it is difficult to make these things plain without appearing to cast blame on my predecessor."

Philip Hankin, as colonial secretary, was in a tricky position. Not only would he be personally affected by the potential outcomes of the issue, he would also be at the very heart of the discussions preparatory to negotiation with Canada. He presided over Musgrave's Executive Council developing the plan. Similarly, he would lead the new session of the legislature when it debated, amended, and voted on that plan. These were enormous responsibilities to shoulder with his limited experience, relying on just innate abilities.

Exacerbating the already onerous tasks faced by Musgrave and Hankin, on November 2, the governor suffered a serious injury. Although an expert horseman, as he mounted a young horse at Government House, it shied and threw him. All his weight came down on his right leg, causing a compound fracture so severe that a shard of bone poked through his riding boot. Staff sent for all four available doctors to attend him. On whether to amputate the leg or try to set it, they were evenly divided.

In those days, surgeons were using chloroform as an anaesthetic. They also experimented with different antiseptics, such as carbolic acid. Of course, this was long before X-ray technology. Musgrave gave responsibility to decide to a Canadian surgeon, Dr. Israel Wood Powell, who chose to attempt keeping the leg. The result confined Musgrave to his bed for months to allow the repositioned bones to set and flesh wounds to heal. He limped for the rest of his life. During the crucial time of the legislative session, it fell to Hankin to act as intermediary between the governor, from his bed, and the members of council and the assembly.

Another response to the Granville dispatch came from forty-three signatories to a petition sent to President Ulysses S. Grant that the United States annex the colony. These few "annexationists" mainly comprised Americans resident in Victoria, but also some Germans and people of the Jewish diaspora. The floods of Americans and other prospectors arriving for the Fraser River gold rushes had by this time abated, but some remained. The pro-confederation *British Colonist* joked that an alternative petition might be made to Queen Victoria that she annex "all American territory north of the Columbia River, our natural border." The editor also pointed out that the annexationist signatories had probably committed the serious crime of sedition.

*

Despite Philip's now onerous workload, he found the time to give another of his popular readings from Dickens. At the meeting of the Mechanics Literary Institute on December 9, he entertained the gathering by reading passages from *Nicholas Nickleby*. He read from the scene describing the conditions and characters in the dreadful boarding school, Dotheboys Hall. The audience listened enthralled as he recounted the awfulness of Mrs. Squeers, Miss Squeers, Miss Tilda Price, and Browdie, her lover. He followed with extracts from *The Ingoldsby Legends*, a series of humorous myths and ghost stories, many in verse, published in popular London weeklies in the 1830s and '40s. The reviewer in the next day's *British Colonist* pronounced that "he read with marked ability," and that it "proved his most successful effort."

CHAPTER 26

Colony to Province, Part 2: Negotiation

For the early part of 1870, Philip Hankin's attention was fully occupied with helping prepare British Columbia's draft terms for joining Canada. His superior, Governor Anthony Musgrave—despite being confined to his bed, recovering from surgery on his broken leg—was keen to pursue this prime aim, which required guiding his Executive Council in drafting the document for debate and approval by the Legislative Assembly.

To convert from being a governed colony to operating as a province within the Dominion, Musgrave needed to reconfigure both the Executive Council and the Assembly. Few of the population had working experience of democratic, representative government. Musgrave knew Canada would expect its new member to function effectively immediately upon joining. He also knew that the community, as it existed, could not form an adequately experienced legislature. They would also need to have in place an electoral system. This meant that a period of transition and preparation for government would be essential. Hankin, similarly inexperienced in such matters, would need to learn and be able to help manage this transition.

In a dispatch to London, Musgrave explained his strategy for reconfiguring the Assembly for the transition to a more democratically elected body. He proposed a new council of fifteen members: three appointed ex officio by the government, two others from the Executive Council, and nine to be elected for districts yet to be specified. He felt they should limit the vote to British subjects for, if non-subjects were included, the vote for confederation would probably not pass. London agreed to this plan and set in motion an official order to endorse it.

Musgrave had hinted to Charles Cox at the Colonial Office how Frederick Seymour had left the running of the colony: "Many matters seem in a terrible mess." Two of these he had already attempted to address. The first was the lack of a treasurer, a complicated situation that had resulted in the chief clerk being left in charge of this crucial function. Musgrave suggested they hold off changing this, pending the restructuring of the entire governance model.

The second problem was that of the courts. When amalgamating the two colonies, they had neglected to establish a single legal system. This resulted in retaining two chief justices of equal stature, one in New Westminster, the other in Victoria. This left a gaping hole in the appeal process. Fortunately, one of those two judges, Joseph Needham, accepted a promotion in Trinidad. With his replacement, they could correct the anomaly by having one nominated the chief justice, the other a puisne, a high court judge but of lesser standing. London agreed to this solution.

Musgrave appointed two men to his Executive Council, both physicians and influential elected members of the Assembly: Dr. John Sebastian Helmcken and Dr. Robert William Weir Carrall. Helmcken was a long-serving official with the HBC, married to one of Sir James Douglas's daughters and a prominent voice in opposition to confederation; Carrall held mining interests in the Cariboo[1] and was just as ardent, but in favour of joining Canada. Musgrave had earlier replaced two vacancies in the Assembly with the gadfly journalist Amor De Cosmos and Francis Jones Barnard, who operated a profitable "express" stagecoach to and from the goldfields, representing Yale.

Still bedridden, Musgrave sent a dispatch to London requesting two months' leave "to visit New York on a matter of personal moment," to begin in April or May, once the legislative session had concluded. He pointed out that they had refused his earlier request for leave before coming to Victoria, while encouraging him to reapply later. He also stated his presence in New York, just as British Columbia's proposal was being reviewed in nearby Ottawa, would enable him to hold discussions with Canada. For this he should receive full pay, since the journey would be official. He also suggested the Crown fund might meet Hankin's entitlement to half his pay while acting as the temporary administrator.

London, probably aware that the purpose of Musgrave's journey was to get married, agreed to the leave, but only at half pay while away. As for Hankin's temporary appointment as administrator and the corresponding increase to his salary paid from Crown funds, they demurred. This seems unfair treatment of both men. Musgrave had to forgo half his salary. Compensating Hankin for the additional responsibilities, as had been done on Seymour's death and for a similar duration, would have been the normal procedure. London's decision seems strange, given that Hankin was an officer who held a favourable view about the union, which they considered necessary for success. Also odd is Philip's omission from his memoir of any mention of the grievance he undoubtedly felt. He usually recalled such matters.

*

On February 15, three days before Philip's thirty-fourth birthday, the Legislative Council assembled and he, as president of the council and colonial secretary, read the governor's speech from the throne on behalf of the incapacitated Governor Musgrave. In it, he first outlined the governor's formal role, then turned to the financial situation of the colony, presenting his estimates for the year ahead. He next broached the question of confederation with Canada. He pointed out that such a

Members of the new Legislative Council on the steps of the legislature building, February 1870. Hankin, wearing a silk top hat, sits in a chair at the top of the stairs.

union was the wish of Her Majesty's government in London, and that a resolution of the colony's problems was urgently needed. It was his view that union with Canada, under favourable terms, was the preferred outcome. They could only achieve this, however, with the clear agreement of the people of British Columbia. The governor had required his Executive Council to prepare a draft of the terms to be presented to Canada to begin negotiations over joining the Dominion. He now needed the legislature to study, debate, and agree to or modify this draft.

At the close of the session, and with the legislature's agreement on the terms of the document to be presented to Canada, a delegation would go to Ottawa for the negotiation. The outcome of the negotiation would then be subject to ratification by a reconstituted legislature, with a majority of elected members. He would prepare an election for seats in the new, expanded legislature in time for debate and their decision of the negotiated terms. This reconfiguration, which he termed "responsible government," would serve to govern the new province properly under confederation, or for whatever form of future they chose for themselves.

Reaction to the speech in Victoria was positive. The *British Colonist* pronounced it "a manly, honest, outspoken, and statesmanlike document." Hankin's skill with the spoken word reinforced the power of Musgrave's text. In London, colonial officialdom minuted, "I should say a good sound sensible Speech . . . & approve." A nervous silence from the Assembly followed mention of "responsible government." It implied that all members' seats would be up for re-election. The Assembly debated the draft terms between March 19 and April 6 and the draft passed. The session closed on April 26.

*

On March 11, prior to the debate on the draft terms, Hankin had written a private letter to the Duke of Buckingham. The duke, although no longer part of the government, still took an interest in the colony and retained a powerful voice in discussions of imperial affairs. The style of Hankin's text shows, as Willard Ireland put it, "that Hankin was a fairly intimate friend" of the duke. He described the current condition of Musgrave:

> *He is now able to get on the sofa and is downstairs in the Drawing room. I hope he may soon now be on Crutches, he was 16 weeks in bed. . . . I like Mr. Musgrave immensely. I never*

wish to serve with a better man, & I think he is as much liked as it is possible for British Columbians to like any Governor.

Philip provided news about Isabel, his wife, and was solicitous about the duchess. He mentioned receiving a long letter from Sir Arthur Edward Kennedy from Africa and that Lady Kennedy and his daughter were with him. He gave brief details of happenings in the province and concluded, "Believe me to be your Grace's very faithful servant," signing it as "Philip J. Hankin."[2]

He sent, by the same mail, a copy of the terms, which he described as "will be proposed to Canada." This hints that he expected this version to be accepted by the Assembly, without alteration. He included a cutting from the *British Colonist* that carried the text of the throne speech and the accompanying editorial. Hankin summarized his reading of the public mind on the question of confederation:

The people here love change, they are never satisfied, and they may find that it is easier to serve Downing Street [the centre of the imperial government, in London] than Ottawa.... [Referring to the concept of responsible government, he felt] they are certainly not fit for it. Some of them hope by that means to get into Office.

He described the "great nuisance, Amor De Cosmos; he is a thorough Democratic ruffian."

We also learn from Hankin's letter that:

Isabel has been very delicate for some time. She never appears to have shaken off the effects of the Yellow Fever she caught in the West Indies, & by the advice of her Medical Man, I am going to send her to California for a few months to stay with a married sister [Kate Patten.]

Convalescing from the same ailment, Isabel had spent some time at Stowe House as a guest of the duchess, and the duke would have remembered her. A few days after Philip's letter, Isabel travelled to San Francisco[3] in the company of Chief Justice Joseph Needham and his family, who were on their way to take up a new post in Trinidad. Hankin himself was not fully fit. According to Susan Nagle's diary, he suffered from lumbago (lower back pain).

Around this time, Susan's and Jessie's diaries revealed Philip received news from Emily, wife of Philip's elder brother, Daniel Bell, then vicar of Christ Church, Ware. His sister-in-law had told him that his youngest brother, Graham, had died in England. Philip did not mention this event in his memoir. Jessie had earlier recorded meeting Graham at her home after he had returned from California, prior to his leaving for England. She wrote, "We said goodbye more affectionately than ever before. I felt that I should never see him again. I hope dear Graham will reach England safely, he is looking better than when he left last October—but still very delicate." She later recalled that he had written to her in January, "the last letter he ever wrote—He is the first friend that I have lost by death 'not lost, but gone before.'" Isabel had also seen Graham before she left for San Francisco.

In her diary for May 9, Susan recorded an item of interest from a letter received from Philip: news of his promotion to commander on half pay. According to Royal Naval records, on April 2, 1870, Hankin was "compulsory retired under 40 years of age. Retired Pay under new regulations £109-10-0 p.annum." This was the event that he mistakenly recorded in his memoir as happening immediately after his wedding, five years earlier (see chapter 18). At this point in his career, it would make more sense for him to decline the promotion (which would require his return to Britain for reassignment) than when he had been a much-disparaged and poorly paid police superintendent, as he recalled in his memoir.

*

Philip recorded little of the eventful year 1870 in his memoir, merely:

> *About a year passed away. And I got on very well with Sir [sic] Anthony Musgrave, who was an extremely pleasant man to serve under. He had two sisters with him and many pleasant dinners were given at Govt House, and occasionally a small dance.*

This brevity may reflect less his disenchantment with his life at age thirty-six than boredom with his memoir project at age seventy-eight. Thereafter, the memoir grows progressively thinner on detail.

A notable omission was the return of Lady Franklin. By then aged seventy-eight, again accompanied by her niece Sophie Cracroft, she

Philip Hankin in middle age. Date and place of photograph uncertain.

paid two brief visits to Victoria on their voyage to Alaska from San Francisco. En route, Sophie noted she would be meeting Musgrave, the new governor. She knew well the family of his fiancée, the Fields, in New York, and:

> *We also hope to find here our queer friend Hankin, a Lieut. in Cap^{tn} Richards ship when we were here 9 years ago, who went with us up the Fraser River—then a harum:scarum fellow. He afterwards left the service, & is now I believe Colonial Secretary here—an important post in which we can hardly fancy him.*

They arrived in Esquimalt on the evening of April 30, aboard the US steamer *Newbern*, the trooping and supply vessel plying between San Francisco and Fort Wrangell in Alaska. They sent messages to Musgrave, Admiral Arthur Farquhar,[4] and Mr. Hankin, who

> *came to us as soon as possible—unaltered in most ways, but stouter. [Hankin then escorted them on a boat tour of the harbour,] landing at his suggestion at a little Indian settlement [Plumper Bay]. . . . We were a lively party . . . & Mr. Hankin*

soon shewed us that he had not lost his fun. . . . We learned too f^{m} Mr. Hankin that we conveyed to him the news of his promotion—i.e. to be Commander on the Retired List, w^{h} was announced to him by a note f^{m} Cap^{tn} Richards.

This note further confirms Hankin's memory of having earlier declined such a promotion was adrift. The next morning Hankin arrived with Anthony Musgrave, nephew and private secretary to the governor. They brought an invitation for the ladies to stay at Government House, "w^{h} of course we were very glad to do." Philip had brought a carriage to convey the ladies to the residence, with a light cart to follow with their luggage and servants. They went by "an excellent road to Victoria" that had been a track, deep in mud, for their earlier visit, and the then-new Point Ellice bridge.

M$^{r.}$ Hankin pointed out all the changes & we passed, also the house in which we lodged with M^{r} & Mrs Moses, the little black barber and his big wife. During the drive, he had been reminding us of all the absurd things w^{h} happened, & the pranks he played, when with us up the Fraser River.

The ladies were most interested in the current situation over the potential union with Canada. Sophie described at length the pros and cons of the issue and the elements to be covered in the negotiation. Upon meeting Musgrave, still in his wheeled lay-chair, they "soon plunged into politics and found complete agreement as to the object of immediate interest."

After lunch, Philip and the younger Musgrave took the ladies on a carriage tour to call upon the bishop, who was away, then upon Sir James Douglas, to find only Lady Douglas and her granddaughter, Miss Helmcken, at home. As they travelled, Philip kept the ladies amused with reminiscences of his earlier pranks, even reciting from memory the Reverend William Crickmer's farewell address at Yale. Curiously, Sophie referred to Philip as "Captain Hankin," despite knowing of his recent promotion to the immediately lower rank of commander. They called upon the Cridges but, running short on time, could only chat from their carriage. They returned to Government House, where a formal dinner party had been arranged, driving around the cricket ground and racetrack of Beacon Hill. They much admired the "great number

Delegates from BC for negotiations on union with Canada disembark from a train, having crossed the continent. Helmcken on step, Carrall with carpet bag, and Trutch with cane. Watercolour by R.J. Banks.

of pretty cottages & country houses, with neat gardens—very different from the dusty, untidy, ragged suburbs of San Francisco."

Sixteen sat down to dinner, the first the governor had given since his long indisposition. His guests included the admiral, flag captain, flag lieutenant, Hankin (Isabel was still in San Francisco), Dr. Israel Wood Powell (who had operated on the host's leg) with his wife, Chief Justice Matthew Baillie Begbie, whom they had met previously at New Westminster, and Mr. and Mrs. Joseph Trutch. Women's suffrage formed an early topic of conversation. Sophie noted, "In the even[g] we had some music and *not* very good singing."

*

On May 14, a three-man delegation boarded the SS *Active* for San Francisco. They were the men whom Musgrave and the executive had selected to carry the revised text of British Columbia's proposed terms for joining Canada: Joseph Trutch, Dr. John Sebastian Helmcken, and Dr. Robert Carrall. They would make an articulate, experienced, and persuasive team. From San Francisco, they crossed the continent by the Union Pacific train. This journey was to change Helmcken's skepticism about the practicality and value of a railroad link with Canada through the Rockies.

They carried terms heavily biased in favour of British Columbia, presumably on the assumption that they would be in for hard bargaining. They included: the construction of such a rail link; Canada taking on BC's debt of over $1 million (about C$30 million in 2025); equivalent positions or generous pensions for government officers ousted by the union; three senators and six members of Parliament; Canada to pay for many aspects of infrastructure; et cetera—a long and costly list. Musgrave wrote to London confirming his complete trust in Trutch, who took three months' leave in London following the negotiation. He could fully brief them in person. The terms negotiated would be subject to ratification by both governments. At a date to be designated by Her Majesty, Queen Victoria, the Colony of British Columbia would join the Dominion of Canada as a province.

CHAPTER 27

Colony to Province, Part 3: Transition

Isabel Hankin stayed in San Francisco with her sister Kate for about ten weeks, convalescing after her latest bout of fever.[1] Hankin seems to have provided her with ample funds to spend on herself. Experiencing such a situation for the first time in her life, apparently, she did just that. When she boarded SS *Active* for the return voyage on June 4, she brought "her wardrobe and a lot of valuable jewelry." Her younger brother, Harry, escorted her for the journey.

Two days out, off a barren, rocky stretch of the northern Californian coast, and in thick fog, *Active*, under the command of a Captain Lyons, struck a rock and was totally wrecked. Lyons got all the passengers and crew safely ashore. He sent a messenger, first by boat 150 miles (240 kilometres) north to Crescent City, then by trail to Jacksonville, the nearest telegraph office, to call for help.

While passengers sheltered on shore, the crew attempted to recover important items: mail bags, passengers' baggage, and some of the cargo. Some local people, together with a few less scrupulous crew members, also scavenged the shoreline and wreck for whatever they could pilfer. Sadly, Isabel and her belongings were not reunited. After two days, the steamship *Pacific*, on its way south, stopped to pick up the castaways, their baggage, and some of the crew, and took them back to San Francisco, where Isabel telegraphed Philip that she was safe.

On June 21, SS *Pelican* steamed into Esquimalt Harbour, bringing the passengers from *Active*, including Isabel and Harry, along with thirty tons of freight from the wrecked vessel. It is not known if the Hankins had insured Isabel's luggage, but the owners of *Active* could not secure insurance on the vessel because of its advanced age and unseaworthiness. Jessie recorded in her diary, "The *Pelican* arrived early this morning. Isabel & Harry were on board. They both look very well in spite of the shipwreck." The very next day, Wednesday, Jessie noted, "Philip, Isabel, Lady Franklin, Miss Musgrave & several officers went to Goldstream."[2] On Saturday, "Philip & Isabel went to San Juan today & intend spending a few days there." Other members of the Goldstream party mentioned by Jessie were the younger Anthony Musgrave; Captain Gregory of *Pelican*; Captain Frederick Anstruther Herbert, RN, of HMS *Scylla*, which had replaced the departed HMS *Charybdis*; and Mrs. George Phillippo, wife of the newly arrived solicitor general. On the party's return from the "al fresco luncheon," the Hankins invited them to "a very elegant little supper."

Lady Franklin and Sophie Cracroft spent their last day visiting Esquimalt Harbour, whose future, Sophie feared, would be to fall into American hands. She also felt that the proposed "union with the Canadian Confederation," with a rail link, "will be most advantageous to B. Columbia."

*

Governor Musgrave was not in Victoria for Lady Franklin's last visit. Despite still needing a wheelchair, he had taken his long-delayed leave in San Francisco, travelling on HMS *Sparrowhawk*. Admiral Arthur Farquhar had placed the vessel at the disposal of the governor. The purpose of Musgrave's trip was to marry Miss Jeanie Lucinda Field, from an enormously wealthy and respected New York family. *Sparrowhawk* arrived first, Musgrave remaining on board to await the bridal party, expected the following day. They were coming by transcontinental express train in Pullman Palace carriages.

On Monday, June 20, the bishop of California conducted the wedding ceremony at Grace Church Cathedral to a select congregation under the rites of the Episcopal Church, but abbreviated to just five minutes. Captain Henry Wentworth Mist, RN, of *Sparrowhawk* stood to support the groom, Governor Musgrave, but there were no bridesmaids or any ostentation. The local correspondent of the *British Colonist* reported the occasion, noting that it was "in pleasant contrast to the pretentious display usually made in this city."

The couple remained in San Francisco for their honeymoon before boarding *Sparrowhawk* for the voyage home. At ten o'clock on the morning of July 2, a signal gun from the Race Rocks lighthouse alerted the town to the imminent arrival of *Sparrowhawk*, bringing the governor and his bride. The arrangements for their welcome went comically awry. The vessel was to have anchored in Esquimalt Harbour, to be met by the admiral's barge and a preliminary welcome by the navy. Sailors would man the yardarms of all the warships then in harbour. The newlyweds would proceed by the barge around to the HBC wharf in Victoria, where the official reception party of dignitaries, including Hankin, with a platoon of the Rifle Volunteers and a band, would celebrate their return.

Instead, *Sparrowhawk* anchored in Victoria's outer harbour. Hankin and some dignitaries, thinking that there had been a change of plan, left and started for Esquimalt. Meanwhile, the barge collected the Musgraves and brought them directly to the HBC wharf, an hour before expected. A few volunteers and bandsmen hastily mustered and played the anthem to the firing of guns by the *Boxer* and the ringing of the town's fire bells. The few spectators cheered as the governor made his way, with difficulty and in obvious pain, to his carriage. Philip arrived back at the wharf just in time to escort the new Mrs. Musgrave, beautifully dressed in black silk and fashionable hat, into the carriage.

The carriage proceeded to the nearby government buildings, where the mayor of Victoria presented an engraved parchment with a loyal address and cordial welcome home. The governor responded appropriately, and the mayor's party withdrew. Climbing once more into the carriage, the couple were driven through the town decorated with bunting and banners of welcome, with townspeople lining the streets, waving flags. On their arrival at Government House, eighteen young ladies dressed in white with blue sashes, Isabel's younger sister Ella Nagle among them, stood in two lines strewing roses in the couple's path as they entered the house. The dignitaries, by this time, had caught up with the proceedings. Together with the young ladies, they were welcomed

Philip Hankin and staff on the steps of the Colonial Secretariat building. On the top step are Hankin, wearing a top hat, and his deputy, Charles Good, on the right.

inside. Over cake and hospitality, toasts and expressions of appreciation were exchanged, then all but the Musgrave household departed.

With the governor's return, Philip Hankin's second period of serving as British Columbia's acting head of government concluded. He reverted to his position as colonial secretary and the governor's right-hand man. One of Governor Musgrave's first acts on his return was to appoint Philip Hankin as chairman of the Pilot Board, replacing Joseph Trutch. His naval experience, especially as a hydrographic surveyor, qualified him well for the role. His status as a commander, RN, retired, with the courtesy title of captain, reinforced his authority.

*

In a dispatch dated July 7, 1870, Sir John Young, Governor General of Canada, reported to his counterpart in British Columbia, announcing "the satisfactory termination of the negotiations between the delegates whom you dispatched and the Ministers of the Dominion." He enclosed a copy of the memorandum covering the terms of agreement. He added "the assurance that such provision shall be made for the retiring pensions of the Public Officers." Musgrave forwarded a copy of the report from Sir John to London, adding:

This result is even more satisfactory than I had anticipated. The terms assented to by the Government of Canada are liberal towards this Colony, and as they embrace an undertaking in respect of a railway—as to the possibility of which I had some doubt . . . I have no hesitation in my belief that they will be accepted with cordiality by the Community at large.

He closed by requesting formal instructions for the creation of a new council, required to ratify the agreement for union. The new colonial secretary in London, John Wodehouse, first Earl of Kimberley, responded that he had already heard the news from Sir John. He "was much gratified that the negotiations had such satisfactory progress."

Musgrave was justified in his belief that the people of the province would agree. The editor of the *British Colonist*, once he knew the terms, was enthusiastic. His editorial praised the governor, "in whose hands Confederation has, on so short a space of time, assumed a form so favourable and so practical." The editor also praised "those gentlemen who have so well discharged their duties in conducting the negotiations with Canada." He praised Canada "for the large and liberal spirit in which she has met the Colony." His only hesitation related to the mention of "responsible government." Even there, he felt, "it is gratifying, however, to know . . . a compromise was made which will fully meet . . . the wishes of the people."

On August 3, Colonial Secretary Hankin, on instructions from the governor, published the dispatch from Canada that included the agreed-upon terms. The agreement about the railway included the provision that the province would grant in trust to Canada a corridor of public land. It would comprise a strip of up to twenty miles (thirty-two kilometres) on either side of the line, for its entire length in British Columbia. Canada agreed to start construction of the railway within two years from agreement and complete it within ten years. It was to connect with the railroad system in Canada, running through the mountains to the Seaboard. This last term would later create much argument over its definition. Vancouver Islanders naturally assumed that it meant somewhere on the south or west coast of the island, perhaps Esquimalt or Port Alberni. In this, they were to be disappointed.

*

Susan Nagle had spent a month in Victoria while her school was closed for the summer. The family enjoyed the brief time that she, Isabel, and Harry were together again. When she returned to Yale in early August, it was still too oppressively hot to restart her classes. A month later, she wrote in her diary, "Much to our astonishment, Charley Hankin made his appearance this evening. He is on his way to Victoria." A few days after that, she mentioned receiving a letter from her mother, with the news that "Isabel too was improving and had decided not to go to England at present." This was the first intimation that her sister had still not fully recovered from the relapse of the ailment that had sent her to San Francisco.

The next news on the matter was in October, when "Isabel left for England accompanied by Charlie Hankin, on September 24," a most puzzling development. Susan also learned:

> *Philip has let his house to the Creases*[3] *and has gone to live with the Phillippo's, what changes take place, I wonder if we shall ever see her again. I sometimes think not.*

Over the next few months, even as the winter set in and the mail had difficulty getting upriver, Susan's journal records receiving letters from Isabel, either to herself or forwarded from her mother. In none of those entries does she mention anything of Isabel's circumstances, where she was living, or the state of her health.

There is, however, an interesting note at the back of Susan's diary covering 1871. It gives as Isabel's address in England: Earlswood Lodge, Red Hill, Surrey. That name was linked to the Royal Earlswood Institution for Mental Defectives, strongly supported by both Queen Victoria and her eldest son, Albert Edward, Prince of Wales. Opened in 1855, it was the first establishment to cater to people with learning disabilities, including Down syndrome, named after an early medical superintendent at Earlswood. Inmates, mainly children, lived in dormitories and tuberculosis was a major cause of death among them.

It is not possible that Isabel had Down syndrome, so what was she doing there? The "Lodge" at Earlswood, in the address she provided, referred to one of the twin gatehouse lodges, distinct from the main building. It seems to have been a separate clinic or sanatorium providing temporary residential care for fee-paying, female patients—such as wives and daughters of military officers serving overseas—needing maternity care or undergoing, say, a minor nervous breakdown. If so, she would have come under the observation and care of Dr. James Beveridge Spence, noted for his enlightened approach to mental disorders. It is possible, of course, that she was pregnant, but the couple remained childless. Hankin does not refer to any of this in the memoir.

*

On September 2, HMS *Beaver* anchored in Esquimalt Harbour, her surveying concluded. The last tasks had been to resurvey, at large scale, Beecher and Pedder Bays, identified as future overspill anchorages for the Esquimalt naval base. Three months later, the trusty but by then very tired vessel steamed round to anchor in James Bay, near the site of the present-day causeway. Staff Commander Daniel Pender and a Lieutenant Coghlan, acting as representatives of the Royal Navy, hauled down the pennant and White Ensign to signify that *Beaver* was no longer on the official list of ships. Two senior officers of the Hudson's Bay Company accepted the handover and ran up the company's flag. By this time, *Beaver* had been in active service for thirty-five years, eight of them as HMS.

A year earlier, Pender had married Amy Marie Gribbell, a sister of Reverend Frank Gribbell. He had come to British Columbia in 1866 to work briefly with William Duncan at Metlakatla. He then came to Victoria, conducting some services at St. John the Divine, and later became rector of St. Paul's, the naval church at Esquimalt. Both Pender and Gribbell were from England's West Country, and both belonged to the Masonic Lodge. Pender was a regular churchgoer.

In late 1870, Pender departed Esquimalt with his wife and daughter, bound for San Francisco and England. He had been on continuous duty, surveying the coasts of British Columbia for thirteen years, serving on HMS *Pumper*, *Hecate*, and *Beaver*. He joined his respected captain, Hydrographer George Henry Richards, in London. There, he worked to complete the seventeen admiralty charts he had most recently surveyed. In 1874, on Richards's retirement, he was promoted to assistant hydrographer until he retired in 1884 with the rank of captain. He died in March 1891.

*

In mid-October, the governor proclaimed a new constitution for the colony. It included the creation of nine electoral districts, based on centres of settlement: three in and around Victoria, another one for Nanaimo and Comox, one for New Westminster, and four more on the mainland. This transition structure was not the full responsible government wished for by a vociferous few and judged premature by Musgrave and London. The Colonial Office in London, through their appointed governor, would continue to be in charge, supported by four officers appointed by London, including Philip Hankin as colonial secretary, and two more members selected from the executive committee. These six would join the nine elected to form the new Legislative Council.

The proclamation also spelled out when and how the nine elections would be held for positions in the next session, to start in January 1871. The only qualification set for electors or candidates was just three months' residence in the district—and, as before, and left unsaid, that candidates be men, and not Indigenous, Chinese, or Hawai'ian. Time did not permit a register of voters before the election, to be held in a few weeks. Musgrave told London that he did not expect any opposition to confederation, just more clamour about responsible government. He was proved correct. The election duly produced sufficient candidates and proceeded without incident. The gadfly Amor De Cosmos was acclaimed as the member for Victoria district. The only business for the next session was to ratify the agreed terms for union with Canada.

*

The election process underway, the governor and his chief officer, Philip Hankin, boarded *Sparrowhawk* for a two-week tour of inspection of some up-island communities. They also planned to visit Knight Inlet, where a dispute had arisen between people of the local Dzawadi community[4] and a party of miners working a promising deposit of copper ore. The officials also invited a photograper, Mr. Green, to accompany them. None of Green's images from the trip seem to have survived. On their way to the scene of the dispute at Knight Inlet, *Sparrowhawk* briefly called into Nanaimo, Fort Rupert, Alert Bay, and logging operations at Menzies and Elk Bays.

Governor Musgrave's report to London noted that at the head of the inlet, on hearing *Sparrowhawk*'s approaching engines, the Dzawadi

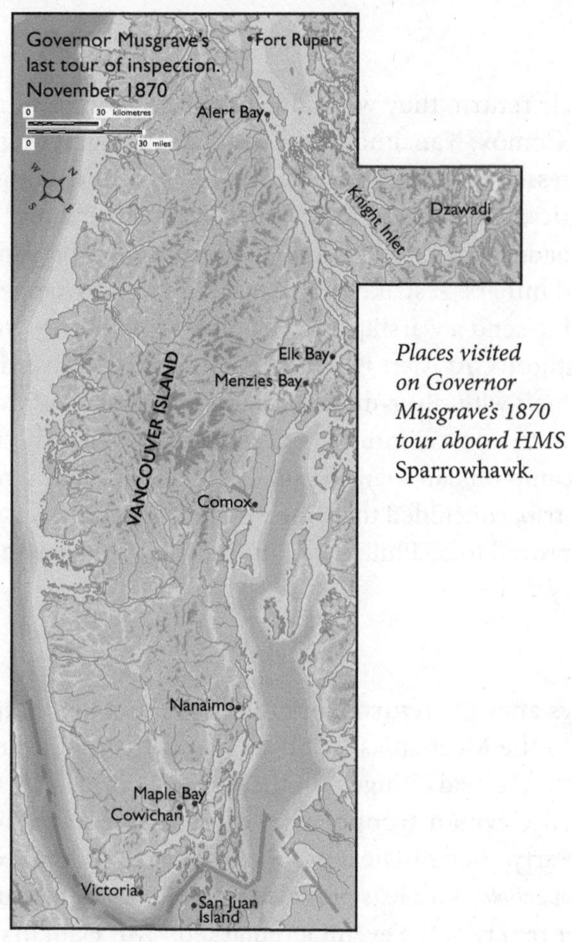

Places visited on Governor Musgrave's 1870 tour aboard HMS Sparrowhawk.

chieftain hurriedly returned all the sacks of ore his people had seized from the miners. When the ships had anchored at the village, the Dzawadi chiefs came aboard, visibly terrified, along with one miner in a placatory mood. With Hankin interpreting in Chinuk Wawa, the Dzawadi explained they supposed the miners to be after gold, which they wished to mine for themselves or be compensated for the land. The miner clarified about the copper and told the visitors that he understood the mistake. He wished to drop any charges of obstruction and taking his ore, on the understanding that he and his men could continue without further trouble. Musgrave, through Hankin, pardoned the Dzawadi. He also admonished the miners to maintain good faith with the local people in their dealings and behaviour. Musgrave reported to London, "I do not apprehend any further difficulty."

On their return, they were able to spend more time meeting the settlers at Comox, Nanaimo, and Cowichan. Musgrave reported being most impressed with the agricultural success of the new and vigorous communities, and of the coal mining centre of Nanaimo. Of the latter place, he made no mention to London of the trouble brewing among the dissatisfied miners. A strike and riots were about to happen. He would soon need to send a warship and a company of marines to support the civilian authority. At Alert Bay and Fort Rupert, the governor presented the local chiefs with silver-mounted batons as symbols of their authority. He called in to a new community of settlers at Maple Bay and the Royal Marines' camp on San Juan Island. The *British Colonist*, reporting the two-week trip, concluded that "the weather, generally, was unpleasant." This tour proved to be Philip Hankin's last voyage aboard a vessel of the Royal Navy.

*

A few days after his return from the trip, Philip gave another of his readings to the Mechanics Institute. It was the first evening of their new season. He read "Bingen on the Rhine," a broadside ballad about a wounded German trooper in the French Foreign Legion; "Bob Sawyer's Party," one of Dickens's *Pickwick Papers*; and excerpts from *David Copperfield*. Vocalists provided interludes between his pieces. The newspaper report of the evening remarked, "Mr. Hankin's reading was in his usual good style, especially his prose." It also noted the attendance of Miss Musgrave and the governor's nephew, Anthony.

*

Governor Musgrave raised with London the question of Hankin's future and that of his other officers under confederation. The terms agreed by Canada included provision for pensions for those not required to serve in the new government. Canada had implied that they would prefer not to provide such pensions but would offer suitable places to most of the affected people. Musgrave wondered if London might find suitable places in other British colonies for those not required by Canada. Of all the officers and magistrates, most likely only Hankin and Phillippo would be affected. Officials in London minuted Musgrave's dispatch about the former:

[Hankin] was appointed in 1868, & has done well there & for some little time administered the Gov^{t}, between Govr Seymour death and Mr. Musgrave's assumption of the Gov^{t}. . . .

I think neither of them are bad men. Mr Hankin I take to be a rough & ready enterprising kind of person, with[ou]^{t} much book learning—Mr Phillippo a respectable lawyer.

The secretary for the colonies eventually replied:

As regards Mr Hankin and M^{r}. Phillippo, . . . I will bear in mind your suggestion that their services should be transferred to some other Colony, but as appointments of like importance and value are comparatively few and the claimants to promotion are many, I fear that there is little chance of my being able to meet your wishes.

In the meantime, Susan recorded in her diary:

Philip has applied for another appt. and thinks he will get a Lieut. Gov. Ship on some of the Islands. Bella [Isabel] is visiting at the Duke of Buckingham's. What a contrast between us two—one a guest at a Dukes, the other teaching at (I might almost say) a ragged school, or next door to it, in a little out of the way part of the world. I hope I am not envious.

She had noted, a few weeks earlier, "Isabel is under the Drs Hands, yet, he gives good hope tho of her recovery."

*

On January 6, 1871, the new Legislative Council met, having dined at Government House the evening before. The first order of business was to elect the Speaker. De Cosmos nominated Dr. John Sebastian Helmcken, who declined, suggesting the colonial secretary had far more experience in this role. Philip Hankin was proposed and accepted unanimously. He took the chair, thanked the members for the honour, then announced a recess. After lunch, Governor Musgrave arrived, wearing full gold-braided civil service dress with knee breeches and a feathered fore-and-aft hat. A guard of honour by the Rifle Volunteers presented arms, with a band playing the national anthem. Anthony, his nephew and private secretary, supported his arm. Speaker Hankin duly received him. Musgrave's speech, delivered "in a loud and clear voice," stressed

Musicians and an escort platoon of Royal Rifle Volunteers assemble behind the Colonial Secretariat building, awaiting the arrival of Governor Musgrave, January 1871.

the significance of the session. He outlined what he was doing to better prepare for the new form of government that a province of Canada would require.

At the end of January 1871, the council passed a motion requesting the Queen to admit British Columbia to the Dominion of Canada. London needed to await Canada's equivalent request before acting. This followed, but only after a contentious debate and vote in the Canadian Senate, on April 5. On June 26, Musgrave proclaimed Her Majesty's assent to the "Constitution Act, 1871," and declared that "it shall take effect on, from, and after the 19th day of July, 1871. . . the thirty fifth year of Her Majesty's reign." He declared July 20 to be a public holiday. Anthony Musgrave was appointed a Companion of the Order of St. Michael and St. George for his services related to this signal development.

Musgrave declined the invitation to be the first lieutenant governor of the new province. He cited as reasons the discrepancy between the lower salary he would receive and the high cost of living in Victoria, together with his injured leg. He learned his successor was to be Joseph Trutch, who had been in England with his wife, and would be returning to Victoria later in July. He would depart on July 25, leaving Philip Hankin in temporary charge of the government for the third time. *Sparrowhawk* would convey the Musgrave party to San Francisco, then return with the Trutches.

Musgrave's most immediate concerns were advice and treatment for his still-bothersome leg from specialists in London, and his wife Jeanie's pregnancy. The couple were anxious to avoid crossing the Rockies and Atlantic in winter. His next post was as governor of Natal, South Africa. He continued with further significant appointments and received a knighthood, as KCMG, in 1875. He died in Queensland in 1888.

Musgrave's departure from Esquimalt was a splendid affair. As the admiral's barge from *Zealous* brought the departing governor's party on board *Sparrowhawk*, all the warships in harbour, including an American sloop, USS *Saranac*,[5] manned the yardarms, and *Zealous* fired a salute of seventeen guns. As the barge passed each ship, there came three hearty cheers. The men of *Sparrowhawk* returned them. The band from *Zealous* played "Home Sweet Home," "Auld Lang Syne" and "other appropriate airs." Once aboard, Admiral Farquhar came to take his leave of the governor. As soon as he had done so and boarded his barge, *Sparrowhawk* got underway and left Esquimalt Harbour at full speed.

*

In May, Susan reported Philip had a painful hip, which worsened and confined him to bed. A doctor diagnosed an abscess. While still suffering, he received a telegram from Isabel saying she would leave England on June 9, with his permission. He replied, enigmatically, "All serene." This seems to indicate that she had been released from Earlswood Lodge and felt fit enough to travel. Although he knew he would be coming back to England, perhaps within a few weeks, he did not wish to dissuade her. Philip noted in his memoir, "I accepted my Pension and retired—returning with my wife to England."

Just before leaving Victoria, on August 15, having handed over his duties as administrator to the new lieutenant governor, Hankin wrote him a letter. He wanted to place on record that he was entitled to the pension agreed effective July 20, the date of union. Philip asked Trutch to inform the authorities in Canada of his request that the regular payments be made to his agent in London. According to the notice in the *British Colonist* on his imminent departure:

> *The Hon. P.J. Hankin sails for England this morning. Mr. Hankin retires with the rank of Captain, RN, on half pay, and with a pension from the Dominion Government of $533.*[6] *He has been many years connected with this Colony in various capacities, during the last three years as Colonial Secretary, and has twice [in fact, three times] been called upon to administer the government. As a public officer, he has been faithful and attentive, and as a citizen has gained the good opinion of all. We wish Mr. Hankin a safe and pleasant voyage home and a prosperous career.*

Philip J. Hankin, commander, RN (retired). Date and place of photograph uncertain.

CHAPTER 28

Private Secretary to a Duke

According to Philip Hankin's memoir, he and Isabel arrived back in England together. This would have been in late September 1871. It is not clear how many of their personal possessions they brought with them, or what happened to the rest. It is reasonable to assume that by this time, they had accumulated a quantity of furniture and possessions. He was an avid reader, so probably would have also built a personal library. As befitted a gentleman and senior official, he would have had an extensive wardrobe. He did not know what the future held but would have been confident that his career would continue to advance; he was in no hurry to pursue a position.

On their arrival, the Duke of Buckingham invited the Hankins to spend a week at Stowe House.[1] Naturally, Philip accepted, and they were "received with the greatest kindness by the Duke & Duchess and their three charming daughters." Isabel had enjoyed their hospitality and care several times and was evidently close friends with the family. Philip too had briefly been a guest at Stowe on his return from Belize. After that week at Stowe, the Hankins began a vacation on the Riviera and Malta. He had visited these places in 1859 as a newly qualified lieutenant aboard HMS *Cadmus* and HMS *Orion*.[2] No sooner had they arrived in Menton, on the French coast near the Italian border, than a letter arrived from the duke.

Buckingham explained that for some time he had been looking for a gentleman to fill the office of private secretary at Stowe. If Hankin cared for the position, it was his.

> *Besides a very comfortable salary [the* Victoria British Colonist *reported it to be £1,000], a pretty little house, 5 mins. walk from Stowe, was offered me, rent free. This kind offer I accepted without any hesitation. I was just starting for Naples and Malta, so returned by one of the P&O Steamers from the latter place to England. I went the day after my arrival to Stowe.*

The Hankins' future for the following decade was settled.

*

On April 13, 1872, the *British Colonist* published a gossipy, anonymous letter from "our English Correspondent," dated February 23. The writer could well have been either Gilbert Sproat, then BC's agent general, or Alfred Waddington, who had previously posted similar reports. The letter reported on some people from Victoria encountered in London, including Sir Arthur Edward Kennedy, who was "in Town, looking none the worse for his five years in Africa. He told us today that he should leave for Hong Kong in a few days." The writer also met

> *Philip Hankin, the luckiest of the lucky; he looks more self-complacent and comfortable than ever. He is now Private Secretary to the Duke of Buckingham and, of course, holds that post and enjoys the pension at the same time. Sir Arthur Kennedy says, 'he is lucky certainly, but a most deserving young man.' You will probably shortly hear of his being in Parliament—oh! The luck of some people.*

It must have been most agreeable for both Hankin and Kennedy, meeting each other again after a gap of five eventful years.

*

The memoir records that Philip spent nearly the next two years at Stowe. In fact, it was over three. Although the duke was no longer in the government, he still had many activities requiring the services of an able lieutenant. He was a member of the House of Lords, the Lord Lieutenant of the county, and Lieutenant Colonel Commandant of the Royal Bucks[3] Hussars, a yeomanry regiment of cavalry with some field guns. Since 1867, he had served as the elected chairman of the Bucks Quarter Sessions.[4] In addition to his dukedom, he held several other hereditary titles.

The Duke of Buckingham and Chandos. Caricature by "Spy" (Carlo Pellegrini) in Vanity Fair *magazine, May 29, 1875.*

Aerial oblique view of Stowe House and grounds, now configured as a prestigious private school.

The third duke was a landowner with a better head for business than his father, who had died bankrupt, leaving horrendous debts. He had been called "the greatest debtor in the world." Much of the family's fortune had vanished. They had auctioned off the furniture, old masters, and silver. All real estate was gone, except for the house and core ten thousand acres of Stowe. The present duke had to maintain what lands remained at Stowe and the immense house itself, as well as attempting to pay off his father's debts. All this, understandably, required considerable and competent management by the duke and his confidential secretary. Philip's memoir, however, records nothing of such details of his work while at Stowe.

*

Hankin did report in his memoir one event during his time there. This was the death, in February 1874, of Caroline, the Duchess of Buckingham. She was the daughter of Robert Harvey of Langley Park, the Sheriff of Buckinghamshire, and she had married the rising Tory politician the Honourable Richard Chandos-Grenville in 1851. Twenty years later, when the Hankins were guests at Stowe, they had three daughters—Lady Mary, then aged nineteen, Lady Anne, eighteen, and Lady Caroline Jemima, thirteen—but no son to inherit the title of duke. As was the tradition in his ducal line, he had chosen an heiress for his bride, to refresh the periodically waning family fortune. In Caroline's case, there could also have been some family connection with the Chandos-Grenvilles. Her brother, Sir Robert, was a captain in the Royal Bucks Hussars, the duke's regiment.

Notwithstanding such strategic considerations, the third duke, his duchess, and their daughters formed a strong, loving relationship. Her passing deeply saddened the duke and everyone at Stowe. Philip's memoir recorded: "The dear Duchess died to the everlasting grief of her family and deeply regretted by all who knew her." She had been especially compassionate to Isabel during the periodic relapses of her unidentified ailment.

*

In the same month his wife died, the duke's close political associate, Benjamin Disraeli, had a major success. His Conservative party was re-elected in a landslide, and he became prime minister for the second time. His agenda would focus on Britain's imperial prestige. A few months later, he invited Buckingham to take the office of governor of the Madras Presidency in India, and the duke accepted. After that of the viceroy, it was the second-most senior position in India, Queen Victoria's "Jewel in the Crown," at the height of the Raj, and was a position of high distinction and financial reward. Buckingham invited Hankin to continue as his private secretary with him in India. Recognizing the benefits, Philip accepted. He was by then thirty-eight years old.

In addition to his three daughters, the duke's family entourage embarking for Madras included his sister Lady Anna Gore-Langton, with her son and daughter. Unknown reasons delayed the party's departure by several months. Their route probably took them through the Suez Canal, opened six years earlier. They eventually arrived in November 1875.

By coincidence, that same month, the astute Disraeli, to everyone's surprise, purchased a forty-four percent shareholding in the Suez Canal Company from the Khedive of Egypt. Previously, British commercial interests, heavily invested in the Cape route to India and the Far East, opposed the canal. Disraeli's coup, however, proved of enormous strategic and financial benefit to the British Empire.

*

Three of Philip Hankin's elder siblings had also served in Madras. His eldest brother, Frederick George, had retired as a lieutenant colonel in the staff corps of the army, based there for many years. His next brother, Edward Lewis, had achieved even higher rank, that of major general in the Indian Army, and also served in a senior role in the Indian Civil Service, based in Madras. Philip's elder sister, Constance Seymour, had also gone out to marry a senior officer of the Madras Native Infantry, but had died young, in childbirth.

*

Isabel, who had been visiting her parents in Victoria for three weeks, joined her husband at Madras soon after. She had travelled via San Francisco, Yokohama, and China. For the first leg of her trip, her mother accompanied her aboard the SS *Pacific*, and they had a lucky escape of timing. On the same journey, two weeks later, the *Pacific* rounded Cape Flattery, heading south in a gale at night, when it struck another vessel and sank. Of the 275 persons aboard, all but one were lost.

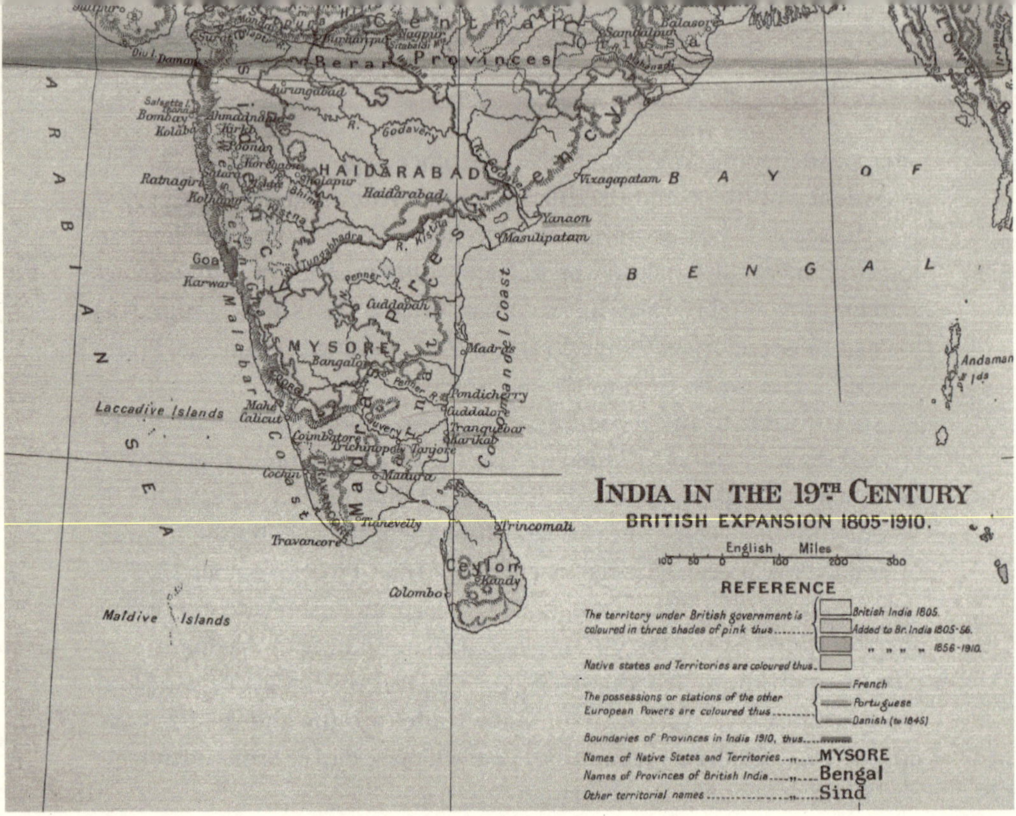

Stanford's map of southern India at the height of the Raj era. The Madras Presidency included much of the southeastern part of the subcontinent.

HMS Serapis*, a troopship converted as a royal yacht for the Prince of Wales's visit to India.*

As a senior official in the governor's staff, Hankin and his wife were provided with a sumptuous villa and a contingent of servants within the fortified compound called Government House. They had come a long way from when they lived above Victoria's police barracks and afterward, when they rented a simple house with a ladder for access and neither shutters nor curtains in Belize.

*

Soon after arriving, the new governor received a royal visitor, Albert Edward, the Prince of Wales, eldest son of Queen Victoria. The prince had set off from London by royal train to Brindisi, a port on the "heel" of Italy, commanding the entrance to the Adriatic. With a huge retinue, he boarded a flotilla of four vessels: the Royal Yacht *Osborne*, HMS *Serapis*, a converted troopship, and two frigates, HMS *Hercules* and *Pallas*. They arrived at Bombay (now Mumbai) on November 8, 1875. Over the next four months, the prince and his party kept a hectic round of public appearances, galas, and ceremonial events with imperial officers and Indian maharajas and nawabs.

After visiting Ceylon (now Sri Lanka) on the morning of December 13, the party arrived by train at Madras (now Chennai). To greet the royal visitor were Governor Buckingham and his officials, including Hankin, the senior of those. Also present were the maharajas and dignitaries of the four states comprising the Presidency of Madras, and military officers, everyone in splendid uniforms. The procession drove through the streets to Government House with 12,500 children from 126 schools and colleges waving flags and singing from elevated stands as they passed. A servant held a golden umbrella over the prince so that onlookers might identify him.

Following introductions between the governor's family and staff and the prince and the senior officers of his retinue, they all took breakfast. The prince changed into his uniform to formally receive each maharaja and nawab paying respects to the imperial visitor. Many of these Indian potentates could trace their lineage back over centuries. A grand levee followed these audiences. Held in the vast banqueting hall, it was "attended by every European and Native who could obtain access to it." After that, the governor gave a state banquet for just the most senior fifty names, in honour of the prince.

Ladies scattering flower petals welcome the Prince of Wales to India.

Except for one day, the anniversary of the death of his father, which the prince observed in seclusion at the governor's country residence Guindy Park, activities filled the next few days. These included formal visits from leaders of local institutions such as universities and Freemasons, as well as return visits to the states' princes, each with the presentation of valuable gifts and their reciprocation.

Several banquets included performances by local dancers and performers. At a lunch put on by "the Club," a social institution found in all parts of the British Empire, the prince tasted the renowned Madras curries. There followed a military review of the eight British and Indian regiments stationed in the presidency. Attended by the seven military members of his suite, the prince, wearing the uniform of the 10th Hussars, acknowledged the salutes of the troops as they passed in review.

One of the final spectacles of the royal visit to Madras took place at the harbour on the evening of December 17. First, from a special stage, the party watched a splendid display of fireworks from both the visiting ships and local craft. The festivity culminated in local fishermen displaying their skills in riding the huge breakers of the Coromandel Coast, "with wildest yells." The party then moved to the railway station for farewell entertainments provided by the local people, comprising traditional songs, dances, and recitals by renowned performers. By then his highness was exhausted, made his excuses, and retired.

The prince was up just four hours later to join a meet of the Madras pack of hounds, hunting jackals. This was the last day of the princely visit to Madras. At five thirty that evening the party boarded the ships to set sail bound for Calcutta (now Kolkata). The total time the prince had spent in Madras was just six days, of which five were crammed with official events. The prince and his retinue were impressed with how much local knowledge Governor Buckingham had gained in the short time he had been in the position. The whole affair must have been invaluable for the duke in meeting all the important people of his region, most for the first time.

Hankin's memoir recorded little of the pomp of the occasion. He did, however, claim to have established a friendship with the prince:

> *One day he took me with him, on board his ship, the 'Serapis,' and showed me his Photographs, and anything he thought would interest me. He was one of the kindest and most charming of men and made one feel quite at ease immediately.*

The prince also presented Philip with a signed photograph of himself, which, together with those of the King and Queen of the Sandwich Islands, Hankin treasured for many years. They were listed in the items when the Hankins auctioned the contents of his house in James Bay in 1903.

*

Hankin recorded another event, the Delhi Durbar, when Queen Victoria was proclaimed Empress of India. Held during the first two weeks of January 1877, the durbar (meaning "court") signified the transfer of control of British India from the East India Company to the Crown. The viceroy, Lord Edward Robert Bulwer-Lytton, presided over the grand occasion. The governor, his family, and senior members of his staff also attended. They witnessed a spectacular assembly of sixty-three maharajas, nizams, nawabs, and intellectuals, many carried in howdahs above richly decorated elephants. Fifteen thousand British and Indian troops paraded in demonstration of the colony's military might.

The Grand Durbar, or court, at Delhi in January 1877 to celebrate Queen Victoria being declared Empress of India. Buckingham and Hankin attended.

During all this glitter and opulence, one lone figure named Ganesh Vasudeo Joshi, wearing "homespun, spotless white *khadi* fabric," rose to deliver a politely worded petition. He requested that "Her Majesty grant to India the same political and social status as is enjoyed by her British subjects." This is considered the beginning of the campaign for a free India.

*

The governor devoted much of his energies during his five-year term of office to easing the effects on the populace of a combination of natural disasters. A prolonged famine followed the failure of two successive rainy seasons, made worse by a cholera epidemic. The overall crisis affected eighteen million people, of whom more than a million died. The duke called upon his extensive political and financial contacts in London, including the lord mayor, to establish and fund a relief program. He created a program to employ over seven hundred thousand workers to build a waterway to connect Madras city with two rivers. It provided all-season communication with the northern parts of his governorship, or "presidency." They named it the Buckingham Canal.

In 1879, in the Rampa region in the northern part of the Madras Presidency, brewing unrest over harsh taxation erupted into a full rebellion. Hill tribes who had led an independent life for centuries had just

The duke, as governor of Madras, conveyed by barge, pays a ceremonial call on the neighbouring Rajah of Travancore at Trivandrum. The hatless man at the bottom of the stairs appears to be Secretary Hankin. Painting by Raja Ravi Varma, 1881.

come under the control of a tyrannical official. Further provoking the situation, the government imposed a new tax on "toddy," their traditional fermented drink. In protest, the local people attacked police stations in an increasing wave of violence. The Madras government sent a massive force of police, infantry, and even cavalry to quell the insurrection. They exiled many captured revolutionaries to the remote Andaman Islands. Afterward, the British government repealed the tax on toddy and put in place conciliatory measures to improve the conditions of the hill tribes.

All these events and measures involved the governor and his effective chief of staff, Philip Hankin. In addition to Hankin, the duke's personal staff included a military secretary, two aides-de-camp and their two assistants, a medical officer, and a bodyguard. Over the five years he spent in India, the workload on the conscientious Hankin proved onerous, although he made no reference to such pressure in the memoir. He does not appear to have taken any leave during that period. In October 1878, the *British Colonist* in Victoria republished an article from the *Bengal Gazette* of August that year, discussing the apparent changes to Philip in just three years:

> *We are sure Captain Hankin will admit [he is] the most hard-worked of men. Can anyone look at that gallant captain, and dare to affirm that his is not an anxious life, or declare that the*

consumption of midnight kerosine is not driving him into a premature grave. 'What has he to do?' We reply, 'What has he not to do?' Note his care worn lineaments, his emaciated frame, his melancholy expression, his gloomy accents, his loss of appetite, his inability to ride, drive, or dance. . . . For no jollier-looking man ever retired from the Navy, with all the pleasant attributes of a sailor, than Captain Hankin, and no more generally popular a functionary is there in the Presidency. . . . [The role] seems to suit him admirably; though it is still open to doubt whether a Governor is wise in bringing a Private Secretary out with him instead of appointing some young official on the spot, who is acquainted with local ways and people.

The following year, 1879, the *British Colonist* for March 25 carried a curious, if erroneous, snippet:

Knighted.—Hon. Philip Hankin, late Colonial Secretary of the Colony of British Columbia, and now in India, has been made a Knight. Lady Hankin is a daughter of Captain Nagle of this city.

There was no knighthood or other official recognition of Hankin's five years of service, in a senior capacity, to the imperial government when, at long last, he retired. In April 1880, William Ewart Gladstone replaced Benjamin Disraeli as prime minister, who appointed William Adam to replace the Duke of Buckingham as governor of Madras. Governor Adam arrived in December of that year. Presumably, the duke, his extended family, and Philip and Isabel Hankin all then returned to Britain. The absence of any decoration for the service he rendered would have been unusual, signifying, perhaps, a falling-out between the duke and Hankin. A deteriorating relationship would have exacerbated the stress commented on by the *Bengal Gazette.* If so, Philip mentioned no such contretemps in the memoir.

CHAPTER 29
Life in Retirement

Philip Hankin's financial situation when he returned to Britain in early 1881 is unclear. Although he had technically been connected with the prestigious Indian Civil Service (ICS), it had been only a temporary position. Nor had he served the minimum of twenty-five years required to qualify for ICS officers' standard pension of £1,000 annually. The memoir does not record his salary while working for the duke at Stowe, but according to the *British Colonist*, it was £1,000. Arrangements for his salary and allowances while in Madras are not mentioned. Nor are details of any bonus or pension the duke might have granted him afterward.

He had two other pensions: £155 from the Royal Navy as a commander, retired, and £533 from Canada for his services to the Colony of British Columbia.[1] These would amount to £688 (about C$134,000 in 2025). Also, during his five years at Stowe and five more in Madras, Hankin's living expenses would have been minimal. He should have been able to save and invest much of his salary and pensions. Financially, he could expect quite a comfortable retirement. He was still only forty-five years old.

Philip gave no hint in his memoir of how his relationship with the duke and his family remained after they all returned to England. Perhaps significantly, he made no further comment about them, or of revisiting Stowe, for the rest of his narrative.

*

Philip Hankin as a distinguished, mature gentleman.
Photograph taken at Muswell Hill, London, 1911.

After Hankin's return from Madras, it becomes progressively more difficult to reconcile the events recorded in the memoir with other evidence of his activities. There are gaps, some of a few years' duration, where he records nothing that happened in his life. Later evidence, however, provides hints of what he had probably been doing, and where. The inevitable result is ambiguity in the chronology of his last decades.

According to the memoir, his first activities on returning were to make a tour of several major cities on the continent, followed by nearly two years in Paris working to improve his French. Contradicting the memoir, a notice in the *British Colonist* reported Philip and Isabel arriving in Victoria on June 30, 1881. Philip records the Victoria visit as following Paris, but the timing does not support that. It can only have been soon after their arrival from India. Isabel's father, Jeremiah Nagle, died the following year, January 6, 1882, and the memoir describes the purpose of the brief visit was "to see her parents." The tour of Europe and the sojourn in Paris must have been later, possibly in late 1881 through 1883.

Next in the memoir comes a curious escapade in the southern United States. Philip had heard gossip about a lucrative opportunity in Florida. A promoter called Friedland had bought land there and was selling off parcels. He told a plausible story that purchasers could establish their own orange groves, then sell the fruit at a profit in New York. Interested but skeptical, Philip went there to see for himself. He found that it was located in a remote area and that several gullible young Englishmen had invested their small savings in the scheme. They had cleared their plots, bought and planted four-inch-high orange seedlings, and prepared to wait seven years for them to bear fruit. Philip learned that, during some winters, sharp frosts would kill off the saplings. Also, mosquitoes and other insects plagued the area, "to say nothing of snakes." He decided the scheme was not for him.

Wanting to cover the costs of his journey, he recalled that Americans admired the works of Dickens, and so he began a series of readings in different towns throughout the southern states. He hired a friend he had made at the orange groves to accompany him as a front man. The man would go ahead to the next town, arrange a venue, and post large notices declaring, "Commander Hankin of the British Navy would arrive on such a date and give readings from Dickens." The tour lasted six weeks. He returned to London via New York. Hankin recalled:

> *This turned out a very good spec. for I managed to make about a hundred dollars a week clear of expenses. . . . Altogether, I made enough money to pay my expenses from England and home again.*

There is no supporting evidence for the timing of the Florida investigation and his subsequent speaking tour, except a link to the next reported episode: "I now settled down in the Isle of Wight for 2 years." The census of 1901 confirms his presence there. This suggests that he set out for Florida perhaps in 1899, leaving a hiatus of nearly two decades of his life from the memoir.

Much later, when he spent part of the years 1906 and 1907 in Vancouver, he offered language lessons, mentioning he had spent ten years living in France and another ten in Germany. These periods, if accurate, would seem to fill most of the missing years in his narrative. It seems a pity that Hankin chose not to recall and write anything of his experiences during those extended periods spent in Europe.

In his accounts of travels in the memoir, Philip usually wrote "I," not "we." Isabel's frail condition, physically and perhaps emotionally, added to their lack of a permanent home or support system in Britain, makes it probable that Isabel accompanied him on most of his peregrinations, but not all. A brief note in the *British Colonist* in December 1887 reported Captain Hankin coming to Vancouver and Victoria with a Colonel George B.B. Hobart, but without mention of Isabel. The men spent a few days, then carried on to San Francisco. Philip had known Hobart well in Madras when he served as military secretary to the duke.

Where and with whom Isabel stayed during her husband's absence is unclear. Possibilities include at Stowe House, or with Mary Jane Hankin, Charles's widow, who, after his death in 1876, continued running their malting business in Great Amwell, near Stanstead Abbotts. It is also possible that by then he and Isabel had taken a house in Ryde, on the Isle of Wight, and made enough friends there for her to be left on her own. The British census for 1901 has them living in Ryde. Philip had known the town when he was a midshipman aboard HMS *Sidon* at Spithead in 1853 (see chapter 3). It was there that his friend Frank Thomson had taken him for dances, and where he had met many other families socially. Thomson had died in 1884, but before that, they had been in contact and the Hankins had become reacquainted with Frank's daughter and her family.

While Ryde continued to be a popular summer resort, "in the winter it was deadly dull . . . like a deserted city." He recorded, "Occasionally, the pleasure of my company was requested to tea, but I got very tired of teas, besides, it was impossible to eat one's dinner afterwards." He then noted:

> *The Wanderlust came over me. I decided to go to Tasmania. . . . My wife said she could be ready in a fortnight, and off we started. We went in a small vessel of 2,000 tons, and the accommodation was unheated. We touched at the Cape, but it was the commencement of the Boer War and we were not allowed to land. Soon after leaving Cape Town, the weather became very cold and rough and our little vessel pitched terribly, but considering the heavy seas we encountered, proved herself a good sea boat. It was, however, 6 weeks before we reached Melbourne.*

The detail about the Boer War would place their journey in 1899. One can only sympathize with Isabel, then fifty-three years old, enduring the fury of the great Southern Ocean in an unheated cabin aboard a tiny ship.

The memoir continues, "We managed luckily to just catch another vessel starting for Hobart, Tasmania." This crossing would have traversed the Bass Strait, just as notorious for rough seas as their crossing from the Cape. Tasmania did not live up to the glowing reports Philip had heard. The temperature in Hobart varied from 98°F (37°C) at eleven thirty a.m. to 40°F (4°C) five hours later, "and we had to sit over a large fire." He noted:

> *[Tasmania] is a wonderful country for apples and greengages, but one can't live on them. . . . I never saw in any country so many house flies, tarantulas, and venomous snakes. I killed two or three of them in the garden. I was very sorry afterwards, that I had not gone to Auckland.*

Philip and the long-suffering Isabel stayed just two months in Hobart before trying the second town on the island, Launceston. They found it "much nicer and prettier than Hobart," but remained only ten days. Next, they visited Melbourne, "a very fine city." After a month, they took a ship via Fiji and the Sandwich Islands to their familiar Victoria. Philip noted in the memoir that he "found the place much grown, and improved, and not many old friends and acquaintances." The *Victoria Daily Times* for June 12, 1902, noted their arrival:

> *Philip Hankin one of the pioneers of British Columbia, who during the past 14 or 15 years has lived in different parts of the world, arrived on the RMS Aorangi yesterday afternoon, accompanied by Mrs. Hankin. Mr. Hankin has travelled about a great deal since last here, and is now more firmly convinced than ever that Victoria is the most charming residential spot he has ever seen. He was in Victoria at the time this place was a colony, and had then taken an interest in public life. Mrs. Hankin is the daughter of the late Capt. Nagle.*

The phrase "taken an interest in public life" was sadly ignorant or dismissive of his contribution as a senior member of the government, including three spells as its head. Hankin's memoir continued:

[We] stayed in rooms for a month, and then built a very pretty little house close to Beacon Hill, with lovely views of the sea and snow-capped mountains.

Later information places this house on "Battery Street, one block from Beacon Hill end of car track"—presumably, the tramcar line. Far from being a "little house," it contained a drawing room, morning room, dining room, kitchen, and at least two bedrooms. It would surely have taken more than a month to locate and acquire the parcel, then construct, finish, and furnish such a residence. They would have had to ship much of their furniture and chattels from England—that, alone, would have taken a few months.

Despite diligent study of the detailed and dated fire insurance plans and annual city gazetteers, providing names of owners, the eminent local historian John Adams and other researchers have found no record of such a house, occupancy by the Hankins, nor of its sale. The most likely candidate seems to be 602 Battery Street, but the record gives the builder of that house as G.S. Carr in 1902 and valued at $1,000. The house remains virtually the same as in a 1910 photo, with a hexagonal turret and splendid views of the strait off today's Dallas Road and the Olympic Mountains beyond. Sadly, the couple could not enjoy their new home for long. Philip wrote:

Now my wife was taken with her last fatal illness, and she expressed a wish to get back to England, so I managed to get rid of the house, and sold the furniture, and we started for England.

The stresses of the long journey had proved too much for her already weakened system. Perhaps to ease further strain at sea, Philip opted to take the new Canadian Pacific Railway (CPR) to the east coast. He continued, "We only reached Hamilton, Ont. Canada, and there my dear wife died and is buried." The date recorded is September 17, 1903. Isabel was fifty-seven.

The auction of their furniture and treasures took place on April 1, 1903, and the list makes fascinating reading. There were mahogany tables, sofas, easy chairs, a rolltop desk, beds, chests of drawers, wardrobe, mirrors, and carpets; just as one would expect in a retired, well-travelled, late-Victorian gentleman's house. There was also a wealth

AUCTION

WEDNESDAY APRIL 1

AT 1 P.M.

Battery street, (one block from Beacon Hill end of car track, at

Capt Hankin's Residence

The above gentleman is leaving for England and has instructed me to sell without reserve, the whole of his valuable and fine collection of

Furniture, Silverware, Pictures, Bric a Brac, and Rare Pieces of China.

Drawing Room—Six Water Colors, Scenes in Venice, Switzerland, England and other countries (in beautiful frames); Hand Painted China Vases; Looking Glasses, etc.; Hungarian Photo Frames; Fine Old Worcester, 100 years old, made for Hon. East Indian Co.) Musical Box; Dresden China; Mahogany Tables; Sofas; Easy Chairs; Cushions; Large Mantle Mirror; Fire Guards; Brass Fender; Rugs; Carpet Squares; Austrian Lace Curtains, etc.

Morning Room—Roll Top Desk, stool; Small Book Case; Easy Chairs; Indian Wicker Chair; Leather Seat Chair; Movable Electric Lamp; Oak Tables; Jap. Table; some very fine Water Colors in Handsome Frames; Photograph of present King Edward VII., with his own Autograph; 2 Photographs of the late King and Queen of Sandwich Islands, with their Autographs; Stevenson's Works; Life and Times of Queen Victoria; Poems of George Sims; Ornaments; Candlesticks; Large Mantle Mirror; Rugs; Brass Fender; Clock; Austrian Lace Curtains; Portiers, etc.

Dining Room—Oak Extension Table; Six Chairs; Oak Side Table; Cushions; Large Mirror; Brass and Nickel Fender; Table Covers; Tapestry Curtains; Oil Paintings; 8 Day Clock; Indian Snake Brass Candlesticks; Solid Silver Queen Anne Tea Set; Cutlery; Austrian Fruit Set; Old Indian Silverware; Vienna Coffee Pot; Hot Water Kettle; Dessert Set, etc.

Kitchen—Albion Range; Linoleum; Tables; Cooking Utensils; Crockery, etc.

Bedrooms—Enameled Bedsteads; Hardwood Bureaus; Washstands; Wire Mattresses; Hair Top Mattresses; Blankets; Bed Linen; 3 Good Chests of Drawers; Wardrobe; Toilet Sets; Carpet Squares, etc.

Goods on view Tuesday, 2 to 5. (Children not allowed on the premises.)

W. T. HARDAKER,

Auctioneer.

Announcement of the auction of the contents of Philip and Isabel Hankin's house in James Bay April 1, 1903. In addition to their furniture and chattels, the sale includes several items of great personal value.

of fine chattels: glassware, curtains, rugs, silver tea services, Dresden chinaware, candlesticks, clocks, and a few books in fine bindings. On the walls hung beautifully framed fine watercolour scenes from Europe.

Also for sale, and most notable, were a framed and signed photograph of King Edward VII, when he was still Prince of Wales, during his 1875 visit to Madras, and similarly, of the late King and Queen of the Sandwich Islands. These last three items were personal gifts to Philip that he had guarded for many years. To abandon them to the vagaries of the open market must have distressed him dreadfully. One wonders, whatever became of them?

*

Immediately following Isabel's funeral, Philip continued his journey, returning to London. He noted, "I arrived a very lonely and unhappy man. I stayed a few days in an hotel and afterwards took some rooms, where I was comfortable but lonely." He sought solace in his customary travelling. He returned to Menton on the Riviera, then on to Madeira and the Canary Islands, staying for a few months with a friend from his earliest days aboard *Plumper*, Charles John Didham, now a captain and retired. Next he went to Cape Town, spending three weeks, and finding just one of his old friends still alive. While in South Africa, he visited Durban and Delagoa Bay (now Maputo in Mozambique), places he had known as a young midshipman aboard HMS *Castor.* This seems a curious choice, since that period of his life had been far from agreeable. He acknowledged, "I liked being at sea better than anything, for I met some interesting people, and chatting with them made me forget my troubles."

Philip tried returning to Hamilton to visit Isabel's grave, "but that only made matters worse." After that, he took a German ship out of Hamburg for Hong Kong, where he stayed a month. From there, he sailed for Victoria via Japan aboard the RMS *Empress of China*, one of Canadian Pacific's luxury ocean liners. According to the press announcement, arriving with him was another retired naval captain, J.H. Adams and his wife. His connection with Philip, if there was any apart from meeting during the voyage, is not known.[2]

The *Victoria Daily Colonist*'s announcement of the ship's arrival on January 31, 1906, stated that "Commander P. Hankin" and the other officer were "on furlough." On February 25, the same newspaper noted, "Capt. Hankin" was staying at the King Edward Hotel. On his retirement

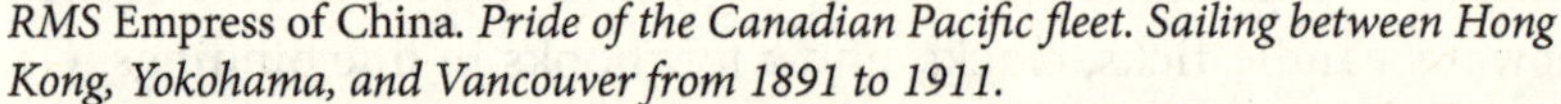

RMS Empress of China. *Pride of the Canadian Pacific fleet. Sailing between Hong Kong, Yokohama, and Vancouver from 1891 to 1911.*

from his position as colonial secretary at the transition to joining Canada, as for all members of the outgoing Executive Council, he was entitled, for life, to be addressed as "the Honourable" whenever in British Columbia. The editor seems to have been oblivious of Hankin's history or neglectful of this protocol.

The few months Philip spent in Victoria during the spring of 1906 provided Captain John Thomas Walbran with an excellent opportunity to secure some first-hand information about "the early days on this coast." Walbran, skipper of the Canadian government's steamship *Quadra*, had become fascinated with the stories behind the coastal place names of British Columbia. He was close to publishing a monumental book on the topic. Having access to an officer who had served aboard both HMS *Plumper* and *Hecate* when many of those names first appeared on charts would surely have been a godsend to the researcher. Philip, too, must have been delighted to have his brain picked in this way and contribute to the record in his later years. Walbran devoted two full pages of his book to Hankin, his history, and the six local toponyms bearing his name.

Walbran and the *Quadra* were fulfilling the exact role suggested by Admiral Denman forty-three years previously for the then newly reinstated Lieutenant Hankin. Walbran commanded a lightly armed patrol vessel, powerful enough to function in the worst of weather off the west coast of the island and farther north. Their mission included regular visits to communicate with the coastal Indigenous population and remote communities, reportedly to reassure them of the government's concern for both their welfare and the consistent application of justice. *Quadra* also acted as a supply and support vessel for the remote lighthouses throughout the west coast. Valuable additional services were to provide hydrographic information updating, or amending as necessary, the work of *Plumper*, *Hecate*, and HMS *Beaver*, and to deter the illicit trade in liquor.

In mid-June 1906, Philip moved to Vancouver, by then a substantial city, far larger and of greater importance than Victoria due to the presence of the terminus for the CPR. He took rooms at 1300 Ninth Avenue (now Broadway) at Fairview. He immediately placed a small announcement running for five days in the *Vancouver Daily World* under "Educational":

Captain John Thomas Walbran researched the history of BC coastal place names, publishing his monumental book on the topic in 1909.

CGS Quadra. *Lighthouse supply and support vessel commanded by Captain Walbran between 1891 and 1903.*

> *Captain Hankin, who has resided ten years in France and ten in Germany, and speaking both languages, is prepared to receive a few pupils, either children or adults, at his residence, 1300, Ninth Avenue, Fairview. . . . Tram passes the door.*

*

Philip left Vancouver in February 1907, travelling via China to England, then "roamed about England" for a while before making another voyage to Cape Town. After three weeks he returned to London, where, in 1911, he rented a flat in a terraced house at 20 Coniston Road, Muswell Hill, a "genteel urban village" on the high northern outskirts of the capital.[3] He rented from his sister-in-law, Charles's widow, Mary, who had inherited the house from her mother, and lived there with her unmarried eldest daughter, Ida Mary, and two female servants. By this time, Philip had engaged a valet, Arthur Wiles, a twenty-six-year-old Scot who remained with him until the outbreak of the war, when he was called up for the army. The census of 1911 confirms the three residents with three servants at the Muswell Hill house.

Hankin left because, he claimed, he found life there tiring and expensive. The latter complaint rings as implausible, given he was well provided for by pension income and would have saved a considerable fortune. It would seem a closer, more mutually supportive relationship with Mary would have been a natural development for them, but that did not happen.

After trying Jersey in the Channel Islands "for a short while," he moved to Southsea, near Portsmouth. He recalled pleasant memories from a half century earlier during brief intervals spent there with the family of his friend, Frank Thomson. He spent the following three years in that house, reading books in French and German and "the only amusement was to ride about on top of the tramcars, or walk about on Palmerston Road [the main commercial street]." He also made a few calls, where he "was immediately invited to tea—I got very tired of tea parties and cake, and found it always took away my appetite for dinner." He had earlier noted the same sentiment about Ryde.

*

In this mood of loneliness and ennui, Philip started writing the memoir of his long life. He began, however, with a denial of his true state of mind. Adopting a confident tone, he wrote:

> *I have had many ups and downs and have travelled several times around the world, and held various positions in many parts of the globe. . . . I have had a long and happy life, and have much to be thankful for, and now, when my call comes, I am quite ready to go, as all I love best, have gone before me.*

As he got to the final years of his narrative, he stated his intention in writing to have been to "interest, and amuse some of my old friends." Very few of those friends could have read the result, which he completed aged seventy-nine, outliving most of them. He acknowledged:

> *I get soon tired, and my memory is beginning to fail me. . . . If I had kept a journal all my life, I could have made it much more interesting, but I have written every word from memory.*

He completed the narrative in 1915, at the height of the horrors of the Great War, but omitted mention of the conflict. He added a forty-three-page coda, eleven percent of the total, to his narrative that makes depressing reading. It comprises a sorrowful litany of his problems finding, managing, and eventually firing a long series of unsatisfactory servants: valets, cook-housekeepers, even impertinent junior maids. Each one proved incompetent, lazy, dishonest, or insubordinate. He acknowledged he was now an old man, reflecting:

> *It is a very difficult thing, to know how, and where to live, even if he has a fairly good income. The loneliness is the worst part. Relations don't care for you and don't want you, unless you are rich, then they all love you. . . . I have tried Hotels, Boarding houses, Lodgings, and what is advertised as a 'Home from Home,' but I have failed to find it. . . .*
>
> *I trust this history I have written of the various scenes in my long life, may interest some of my old friends, and encourage young men who go to the colonies to* <u>*work*</u> *and to be willing to accept the first chance they get, and not to expect an appointment at £500 a year, the day they arrive, and if a weary task they find it, Persevere, and never mind it.*

This was the last page of his coda and the conclusion of his memoir. He entrusted his manuscript to his friend in Ottawa, E.L. Britain, in 1922.

*

Documentary evidence of Philip Hankin's last few years is sparse. The *Colonist* of Victoria for October 28, 1919, reported him having arrived there some two weeks earlier and gone to Duncan. Presumably, this was to visit Susan, Isabel's sister, by then wife of Reverend David Holmes and mother of several children. Susan had stopped keeping her diary a few years earlier, so this theory is unconfirmed. An alternate possibility is that he visited a member of the Gore-Langton family. Lady Anna Gore-Langton, the duke's sister, and her two children had accompanied Hankin and the Duke of Buckingham to Madras previously. According to Bosher's *Imperial Vancouver Island*, several members of that lineage came to settle in the Cowichan Valley. Hankin could well have maintained correspondence with them after he left the duke's service.

Philip returned to Victoria to stay at the Union Club while he looked up the few old acquaintances of his who remained, such as Dr. John Sebastian Helmcken and James Anderson of the Natural History Society. He also visited the offices of the Victoria and Island Development Association, whose mission was to attract more agricultural settlers to emigrate from Britain and establish farms.

Three years later, on January 26, 1922, his name appeared on the passenger manifest of SS *Ballarat*, out of London, bound for Australia. Also listed was his then valet, Alfred Sheppard, aged twenty-two. They gave their address in the United Kingdom as "c/o Holt & Co, 44 Charing Cross NW." This was Philip's bank, which specialized in military and naval officers' accounts. They are still active as a bank, but their archives retain no record of Commander Philip Hankin.

*

The electoral register for Brighton, Sussex, for 1923 lists Philip Hankin as resident at 8 Hallyburton Road, Aldrington, Hove, and the sole occupant of that house. That same year, according to the death certificate, he died at that address, on November 28, of "1 Senile Decay, 2 Cardiac Failure 14 days. No PM [Post Mortem]. Signed, F.J. Borrer. Present at death." Philip Hankin was eighty-seven.

He would have left a considerable financial legacy, but no will or probate has been found. There was no memorial service, eulogy, or obituary, nor any record of his burial or other disposal of his remains. Philip Hankin just seems to have vanished from this world—unremembered, until recently, except for his memoir, the Huu-ay-aht word list, and the entry in Walbran's book highlighting a few toponyms on Vancouver Island. Such was the lamentable end for a man whose life and times had been a roller coaster of adventure, discovery, hardship, luxury, responsibility, risk, social prominence, and, toward the end, abject loneliness. Philip Hankin departed the turmoil that had been his life in desolate obscurity.

Afterword

While writing this book, I mentioned it in conversation with a noted local journalist and keen historian. The name Philip Hankin did not register with him, so he asked, "What did he do?" I could not provide a brief answer. Hankin lived a long life during epic times for our regional history, experienced worldwide travels, and took part in government at a senior level during several momentous changes. No single accomplishment or reason for fame or notoriety emerges.

Who, then, was Philip Hankin, and why remember his name? Having now completed a chronological account of his life and times, I am in a better position to respond. I can attempt to evaluate his contribution, motives, personality, talents, and shortcomings. While his memoir, written from memory at an advanced age, provides a basis to begin, it reveals neither the complete story of his life nor the essence of Hankin, the person. To form my opinion, I needed to compare other accounts of the events he recalled. I am now better able to see what really unfolded, and how he must have seemed to others he encountered. But puzzles persist.

I remain impressed with the man in several aspects, and less so in others. These views, of course, are subjective, and will no doubt differ from those of others who have studied the man and his life's trajectory. Should further contemporaneous material emerge, shedding more or different light on Hankin and his story, I am prepared to adjust my opinions. I sincerely hope more becomes known, since there remain several questions for which I need answers, areas of his life and personality where I seek clarification.

*

I begin with the positive characteristics of Philip Hankin. Despite his skimpy early education, followed by some brutal treatment during his formative years at sea, he showed innate intelligence and an aptitude for learning. He overcame a woeful lack of even the most elementary knowledge of mathematics, especially geometry. He soon learned the techniques of hydrographic surveying once exposed to on-the-job training by a sympathetic master of the science, Captain George Henry Richards, RN. He even produced a very creditable topographic map of a journey over difficult and hitherto unknown territory. Hankin showed effective leadership when, under trying conditions, he commanded a small party of men hauling a quantity of massive stone blocks up a two-hundred-foot cliff to construct the plinth and obelisk to mark the 49th parallel at Point Roberts.

He rapidly gained a working knowledge of several west coast Indigenous dialects. For the first time, he and a collaborator, Thomas Roberts, known as "Friday," produced a three-hundred-word dictionary with thirty-five useful phrases and a complete Lord's Prayer in the Huu-ay-aht language. Through no fault of his own, the document went unpublished, was shelved—miscredited and in obscurity—until my fortunate discovery of its existence (see appendix 2). Hankin proved adept at acquiring other languages, except for Dutch, when, hilariously, his slight smattering was taken for a more fluent mastery. He learned French and German sufficiently well to offer private lessons in them.

His knowledge of Indigenous languages and social protocols triggered his participation, as a lowly civilian clerk, during a most unfortunate demonstration of imperial wrath. His evident courage and skills at negotiation impressed even a battle-hardened admiral, Joseph Denman. This resulted in his naval rank of lieutenant being restored, and his appointment as commissioner of police. He performed commendably in this role, despite severe political opposition to his superior, then-Governor Arthur Edward Kennedy, pressuring the police as a pretext. The only voices critical of Hankin's performance in this office were those less enthusiastic of probity and efficiency in how the law should be applied.

He was later dropped into a position of significant administrative responsibility, replacing a man—William Alexander George Young—far more educated and experienced in the role. Once there, to the astonishment of almost everyone, Hankin again carried out his duties admirably under the most trying circumstances.

He impressed several senior men of experience and sound judgement, such as Richards, Kennedy, Denman, Musgrave, and the Duke of Buckingham. They all provided glowing letters of reference or, in the latter case, entrusted him with a situation of high confidence for over a decade. In the final version of the legislative body before the colony joined the Dominion, Hankin's peers elected him Speaker, in clear acknowledgement of his impartiality, negotiating abilities, and trustworthiness. His office required that, on four occasions, he take on the role of administrator, the temporary head of government, and each time, he handled the responsibilities with aplomb.

Hankin enjoyed talents in social settings. He proved an excellent dancer, and therefore was popular with women, particularly those younger, eager partygoers. Even later in life he surprised a southern belle on a Mississippi steamboat with how light he was on his feet on the dance floor, despite his expanding girth. He had a fine tenor voice and enjoyed singing hymns in church. A natural actor, he performed dramatic readings from Dickens and others, highly popular both in the Victoria community and at paid performances across the southern United States. Appointed aide-de-camp to Lady Franklin, Hankin's pranks and repartee entertained, mostly, the ladies throughout their visit. His unexpected dancing of the hornpipe was the encored highlight of a concert put on by the Royal Engineers in Lady Franklin's honour.

His cooking of a chicken curry for the Queen of the Sandwich Islands proved a success and the royal couple thanked him with signed portraits. That same skill fostered the bonding with Richards while they were out on fieldwork.

*

Several aspects of his character were far less praiseworthy, especially by today's standards. Among them was the incident aboard *Orion* in the Mediterranean when he played a juvenile prank that ill befitted his rank. To a captain whom Hankin called "a nice man," and who sincerely believed in an alternate theory of medicine, he pretended to be a fellow enthusiast. He took advantage of a solicitous gesture to desert his post and poke fun at the respected senior officer while doing so.

Among his pranks intended for the amusement of the elderly and revered Lady Franklin and her companion, Sophie Cracroft, he showed a disagreeable strain of snobbery. He mocked the genuine, if unsophisticated, language and manners of a respectable couple who had welcomed the distinguished visitors into their home. Similarly, he ridiculed the clergyman Crickmer's somewhat verbose farewell address to the ladies after their visit to the frontier town of Yale. In significant contrast to Hankin's snide sneers, Lady Franklin accepted Crickmer's sentiments with appropriate grace. On that same trip, his practical jokes involving Indigenous artifacts and a swaddled baby were inconsiderate and tasteless, even in those more socially stratified times. Today, they would be viewed as abhorrent and totally reprehensible.

Hankin showed a thoroughly unpleasant side of his nature during *Hecate*'s return voyage to London in 1863. He cruelly goaded a fellow messmate, Jack Gowlland, into an unseemly shouting match. Clearly, animosity between the two had been long simmering. The roots of their squabble, and perhaps rivalry, seem to have started during their social life at dances and outings ashore in Victoria. The furious mutual slanging erupted as they crossed the enervating doldrums of the Indian Ocean. The aftermath revealed Hankin had been keeping scurrilous notes about Gowlland and other fellow officers. He even allowed them to become public and denied having authored them.

Fortunately, such examples of ignoble behaviour on Hankin's part seemed to have ended once he matured. Following the tribulations of his journeys to and from Barkerville, and during his brief time there, he seems to have emerged from his persona of an irresponsible jester to one of more gravitas.

Whatever occurred at Barkerville marked a radical change in Hankin's character. His account of those few weeks seems implausible. He failed to mention in his memoir that two of his brothers were active partners in the most successful of the mining operations, Billy Barker's syndicate. It would have been impossible for him not to have known they were there and sought to share in their prosperity, even as a common day labourer. He had been with Charles to call upon Daniel Pender in Esquimalt only a few weeks before he says he arrived at Barkerville, down to his last 50 cents. Why would he not call on his brothers? If he did, what transpired? It must have been an encounter so traumatic that he felt unable to mention his brothers' names in his entire memoir.

That omission, which included all of his family, except the few times he visited his father between voyages, is most puzzling. His father's personality must have been a key factor. Daniel's preference for babies over children, and hence the long, uninterrupted series of pregnancies of his wife until her early death, would seem significant. So, too, was his preferential treatment of some of his sons—sending them away for expensive schooling—while leaving others, especially Philip, semi-educated.

The father neglected a traditional succession plan of preparing the eldest, or even any of his sons, to take on the role of master of a heritage estate with large acreage. Instead, he appears to have steadily sold off his land holdings and, eventually, Thele House. Money troubles would seem an explanation. He was a keen breeder and racer of horses. Might he have also been an unsuccessful gambler? Philip's memoir offers no clue.

Daniel Hankin's ill-fated plan to emigrate to New Zealand formed part of this deterioration in the family's wealth. To consider relocating to a remote colonial outpost, to pioneer a new agricultural life on the pretext that the sea voyage would be of benefit to his ailing wife, is preposterous. It was also an ill-considered, high-stakes gamble, reinforcing the possibility of an addiction. He came to the obvious realization that he could not carry out a pioneering venture on his own and ordered Philip to resign from the navy to provide some essential help. Then, rather than grooming his teenaged son to help with the transition, he ordered Philip to take a job in London as an office menial. Altogether, it must have been most disruptive to the boy's sense of self-worth and his bonds with family.

Another puzzling quirk played on Hankin's frame of mind when he wrote his memoir. He omitted any mention of the Huu-ay-aht Thomas Roberts, known to him as Friday, and the word list they prepared. It is clear from Captain Richards's comments that the two had, initially, a very close relationship. The effort and rapport needed to collaborate in creating such a document must have been exceptional. They did so with no pre-existing list for reference, nor a common language. Other sources reveal that, as well as the two periods aboard *Hecate*, the two men later served together on other occasions. They were both on *Sutlej* during the Ahousaht reprisal mission and on *Scout* for the farewell voyage of Governor Kennedy, as well as working together on a serious court case—the murder of William "Eddy" Banfield. So, why would Hankin obliterate Thomas Roberts and their joint project from the record of his life? Something traumatic must have transpired between them.

*

Philip's relationship with women is also interesting. He hardly knew his mother, constantly preoccupied with the latest infant. He grew up with two sisters: Constance, three years his senior, and Alice, eight years his junior. Interacting with them would have provided some experience in the tricky art of navigating the differences between the sexes, an essential life skill. His first encounters with female counterparts other than siblings happened when, as a seventeen-year-old, he attended parties with Frank Thomson at Winchester and Ryde. Here he learned to dance and exchange courtesies with girls of his own age and class, but he does not seem to have formed any near-romantic ties.

In Victoria, his social life improved. Young officers on ships were prized participants at functions ashore, including balls, parties, and picnic excursions. They were also potential "catches" for the unmarried daughters of settlers and officials. The officers delighted in inviting the same settlers, with their daughters, to events aboard their ships. Hankin was in his element at all such occasions, mingling with growing comfort among different strata of society. Again, he does not seem to have formed any amorous attachment during this time, but he remembered the names of many of the girls when he wrote his memoir. The dramatic spat with Gowlland revealed that sometimes he might have taken things too far. This would have been more consistent with his persona as a prankster, rather than a lothario.

Later, he and his brothers formed part of the social circle that centred on the three Nagle sisters. Philip's marriage to Isabel came exactly as he transitioned into responsibility. Already embarked on his career as a government official, on a meagre salary, and with nothing saved, his decision seems premature. Taking a wife at such a time seems more of a cool calculation to appear more conservative and trustworthy rather than the result of love. It was not for money, as Isabel had none. The memoir treats it as an unremarkable development, only mentioned in passing. There was no sign of courtship, merely the formality of asking permission of her parents. Curiously, nowhere in the memoir does he refer to her by name, merely, "my wife" or "my dear wife."

They were childless; however, they were fond of and supported each other. Isabel, from the outset, was of poor health, and the bout of yellow fever hit her hard, with long-lasting effects. Philip was always solicitous, ensuring she could convalesce, in Cuba, in San Francisco, and at Stowe. Even as she approached the end of her life and they had finally established a home in James Bay, upon her wish to return to England, he showed no reluctance in selling up everything to accommodate her need. Isabel was supportive throughout his dramatic, variable career. Even in retirement, she seems to have accepted his affliction of wanderlust, agreeing to up sticks and try life in Tasmania at just two weeks' notice. Many a wife, less forbearing, would have hesitated or argued. After Isabel's death, he was once more a changed man. He grieved deeply, and sank into lonely depression until his own, solitary passing.

*

Before Hankin reached that stage, he underwent yet another transition in his life as he returned to England in 1881 after his years in India. Judging from the report in the *Bengal Gazette*, his life there had proved exhausting, sapping any remaining energy and spirit. The next three decades of his life, even before losing his wife, blurred in his recollection. He wandered aimlessly, without purpose or roots. He admitted to feeling most comfortable when going somewhere, anywhere, on a ship. While he made new acquaintances, none were permanent or profound. He lost connection with previous friends such as Richards, Pender, and even the Buckingham family. For him, wanderlust became a dominant obsession. This compulsion later combined with his urge to learn other languages. He devoted almost two decades to the study of French and German, acquiring fluency in both.

Following his bereavement, he shared a house with his sister-in-law Mary, by then a widow, and her grown daughter in Muswell Hill, a comfortable middle-class suburb of London. Their relationship failed to develop, which seems a pity. His urge to wander overcame any need for stability for his remaining years, so he moved on. The pretext for leaving, he claimed, was financial necessity. This does not seem convincing, given his two pensions and opportunities for accumulating savings.

His incessant travelling would have been expensive, but no threat to his probable wealth. In his years after Madras, he might have become something of a miser, begrudging minor expenses while hoarding his savings, except to satisfy an overwhelming craving to keep moving.

*

Overall, I believe Philip Hankin's life was remarkable and well worth recounting. His description of the life of a midshipman in the mid-Victorian Royal Navy—chasing slavers around Africa while at the mercy of irrational bullies such as Christopher Wyvill and William Henry Haswell—is instructive. Those experiences affected his attitude toward the service and redirected the trajectory of his life. In a different way, the philosophy of the old salt aboard *Seringapatam* helped mould his approach to adversity. The man had counselled, "Never say die, lad, s'long as there's a shot in the locker!" Philip would summon up this maxim much later, as he experienced hardship and despair.

The Hankin memoir contributes an interesting perspective to the early phases and political developments in Victoria and British Columbia. He witnessed key events of the region's transition from a remote and tiny outpost of Empire to a busy hub of gold-fuelled frenzy. He helped add detail to the largely blank charts and maps of Vancouver Island. He communicated with Indigenous communities at the beginning of their contact with resident outsiders, observing the ravages of smallpox and other European-introduced pestilence. He was one of the first to study and record one of the west coast dialects. He used that knowledge to help a senior naval officer exact brutal judicial redress for contravention of the incomers' laws.

London's decision to unite the two British colonies on the west coast of North America directly affected Hankin. He lost one job but gained a career advancement. He was involved when that so-called "united" colony joined confederation with Canada. He was successively right-hand man to Governors Kennedy, Seymour, and Musgrave, present when key decisions were discussed and made. He helped bring about the smooth administrative transition from colony to province.

Hankin's memoir adds an important perspective to the interaction between the Royal Navy personnel on station and the civilian and Indigenous communities during tumultuous societal changes on

Vancouver Island. Many times, he acted as a bridge between the three cultures.

His life after leaving the service of British Columbia, as recounted in his memoir, is of lesser general interest. It reveals little new to the knowledge of life in one of England's most prestigious households, that of the Duke of Buckingham at Stowe, nor of India under the Raj. He had witnessed both during his nine years' service with the duke. His long period of wanderlust adds virtually nothing of further value for the reader, apart from a few amusing anecdotes, such as the foray into an orange business in Florida and dancing with a southern belle on a Mississippi paddlewheeler.

His last few years are a gloomy account of a man—once the life and soul of a party, then an able public servant and assistant to a duke—sinking progressively deeper into depression and solitude as he wandered the world. Philip Hankin's story could well have formed the basis for one of the more melancholic pieces of his hero, Charles Dickens.

APPENDIX 1

Timeline of Philip Hankin on Vancouver Island

The following table puts Philip Hankin's life into historical context relative to the Vancouver Island region.

Vancouver Island Region		Date	Philip Hankin
Earliest signs of human activity on this coast.	◄	13,500 years BP	
Earliest evidence of continuous human settlement from Yuquot and Marpole middens.	◄	4,400–4,000 years BP	
First confirmed contact by Europeans made by Juan José Pérez Hernández.	◄	August 5, 1774	
James Cook arrives at Nootka Sound.	◄	March 31, 1778	
First circumnavigations of Vancouver Island by George Vancouver and Spaniards Dionisio Alcalá Galiano and Cayetano Valdés y Flores.	◄	Summer/fall 1792	
Hudson's Bay Company trading for furs. Establishes Fort Vancouver (Oregon Territory).	◄	1825–1829	
		► February 18, 1836	Born, Stanstead Abbotts, Hertfordshire, England.

Vancouver Island Region	Date	Philip Hankin
James Douglas establishes Fort Victoria. ◄	1843	
Britain grants contract for colonization of Vancouver Island to HBC. ◄	January 1849	
	► May 12, 1849	Joins Royal Navy as midshipman.
Richard Blanshard arrives in Victoria to proclaim Vancouver Island as a British colony. ◄	March 11, 1850	
Blanshard leaves. Douglas becomes governor. ◄	September 1, 1851	
Douglas reports to London that gold discovered on Fraser and Thompson Rivers. ◄	September 21, 1857	
	► November 10, 1857	Arrives at Esquimalt in HMS *Plumper.*
Mainland proclaimed second British colony as British Columbia. Seymour appointed governor. Kennedy appointed governor of Vancouver Island. ◄	August 1858	
	► October 1858	Returns to Britain on promotion to lieutenant.
	► December 23, 1860	Arrives at Esquimalt on HMS *Hecate.*
	► 1861	Compiles Huu-ay-aht word list with Thomas "Friday" Roberts.
	► December 28, 1862	Leaves Esquimalt aboard *Hecate.*

Vancouver Island Region	Date	Philip Hankin
	► January 1864	Returns to Britain. Resigns commission.
	► March–September 1864	Returns to Victoria as civilian; goes to Barkerville.
	► October 1864	Clerk in government service; Ahousaht reprisal incident.
	► Late December 1864	Superintendent of police.
	► February 4, 1865	Reinstated in Royal Navy at old rank.
	► August 3, 1865	Marries Isabel Nagle.
The two colonies are united as British Columbia. Seymour remains as governor. Kennedy returns to Britain. ◄	August 6, 1866	
	► February 1867	Returns to England; meets Duke of Buckingham.
	► 1867–1868	Colonial secretary of British Honduras.
	► November 4, 1868	Posted as colonial secretary of British Columbia.
Seymour dies. ◄	► June–August 1869	Administrator (acting head of government).
Musgrave arrives as governor. ◄	► August 23, 1869	Resumes post of colonial secretary.
	► April 2, 1870	Retired from Royal Navy as commander.
	► January 1871	Elected Speaker of Legislative Assembly.

Vancouver Island Region	Date	Philip Hankin
British Columbia joins Dominion of Canada. Musgrave returns to Britain. Trutch appointed lieutenant governor of the province of British Columbia. ◄	July 20, 1871	
	► August 16, 1871	Retires on two pensions; returns to Britain.
	► February 1872–spring 1881	Private secretary to Duke of Buckingham.
	► Spring 1875–spring 1881	With duke in Madras.
	► Spring 1881	Returns to Britain; retires; wanderlust begins.
	► June 1881	Philip and Isabel visit Victoria.
	► December 1887	Brief visit to Vancouver and Victoria.
	► 1889 (approximate)	Philip's adventures in southern US.
Queen Victoria dies, succeeded by Edward VII. ◄	January 22, 1901	
	► Summer 1902	Philip and Isabel arrive in Victoria. Acquire house on Battery St., James Bay.
	► Summer 1903	Sell up and return to Britain; Isabel dies on journey.
	► January 31–mid-June 1906	Visits Victoria.
	► Mid-June 1906–February 1907	Moves to Vancouver. Offers language lessons.

Vancouver Island Region	Date	Philip Hankin
Edward VII dies, succeeded by George V. ◄	May 6, 1910	
	► 1912–1915	Writes memoir.
	► October 1919	Visits Victoria and Duncan.
	► 1920 (approximate)	Philip gives memoir to E.L. Britain.
	► November 28, 1923	Dies in Hove, Sussex, England.
	► May 1954	BC Archives receives memoir.

APPENDIX 2
Word List

Introduction

In April 1861, Lieutenant Philip Hankin, RN, was serving aboard HMS *Hecate* during a hydrographic charting mission to the waters around Vancouver Island. While surveying Barkley Sound, his captain, George Henry Richards, had employed a young fisherman from Huu-ay-aht Nation as a sailor, but specifically to assist with his knowledge of the local waters, communities, and physical toponyms.

Hankin, with some talent for acquiring languages, monopolized the man's time aboard to study and learn the Huu-ay-aht dialect of the Southern Wakashan language and, by extension, those of neighbouring, related groups of the Nuu-chah-nulth First Nations.

In this process, Hankin compiled lists of words and phrases in what a subsequent unknown editor termed "a vocabulary of the language spoken by the Natives of Barkley Sound." He also claimed to have consulted speakers from Clayoquot and Nootka Sounds, to refine the orthography, as necessary.

Besides lists of words and phrases with their meanings in English, he began another set of lists for Chinook Jargon or Chinuk Wawa, the lingua franca used throughout the region by different language groups and foreign traders, including the Hudson's Bay Company employees.

Finally, he sketched a few Indigenous artifacts he called "weapons," but which were traditional and fishing devices.

People Involved

The fisherman's name, as provided by missionaries, was Thomas Roberts, but Richards, Hankin and the crew knew him as "Friday." He was a member of the Huu-ay-aht people, whose traditional territory is the southeastern side of Barkley Sound, including several islands.

Roberts was an intelligent individual. As Hankin was learning his language, Roberts gained a working knowledge of English. This, together with his knowledge of the local waters including Alberni Inlet, later provided him with employment as a pilot for shipping to and from the lumber mill at the head of the inlet.

Philip Hankin, a twenty-five-year-old lieutenant in the Royal Navy, with minimal formal education except for junior naval officers' training, had an innate aptitude for languages and empathy and respect for different cultures. He also quickly became adept at hydrographic and topographic surveying, impressing his captain.

George Henry Richards, captain of HMS *Hecate*, had vast experience of hydrography in waters little known to Europeans. He was also highly skilled at managing and motivating his subordinates, and empathetic with the local people. After this voyage he received the appointment of Hydrographer, the head of that service in the Royal Navy, the most experienced and active in the world in that era.

Title and Description of the Document

The document, written in Hankin's hand, has no title, merely his name and rank. In another hand, presumably by a subsequent editor, is an annotation, "Vocabulary of the Natives of Barkley Sound, Vancouver Island," with a subtitle, "followed by a short list of Chi-nook [Chinuk Wawa] words supposed to be a trading jargon." The words "supposed to be a" have been struck through and replaced with "which is the common." Another annotation is "Recd. 10 Dec. 1861."

Hankin's manuscript, written in ink with a fine nib, appears to be a series of common soft-cover school exercise books with faintly ruled pages.

The book has been subsequently rebound in navy-blue boards, perhaps for incorporation into a library. Printed in gold on the spine is the presumed editor's title. There are several editorial annotations, in soft pencil, throughout the text.

Hankin would have kept notes of his conversations with Thomas "Friday" Roberts during the survey season of 1861. The period while *Hecate* was undergoing repairs in San Francisco provided opportunity for him to compile those notes into a coherent word list, perhaps in consultation with Roberts, who was also aboard. Hankin does not credit Roberts, or Friday, as his source in the document or in his memoir, but it is clear from Captain Richards's journal that they spent much time together. Officers' notes on such observations were not considered personal property, but official mission documents. Hankin handed the word list over, although still incomplete, to Richards soon after *Hecate* returned to Esquimalt and before Hankin began erecting the boundary obelisque (see chapter 10).

Richards sent it to the Hydrographic Office in London where, according to the annotation, it was "rec'd 10 December 1861." Much later, after editing and consideration for publication, the document was rebound and taken into the Admiralty Library at the Naval Historical Branch, Portsmouth, with the call number MSS 94. It was never published.

Structure of the Document

After a short page of introductory remarks by Hankin, there follow 19 double-page spreads showing a total of 302 English words with their Southern Wakashan translations. The words are grouped alphabetically under the English initial letter, but not listed alphabetically within each letter group. A single page of numerals from 1 through 900 follows. Between the pages for "B" and "C" is a page devoted to a translation of the Lord's Prayer. The presumed editor has marked it to be moved to the end of the vocabulary.

The next section covers 35 useful phases, with their translations and explanations of subtle differences, grouped according to the type of remark or opening words: "Come here . . . ," "Go away . . . ," "I want . . . ," and "Where are . . . ."

A single page entitled "The Different Tribes on the West Coast of Vancouver Island with the Estimated Number of Natives" follows the phrases. The tribes are grouped into Barkley Sound, Clayoquot Sound, and Nootka Sound. He lists 16 tribes with a total population of 2,350. He makes no differentiation between men, women, or children. The largest tribe listed is "Car-ūket" (with a bar above the "u") at 600. Thomas Roberts's people, the Huu-ay-aht, are listed as "Oohīat" (with a bar above the "i"), with 200. In his introduction, Hankin explains his use of a bar above a vowel is to indicate that it is pronounced long—"oo" and "eye."

Following the sections covering Southern Wakashan are two sections of "Chin nook." The first is, again, an alphabetical grouping of words, but this time alphabetized in Chinuk Wawa with their English translations on the same page. The list goes only as far as "Q," presumably left incomplete due to lack of time. For the second section of Chinuk Wawa, Hankin provides 46 "Examples in Chin ook" composed of useful phrases, questions, and answers. The lists on many pages are short, again hinting he could not finish compiling his notes before handing them over to Richards. This curtailment could be the reason for the lists not being published.

The last two pages show fine sketches of eleven artifacts with their English and Wakashan names. He labelled them: "Fish rake," "Fish Spear," "War paddle," "Common paddle," "Bow," "Arrow," "Point of an arrow" (decorated), "War Club," "Fish Club," "Fish hook" (for halibut), and "Indian Antidote against diseases" (a two-faced ceremonial rattle). He does not provide Wakashan terms for the war club, the fish club, or the rattle.

I have endeavoured in compiling the following vocabulary of the language spoken by the Natives of Barclay Sound, on the West Coast of Vancouver Island, to secure a faithful reproduction of the sounds (as [illegible]) ~~(from the writing)~~ when read ~~by a third person, having no personal communications with either writer, or speaker.~~

The vocabulary has been compiled with ~~the greatest~~ care, strictly according to the English pro[illegible] [illegible] and written down from the mouths of different intelligent Natives. Words obtained from one Indian have been ~~most~~ carefully compared with the testimony of others, and any defect, or peculiarity of pronunciation has been immediately corrected.

The Barclay Sound language differs slightly ~~[illegible]~~ from that spoken at ~~[illegible]~~ Clayoquot Sound (pronounced Clak-o-ot) and a considerable difference exists at Nootka, but the Indians all understand the language of Barclay Sound in a greater, or less degree.

~~The words are carefully accented long, or short, according to their pronunciation thus (ā long,) in Father, (ă short) in hat.~~

I have also annexed a sketch of the different weapons, originally used by the Natives of Vancouver Island, which have of late years been superseded by the use of the Rifle, and long muskets with flint locks traded from the Hudson Bay Company—

C

Cat
Canoe
Carry
Clams
Coat
Come here
Cough
Change
Chin
Codfish (Indian)
Cockles
Cypress (yellow)
Cut, (to cut a piece of wood)
with scissors
Cast off
Cold
Cone of (pine tree)
Cedar
Codfish (English)
To cut with scissors
Crow (a)
Chair (a)
Cranberries (red)
(black)

Ohiet Mark1.

C

pish-pish
chăr-pŭtz
mă-whăr
hăt-chĭn
kă-pŏ
chōō-quăr
wăr-wŭs-ăr-kăr
hōw-ōō-yĕr
ă-nē-klŏck-sŭlk
tōōsh-kōōrk
hŏ-pissĕy
āitle-mŏp-pŭt
ŭk-hărt-ă-chĭttle
klŏck-sărp-ĕy
chĕt-ăr shittle
săt-tŏ
hŏm-miss
kŭm-măh
klăppē-yĕk
kāir-ĭn
quăr-āitz-ōōs
āit-tōōp
tĭ-sĭn

"Go away" "Go." - "Go on" -

There are several Indian words for this, according to the sense in which they are used.

In speaking to an Indian on shore, telling him to "go away", the equivalent to "clătter-wĕr" in Chinook, the correct word to use is; Wăăr-ālchĕy

Go away, I'm busy, use - "āitler-sōōt-jĕ, ō-ōōsh-tĭk-hăr"

Go away, "be off with you." Kor-aitchy

Go on, if speaking to a man in a canoe, who is paddling you use - klă-huk, or klă-ar-shē

Go with him (on shore)

Do - (in a canoe)

Hankin grouped the English words in pages under their first letter, but not alphabetically within each page, with their corresponding translations on the facing page. The words "Omit marks" and other annotations seem to have been added by another hand.

Numerals

1	Tsow-wŭk
2	Ărt-tĕr
3	Kŭtsĕ-tsăr
4	Mōō
5	Sootchăr
6	Nōōpōō
7	Ărtlĕ-pōō
8	Ărtlĕr-kŏlk
9	Tsow-wŏk-kŏlk
10	Hiŭ
11	Hiŭ-ish tsow-wŭk
12	— Do — Ărtlĕr
13	— Do — Kărtsĕ-tsăr
14	— Do — Moo
15	— Do — Sootchar
16	— Do — Nōōpōō
17	— Do — Ărtlĕ-pōō
18	— Do — Ărtlĕr-kolk
19	— Do — Tsow-wok-kolk
20	Tsăr-ketz
21	Tsar-ketz-ish tsow-wŭk
30	Kŭt-chĭt-sĕk
31	Kŭt-chit-sĕk, ish tsow-wuk
40	Mōō-yĕk
41	Mooyek ish tsow-wuk
50	Soot-chĕk
51	Soot-chĕk ish tsow-wŭk
60	Nōō-pōōk
61	Noo-pook ish tsow-wuk
70	Ărtlĕ-pōōk
71	Artle-pook ish tsow-wuk
80	Ărtlĕr-kŏlk-yĕk
81	Ărtlĕr-kŏlk-yĕk ish tsowŭk
90	Tsow-wŏk-kŏlk-yĕk
91	Tsow-wok kolk yek ish tsowuk
100	Hiŭk
101	Hiŭk ish tsowŭk
200	Ărtlĕ-pĕ-took
300	Kărtchĕ-sork-pĕ tŏrk
400	Mōōyĕk-pĕ-tŏrk
500	Sootchĕk-pĕ tŏrk
600	Nōōpook-pĕ tŏrk
700	Ărtlĕ-pook-pĕ tŏrk
800	Ărtlĕr-kŏlk pĕ tŏrk
900	Tsow-wŏk-kolk pe tork

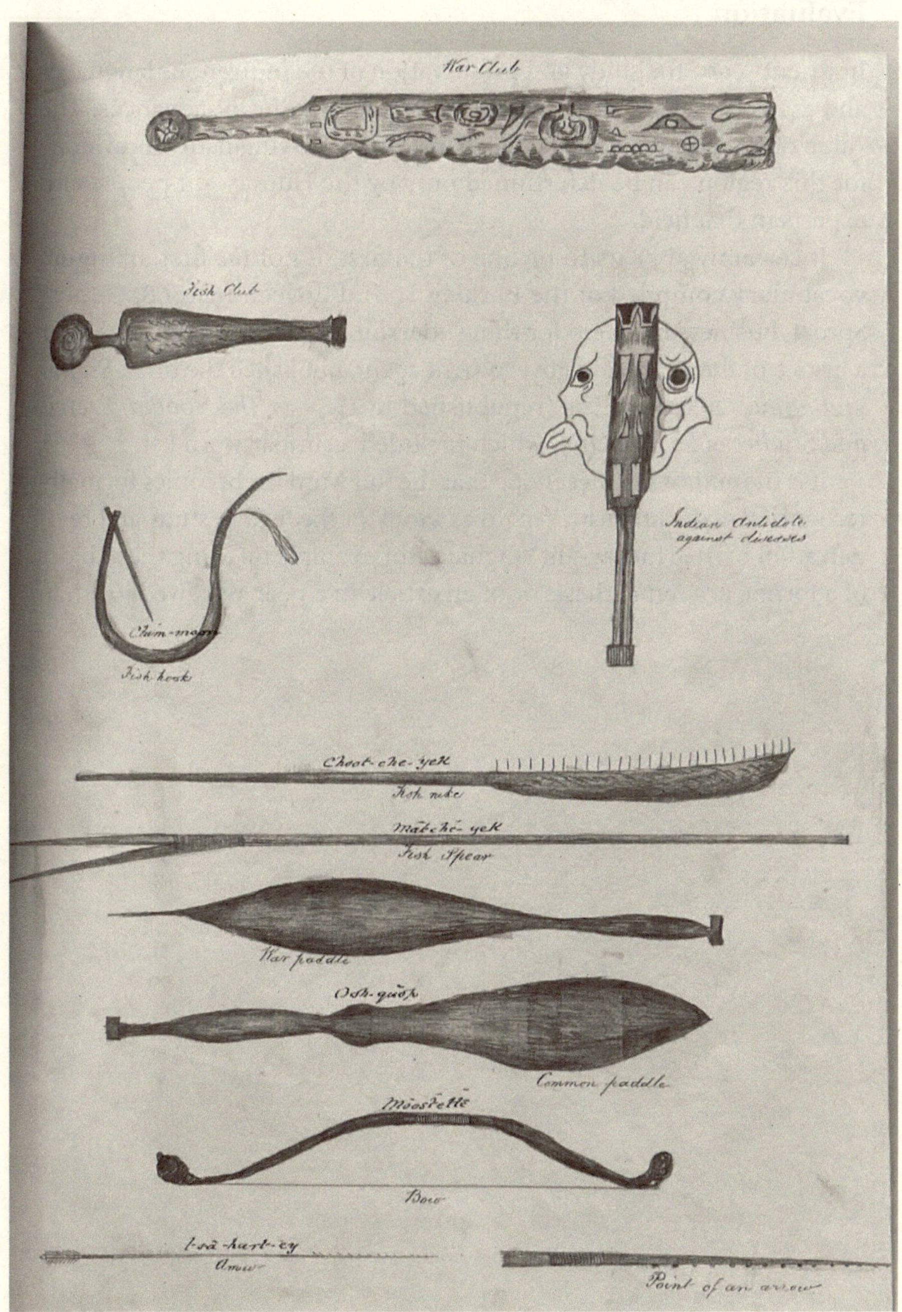
War Club
Fish Club
Indian Antidote against diseases
Chim-moon
Fish hook
Choot-che-yek
Fish rake
Mâtchê-yek
Fish Spear
War paddle
Osh-quop
Common paddle
Moostelle
Bow
I-sa-hart-ey
Arrow
Point of an arrow

Evaluation

In recent years, the study and preservation of the Indigenous languages and dialects of Vancouver Island have seen significant advances. The value of the contribution Hankin's list makes to linguistic knowledge for this region can be determined only by the Huu-ay-aht people and experts in that field.

It certainly appears to be one of the first, if not *the* first, bilingual vocabulary compiled of the Barkley Sound dialect. In 1868, Gilbert Sproat, business manager for the Anderson lumber company and later a justice of the peace and government agent, published the book *Scenes and Studies of Savage Life* (republished in 1989 as *The Nootka: Scenes and Studies of Savage Life*), which included a similar word list.

It is the author's earnest hope that the full word list becomes formally recognized in the linguistic record as a tool for the further study and revitalization of the Huu-ay-aht language, for example by being the subject of a formal academic thesis or of an article in a peer-reviewed journal.

The Ethnolinguistic Value of Philip Hankin's Word Lists of Barkley Sound Nuu-chah-nulth and Chinuk Wawa Trade Language

By Dr. Henry Kammler

Department of Ethnology, Institute of Social and Cultural Anthropology, Ludwig-Maximilians University of Munich, Germany

Philip Hankin's lists of words and phrases of the two languages Nuu-chah-nulth (specifically the Huu-ay-aht variant of the Barkley Sound dialect) and Chinuk Wawa make a remarkable and outstanding document for the ethnohistory and linguistics of Vancouver Island's southwestern coastline.

Being from 1860–1861, it is the earliest known source of substantial language data for the Barkley Sound dialect. It predates by a few years the writings of Gilbert Malcolm Sproat and Reverend Christopher Knipe, who had been in the Alberni area circa 1861–1864 and who both published books containing vocabularies from Barkley Sound in London in 1868. These two gentlemen's word lists are partially identical, even though neither author mentions the other. If this is not a case of plagiarism, they may have copied from a hitherto undiscovered third source, possibly William Eddy Banfield. Banfield arrived in Barkley Sound in 1858 as one of the first newcomer-settlers. He reportedly acquired a certain fluency in the local language (see bibliography, Mayne, 1862) and acted as a government agent until he drowned in 1862. It is important to note that Hankin's writings constitute a source independent of the other ones mentioned.

It can be assumed that Hankin was familiar with the most popular travel accounts of the West Coast, like reports of James Cook's third voyage and John Jewitt's 1816 captivity narrative. Such travel literature often contained short vocabulary lists which may have inspired him. He was also aware of the difficulties of presenting foreign speech sounds through the means of the English orthography. His hearing was sharp enough to grasp that there was distinction of long and short vowels in Southern Wakashan: "The words are carefully accented long or short, according to their pronunciation. Thus ā long in Fāther, ă short in hăt."

Such use of diacritics for the purpose of "pronunciation re-spelling" was already an established practice at Hankin's time, for example in John Ogilvie's popular *The Imperial Dictionary* (1840). A scholar with a working knowledge of Southern Wakashan can easily identify the majority of the documented expressions.

Hankin's writings provide very valuable insights and allow for some new discoveries in terms of lexicon, grammatical forms, intercultural communication and numeric systems. Chinuk Wawa itself must have been fairly new on Vancouver Island's west coast at the time of Hankin's visit. A few of Hankin's words represent a true mystery and will need further inspection. One example is his "*saarktikkā*" for "ship" occurring on several pages. It has nothing in common with any thinkable word for ship, vessel, on board, et cetera. The sequence "*saarkti*" could be a representation of the last three syllables of Hankin's ship's name HMS *Hecate*.

When it comes to grammatical elements, Hankin also secured interesting data. Thus he gives a phrase that includes an expression for "slightly, a bit" (*-t̓a·na*) that in the modern variants is considered typical only for dialects north of Barkley Sound. Southern Wakashan is very rich in synonyms, but the lexical base is becoming narrower with the dwindling speech community under the conditions of severe language endangerment. Sources like Hankin's help in documenting authentic use of words and grammatical forms that today's primary speakers may not be familiar with.

The numerals recorded by Hankin are clearly Barkley Sound dialect, at least up to 29. Starting with 30, he presents the language as having a decimal system like English. However, the local language uses units of 20s; it has a vigesimal system. So what Hankin took as 3×10 = 30 (*qač̓ciiq*) is actually 3×20 = 60, and *muuyiiq* is 4×20 = 80. Mistaking the Indigenous system based on twenties for a ten-based one in European language sources goes back to as early as the first contact period of the 1780s. Joseph Ingraham, first mate on the US ship *Columbia*, who compiled a word list at Nootka Sound in 1789, made the same assumption. So he glossed his "*mooyak*," or more accurately *muuyiiq*, as 40 when it should have been 80. Not surprisingly, Ingraham was also erroneously convinced that his Southern Wakashan hosts "cannot count higher than one hundred." All of Hankin's hundreds show the sequence "*-pě-těrk*," or

-pitiiq, which may indicate that this was a valid strategy (alongside other ones documented elsewhere) to represent higher numbers ascending into the thousands in the traditional language. Ingraham's prejudice could not have been farther from the truth.

Hankin's material also allows for observations on *intercultural communication*. Among his conversational phrases he has a series starting with "I want to see (. . .)" and complemented by "(. . .) you, (. . .) your mother, (. . .) your sister" for each of which Friday offers the predicate "năh-naanitch ŭp ŭs," or *ńańaačapis*: "let me see in detail, let me examine."

The sampled pages also reveal that his Huu-ay-aht consultant in many instances either simplified his language for Hankin or that he translated word by word, and in this manner came up with what would be ungrammatical in his mother tongue.

In a similar vein, Hankin's "The Lord's Prayer" consists of several lines in the Barkley Sound dialect, but it can hardly count as the first connected text written down in the language. It represents words strung together as one-to-one correspondences of the English version, obscuring the message at the sentence and text levels. Hankin's units of translation in conversational phrases were mostly the whole clauses, so many of their Barkley Sound correspondences are eloquent sentences in the language, except where Hankin must have tried a word-by-word prompting.

Hankin's list for Chinook Jargon, or Chinuk Wawa, is rather short. He obviously did not elicit it from speakers because the entries are from Chinuk Wawa to English in more or less alphabetical order. He probably compiled the list from a written source or several sources, though he would not have missed the chance to check the headwords with speakers of this trade language (some of his Chinuk Wawa entries show accented vowels like the ones employed in his Barkley Sound material). At the time of HMS *Hecate*'s survey of Vancouver Island, there were very few printed materials for Chinuk Wawa available.

Hankin's approach to Chinuk Wawa indicates that it was not a language spoken by his Huu-ay-aht consultant. The list is very distinct from the data taken down from the fluent speakers of Southern Wakashan. To put it differently: As a visitor to Barkley Sound in the 1860s, you could make little use of Chinuk Wawa. You had better learn the local language. Hankin made the effort.

Philip Hankin's manuscript is a trove of extremely valuable linguistic and ethnohistorical information for Barkley Sound, especially the Huu-ay-aht and other Nuu-chah-nulth First Nations. It offers unique lexical items and idiomatic expressions of the Huu-ay-aht language as it was in the 1860s and allows glimpses into the quickly changing linguistic landscape of the time.

Acknowledgements

The economics of my work on this project were improved enormously by:

- BC Arts Council's grant under the program of Project Assistance for Creative Writers.
- Director, Royal BC Museum and Archives, for the most considerate and timely waiving of image reproduction fees.

The author and publisher respectfully acknowledge, with gratitude, the cooperation of the Huu-ay-aht Nation's ḥaw̓iiḥ council of Hereditary Chiefs in supporting the inclusion in this book of part of the word list of their language developed by collaboration between Thomas Roberts and Philip Hankin. In particular, we thank Ḥaw̓iił ḥapinyuuk (Tommy Happynook) and hinatinyis (Brittany Johnson) Coté for their support and efforts to identify Thomas Roberts.

My sincere thanks go to all those who assisted my research for this book. They include:

- John Adams, for sharing his knowledge of the history of houses on Battery Street.
- Judy Carlson, Alberni Museum and Archives.
- Dick Dixon, Stanstead Abbotts Local History Society.
- Marie Elliott, who kindly shared her notes related to her book *Gold in British Columbia*.
- Ron Greene, for generously providing some images.
- James Gorton, Hudson's Bay Company Archives, Winnipeg, Manitoba.
- Sharon Keen, for her assiduous delving into BC Archives and the BC legislature library.
- Christian Keller, Barkerville Historic Town and Park, for material on the Hankin brothers.
- Jesse Robertson, for kindly sharing some sources on Thomas "Friday" Roberts.

- Genealogist Sherri Robinson, who was of huge help in finding the Hankin family data.
- Alan Twigg, for help with material on Belize/British Honduras.
- Joanna Vink, Melbourne, Australia, for sharing her research into the Gowlland story.
- Angus Weller for his cartography.
- Jade Wells, for photographing the Huu-ay-aht word list.
- John Williams, head archivist at UK Hydrographic Office, Taunton, UK.
- Jennifer Wraight, Admiralty Library, Portsmouth, UK.
- Carol-Ann Zenger, Anglican Church of St. John the Divine, Victoria, BC.

My grateful appreciation goes to Richard Mackie for providing the foreword.

Similarly, to Adam Werle and Henry Kammler for their expert review and evaluation of the word list.

I am beholden to Tori Elliott and her team at TouchWood Editions, for their professionalism in the design, production and publication of this, my fourth book with them.

I thank my dear wife, Jean, for her support during this long project, in addition to her skills as an editor. For all this, and more, I have dedicated this book to her.

Notes

Introduction

1. BC Archives call number: old manuscripts E/B/H19.

Chapter 1

1. The Hankin surname appears to have derived from the Anglo-Saxon Johan-kin.
2. "Thele," too, is of Old English origin, meaning board or plank.
3. A wickerwork contraption with three wheels, precursor to a wheelchair, first used in the spa town of Bath.
4. No records survive of the names of pupils attending any of the three senior schools in Ware between 1849 and 1855, when they were amalgamated.
5. The four rules were: addition, subtraction, multiplication, and division. The rule of three related to proportion: As *a* is to *b*, so *c* is to *x*. Knowing the three values *a*, *b*, and *c*, what is the value of *x*? Answers: $x = b \times c \div a$. Or, $x = a \times b \div c$.
6. Probably Psalm 103.

Chapter 2

1. See Prime, in bibliography.
2. *Pictorial History of South Africa*, p. 272.
3. Philip's aunt, Christiana, had been a noted campaigner in the anti-slavery movement and had published two books on the subject.
4. The adventure novelist R.M. Ballantyne would twice quote this rousing message in his books *The Lighthouse* (1865) and *Black Ivory* (1873). Ballantyne had worked in Canada with the Hudson's Bay Company during the 1840s.

Chapter 3

1. Thomson, a few years older than Philip, later twice commanded Queen Victoria's royal yacht, HMY *Victoria and Albert*, and HMS *Challenger* during the Royal Society's around-the-world oceanographic exploring expedition of 1872–76.
2. Now Quelimane, a port in Mozambique on the delta of the Zambezi River, on the Indian Ocean.

Chapter 4

1. For more detailed accounts of these explorations, see Layland, 2013 and 2016.
2. Termed "gazetting," referring to being registered in the official *London Gazette.*
3. From his description, the birds behaved more like sandpipers, probably grey-breasted seedsnipe, but just as tasty.
4. Indigenous inhabitants of the Tierra del Fuego archipelago, now identified as Selknam, Yagan, or Kawesqar people. They are currently considered as probably descended from the Paleoindian peoples who travelled south from Beringia, down the kelp highway thirteen thousand years ago, or possibly far earlier.
5. In 1520, Magellan's officers had associated these people with the mythological creatures "Patagones" ("big-feet"), which gave the name to the region at the southern tip of South America.

Chapter 5

1. Now separated by the negotiated boundary into the San Juan Islands (US), and the Southern Gulf Islands (BC).
2. Three such huts were originally built, belatedly, as a hospital for cases from the Kamchatka theatre of the Crimean War.
3. With a Captain Jeremiah Nagle as skipper. More will be heard about this man and his family in chapter 19.

Chapter 6

1. Hecate, in Greek mythology, was the three-headed goddess of crossroads and the underworld, also associated with wilderness and childbirth.
2. This area had been visited by a Royal Navy surveying ship, HMS *Beagle*, in 1834 (with Charles Darwin aboard), but was not properly charted until 1869. Richard Charles Mayne, by then a captain and commanding his own ship, HMS *Nassau*, made a detailed chart of its 255 miles (410 kilometres) of channels and twenty anchorages and havens.

Chapter 7

1. For a more detailed account of *Plumper*'s surveying operations during 1860, see Dorricott and Cullon, 2012.
2. The scientific work of these officers is recounted in *In Nature's Realm*, Layland, 2019.
3. Amor De Cosmos founded the *British Colonist* in 1858, later changed to the *Daily Colonist*. In 1980, it merged with the *Victoria Daily Times* that had first been published in 1884. The name is now the *Times Colonist*.

4. This figure includes white people only. Imperial authorities of the era did not count Indigenous, Asian, African, or Hawai'ian people.
5. At the narrows, periods of slack tide are usually limited to a few minutes.

Chapter 8

1. Commander George Henry Richards, RN, had been involved in one of the many searches for her husband's vessels by the Royal Navy. Had he not already been committed to the Northwest Boundary Commission, he would have been her first choice to lead the *Fox* expedition, which she had funded personally.
2. Sophie wrote a continuous series of long letters addressed to "My dearest ones" while with her aunt. Dorothy Blakey Smith of the Provincial Archives has collated and annotated those of local interest.
3. The church was at the junction of Douglas and Fisgard Streets, the site now occupied by the Hudson building. Rebuilt, the church of St. John the Divine is now on Quadra at Mason Street.
4. Harris would later represent Esquimalt in the Legislative Assembly until resigning to become the first mayor of the City of Victoria.
5. Chinook Jargon, or Chinuk Wawa, was a trading language used throughout the west coast from Oregon to Alaska. It is based on the language of the Chinook people of the Columbia River estuary, but simplified and laced with English, French, and Spanish words. Most Hudson's Bay Company people used it comfortably and a few words are still in use, such as *skookum*, meaning "big" or "strong"; *chuck*, meaning "water"; and *potlatch*, meaning "to give."
6. Carved by George Gunya, it is now in the National Museum of the American Indian in New York.
7. The name of the pretty actress was Lulu, after whom the gallant Colonel Richard Clement Moody named a nearby island.
8. Moody was also the lieutenant governor and surveyor general of the new colony of British Columbia.

Chapter 9

1. For detailed accounts of Mayne's sortie and Banfield's tragic story, see Layland, 2016.
2. See notes on Hankin's manuscript word lists of Huu-ay-aht and Chinuk Wawa, appendix 2.
3. The bank was later named "Swiftsure."
4. In 1876, that same ship foundered and sank while attempting to transit Seymour Narrows on the east coast of Vancouver Island.

Chapter 10

1. Not to mention knowing the obdurate nature of his counterpart, Archibald Campbell.
2. For more on Launders's work, as a sapper and after he remained with the Lands Office in Victoria, see Layland, 2013.
3. Visited by George Vancouver and called Cheslakee's Village. See Layland, 2016, chapter 5.
4. Which Richards renamed Cape Cook, on the Brooks Peninsula.

Chapter 11

1. See Layland, 2016, chapter 5.
2. Huu-ay-aht, Ehattesaht, and Kyuquot are all dialects of the Wakashan language group.
3. None of the party seems to have understood that the lakes were filled with large trout, ample for their sustenance and easy to catch.
4. For a more detailed account of this journey, see Layland, 2016, chapter 14.

Chapter 12

1. This was the hereditary name for chiefs of the Mowachaht. Men of the same name had greeted James Cook, George Vancouver, Juan Francisco de la Bodega y Quadra, and the fur traders after sea otter pelts.
2. A senior level of the paymaster scale.
3. Then identified as a potential route to the Cariboo goldfields.
4. Gowlland's journal.

Chapter 13

1. According to Gowlland, during their previous visit to San Francisco for repairs, four men had deserted, but were captured and returned to *Hecate*.
2. This was the time of the Lancashire Cotton Famine. The area's principal industry was that of spinning and weaving textiles, particularly cotton. A disastrous combination of factors caused an industry-wide depression, resulting in hundreds of thousands of workers being laid off and their families starving. There was a related massive emigration. It lasted from 1861 to 1865.
3. See Layland, 2013, 2016, and 2019.
4. This conflicts with Hankin's account of the 1857 visit aboard *Plumper*, when Synge was there.
5. King Kamehameha IV died of chronic asthma just a few months after *Hecate*'s visit.

6. This will have meant, at the time, 180° in longitude, east and west, from the Greenwich meridian. It was confirmed in 1884 but with a few diversions made for the convenience of some island territories. It is where the days change.
7. A project by the Queensland colonial government to subsidize settlement of the heavily wooded "outback" by unemployed cotton mill workers from Lancashire proved ill-considered and unsuccessful.

Chapter 14

1. The original manuscript is now in the Mitchell State Library of New South Wales, Australia. Joanna Vink, in Australia, has edited and published Gowlland's diary and letters.
2. Ostracized.

Chapter 15

1. Daniel Hankin remained, however, on the electoral registry for the years 1861 to 1867 as "occupier" of the Pertenhall property Wood End.
2. See Pender, in bibliography.
3. See chapter 8.
4. See Smith, 1974.

Chapter 16

1. See Layland, 2013, chapter 17.
2. Kennedy mentioned in a dispatch to London that Governor Stephen Hill of Antigua in the West Indies had also "strongly recommended" Hankin. This is puzzling, since the connection between Hill and Hankin is unknown.
3. See Layland, 2016, chapter 12.
4. For a detailed account of the *Kingfisher* incident, the context, and the reprisal action, see Gough, *Gunboat Frontier*, 1984.
5. See chapter 9.
6. Sailors' slang for an improvised conference, typically between two groups without a shared language or culture.
7. Admiralty chart #569 series B1 remained incomplete. It lacked soundings in Shelter and Herbert arms and any detail for Bedwell. His officers would work on such details during *Hecate*'s voyage home.
8. Philip does not mention his having been in Clayoquot, but he was aboard *Hecate* at the time of its survey and took part in the boat work.
9. In 1891, the Canadian government took up Denman's concept for an official coastal vessel by commissioning and deploying CGS *Quadra* under the command of Captain John T. Walbran. See Layland, 2013, chapter 20; also this book, chapter 29.

Chapter 17

1. Kennedy was not knighted until 1867.
2. Botanist and leader of the Vancouver Island Exploring Expedition of 1864. See Layland, 2013, chapter 17.
3. See Layland, 2016, chapter 12.
4. Refer to the full story in Layland, 2016, chapter 14.

Chapter 18

1. Uncle to the surveyor Joseph Despard Pemberton.
2. Technically, William Young had also been "acting," but the position was understood to be his and to be resumed on his return from long leave.
3. Lawyer and long-serving parliamentarian, the larger-than-life Richard McBride, premier of the province of BC from 1903 until 1915, who brought it from virtual bankruptcy through an expansive boom and to an eventual bust.
4. See chapter 8.
5. Hankin did not know Kwak'wala, the language of the Ligwildaxw, so they probably communicated in Chinuk Wawa.
6. See Layland, 2013, chapter 17.
7. Head teacher at the Anglican school for Indigenous children, prior to the now-notorious residential school era.
8. The newspaper later recorded that on that day the temperature in the shade in Victoria had registered 92°F (33°C).
9. The riders were Jessie, Susan, Harry and Fred Nagle, Captain Fox, Mr. Fowler, Graham Hankin, and Police Inspector Welsh.
10. It was £485. His annual rate of pay as a commander would have been just over £300 plus £45 if in command of a vessel.

Chapter 19

1. Robert Louis Smith, in his master's thesis of 1973, thoroughly studied and described the complex politics of the two colonies in this era.
2. Rifles and muskets—more than enough to arm a good-sized militia or a formidable insurgency force.
3. This same year, Philip's brother Graham also briefly served as a temporary junior clerk with the same firm.
4. *Missionary Expedition to Vancouvers Island* by J.X. Willémar and Mr H. Guillod, 1868, vol. 3, H/A/So2, Society for the Propagation of the Gospel papers, BC Archives.
5. "Memoranda of a Trip Round Vancouver Island," file MS-2443.9, BC Archives.
6. Shetlander John Paton Booth would become a significant figure in provincial politics from 1871.

Chapter 20

1. The same man who, three years earlier, had so generously lent the penniless Hankin $60 for the wagon fare on his departure from Barkerville. See chapter 15.
2. A serious viral infection from the bite of mosquitoes. Prior to the discovery of a vaccine, mortality was about fifty percent. People of European origin, lacking immunity, were highly susceptible.
3. Austin had been in office since 1864 and had been preceded by Frederick Seymour.

Chapter 21

1. Former chief justice, Vancouver Island.

Chapter 22

1. Rear Admiral the Honourable George Fowler Hastings, commander-in-chief, Pacific.
2. A powerful and graceful four-gun, screw-assisted, three-masted gun vessel launched in 1856, serving in Esquimalt between 1866 and '72.
3. This was the same man who, while drunk, was duped into causing Victoria to be the capital of the united province.
4. The first British ironclad warship to enter the Pacific, 252 feet (77 metres) overall, 3-masted, advanced steam assisted, 24 guns. Captain Richard Dawkins, RN.

Chapter 23

1. Title accorded to members of the Legislative Council.
2. A reference to the reprisal action against the Ahousaht. See chapter 16.
3. The *British Colonist* noted, "upon which considerable sums of money are depending. A general disposition is manifested to suspend business, and few, if any, stores will be opened."

Chapter 24

1. He misremembered. It had been in 1864, five years previously.
2. Another slip of the memory: he had earlier recorded that he had "not the half of 50 dollars left" when he set out for the Cariboo.
3. Today, his treatment would amount to "constructive dismissal."
4. See chapter 16.

Chapter 25

1. In his memoir he misremembered it as six months.
2. Officer commanding the British camp on the still-disputed San Juan Island.
3. No relation to William Alexander George Young, RN.
4. Apparently ignoring the other exceptions, Newfoundland and Prince Edward Island.
5. Notably, Musgrave omitted the contribution of the Royal Engineers.

Chapter 26

1. On his arrival in 1865, Carrall practised medicine in Nanaimo for two years, then moved to Barkerville to continue to practise. He also invested in mining syndicates and would have known Charles Hankin well.
2. See bibliography for the full text of the letter and Ireland's analysis.
3. This was aboard the elderly SS *Active*, making the regular run that the SS *Commodore* used to run under Captain Jeremiah Nagle, Isabel's father.
4. Rear Admiral the Honourable Arthur Farquhar, the new commander-in-chief, Pacific Station.

Chapter 27

1. Hankin always attributed such relapses as linked to yellow fever contracted in Cuba. That disease is not known for repeated bouts, so Isabel might have been misdiagnosed. She had been unwell even before leaving Victoria in early 1867, so there could have been an underlying condition that surfaced periodically.
2. A popular, rustic destination for genteel excursions and picnics, especially when the salmon were spawning; it is now a provincial park.
3. Henry Pering Pellew Crease had been attorney general but had been elevated to the bench as a puisne, or junior, judge. His wife, Sarah, was a talented botanical artist—see Layland, 2019.
4. A group within the Kwakwaka'wakw First Nation.
5. Destined for a calamitous end four years later, while attempting to transit Seymour Narrows.
6. His retired rank was commander, not captain, and the pension was £533, not $533.

Chapter 28

1. See sidebar, pp. 216–17, chapter 20.
2. See chapter 6.
3. "Bucks" is the commonly used abbreviation for Buckinghamshire.
4. The local court where justices of the peace, sitting with a jury, heard non-capital crimes and civil cases.

Chapter 29

1. According to the Dominion estimates for 1887, his annual pension was recorded as $2,595.56.
2. Captain Adams does not appear in Philip's memoir, nor is he listed as having commanded a ship of the Royal Navy, according to the website The Victorian Royal Navy (see bibliography).
3. Muswell Hill became very fashionable with the opening of Alexandra Palace nearby in 1873. It remains a highly desirable location.

Bibliography

Akrigg, G.P.V., and Helen B. Akrigg. *British Columbia Chronicle 1847–1871: Gold and Colonists.* Discovery Press, 1977.

Ball, Sir Robert. *A Manual of Scientific Enquiry . . . Officers in Her Majesty's Navy and Travellers in General.* 5th ed. Eyre and Spottiswood, 1886 (first published 1849).

Barman, Jean. *British Columbia in the Balance: 1846–1871.* Harbour Publishing Co. Ltd., 2022.

Bentley-Crunch, Dana. *Edward VIII: Image of an Era, 1841–1910.* HMSO Publications, 1992.

Bosher, J.F. *Imperial Vancouver Island Who was Who 1850–1950.* Writersworld, 2012.

Bushby, Arthur Thomas. *The Journal of . . . 1858–1859.* Edited by Dorothy Blakey Smith. *British Columbia Historical Quarterly*, January–October, 1957–1958.

Cracroft, Sophia. *Lady Franklin Visits the Pacific Northwest: being extracts from the diary of Miss Sophia Cracroft . . . February to April 1861 and April to July 1870.* Edited by Dorothy Blakey Smith. Provincial Archives of BC, memoir no. 11, 1974.

Duffus, Maureen. *A Most Unusual Colony: Vancouver Island 1849–1860.* Desktop Publishing, 1996.

Elliott, Marie. *Gold in British Columbia: Discovery to Confederation.* Ronsdale Press, 2020.

Fox, Lt. Cecil H., RN. *Manual of Seamanship for Boys and Seamen of the Royal Navy, 1904* (reprinted). Algrove Publishing, 2003.

Gregson, Harry. *A History of Victoria, 1842–1970.* Victoria Observer Publishing, 1970.

Gough, Barry. *Gunboat Frontier: British Maritime Authority and Northwest Coast Indians 1846–1880.* University of British Columbia Press, 1984.

Gowlland, John Thomas Ewing. *My Dearest Gennie.* Edited by Joanna Vink. Calwell ACT, Australia: Inspiring Publishers, 2013.

———. *Narrative by J.T. Gowlland, Voyage of HMS* Hecate *Sydney to London 1863*. Edited by G.C. Ingleton. Transcript is in Mitchell Library, State Library of NSW, Australia, Microfilm CY Reel 4803.

Guillod, Henry. "Extracts from the journal . . ." *Tenth Annual Report of the Columbia Mission for the Year 1866*, p. 25. Rivingtons, Waterloo Place, 1869.

Hankin, Captain Philip J. Untitled manuscript memoirs, 1914. BC Archives collection, B 01332 and microfilm box 68 file 706a.

Hazlitt, William Carew. *The Great Gold Fields of Cariboo*. Foreword by Barry Gough. Klanak Press. 1974.

Holmes, Susan Abercrombie (Nagle), *1840–1921*. Provincial Archives of BC, MS-2576 Series 1865-1911.

Ireland, Willard E. "An Official Speaks Out: Letter of the Hon. Philip J. Hankin to the Duke of Buckingham, March 11, 1870." *British Columbia Historical Quarterly*, vol. 13, 1949.

Jewitt, John R. *White Slaves of the Nootka: Narrative of the Adventures and Sufferings of John R. Jewitt While a Captive of the Nootka Indians*. Heritage House, 1990.

Kemp, Peter, ed. *The Oxford Companion to Ships & the Sea*. Oxford University Press, 1976.

Layland, Michael, *The Land of Heart's Delight: Early Maps and Charts of Vancouver Island*. TouchWood Editions, 2013.

———. *A Perfect Eden: Encounters by Early Explorers of Vancouver Island*. TouchWood Editions, 2016.

———. *In Nature's Realm: Early Naturalists Explore Vancouver Island*. TouchWood Editions, 2019.

Ludditt, Fred. *Barkerville Days*. Mitchell Press, 1969.

Mackie, Richard Somerset. *The Wilderness Profound: Victorian Life on the Gulf of Georgia*. Sono Nis Press, 1995.

Mayne, Richard Charles. *Four Years in British Columbia and Vancouver Island*. Murray, 1862.

McGoogan, Ken. *Lady Franklin's Revenge*. Bantam Press, 2006.

Mynett, Geoff. *River of Mists: People of the Upper Skeena 1821–1930*. Caitlin Press, 2022.

———. *The Eventful Life of Philip Hankin: Worldwide Traveller and Witness to British Columbia's Early History*. Caitlin Press, 2023.

Pender, Daniel. *Captain's Letter—Pender 1862–1866*. Taunton, UK: Hydrographic Office Surveyors Letters SL56.

Pictorial History of South Africa. Odhams Press, 1938.

Porcher, E.A. *A Tour of Duty in the Pacific Northwest: E.A. Porcher and H.M.S. Sparrowhawk, 1865–1968.* Edited by Dwight L. Smith. University of Alaska Press, 2000.

Prime, Adam John. "The Indian Army's British Officer Corps, 1861–1921." PhD diss., University of Leicester, UK, February 2018.

Richards, G.H. *The Private Journal of Captain G.H. Richards: The Vancouver Island Survey (1860–1862).* Edited by Linda Dorricott and Deidre Cullon. Ronsdale Press, 2012.

Ritchie, G.S. *The Admiralty Chart: British Naval Hydrography in the Nineteenth Century.* Hollis & Carter, 1967.

Russell, William Howard. *The Prince of Wales Tour: A Diary in India.* R. Worthington, 1877.

Sandilands, R.W. *The History of Hydrographic Surveying in British Columbia.* Paper read before BC Historical Society, Victoria Branch, January 2, 1965. University of Victoria Library, VK597 C3252.

Smith, Robert Louis, "Governor Kennedy of Vancouver Island and the Politics of Union 1864–1866." MA thesis, University of Victoria, 1973. Special Collections, University of Victoria Library, BC: Call # FC 3822.1 K45 S 5.

———. "The Hankin Appointment, 1868." *BC Studies* 22, 1974.

Sproat, Gilbert. *The Nootka: Scenes and Studies of Savage Life.* Edited by Charles Lillard. Sono Nis, 1987.

Sterritt, Neil J. *Mapping My Way Home: A Gitxsan History.* Creekstone Press, 2016.

Twigg, Alan. *Understanding Belize: A Historical Guide.* Harbour Publishing, 2006.

Underhill, Stuart. *The Iron Church: 1860–1985.* Braemar Books, 1984.

Verney, Edmund Hope. *Vancouver Island Letters of Edmund Hope Verney, 1862–65.* Edited by Allan Pritchard. UBC Press, 1996.

Walbran, John T. *British Columbia Coast Names: Their Origin and History.* Douglas & McIntyre, 1971.

Williams, David R. *The Man for a New Country: Sir Matthew Baillie Begbie.* Gray's Publishing, 1977.

Online Sources

In addition to the books and technical journals included in the bibliography, I have consulted the following databases available online:

Barkerville Historic Town (https://www.barkerville@barkerville.com)

BC Geographical Names (apps.gov.bc.ca/pub/bcgnws/web/)

British Colonist 1858–1980, The (https://britishcolonist.ca/)

Canadian Encyclopedia, The (https://www.thecanadianencyclopedia.ca/en)

Colonial Despatches (https://bcgenesis.uvic.ca/)

Dictionary of Canadian Biography, The (www.biographi.ca/en/index.php&)

Government of British Columbia First Nations A–Z Listing (www2.gov.bc.ca/gov/content/environment/natural-resource-stewardship/consulting-with-first-nations/first-nations-negotiations/first-nations-a-z-listing)

Hudson's Bay Company Archives, The (https://www.gov.mb.ca/chc/archives/hbca/)

Land Titles Office, Historic Records (https://vault.library.uvic.ca/collections/505a74f4-d7bf-44d2-a5d0-96b2c6ddf2a8?locale=en)

Legislative Library of BC (https://www.leg.bc.ca/learn-about-us/legislative-library)

Stanstead Abbotts Local History Society (https://www.salhs.org.uk/)

UK Hydrographic Office Archive, The (https://www.gov.uk/guidance/the-ukho-archive)

Victorian Royal Navy, The (https://www.pdavis.nl/index.htm)

Victoria's Victoria (https://web.uvic.ca/vv/)

List of Illustrations

Image	Page

Index

CREDIT: TORI ELLIOTT

Born and educated in London, **Michael Layland** trained as an officer, surveyor, and mapmaker in the British Army's Royal Engineers, serving in England, Scotland, Africa, and the Middle East. In his civilian career, he managed mapping-related projects in South and Central America, the Middle East, and North and West Africa. He managed a company taking explorers into Antarctica, and was later a consultant to a forefront computer mapper in BC.

Michael became a Canadian citizen in 1986 and six years later, he and his wife, Jean, moved to Victoria. He is the author of *The Land of Heart's Delight* (2013), *A Perfect Eden* (2016), and *In Nature's Realm* (2019), award-winning books about the cartography, exploration, and natural history of Vancouver Island, respectively, as well as many articles on the same scholarship. He is a former president of the Victoria Historical Society, and his unique in-depth knowledge of maps and mapping, combined with his knowledge of Vancouver Island history, led to him being called as an expert witness for an Indigenous land claim heard by the Supreme Court of British Columbia.

For *Turmoil*, he explored new territory: the biography of an intriguing character who made brief appearances in his earlier books.

MICHAELLAYLAND.COM